GEN 13

ROAD TRIP

Writer:
Gail Simone

Pencilers:
Alvin Lee (#7)
Carlo Barberi (#8-10)
Barberi with Sunny Lee (#11-12)
Kevin West and Sunny Lee (#13)

Inkers:
M3th (#7)
Drew Geraci (#8-9)
Geraci with Barberi (#10-12)
Geraci with Jon Mills and
Dan Davis (#13)

Colors:
Carrie Strachan (#7, 9, 11-13)
Carrie Strachan with Randy Mayor (#8)
Carrie Strachan with Jonny Rench (#10)

Letters:
Pat Brosseau

Collected Edition Cover by
Carlo Barberi, Drew Geraci
and Carrie Strachan

Original Series Covers by Talent Caldwell,
Matt "Batt" Banning and Carrie Strachan (#7)
Carlo Barberi, Drew Geraci and Carrie Strachan
(#8-13)

GEN13 created by Jim Lee,
Brandon Choi and J. Scott Campbell

ISBN: 978-1-4012-1649-8

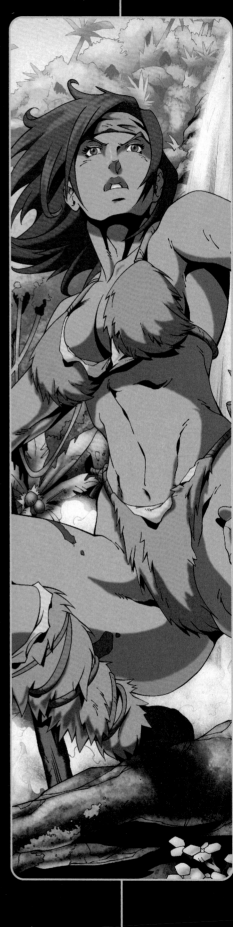

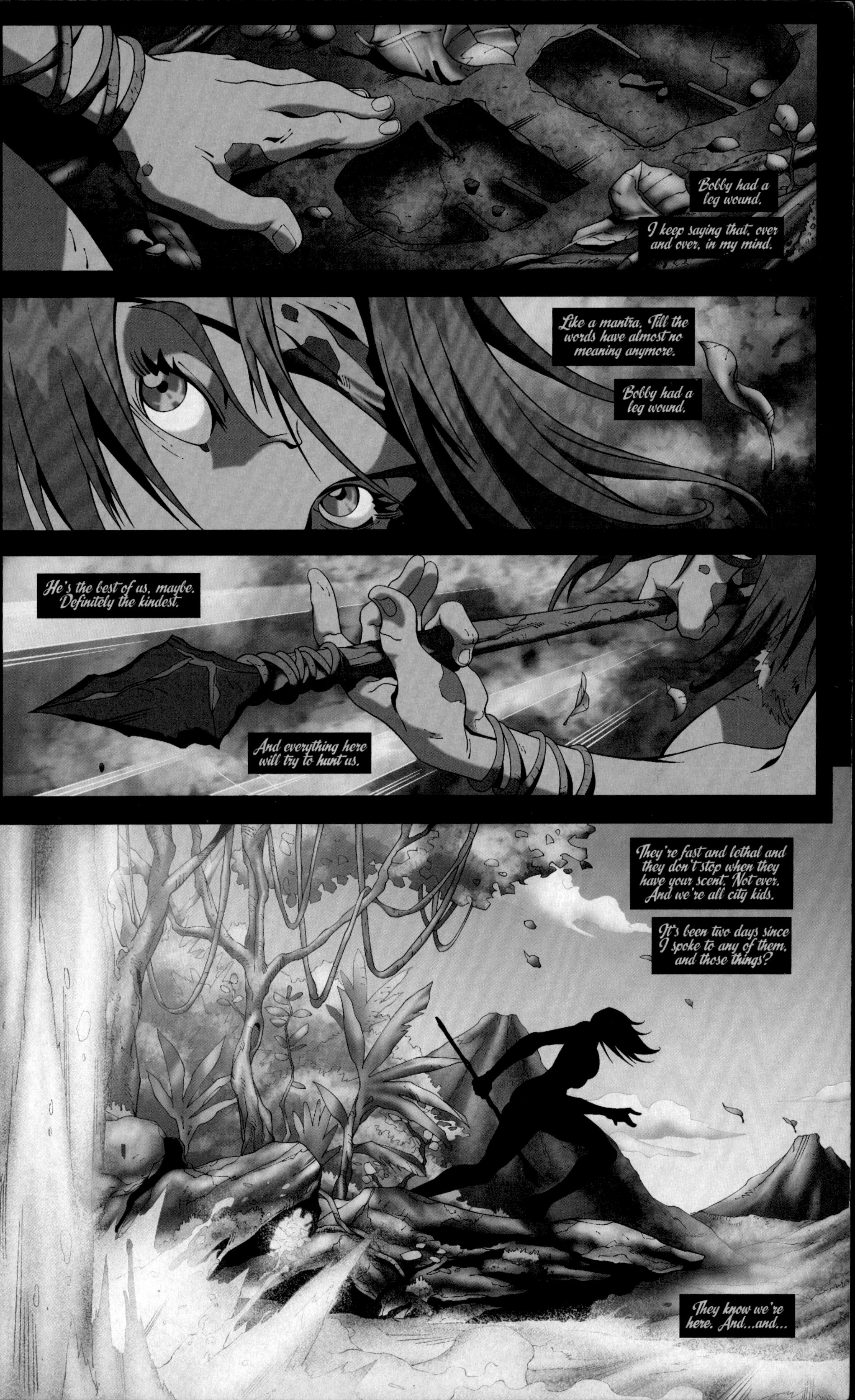
Bobby had a leg wound.
I keep saying that, over and over, in my mind.
Like a mantra. Till the words have almost no meaning anymore.
Bobby had a leg wound.
He's the best of us, maybe. Definitely the kindest.
And everything here will try to hunt us.
They're fast and lethal and they don't stop when they have your scent. Not ever. And we're all city kids.
It's been two days since I spoke to any of them, and those things?
They know we're here. And...and...

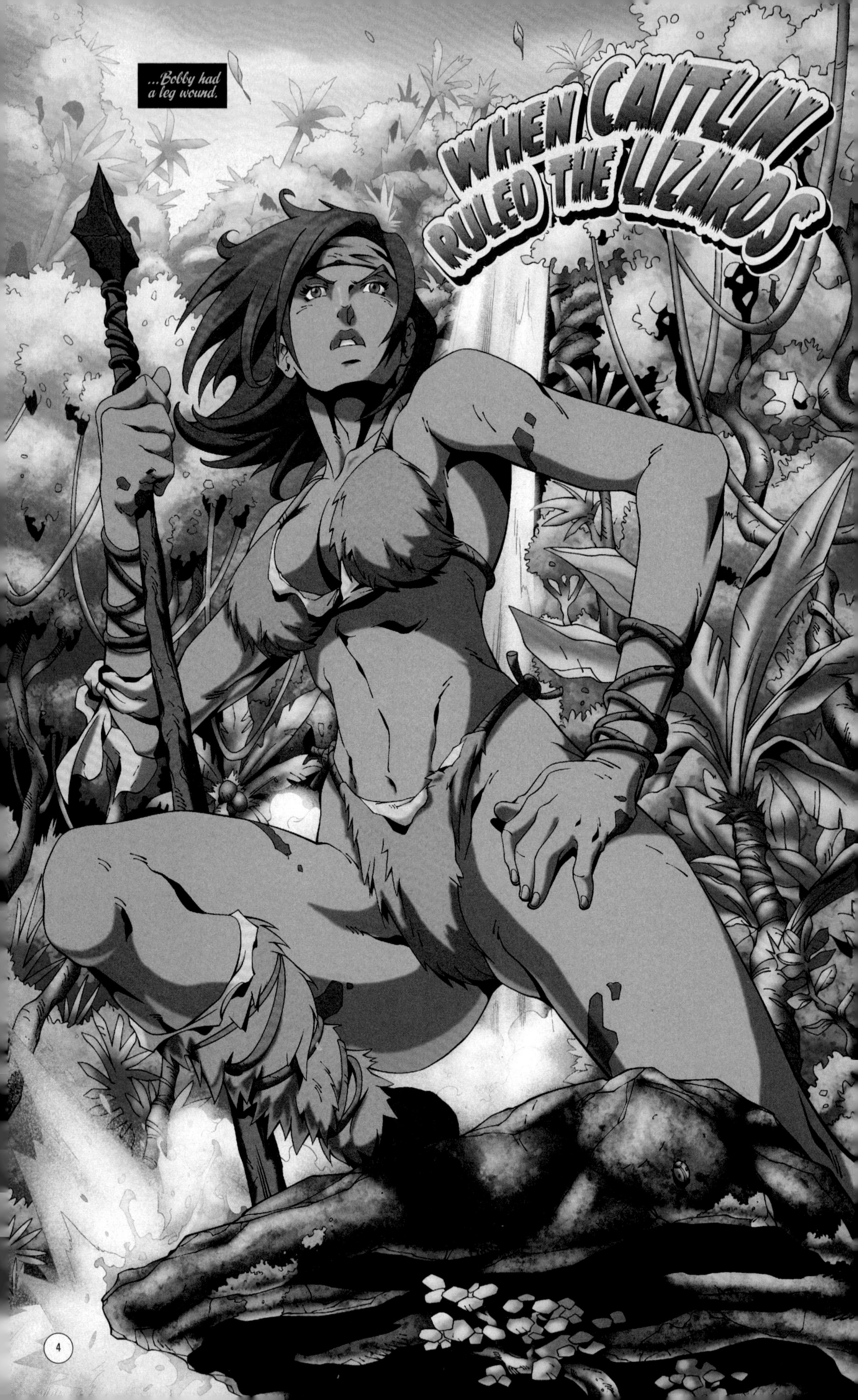
...Bobby had a leg wound.
WHEN CAITLIN RULED THE LIZARDS

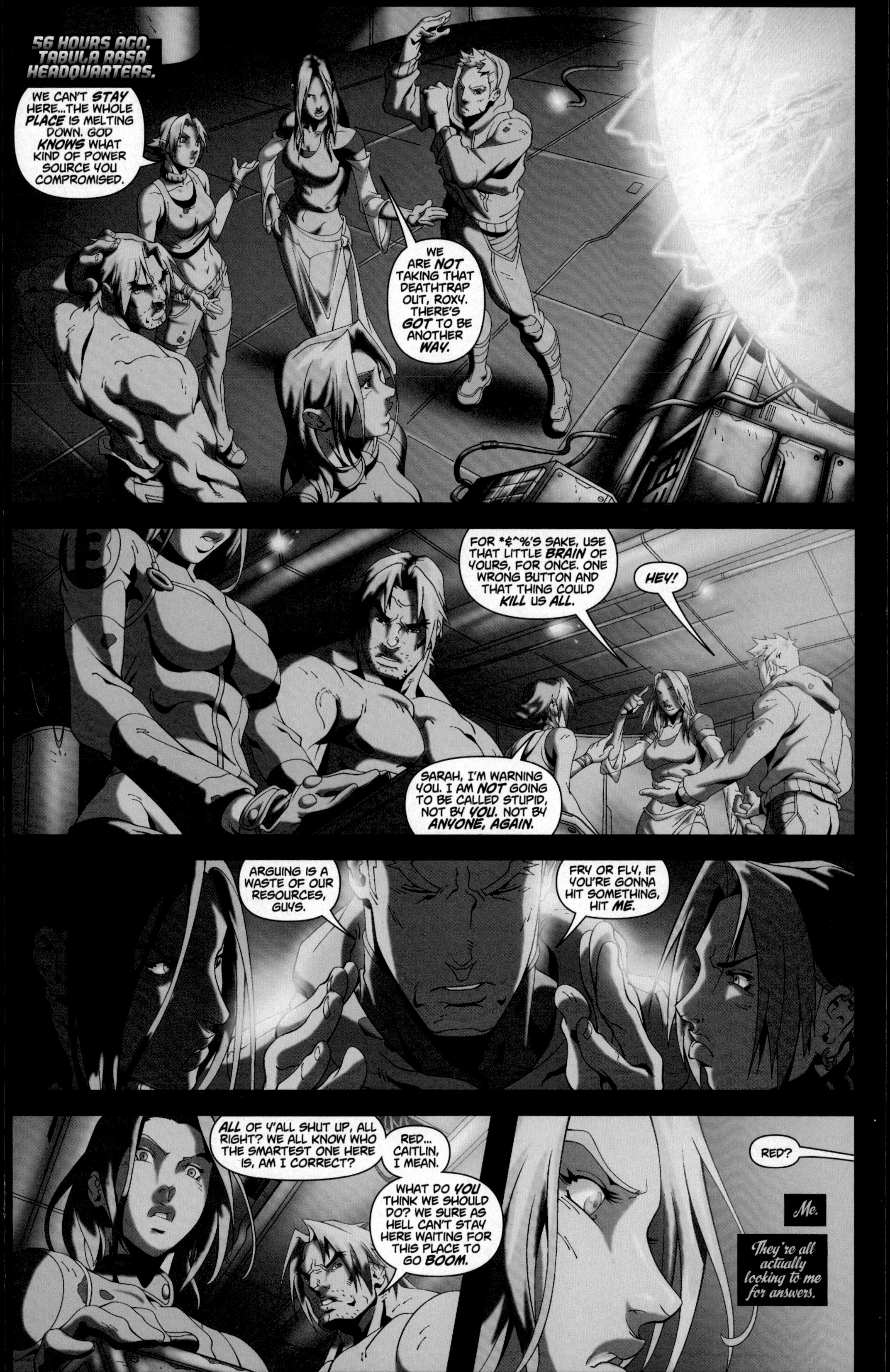

56 HOURS AGO, TABULA RASA HEADQUARTERS.
WE CAN'T STAY HERE...THE WHOLE PLACE IS MELTING DOWN. GOD KNOWS WHAT KIND OF POWER SOURCE YOU COMPROMISED.
WE ARE NOT TAKING THAT DEATHTRAP OUT, ROXY. THERE'S GOT TO BE ANOTHER WAY.
FOR *&^%'S SAKE, USE THAT LITTLE BRAIN OF YOURS, FOR ONCE. ONE WRONG BUTTON AND THAT THING COULD KILL US ALL.
HEY!
SARAH, I'M WARNING YOU. I AM NOT GOING TO BE CALLED STUPID, NOT BY YOU. NOT BY ANYONE, AGAIN.
ARGUING IS A WASTE OF OUR RESOURCES, GUYS.
FRY OR FLY, IF YOU'RE GONNA HIT SOMETHING, HIT ME.
ALL OF Y'ALL SHUT UP, ALL RIGHT? WE ALL KNOW WHO THE SMARTEST ONE HERE IS, AM I CORRECT?
RED... CAITLIN, I MEAN.
WHAT DO YOU THINK WE SHOULD DO? WE SURE AS HELL CAN'T STAY HERE WAITING FOR THIS PLACE TO GO BOOM.
RED?
Me.
They're all actually looking to me for answers.

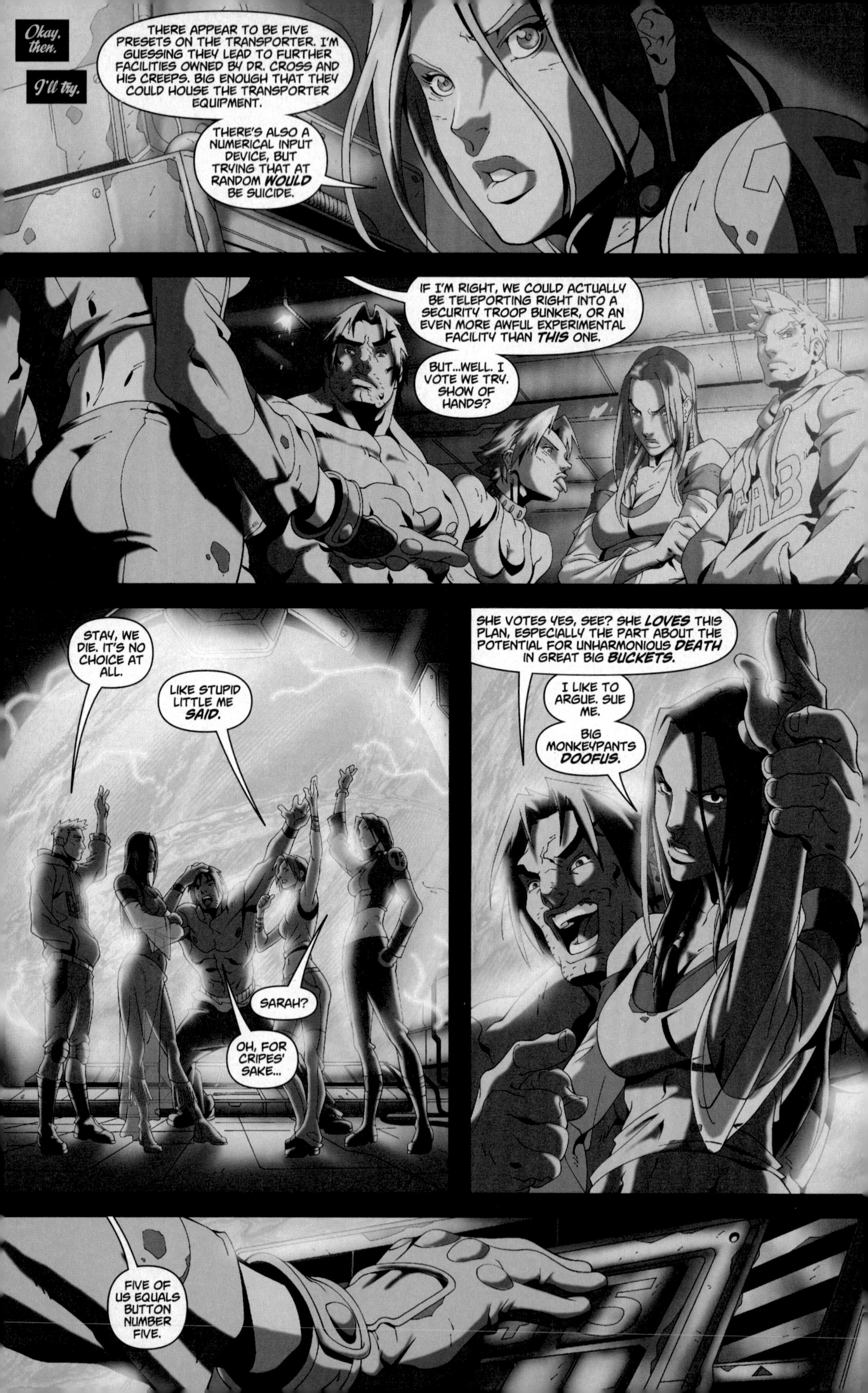
Okay, then.
I'll try.
THERE APPEAR TO BE FIVE PRESETS ON THE TRANSPORTER. I'M GUESSING THEY LEAD TO FURTHER FACILITIES OWNED BY DR. CROSS AND HIS CREEPS. BIG ENOUGH THAT THEY COULD HOUSE THE TRANSPORTER EQUIPMENT.
THERE'S ALSO A NUMERICAL INPUT DEVICE, BUT TRYING THAT AT RANDOM WOULD BE SUICIDE.
IF I'M RIGHT, WE COULD ACTUALLY BE TELEPORTING RIGHT INTO A SECURITY TROOP BUNKER, OR AN EVEN MORE AWFUL EXPERIMENTAL FACILITY THAN THIS ONE.
BUT...WELL. I VOTE WE TRY. SHOW OF HANDS?
STAY, WE DIE. IT'S NO CHOICE AT ALL.
LIKE STUPID LITTLE ME SAID.
SARAH?
OH, FOR CRIPES' SAKE...
SHE VOTES YES, SEE? SHE LOVES THIS PLAN, ESPECIALLY THE PART ABOUT THE POTENTIAL FOR UNHARMONIOUS DEATH IN GREAT BIG BUCKETS.
I LIKE TO ARGUE. SUE ME.
BIG MONKEYPANTS DOOFUS.
FIVE OF US EQUALS BUTTON NUMBER FIVE.

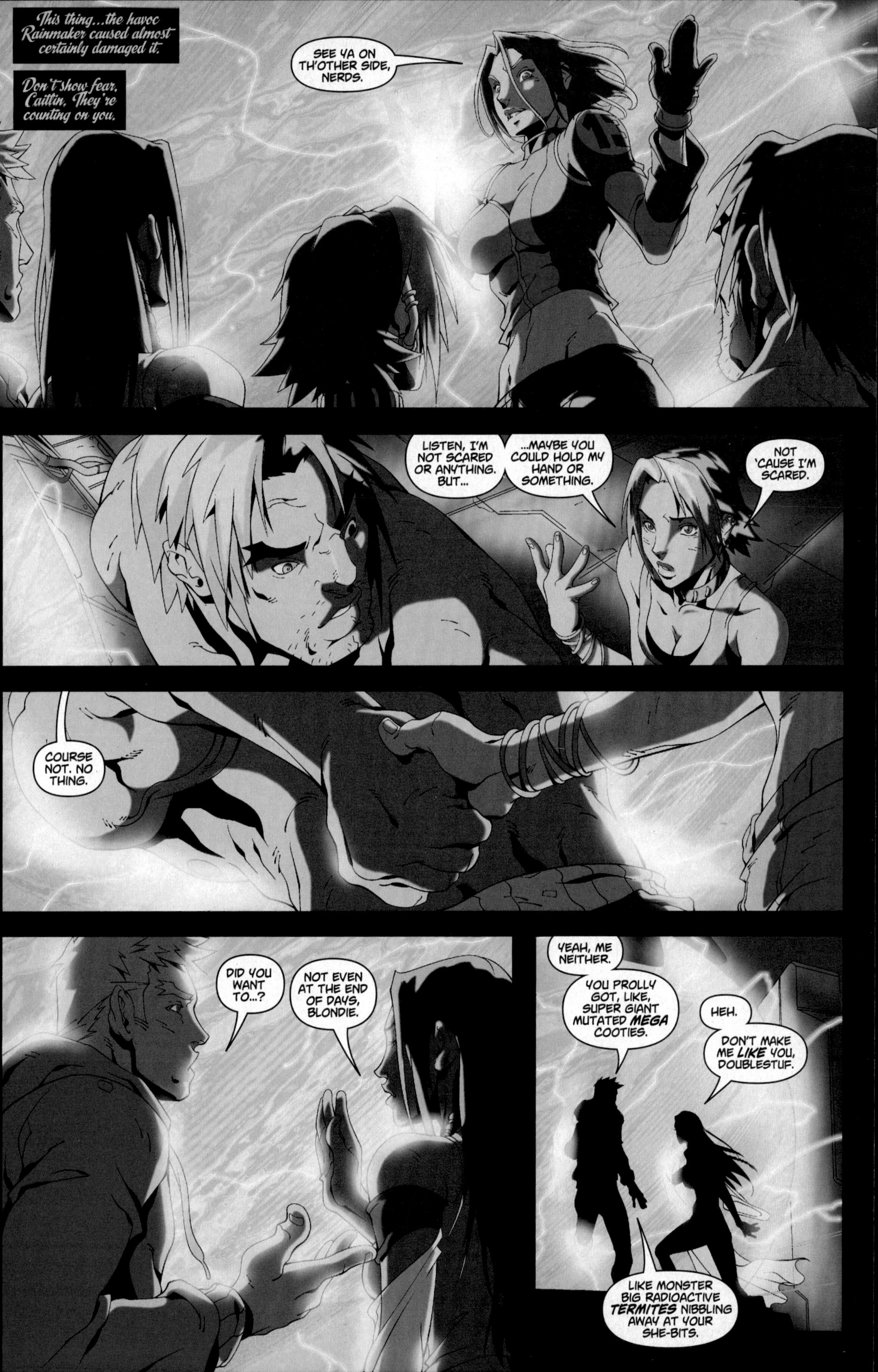
This thing...the havoc Rainmaker caused almost certainly damaged it.
Don't show fear, Caitlin. They're counting on you.
SEE YA ON TH'OTHER SIDE, NERDS.
LISTEN, I'M NOT SCARED OR ANYTHING. BUT...
...MAYBE YOU COULD HOLD MY HAND OR SOMETHING.
NOT 'CAUSE I'M SCARED.
COURSE NOT. NO THING.
DID YOU WANT TO...?
NOT EVEN AT THE END OF DAYS, BLONDIE.
YEAH, ME NEITHER.
YOU PROLLY GOT, LIKE, SUPER GIANT MUTATED MEGA COOTIES.
HEH.
DON'T MAKE ME LIKE YOU, DOUBLESTUF.
LIKE MONSTER BIG RADIOACTIVE TERMITES NIBBLING AWAY AT YOUR SHE-BITS.

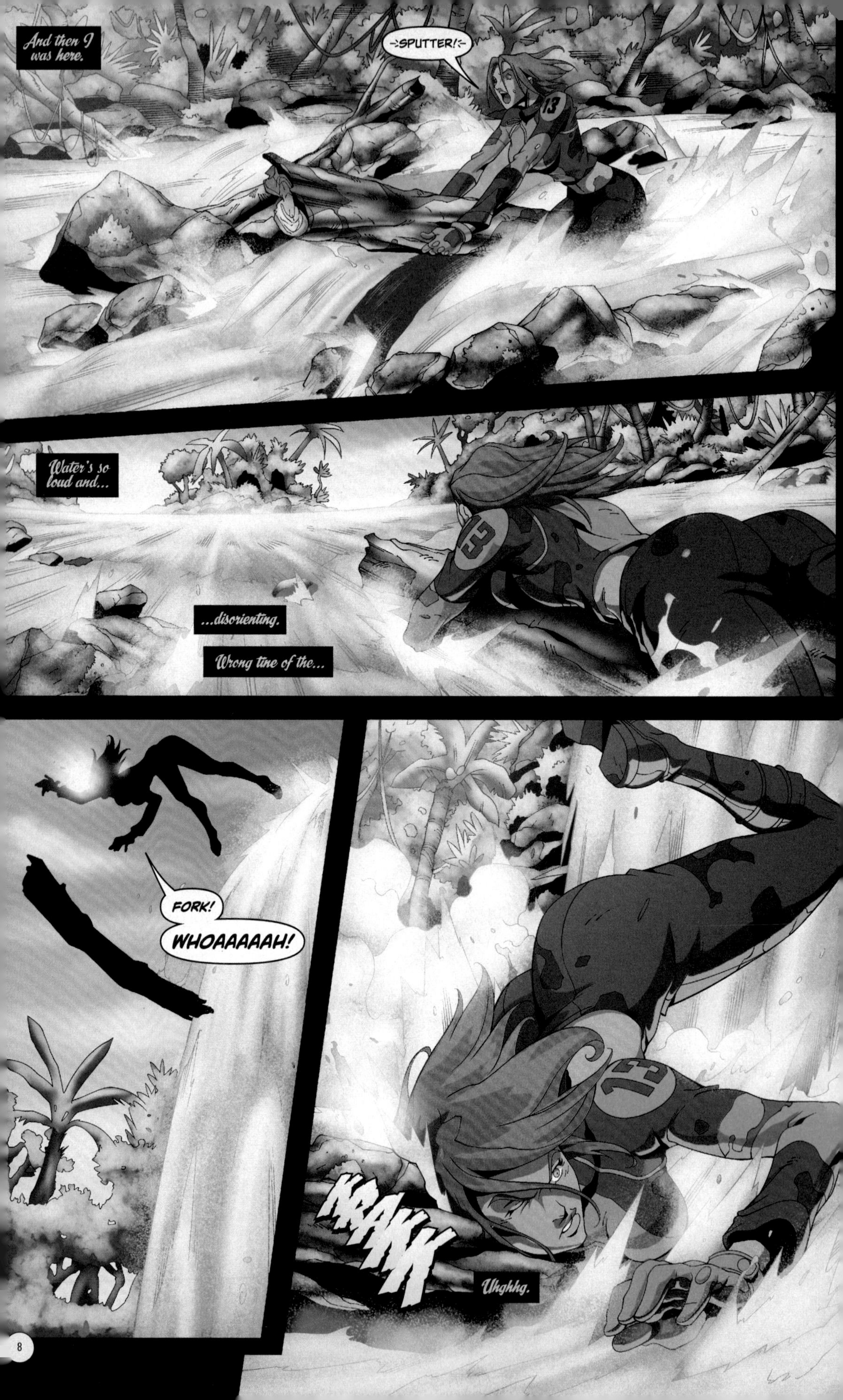

And then I was here.
-SPUTTER!-
Water's so loud and...
...disorienting.
Wrong tine of the...
FORK!
WHOAAAAAH!
KRAKK
Uhghhg.

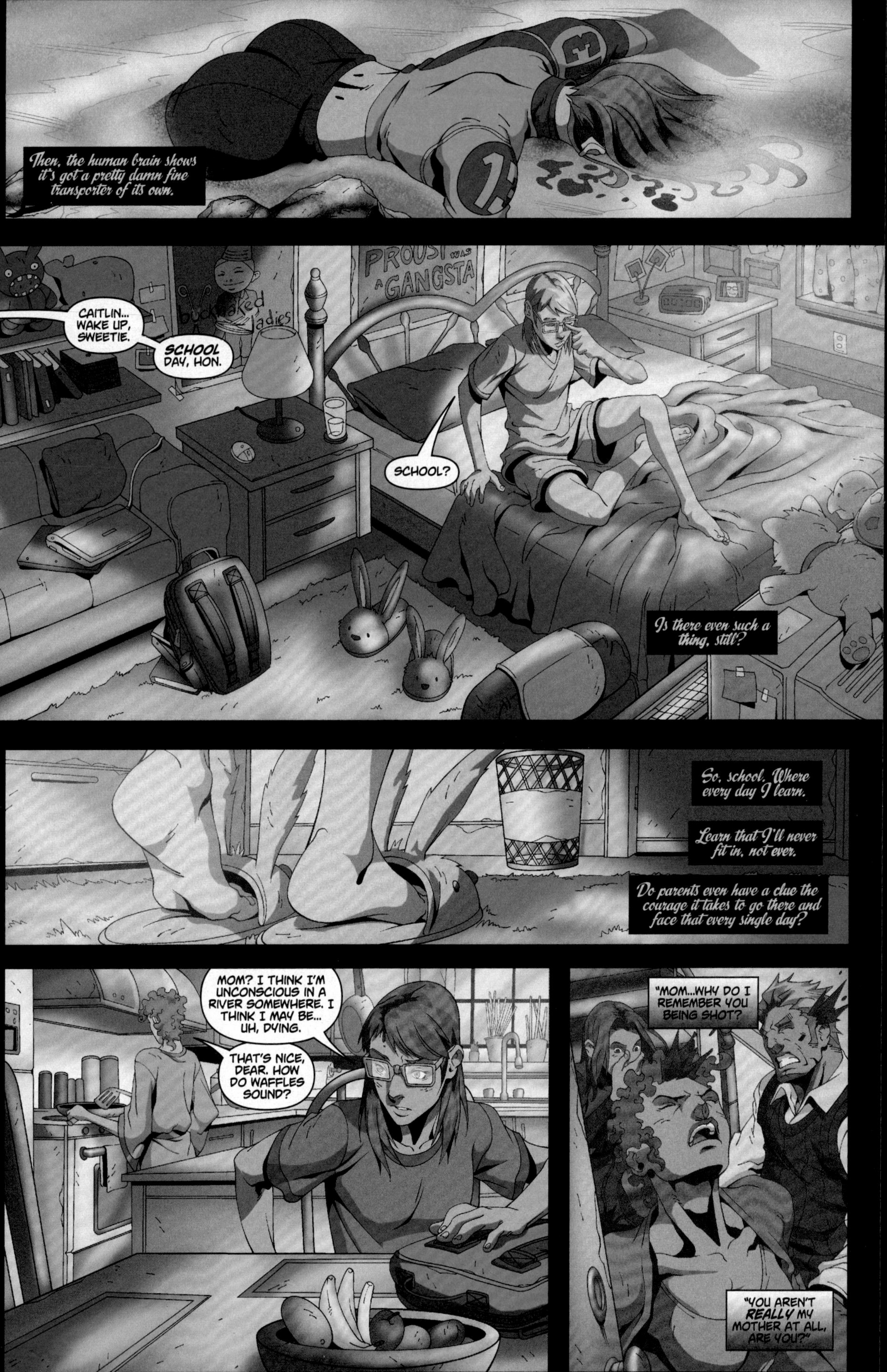
Then, the human brain shows it's got a pretty damn fine transporter of its own.
PROUST WAS A GANGSTA
CAITLIN... WAKE UP, SWEETIE.
SCHOOL DAY, HON.
SCHOOL?
Is there even such a thing, still?
So, school. Where every day I learn.
Learn that I'll never fit in, not ever.
Do parents even have a clue the courage it takes to go there and face that every single day?
MOM? I THINK I'M UNCONSCIOUS IN A RIVER SOMEWHERE. I THINK I MAY BE... UH, DYING.
THAT'S NICE, DEAR. HOW DO WAFFLES SOUND?
"MOM...WHY DO I REMEMBER YOU BEING SHOT?
"YOU AREN'T REALLY MY MOTHER AT ALL, ARE YOU?"

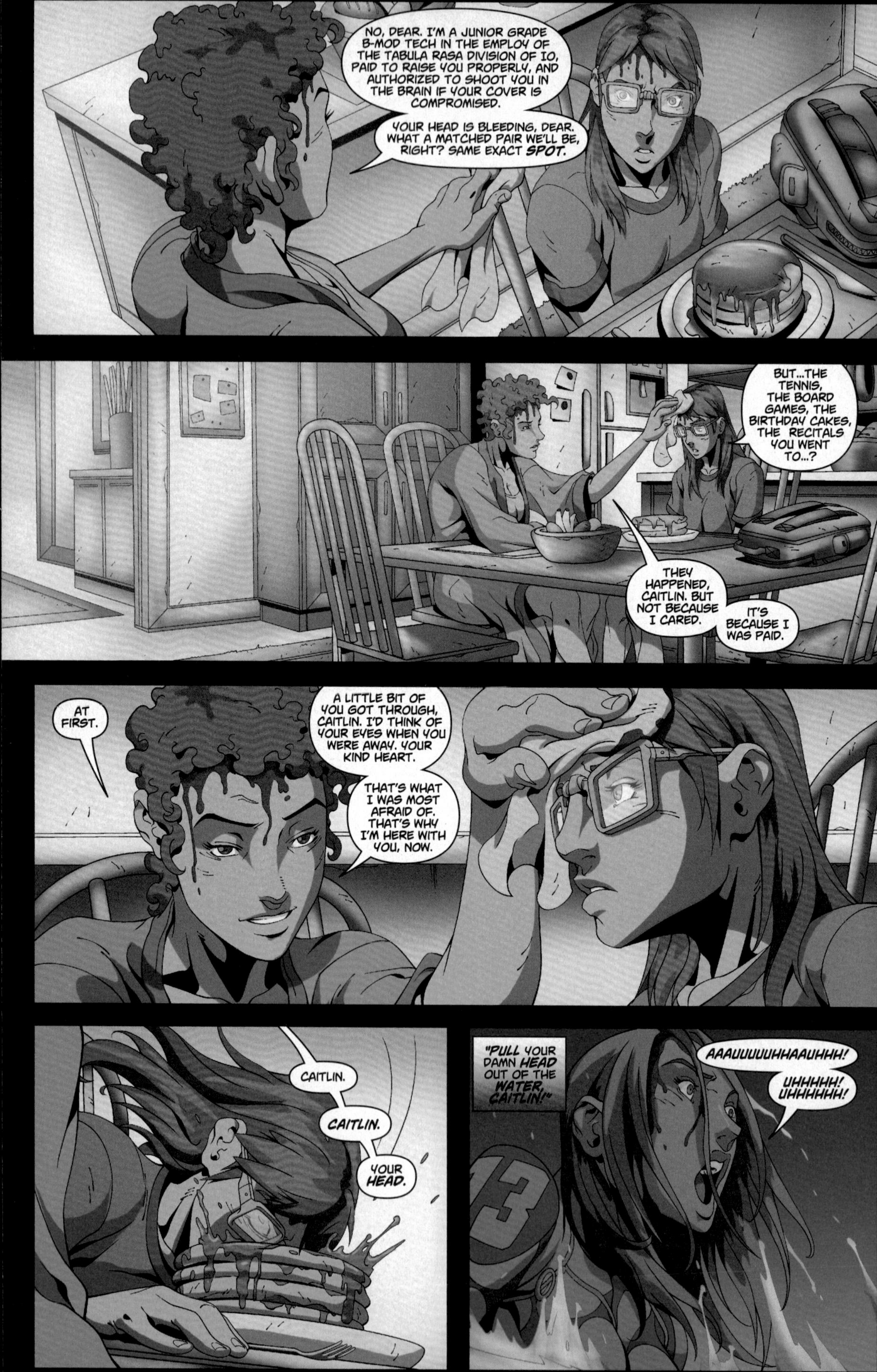
NO, DEAR. I'M A JUNIOR GRADE B-MOD TECH IN THE EMPLOY OF THE TABULA RASA DIVISION OF IO, PAID TO RAISE YOU PROPERLY, AND AUTHORIZED TO SHOOT YOU IN THE BRAIN IF YOUR COVER IS COMPROMISED.
YOUR HEAD IS BLEEDING, DEAR. WHAT A MATCHED PAIR WE'LL BE, RIGHT? SAME EXACT SPOT.
BUT...THE TENNIS, THE BOARD GAMES, THE BIRTHDAY CAKES, THE RECITALS YOU WENT TO...?
THEY HAPPENED, CAITLIN. BUT NOT BECAUSE I CARED.
IT'S BECAUSE I WAS PAID.
AT FIRST.
A LITTLE BIT OF YOU GOT THROUGH, CAITLIN. I'D THINK OF YOUR EYES WHEN YOU WERE AWAY. YOUR KIND HEART.
THAT'S WHAT I WAS MOST AFRAID OF. THAT'S WHY I'M HERE WITH YOU, NOW.
CAITLIN.
CAITLIN.
YOUR HEAD.
"PULL YOUR DAMN HEAD OUT OF THE WATER, CAITLIN!"
AAAUUUUUHHAAUHHH!
UHHHHHH! UHHHHHHH!

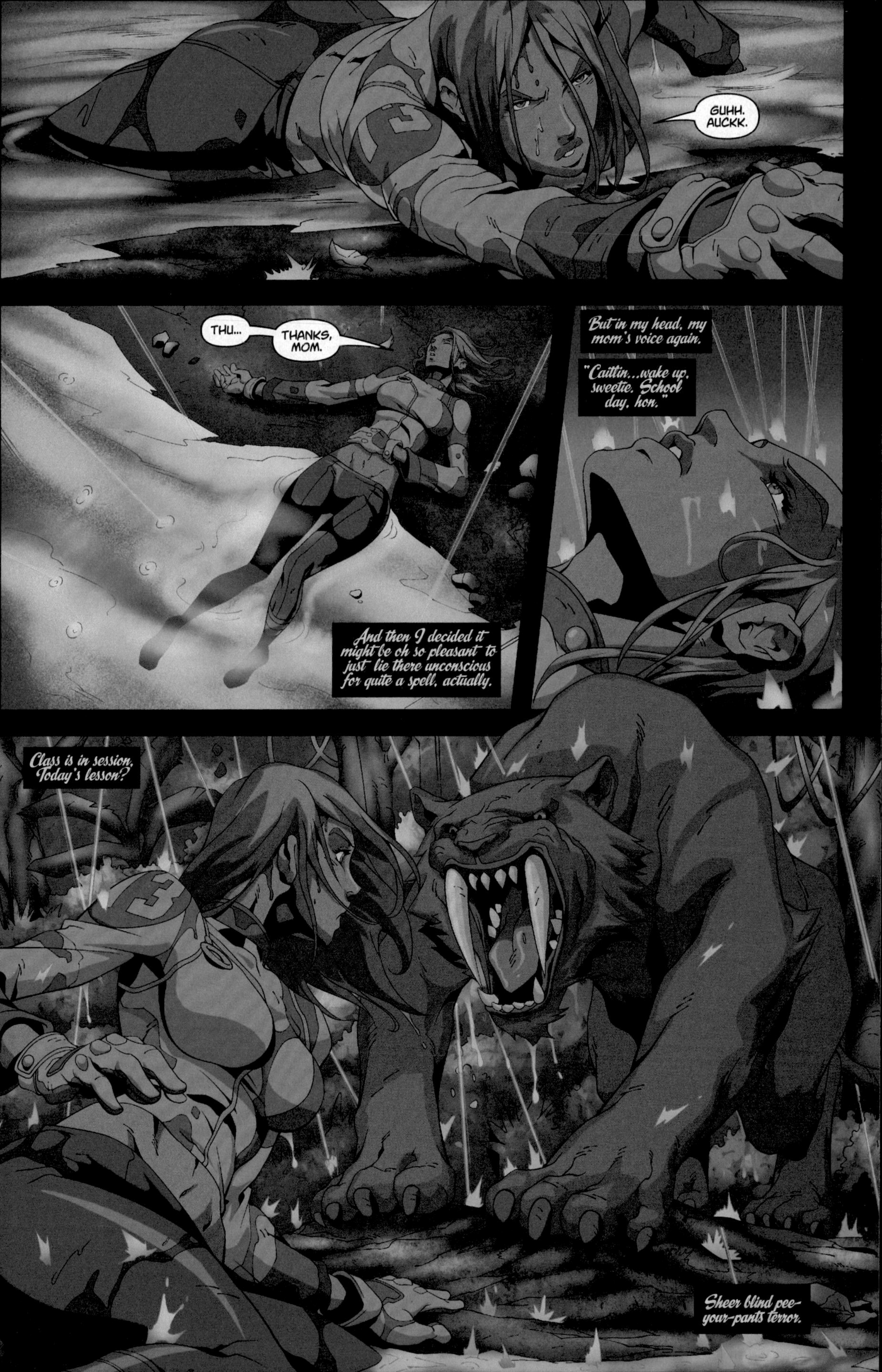
GUHH. AUCKK.
THU...
THANKS, MOM.
And then I decided it might be oh so pleasant to just lie there unconscious for quite a spell, actually.
But in my head, my mom's voice again.
"Caitlin...wake up, sweetie. School day, hon."
Class is in session. Today's lesson?
Sheer blind pee-your-pants terror.

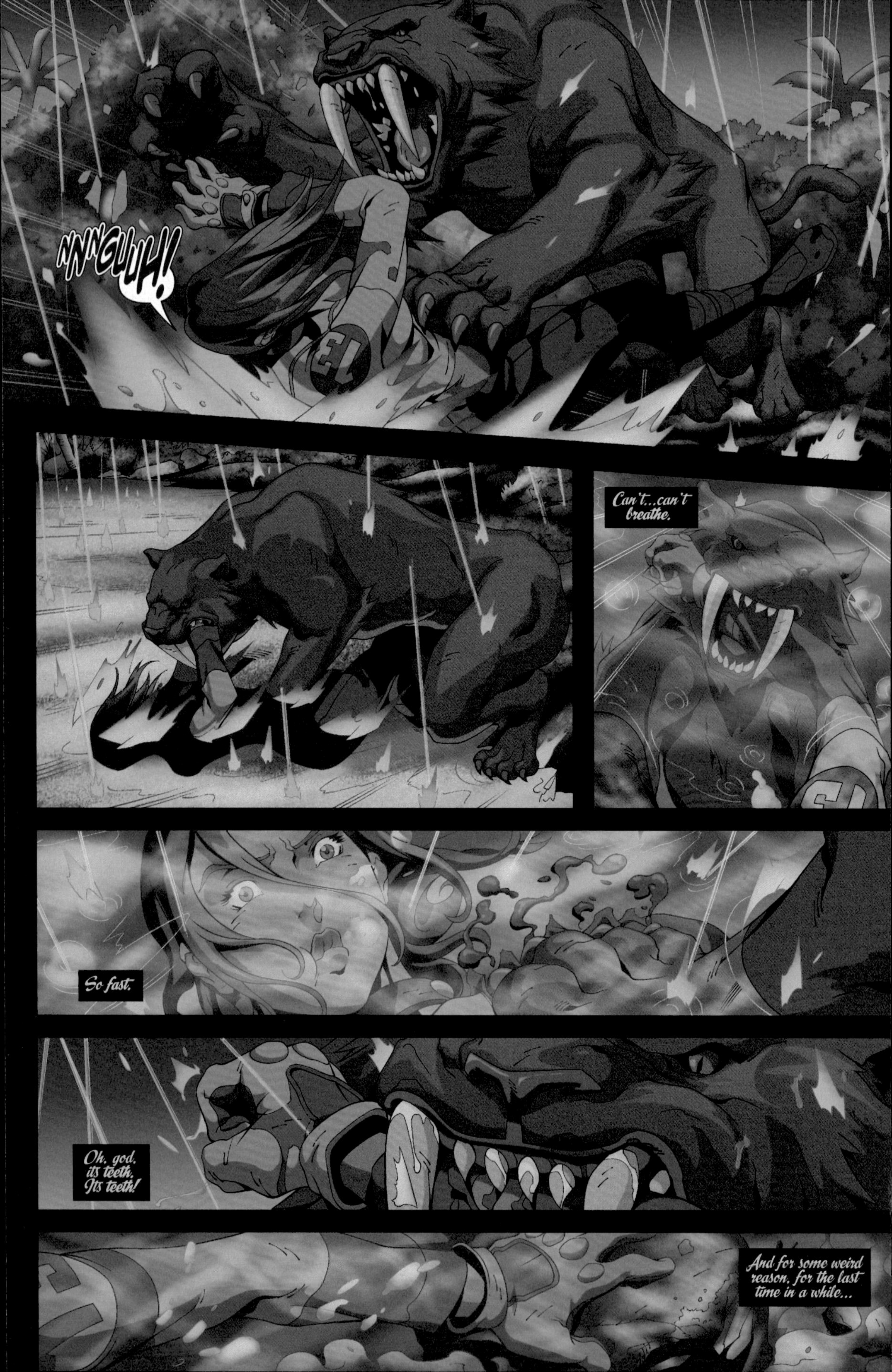
NNNGUUUH!
Can't...can't breathe.
So fast.
Oh, god, its teeth. Its teeth!
And for some weird reason, for the last time in a while...

...I think again of school.

AHUH. AHUH. AHUH.

Either that smersh on my head was a lot harder than I thought, or I just killed a Smilodon neogaeus.

I ALMOST PREFER THE CONCUSSION THEORY.

Shelter. I need shelter, and soon.

There could be a lot more of those things, for all I know.

In Golding's Lord Of The Flies, there's a heart-wrenching scene where the shipwrecked boys are rescued from their island by an English freighter.

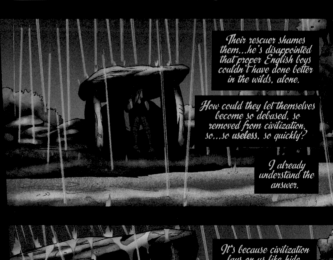

Their rescuer shames them...he's disappointed that proper English boys couldn't have done better in the wilds, alone.

How could they let themselves become so debased, so removed from civilization, so...so useless, so quickly?

I already understand the answer.

It's because civilization lays on us like hide a thousand layers deep.

I try to sleep, fins in the water, voices I can't quite hear in the air around me, fins in the water, fins in the water.

And teeth I'm afraid to imagine.

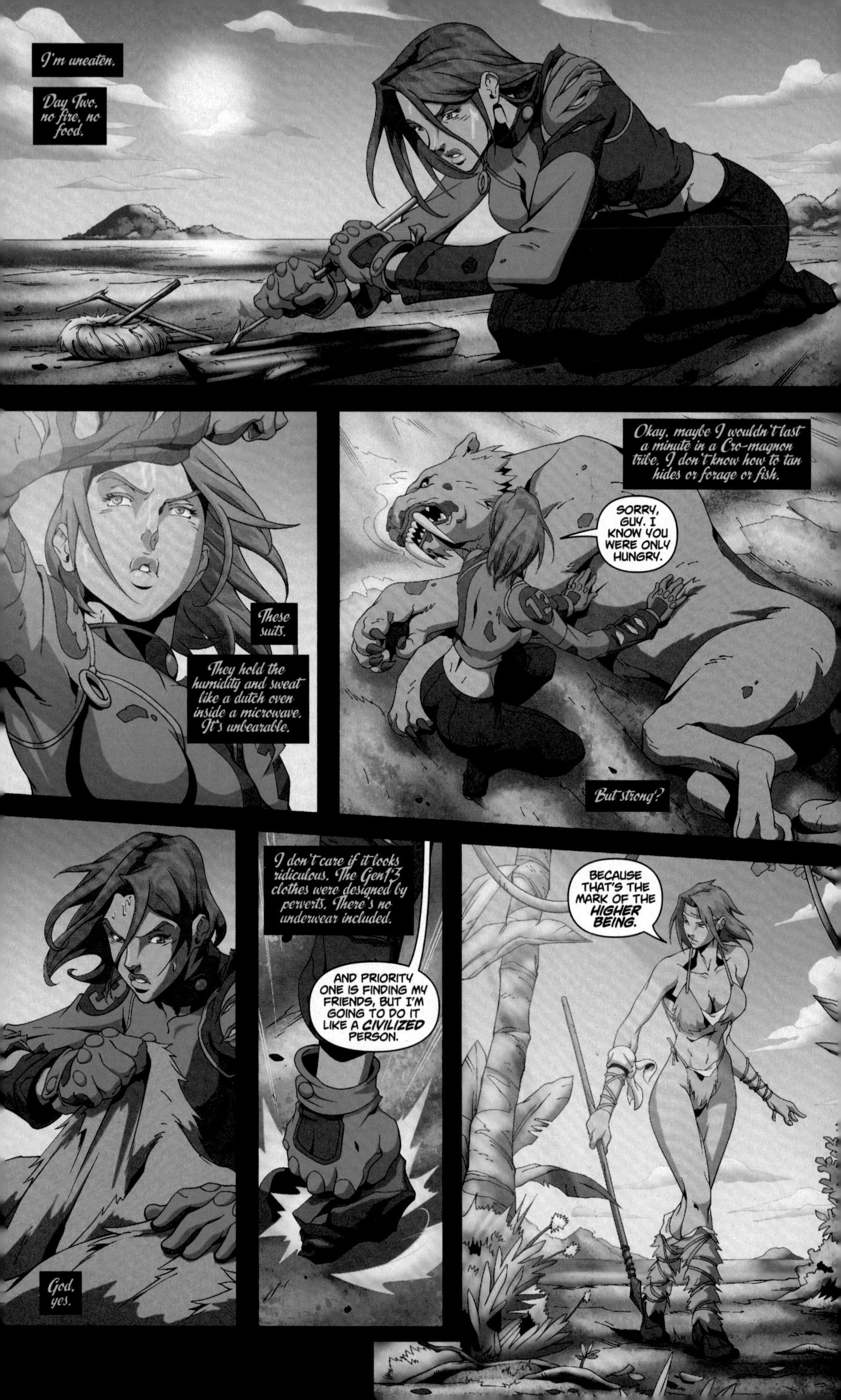

I'm uneaten.
Day Two, no fire, no food.
These suits.
They hold the humidity and sweat like a dutch oven inside a microwave. It's unbearable.
Okay, maybe I wouldn't last a minute in a Cro-magnon tribe. I don't know how to tan hides or forage or fish.
SORRY, GUY. I KNOW YOU WERE ONLY HUNGRY.
But strong?
God, yes.
I don't care if it looks ridiculous. The Gen13 clothes were designed by perverts. There's no underwear included.
AND PRIORITY ONE IS FINDING MY FRIENDS, BUT I'M GOING TO DO IT LIKE A CIVILIZED PERSON.
BECAUSE THAT'S THE MARK OF THE HIGHER BEING.

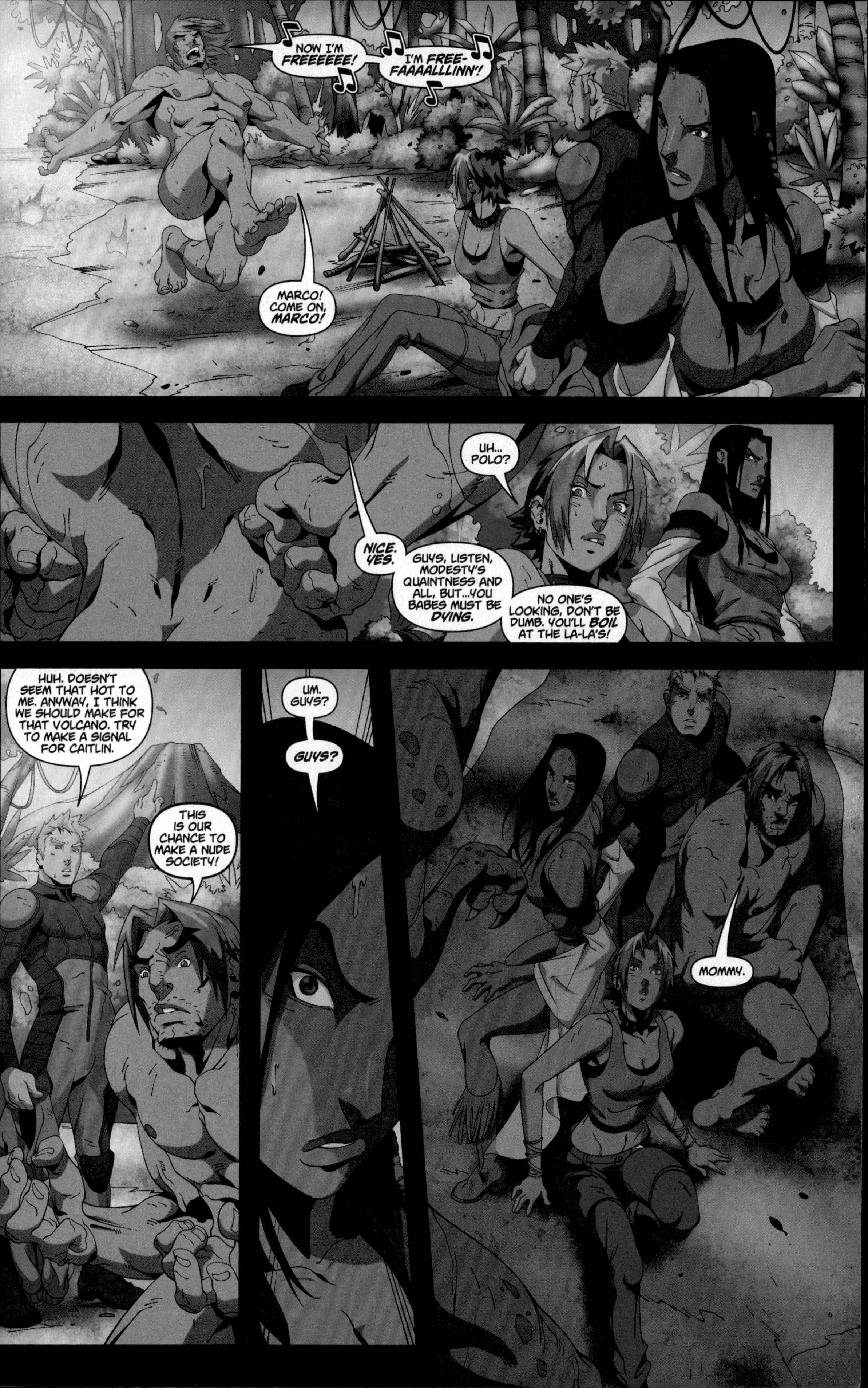
NOW I'M FREEEEEEE!
I'M FREE-FAAAALLLINN'!
MARCO! COME ON, MARCO!
UH... POLO?
NICE. YES.
GUYS, LISTEN, MODESTY'S QUAINTNESS AND ALL, BUT...YOU BABES MUST BE DYING.
NO ONE'S LOOKING, DON'T BE DUMB. YOU'LL BOIL AT THE LA-LA'S!
HUH. DOESN'T SEEM THAT HOT TO ME. ANYWAY, I THINK WE SHOULD MAKE FOR THAT VOLCANO. TRY TO MAKE A SIGNAL FOR CAITLIN.
THIS IS OUR CHANCE TO MAKE A NUDE SOCIETY!
UM. GUYS?
GUYS?
MOMMY.

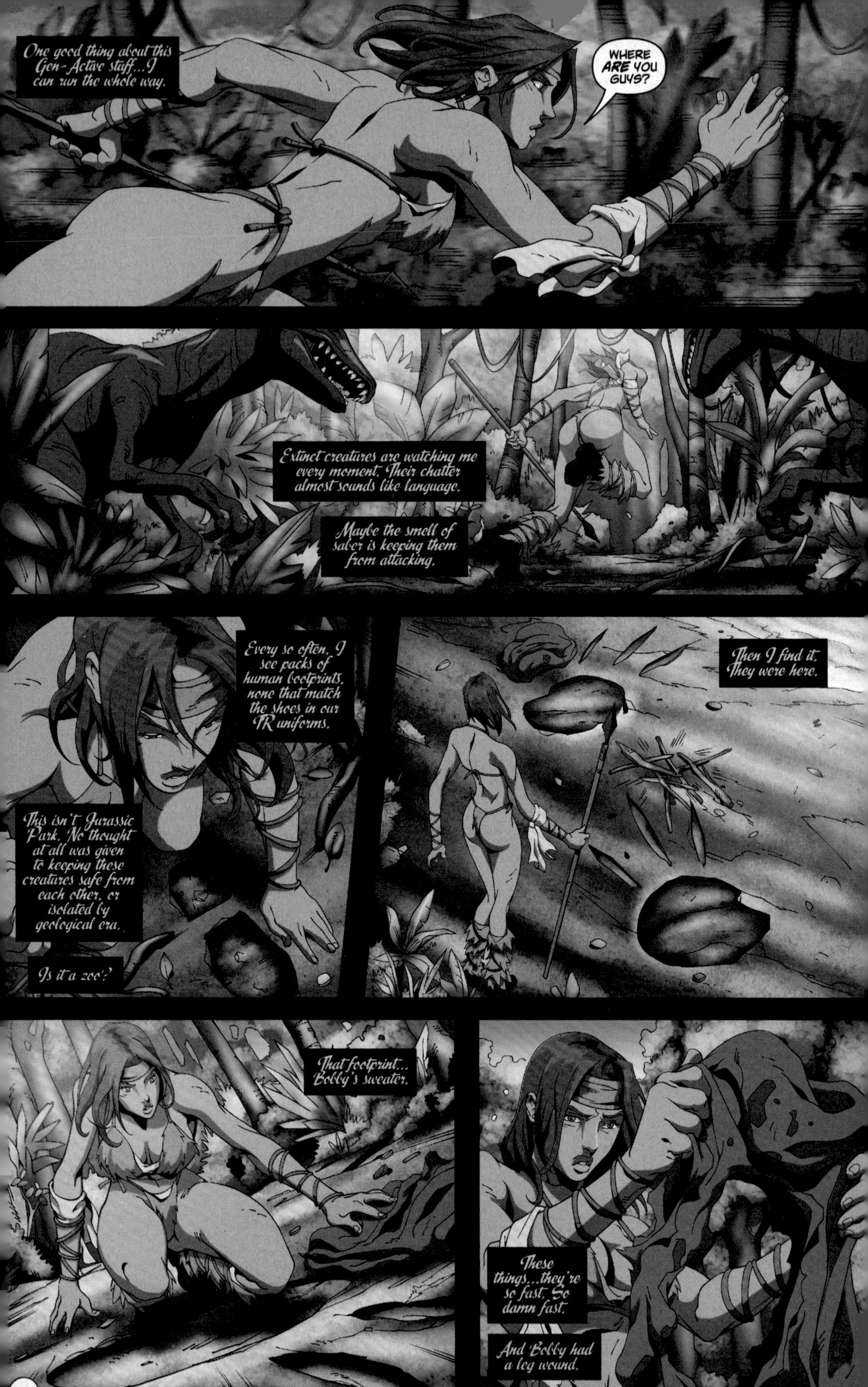
One good thing about this Gen-Active stuff...I can run the whole way.
WHERE ARE YOU GUYS?
Extinct creatures are watching me every moment. Their chatter almost sounds like language.
Maybe the smell of saber is keeping them from attacking.
Every so often, I see packs of human bootprints, none that match the shoes in our TR uniforms.
This isn't Jurassic Park. No thought at all was given to keeping these creatures safe from each other, or isolated by geological era.
Is it a zoo?
Then I find it. They were here.
That footprint... Bobby's sweater.
These things...they're so fast. So damn fast.
And Bobby had a leg wound.

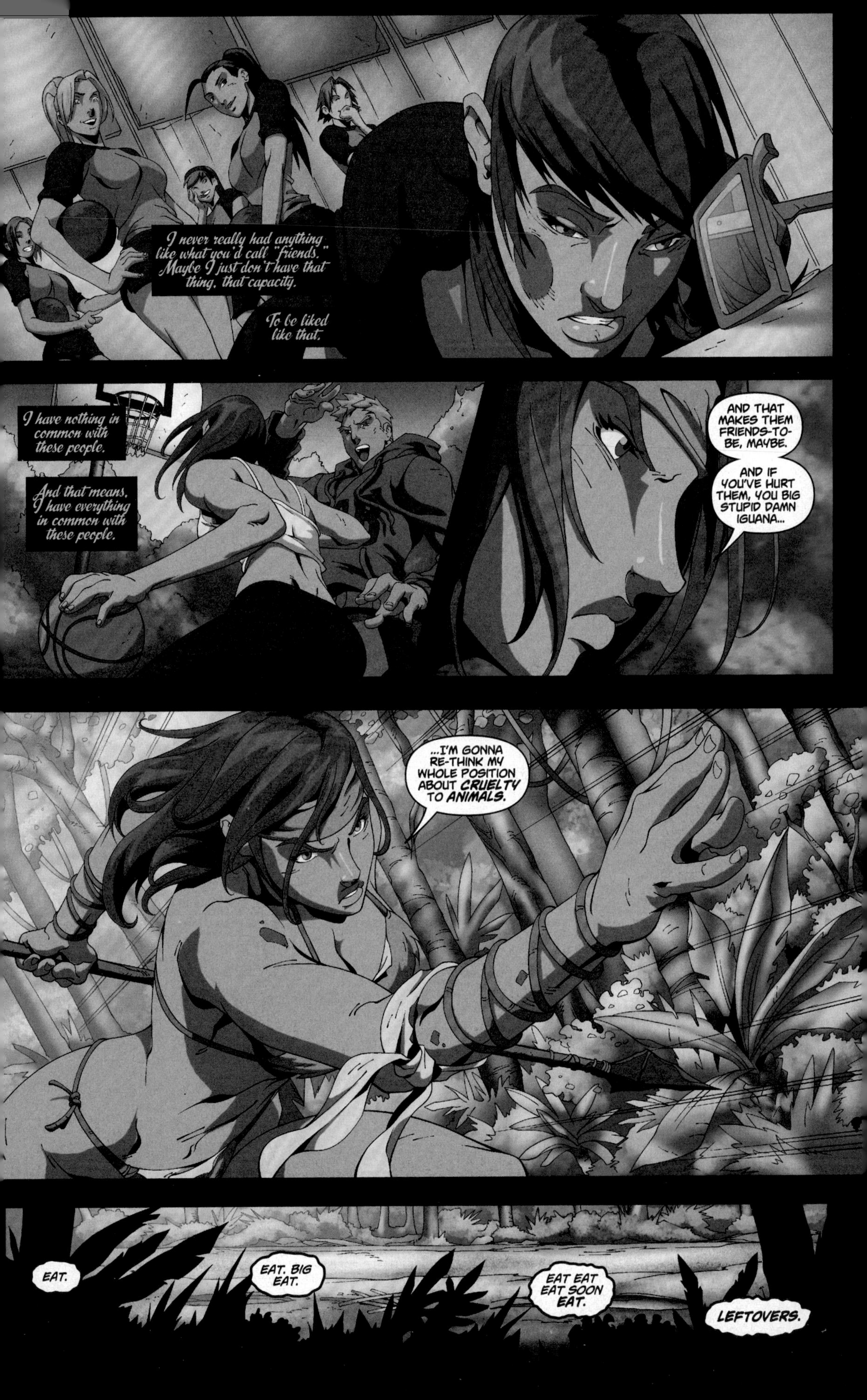
I never really had anything like what you'd call "friends." Maybe I just don't have that thing, that capacity.
To be liked like that.
I have nothing in common with these people.
And that means, I have everything in common with these people.
AND THAT MAKES THEM FRIENDS-TO-BE, MAYBE.
AND IF YOU'VE HURT THEM, YOU BIG STUPID DAMN IGUANA...
...I'M GONNA RE-THINK MY WHOLE POSITION ABOUT CRUELTY TO ANIMALS.
EAT.
EAT. BIG EAT.
EAT EAT EAT SOON EAT.
LEFTOVERS.

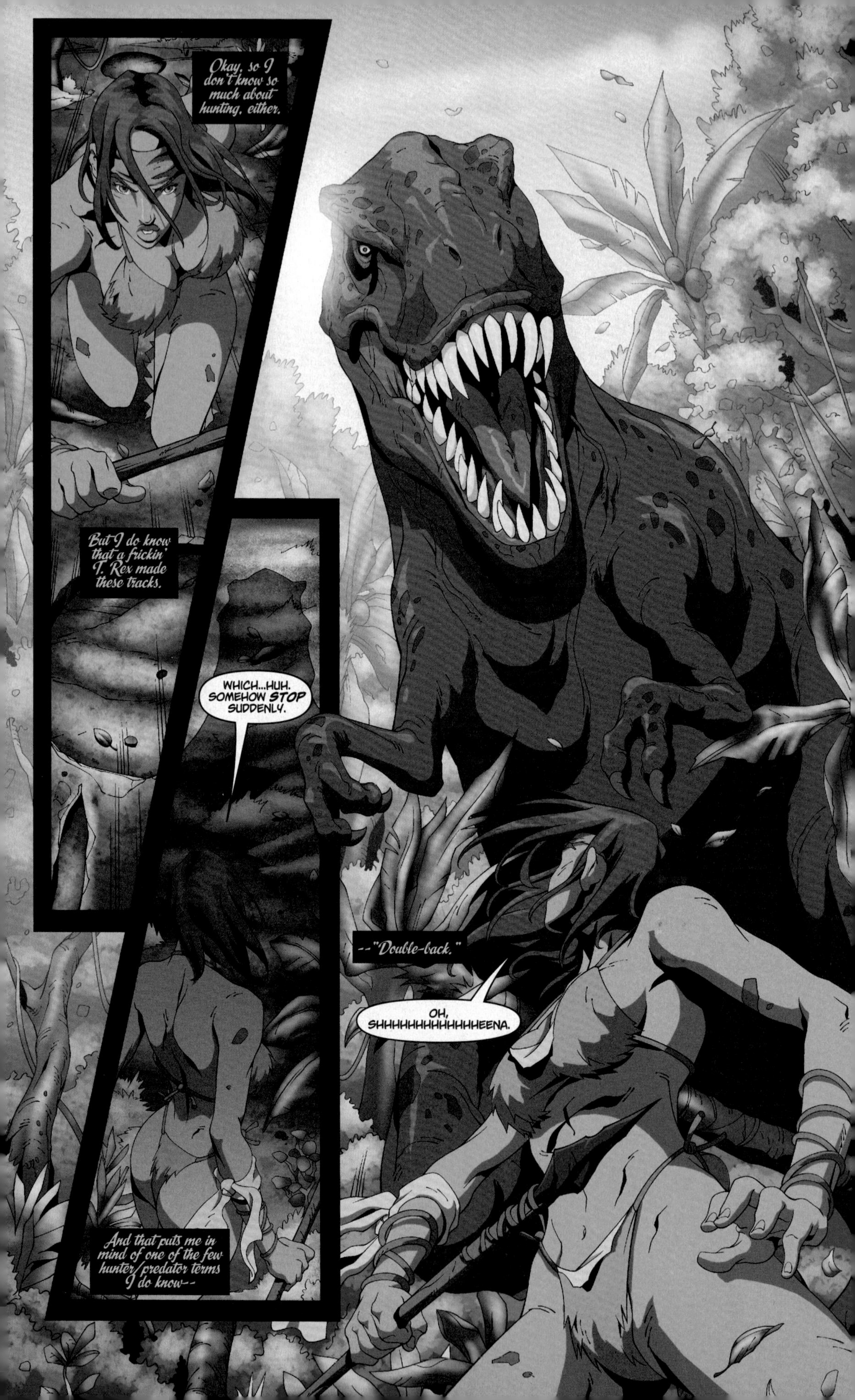
Okay, so I don't know so much about hunting, either.
But I do know that a frickin' T. Rex made these tracks.
WHICH...HUH. SOMEHOW STOP SUDDENLY.
And that puts me in mind of one of the few hunter/predator terms I do know--
--"Double-back."
OH, SHHHHHHHHHHHHHEENA.

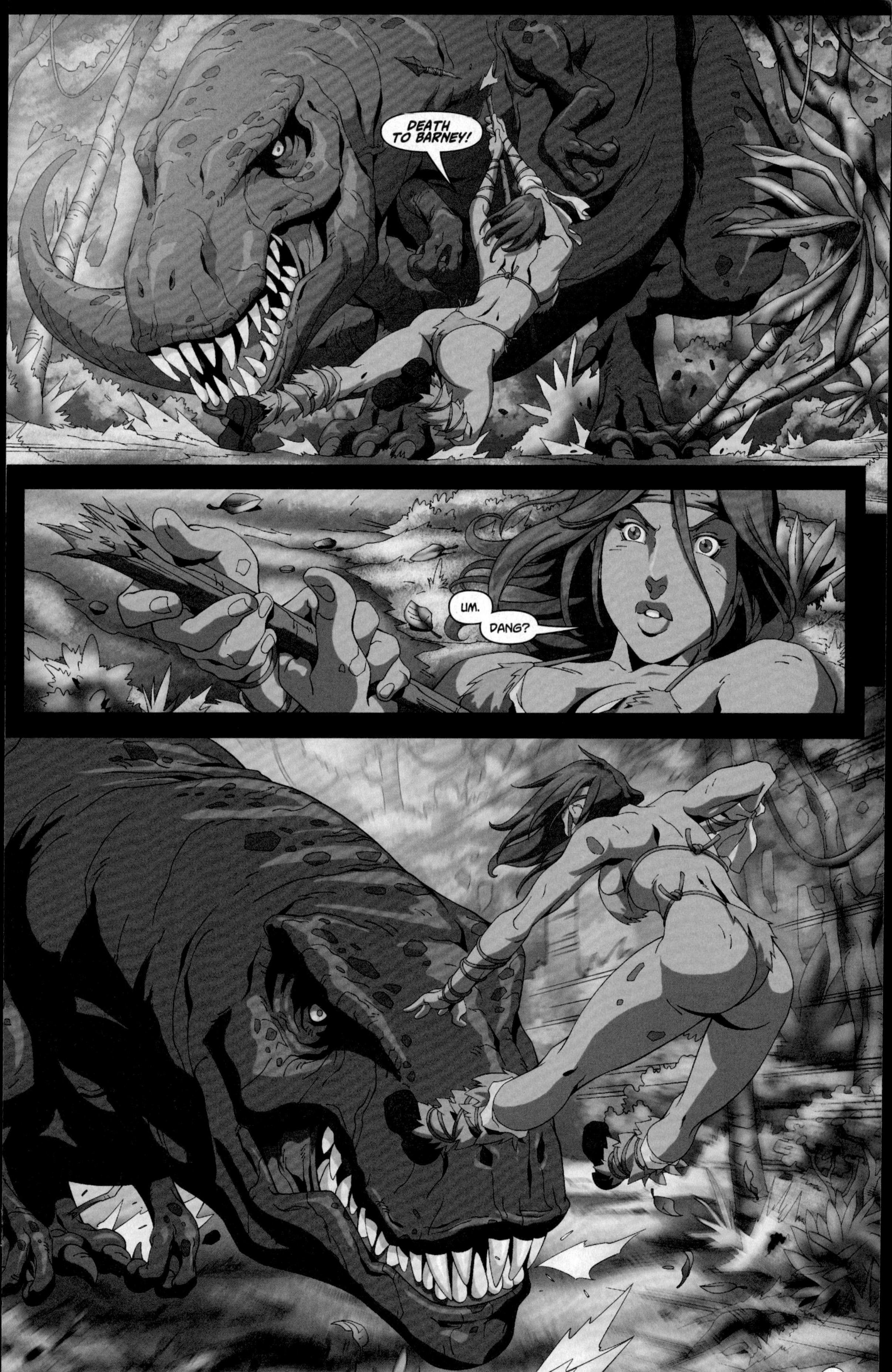
DEATH TO BARNEY!
UM.
DANG?

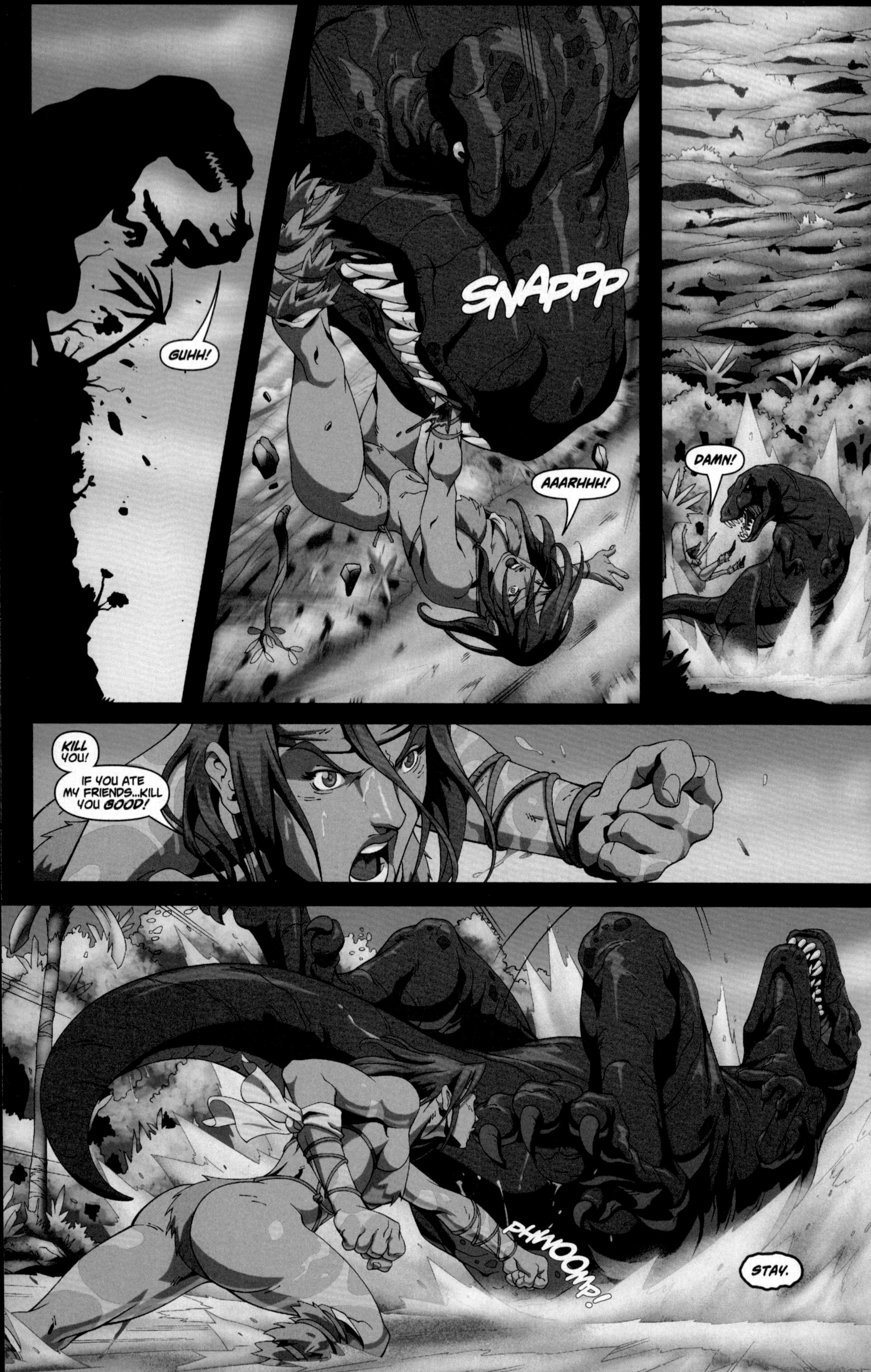
GUHH!
SNAPPP
AAARHHH!
DAMN!
KILL YOU!
IF YOU ATE MY FRIENDS...KILL YOU GOOD!
PHWOOMP!
STAY.

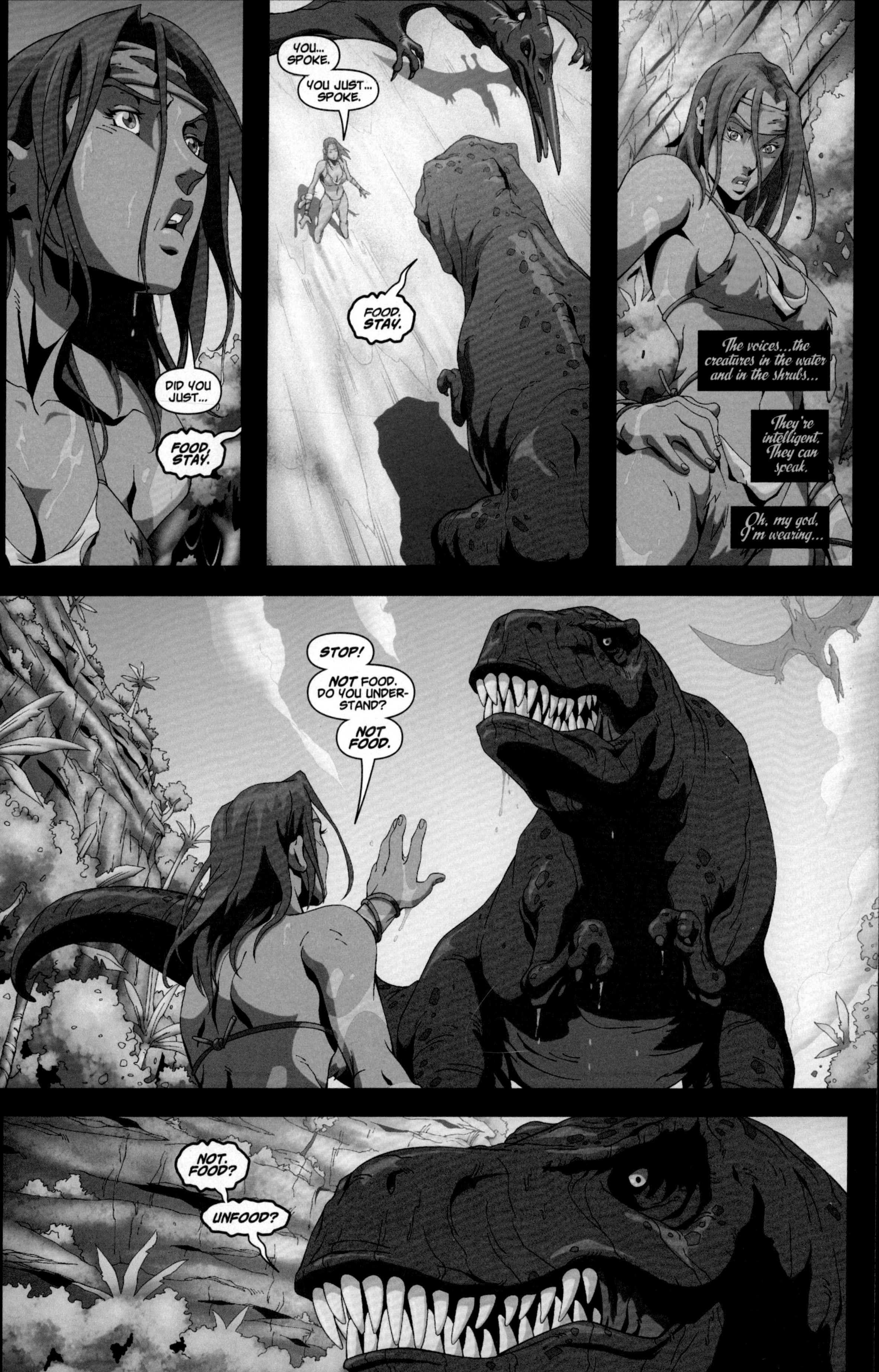
DID YOU JUST...
FOOD, STAY.
YOU... SPOKE.
YOU JUST... SPOKE.
FOOD. STAY.
The voices...the creatures in the water and in the shrubs...
They're intelligent. They can speak.
Oh, my god, I'm wearing...
STOP!
NOT FOOD. DO YOU UNDERSTAND?
NOT FOOD.
NOT. FOOD?
UNFOOD?

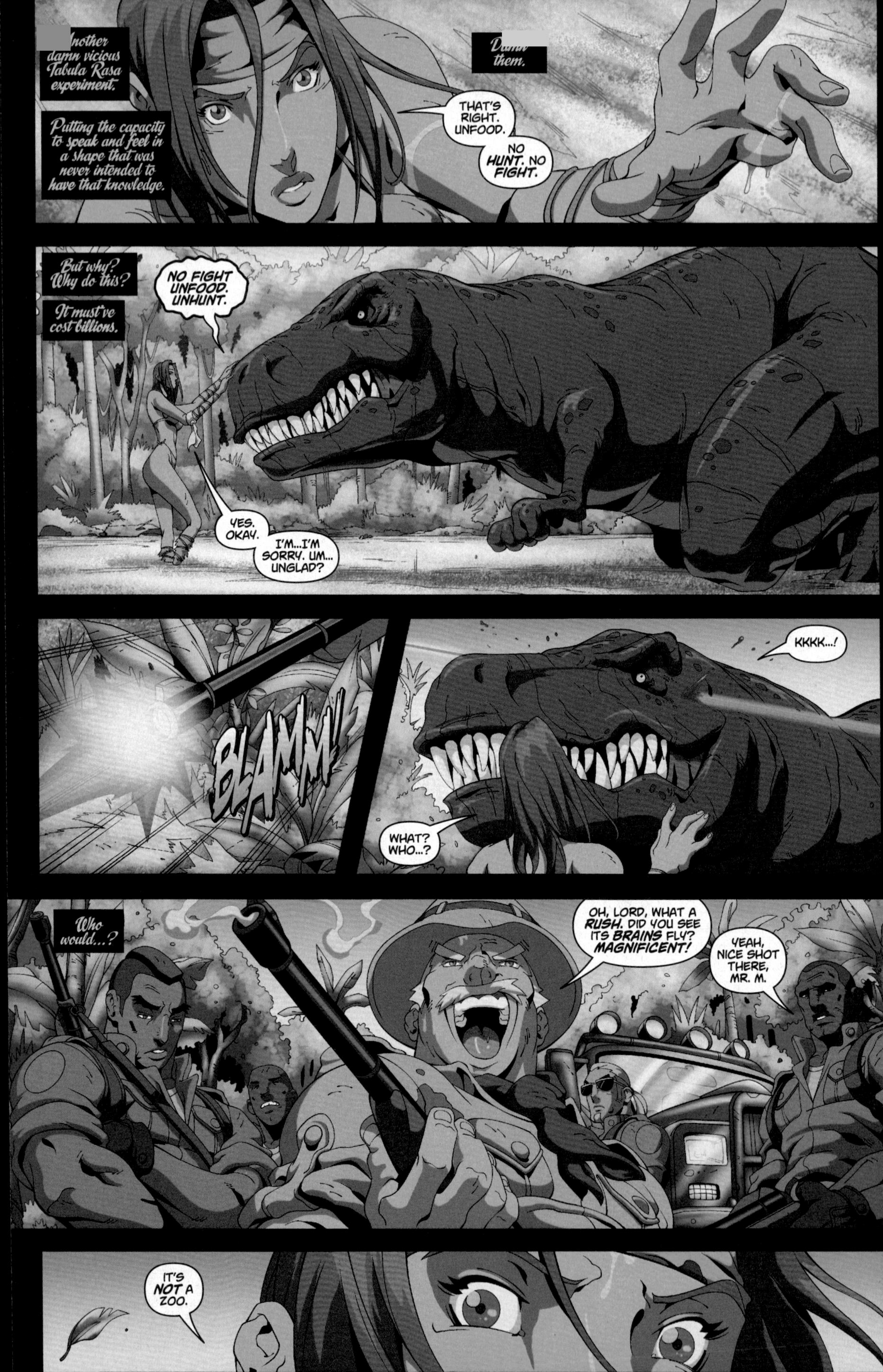
nother damn vicious Tabula Rasa experiment.
Putting the capacity to speak and feel in a shape that was never intended to have that knowledge.
Damn them.
THAT'S RIGHT. UNFOOD.
NO HUNT. NO FIGHT.
But why? Why do this?
It must've cost billions.
NO FIGHT UNFOOD. UNHUNT.
YES. OKAY.
I'M...I'M SORRY. UM... UNGLAD?
BLAMM!
KKKK...!
WHAT? WHO...?
Who would...?
OH, LORD, WHAT A RUSH. DID YOU SEE ITS BRAINS FLY? MAGNIFICENT!
YEAH, NICE SHOT THERE, MR. M.
IT'S NOT A ZOO.

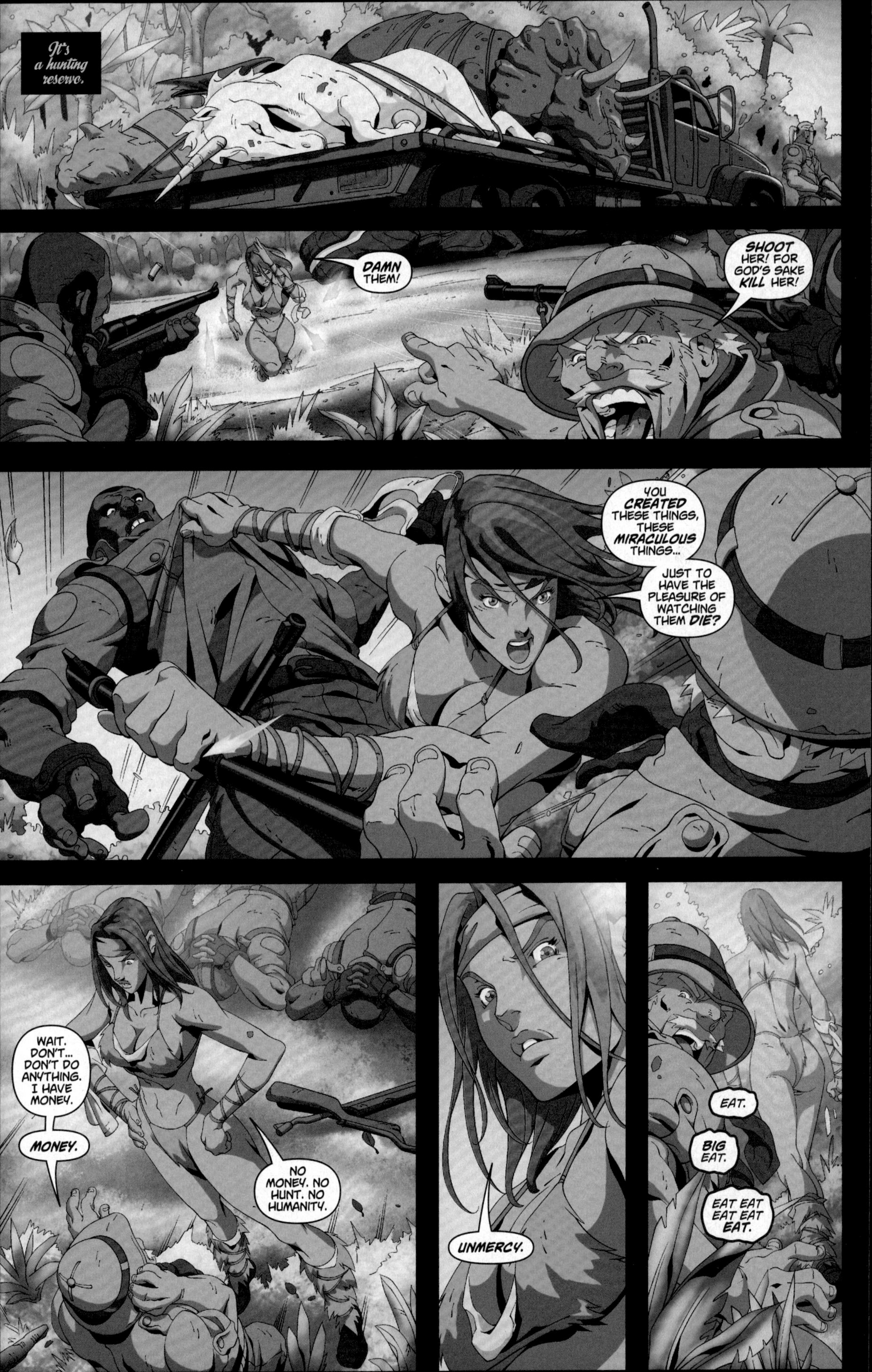
It's a hunting reserve.
DAMN THEM!
SHOOT HER! FOR GOD'S SAKE KILL HER!
YOU CREATED THESE THINGS, THESE MIRACULOUS THINGS...
JUST TO HAVE THE PLEASURE OF WATCHING THEM DIE?
WAIT. DON'T... DON'T DO ANYTHING. I HAVE MONEY.
MONEY.
NO MONEY. NO HUNT. NO HUMANITY.
UNMERCY.
EAT.
BIG EAT.
EAT EAT EAT EAT EAT.

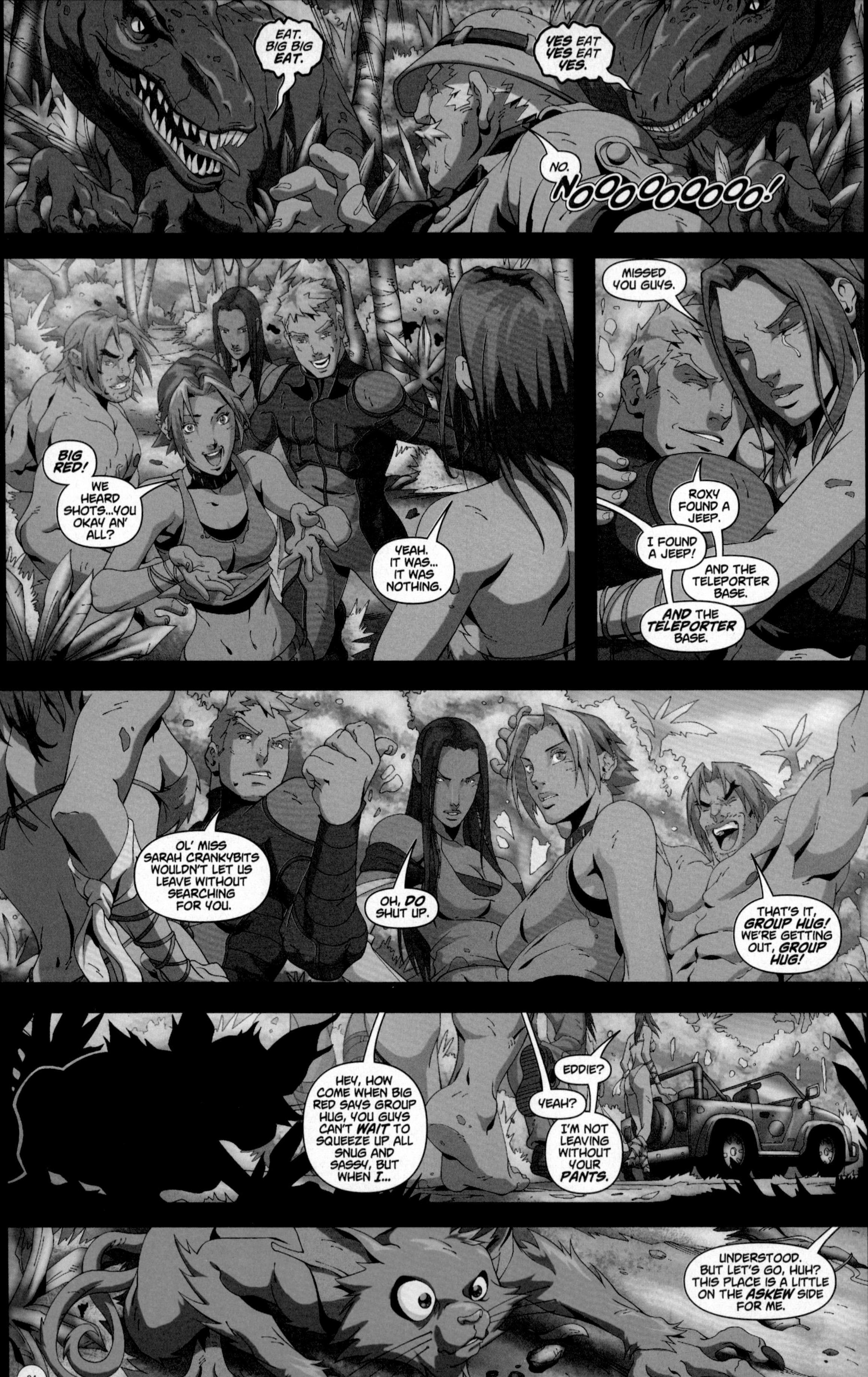

EAT. BIG BIG EAT.
YES EAT YES EAT YES.
NO. NOOOOOOOOOO!
BIG RED!
WE HEARD SHOTS...YOU OKAY AN' ALL?
YEAH. IT WAS... IT WAS NOTHING.
MISSED YOU GUYS.
ROXY FOUND A JEEP.
I FOUND A JEEP!
AND THE TELEPORTER BASE.
AND THE TELEPORTER BASE.
OL' MISS SARAH CRANKYBITS WOULDN'T LET US LEAVE WITHOUT SEARCHING FOR YOU.
OH, DO SHUT UP.
THAT'S IT, GROUP HUG! WE'RE GETTING OUT, GROUP HUG!
HEY, HOW COME WHEN BIG RED SAYS GROUP HUG, YOU GUYS CAN'T WAIT TO SQUEEZE UP ALL SNUG AND SASSY, BUT WHEN I...
EDDIE?
YEAH?
I'M NOT LEAVING WITHOUT YOUR PANTS.
UNDERSTOOD. BUT LET'S GO, HUH? THIS PLACE IS A LITTLE ON THE ASKEW SIDE FOR ME.

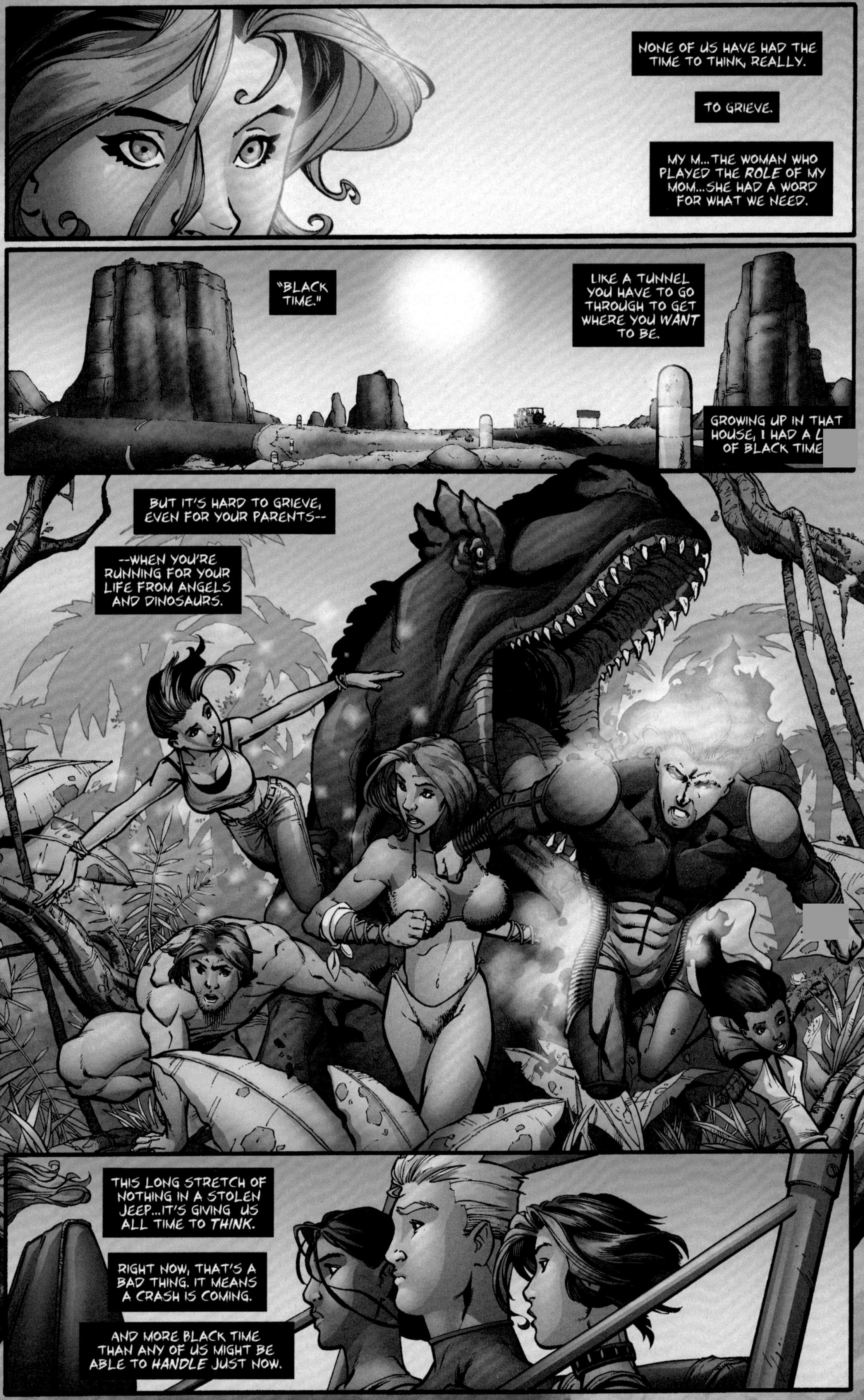
NONE OF US HAVE HAD THE TIME TO THINK, REALLY.
TO GRIEVE.
MY M...THE WOMAN WHO PLAYED THE *ROLE* OF MY MOM...SHE HAD A WORD FOR WHAT WE NEED.
"BLACK TIME."
LIKE A TUNNEL YOU HAVE TO GO THROUGH TO GET WHERE YOU *WANT* TO BE.
GROWING UP IN THAT HOUSE, I HAD A L
OF BLACK TIME
BUT IT'S HARD TO GRIEVE, EVEN FOR YOUR PARENTS--
--WHEN YOU'RE RUNNING FOR YOUR LIFE FROM ANGELS AND DINOSAURS.
THIS LONG STRETCH OF NOTHING IN A STOLEN JEEP...IT'S GIVING US ALL TIME TO *THINK*.
RIGHT NOW, THAT'S A BAD THING. IT MEANS A CRASH IS COMING.
AND MORE BLACK TIME THAN ANY OF US MIGHT BE ABLE TO *HANDLE* JUST NOW.

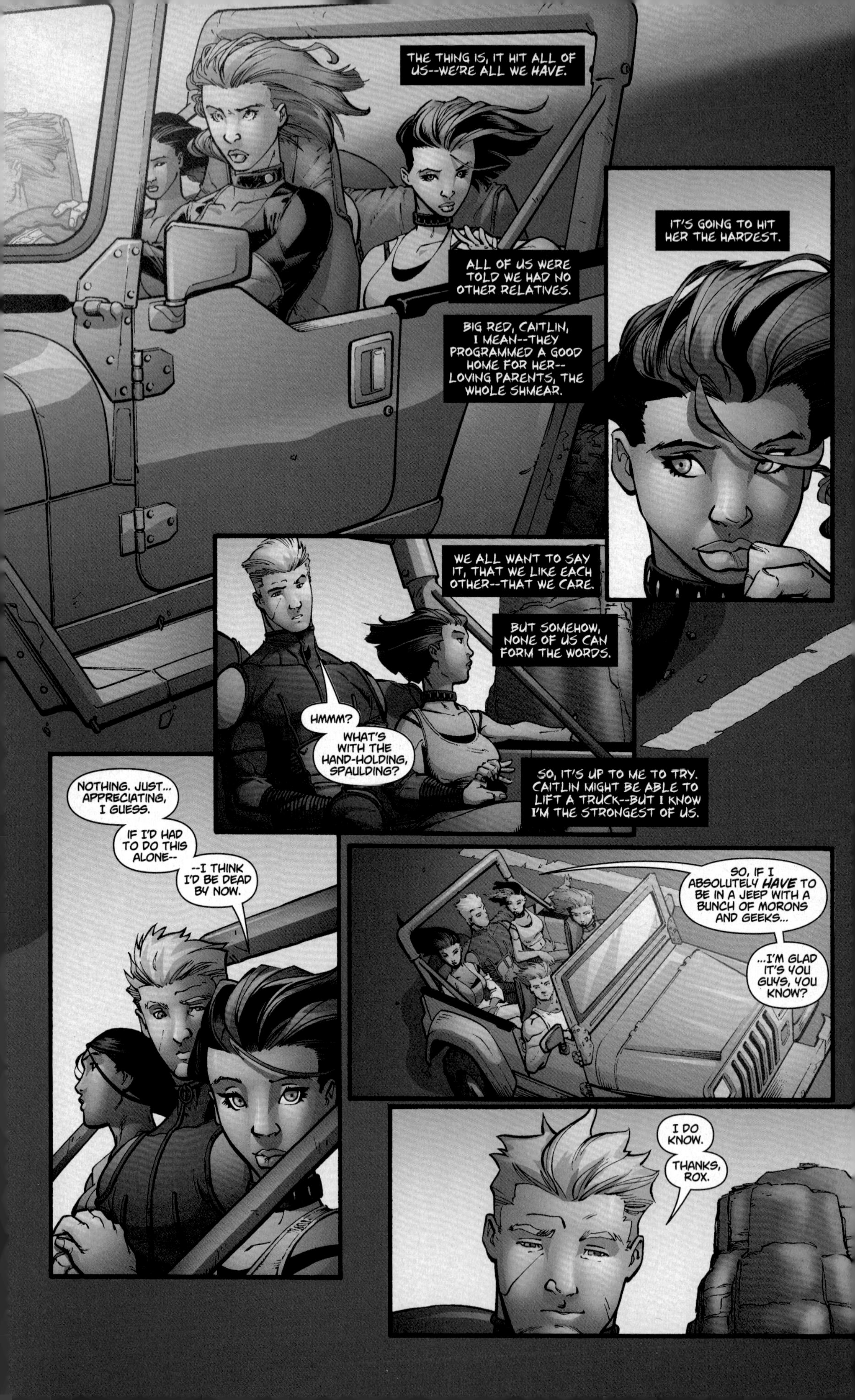
THE THING IS, IT HIT ALL OF US--WE'RE ALL WE HAVE.
ALL OF US WERE TOLD WE HAD NO OTHER RELATIVES.
BIG RED, CAITLIN, I MEAN--THEY PROGRAMMED A GOOD HOME FOR HER--LOVING PARENTS, THE WHOLE SHMEAR.
IT'S GOING TO HIT HER THE HARDEST.
WE ALL WANT TO SAY IT, THAT WE LIKE EACH OTHER--THAT WE CARE.
BUT SOMEHOW, NONE OF US CAN FORM THE WORDS.
HMMM? WHAT'S WITH THE HAND-HOLDING, SPAULDING?
SO, IT'S UP TO ME TO TRY. CAITLIN MIGHT BE ABLE TO LIFT A TRUCK--BUT I KNOW I'M THE STRONGEST OF US.
NOTHING. JUST... APPRECIATING, I GUESS.
IF I'D HAD TO DO THIS ALONE--
--I THINK I'D BE DEAD BY NOW.
SO, IF I ABSOLUTELY HAVE TO BE IN A JEEP WITH A BUNCH OF MORONS AND GEEKS...
...I'M GLAD IT'S YOU GUYS, YOU KNOW?
I DO KNOW.
THANKS, ROX.

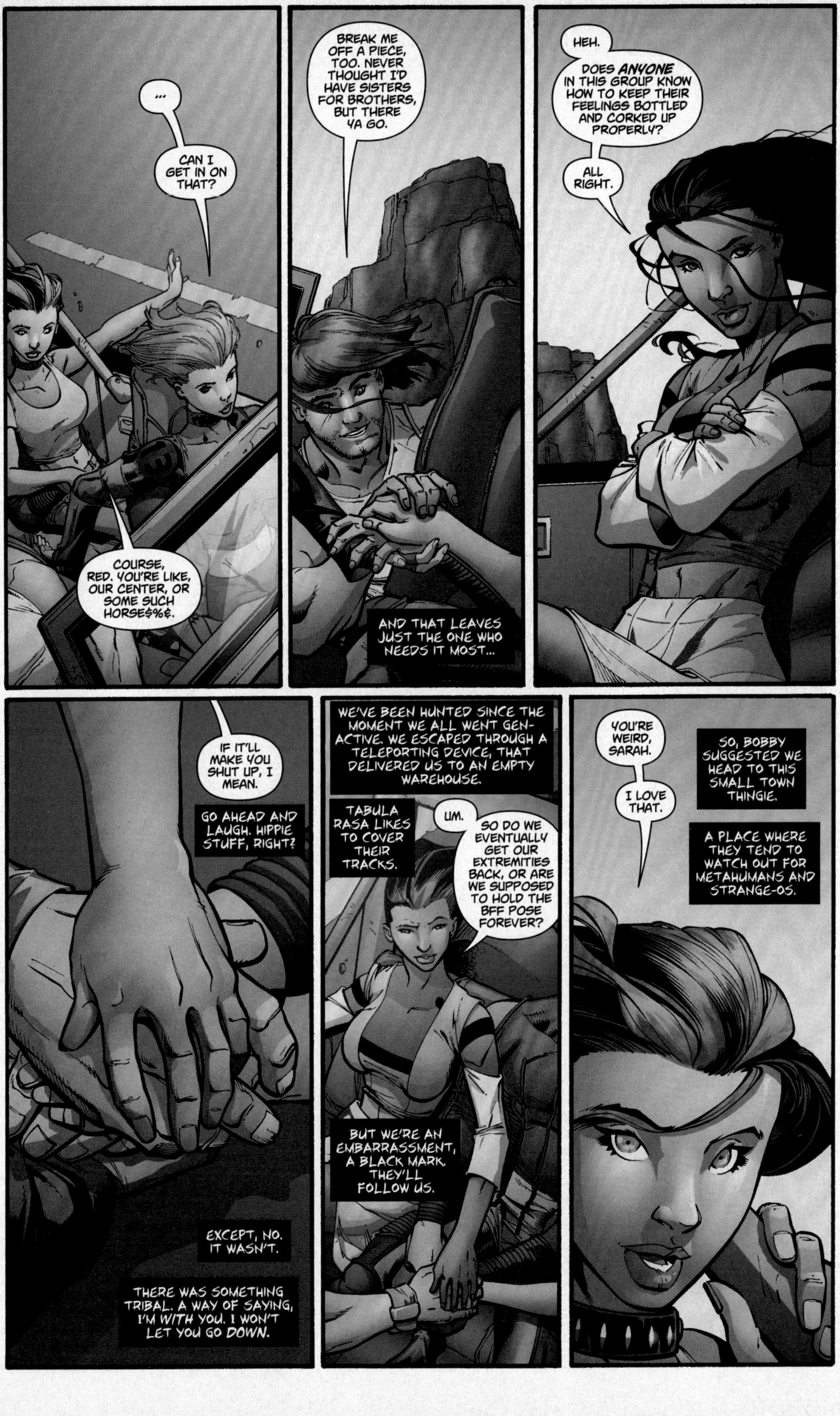
...
CAN I GET IN ON THAT?
COURSE, RED. YOU'RE LIKE, OUR CENTER, OR SOME SUCH HORSE$%&.
BREAK ME OFF A PIECE, TOO. NEVER THOUGHT I'D HAVE SISTERS FOR BROTHERS, BUT THERE YA GO.
AND THAT LEAVES JUST THE ONE WHO NEEDS IT MOST...
HEH.
DOES ANYONE IN THIS GROUP KNOW HOW TO KEEP THEIR FEELINGS BOTTLED AND CORKED UP PROPERLY?
ALL RIGHT.
IF IT'LL MAKE YOU SHUT UP, I MEAN.
GO AHEAD AND LAUGH. HIPPIE STUFF, RIGHT?
EXCEPT, NO. IT WASN'T.
THERE WAS SOMETHING TRIBAL. A WAY OF SAYING, I'M WITH YOU. I WON'T LET YOU GO DOWN.
WE'VE BEEN HUNTED SINCE THE MOMENT WE ALL WENT GEN-ACTIVE. WE ESCAPED THROUGH A TELEPORTING DEVICE, THAT DELIVERED US TO AN EMPTY WAREHOUSE.
TABULA RASA LIKES TO COVER THEIR TRACKS.
UM.
SO DO WE EVENTUALLY GET OUR EXTREMITIES BACK, OR ARE WE SUPPOSED TO HOLD THE BFF POSE FOREVER?
BUT WE'RE AN EMBARRASSMENT, A BLACK MARK. THEY'LL FOLLOW US.
YOU'RE WEIRD, SARAH.
I LOVE THAT.
SO, BOBBY SUGGESTED WE HEAD TO THIS SMALL TOWN THINGIE.
A PLACE WHERE THEY TEND TO WATCH OUT FOR METAHUMANS AND STRANGE-OS.

ROAD TRIP
CLUB KIDS

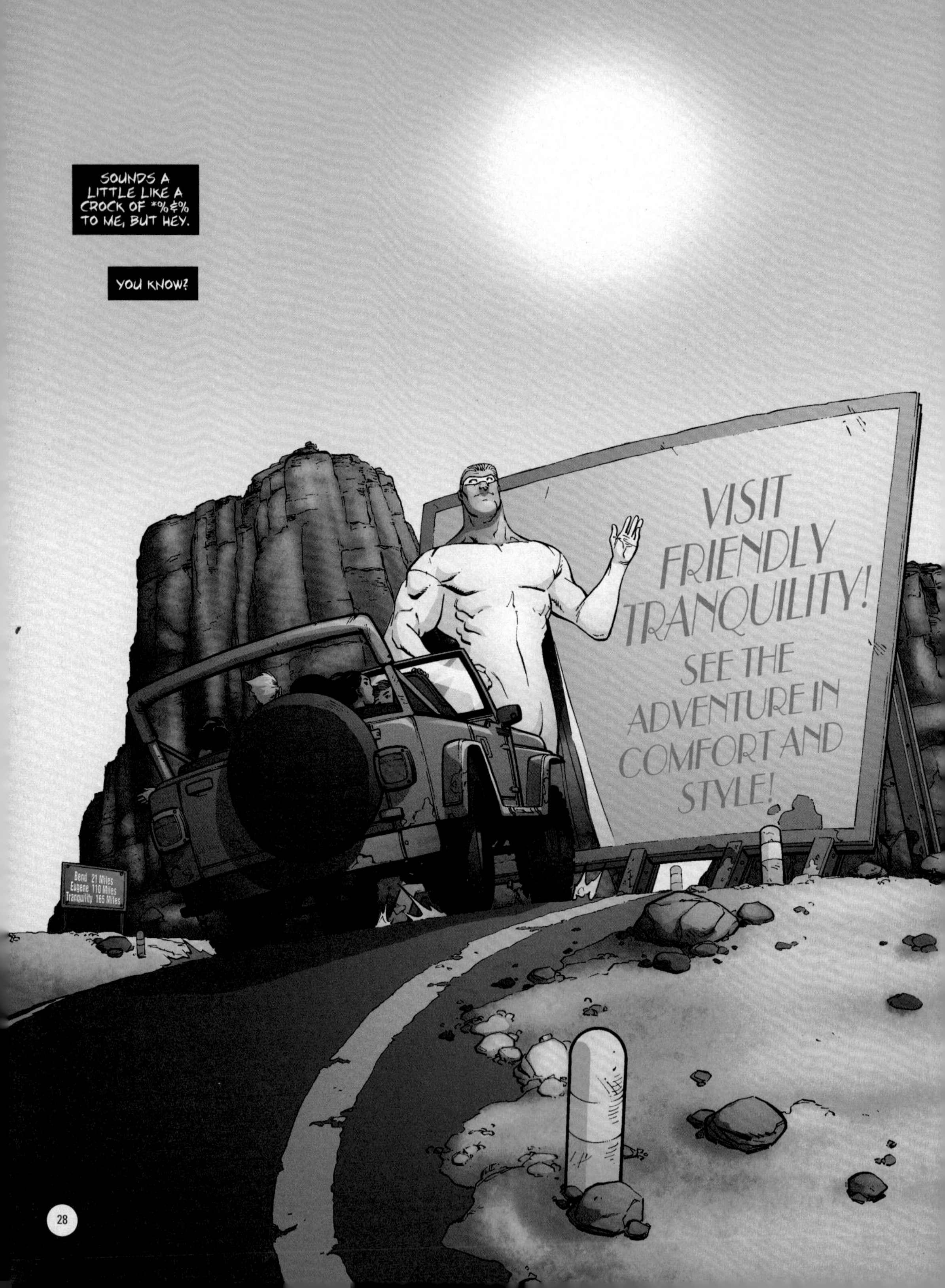

SOUNDS A LITTLE LIKE A CROCK OF *%&% TO ME, BUT HEY.
YOU KNOW?
VISIT FRIENDLY TRANQUILITY!
SEE THE ADVENTURE IN COMFORT AND STYLE!
Bend 21 Miles
Eugene 110 Miles
Tranquility 165 Miles

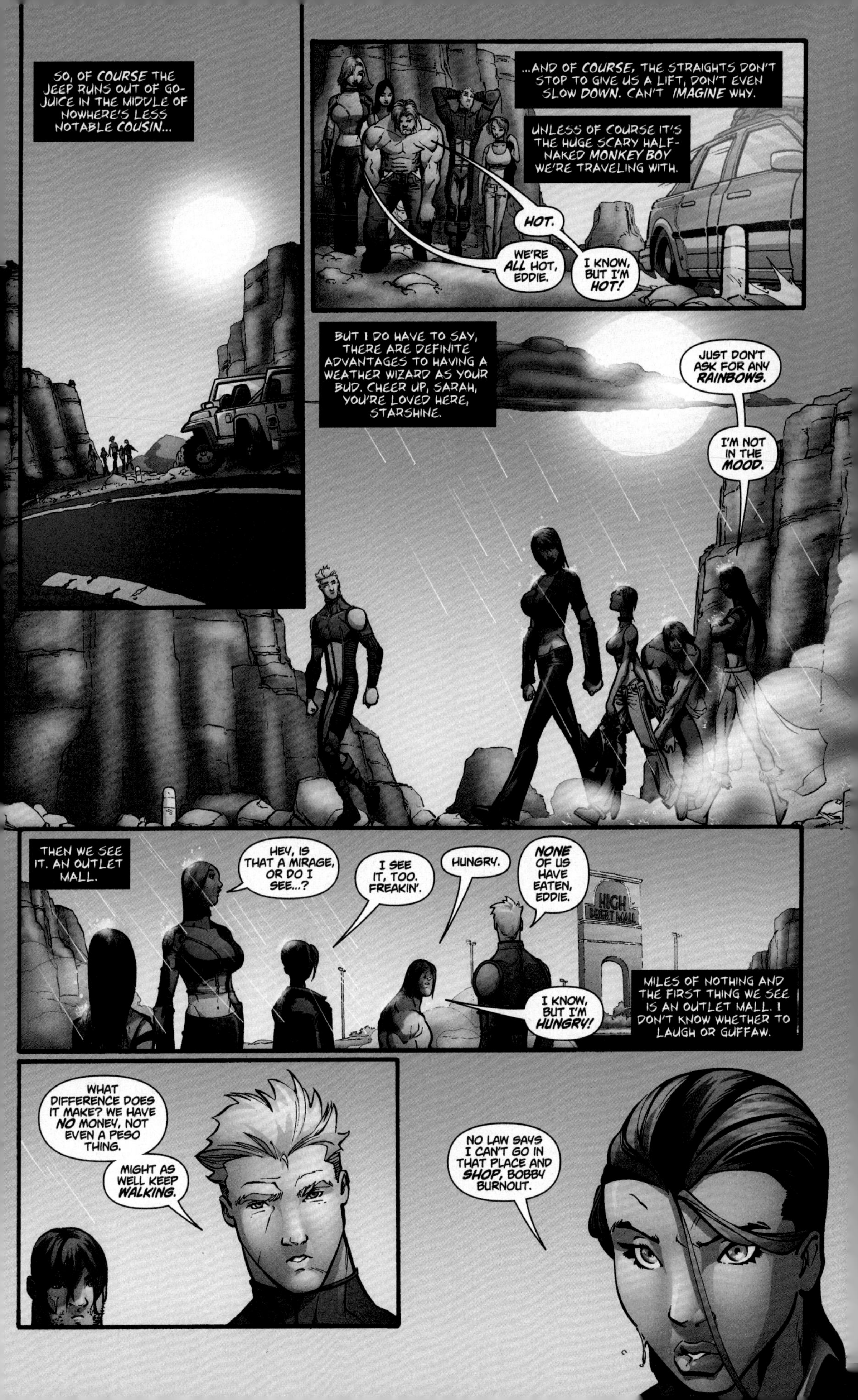
SO, OF COURSE THE JEEP RUNS OUT OF GO-JUICE IN THE MIDDLE OF NOWHERE'S LESS NOTABLE COUSIN...
...AND OF COURSE, THE STRAIGHTS DON'T STOP TO GIVE US A LIFT, DON'T EVEN SLOW DOWN. CAN'T IMAGINE WHY.
UNLESS OF COURSE IT'S THE HUGE SCARY HALF-NAKED MONKEY BOY WE'RE TRAVELING WITH.
HOT.
WE'RE ALL HOT, EDDIE.
I KNOW, BUT I'M HOT!
BUT I DO HAVE TO SAY, THERE ARE DEFINITE ADVANTAGES TO HAVING A WEATHER WIZARD AS YOUR BUD. CHEER UP, SARAH, YOU'RE LOVED HERE, STARSHINE.
JUST DON'T ASK FOR ANY RAINBOWS.
I'M NOT IN THE MOOD.
THEN WE SEE IT. AN OUTLET MALL.
HEY, IS THAT A MIRAGE, OR DO I SEE...?
I SEE IT, TOO. FREAKIN'.
HUNGRY.
NONE OF US HAVE EATEN, EDDIE.
HIGH DESERT MALL
I KNOW, BUT I'M HUNGRY!
MILES OF NOTHING AND THE FIRST THING WE SEE IS AN OUTLET MALL. I DON'T KNOW WHETHER TO LAUGH OR GUFFAW.
WHAT DIFFERENCE DOES IT MAKE? WE HAVE NO MONEY, NOT EVEN A PESO THING.
MIGHT AS WELL KEEP WALKING.
NO LAW SAYS I CAN'T GO IN THAT PLACE AND SHOP, BOBBY BURNOUT.

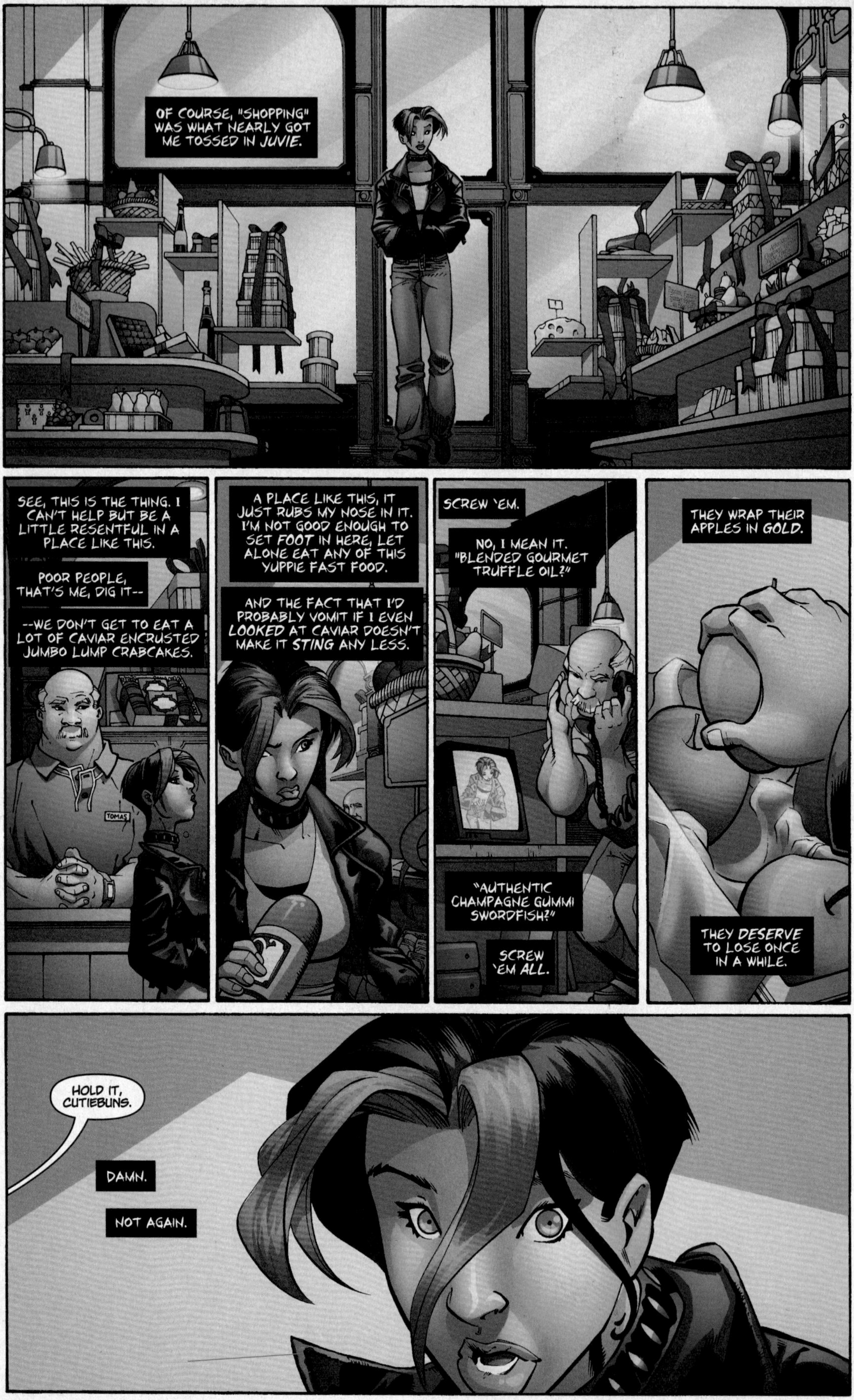
OF COURSE, "SHOPPING" WAS WHAT NEARLY GOT ME TOSSED IN JUVIE.
SEE, THIS IS THE THING. I CAN'T HELP BUT BE A LITTLE RESENTFUL IN A PLACE LIKE THIS.
POOR PEOPLE, THAT'S ME, DIG IT--
--WE DON'T GET TO EAT A LOT OF CAVIAR ENCRUSTED JUMBO LUMP CRABCAKES.
TOMAS
A PLACE LIKE THIS, IT JUST RUBS MY NOSE IN IT. I'M NOT GOOD ENOUGH TO SET FOOT IN HERE, LET ALONE EAT ANY OF THIS YUPPIE FAST FOOD.
AND THE FACT THAT I'D PROBABLY VOMIT IF I EVEN LOOKED AT CAVIAR DOESN'T MAKE IT STING ANY LESS.
SCREW 'EM.
NO, I MEAN IT. "BLENDED GOURMET TRUFFLE OIL?"
"AUTHENTIC CHAMPAGNE GUMMI SWORDFISH?"
SCREW 'EM ALL.
THEY WRAP THEIR APPLES IN GOLD.
THEY DESERVE TO LOSE ONCE IN A WHILE.
HOLD IT, CUTIEBUNS.
DAMN.
NOT AGAIN.

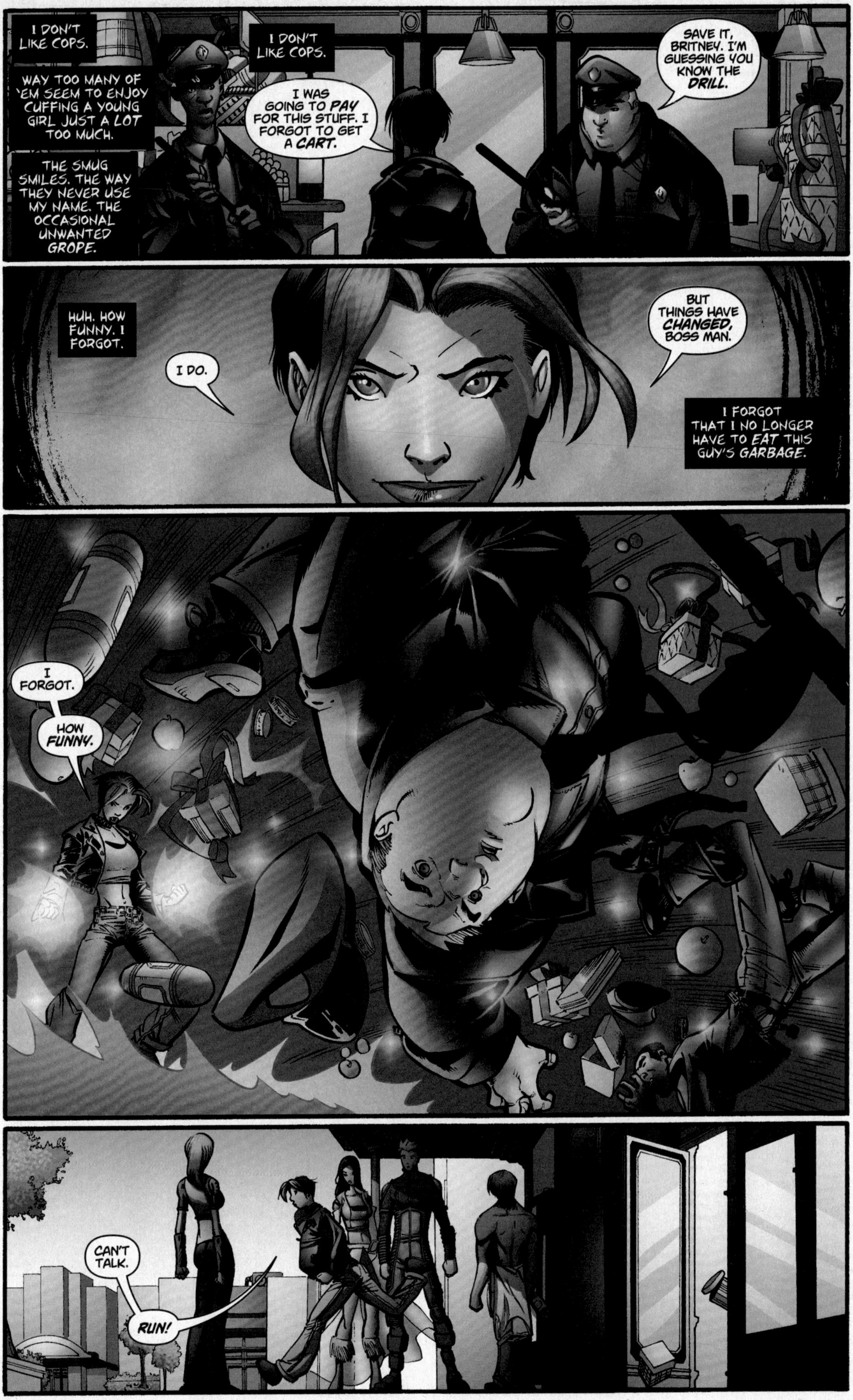
I DON'T LIKE COPS.
WAY TOO MANY OF 'EM SEEM TO ENJOY CUFFING A YOUNG GIRL JUST A LOT TOO MUCH.
THE SMUG SMILES. THE WAY THEY NEVER USE MY NAME. THE OCCASIONAL UNWANTED GROPE.
I DON'T LIKE COPS.
I WAS GOING TO PAY FOR THIS STUFF. I FORGOT TO GET A CART.
SAVE IT, BRITNEY. I'M GUESSING YOU KNOW THE DRILL.
HUH. HOW FUNNY. I FORGOT.
I DO.
BUT THINGS HAVE CHANGED, BOSS MAN.
I FORGOT THAT I NO LONGER HAVE TO EAT THIS GUY'S GARBAGE.
I FORGOT.
HOW FUNNY.
CAN'T TALK.
RUN!

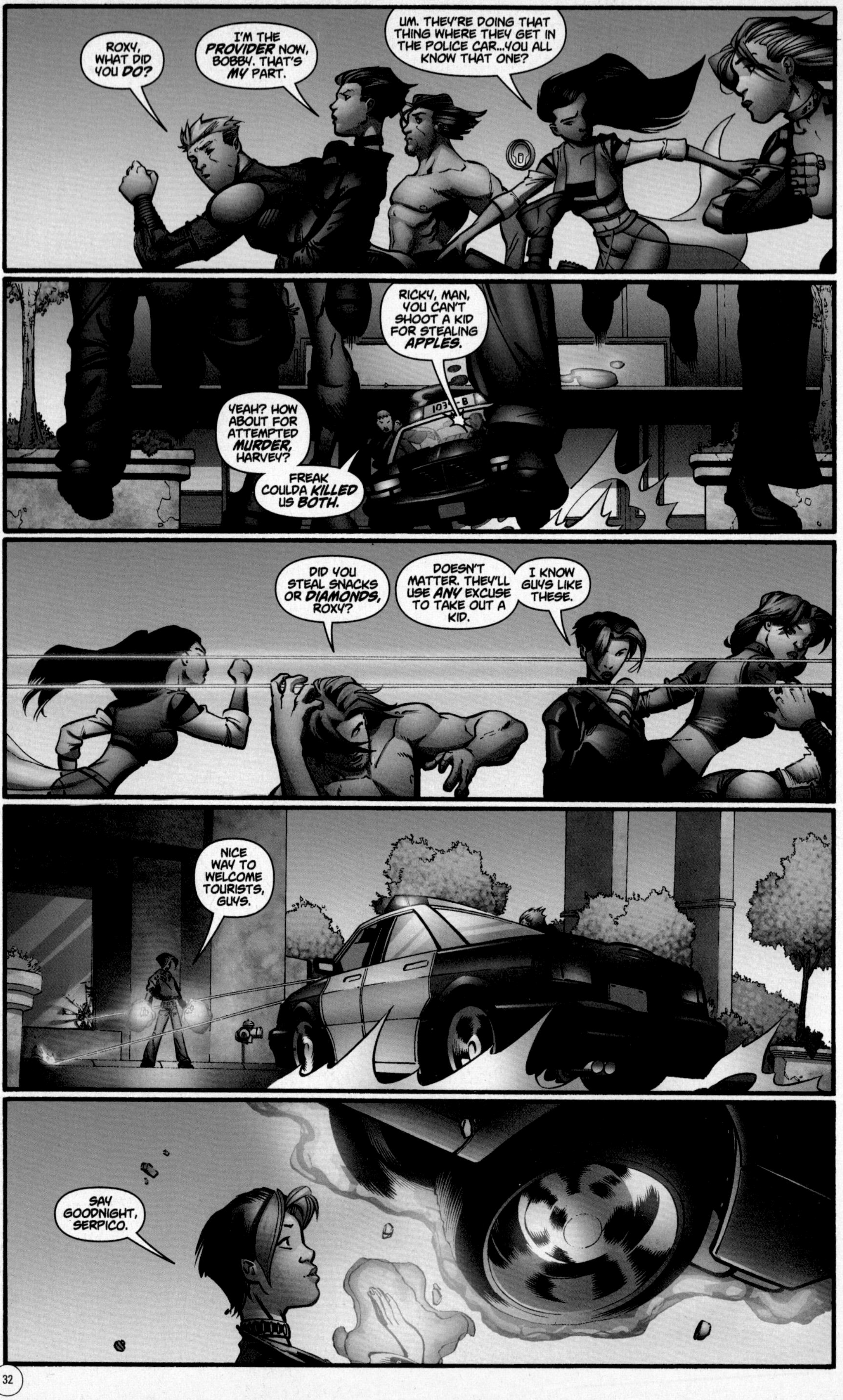
ROXY, WHAT DID YOU DO?
I'M THE PROVIDER NOW, BOBBY. THAT'S MY PART.
UM. THEY'RE DOING THAT THING WHERE THEY GET IN THE POLICE CAR...YOU ALL KNOW THAT ONE?
RICKY, MAN, YOU CAN'T SHOOT A KID FOR STEALING APPLES.
YEAH? HOW ABOUT FOR ATTEMPTED MURDER, HARVEY?
FREAK COULDA KILLED US BOTH.
DID YOU STEAL SNACKS OR DIAMONDS, ROXY?
DOESN'T MATTER. THEY'LL USE ANY EXCUSE TO TAKE OUT A KID.
I KNOW GUYS LIKE THESE.
NICE WAY TO WELCOME TOURISTS, GUYS.
SAY GOODNIGHT, SERPICO.

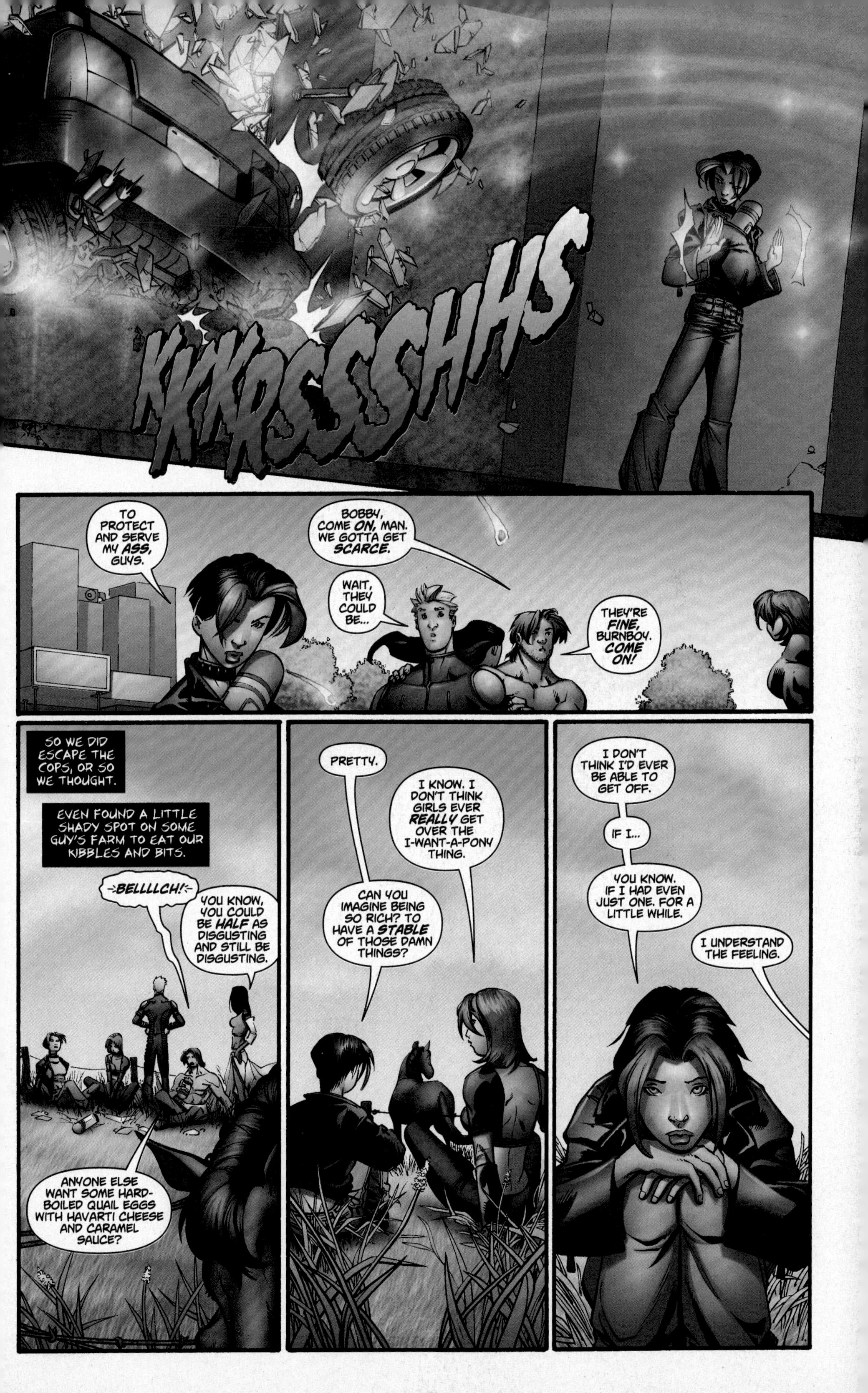
KKKRSSSCHHS
TO PROTECT AND SERVE MY ASS, GUYS.
BOBBY, COME ON, MAN. WE GOTTA GET SCARCE.
WAIT, THEY COULD BE...
THEY'RE FINE, BURNBOY. COME ON!
SO WE DID ESCAPE THE COPS, OR SO WE THOUGHT.
EVEN FOUND A LITTLE SHADY SPOT ON SOME GUY'S FARM TO EAT OUR KIBBLES AND BITS.
-BELLLLCH!-
YOU KNOW, YOU COULD BE HALF AS DISGUSTING AND STILL BE DISGUSTING.
ANYONE ELSE WANT SOME HARD-BOILED QUAIL EGGS WITH HAVARTI CHEESE AND CARAMEL SAUCE?
PRETTY.
I KNOW. I DON'T THINK GIRLS EVER REALLY GET OVER THE I-WANT-A-PONY THING.
CAN YOU IMAGINE BEING SO RICH? TO HAVE A STABLE OF THOSE DAMN THINGS?
I DON'T THINK I'D EVER BE ABLE TO GET OFF.
IF I...
YOU KNOW. IF I HAD EVEN JUST ONE. FOR A LITTLE WHILE.
I UNDERSTAND THE FEELING.

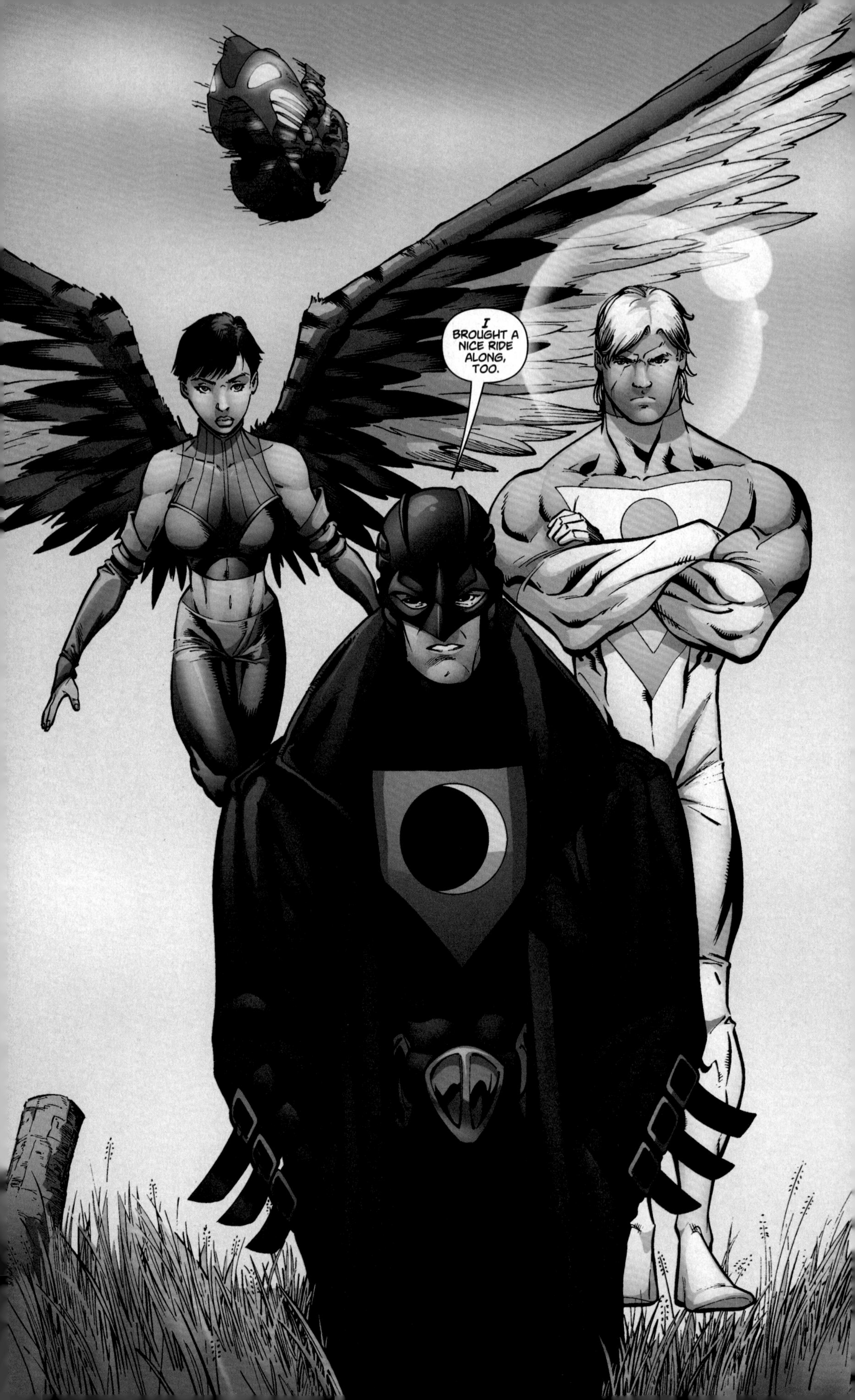
I BROUGHT A NICE RIDE ALONG, TOO.

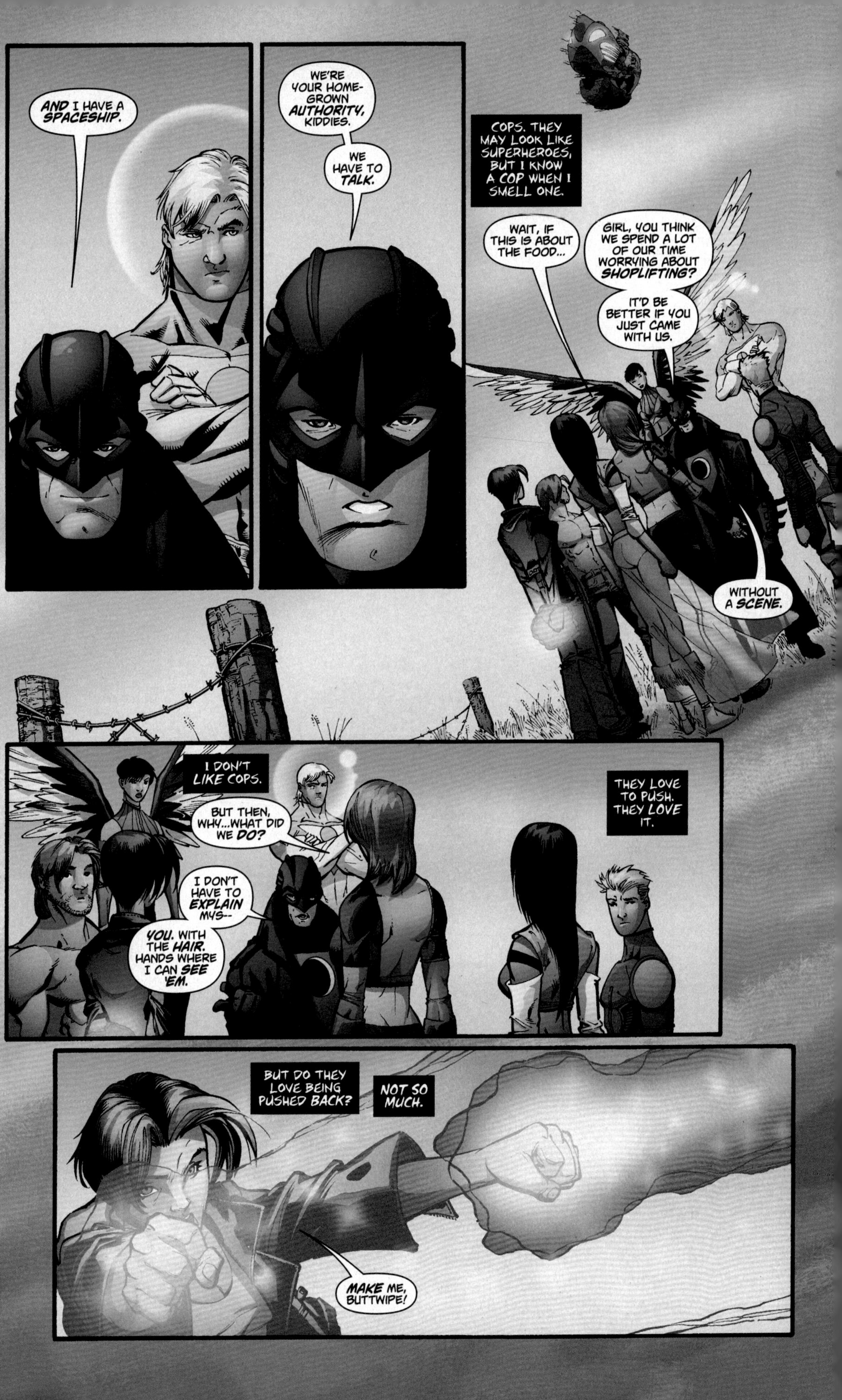
AND I HAVE A SPACESHIP.
WE'RE YOUR HOME-GROWN AUTHORITY, KIDDIES.
WE HAVE TO TALK.
COPS. THEY MAY LOOK LIKE SUPERHEROES, BUT I KNOW A COP WHEN I SMELL ONE.
WAIT, IF THIS IS ABOUT THE FOOD...
GIRL, YOU THINK WE SPEND A LOT OF OUR TIME WORRYING ABOUT SHOPLIFTING?
IT'D BE BETTER IF YOU JUST CAME WITH US.
WITHOUT A SCENE.
I DON'T LIKE COPS.
BUT THEN, WHY...WHAT DID WE DO?
THEY LOVE TO PUSH. THEY LOVE IT.
I DON'T HAVE TO EXPLAIN MYS--
YOU. WITH THE HAIR. HANDS WHERE I CAN SEE 'EM.
BUT DO THEY LOVE BEING PUSHED BACK?
NOT SO MUCH.
MAKE ME, BUTTWIPE!

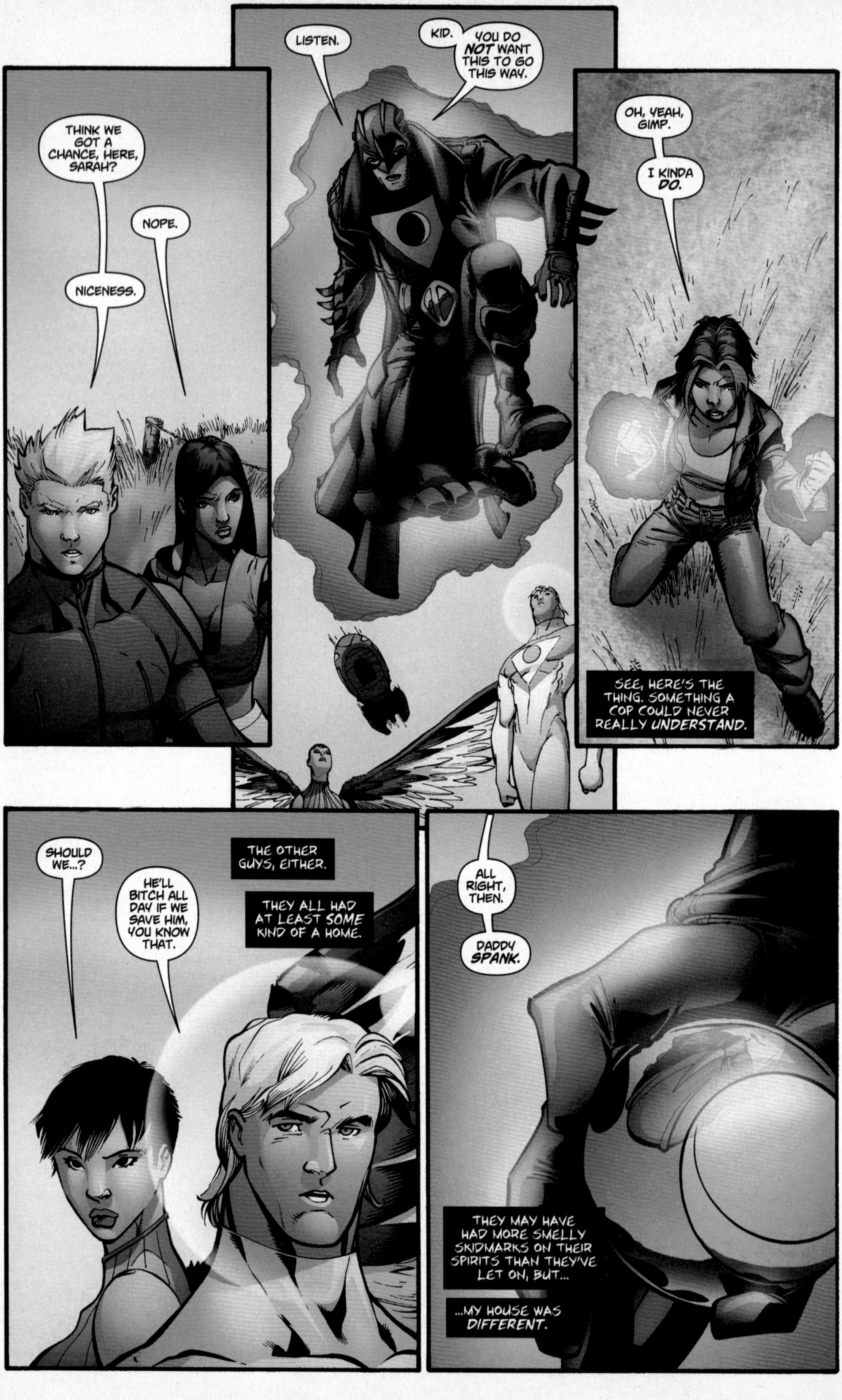
THINK WE GOT A CHANCE, HERE, SARAH?
NOPE.
NICENESS.
LISTEN.
KID.
YOU DO NOT WANT THIS TO GO THIS WAY.
OH, YEAH, GIMP.
I KINDA DO.
SEE, HERE'S THE THING. SOMETHING A COP COULD NEVER REALLY UNDERSTAND.
SHOULD WE...?
HE'LL BITCH ALL DAY IF WE SAVE HIM, YOU KNOW THAT.
THE OTHER GUYS, EITHER.
THEY ALL HAD AT LEAST SOME KIND OF A HOME.
ALL RIGHT, THEN.
DADDY SPANK.
THEY MAY HAVE HAD MORE SMELLY SKIDMARKS ON THEIR SPIRITS THAN THEY'VE LET ON, BUT...
...MY HOUSE WAS DIFFERENT.

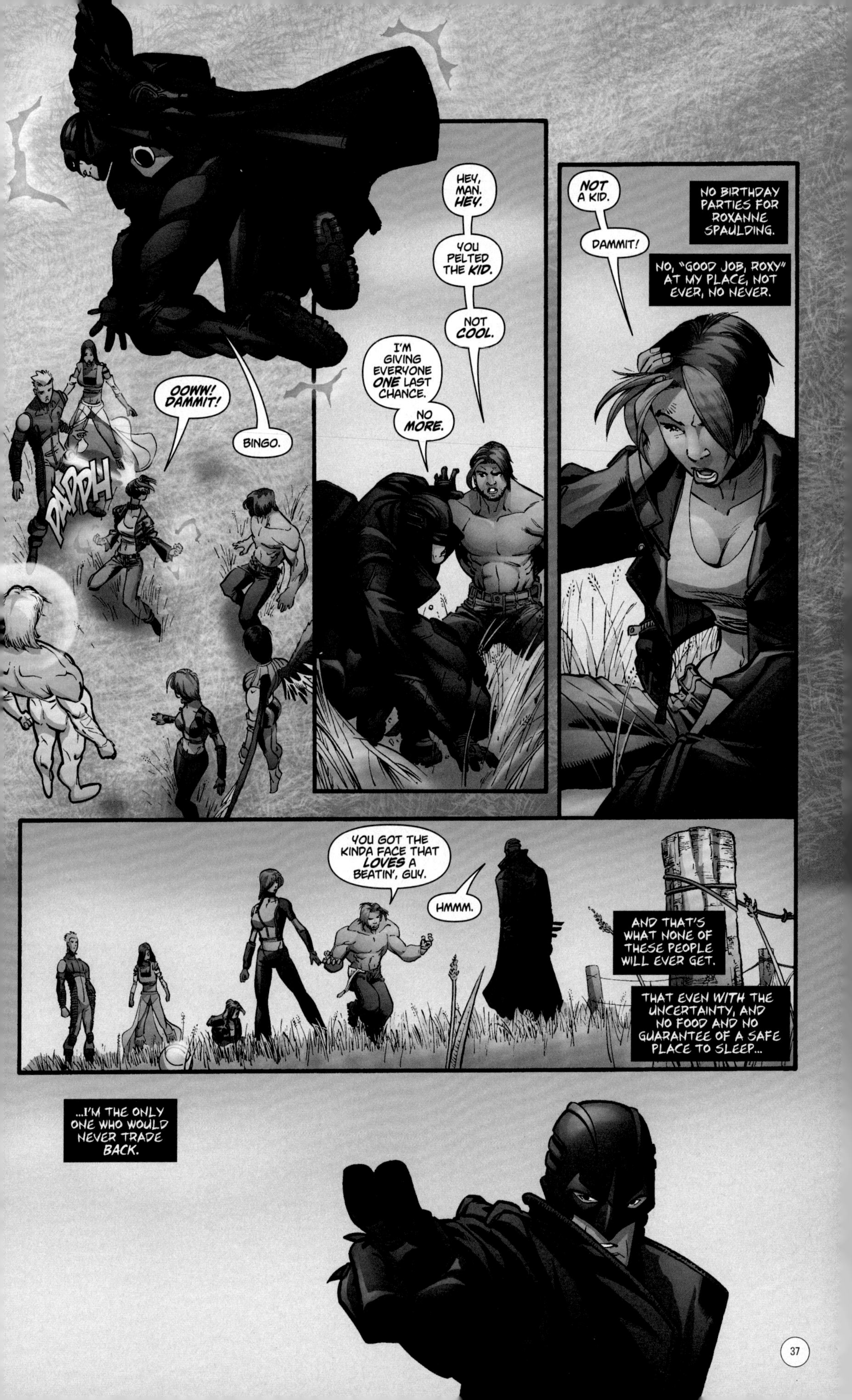
OOWW! DAMMIT!
BINGO.
PAPPH
HEY, MAN. HEY.
YOU PELTED THE KID.
NOT COOL.
I'M GIVING EVERYONE ONE LAST CHANCE.
NO MORE.
NOT A KID.
DAMMIT!
NO BIRTHDAY PARTIES FOR ROXANNE SPAULDING.
NO, "GOOD JOB, ROXY" AT MY PLACE, NOT EVER, NO NEVER.
YOU GOT THE KINDA FACE THAT LOVES A BEATIN', GUY.
HMMM.
AND THAT'S WHAT NONE OF THESE PEOPLE WILL EVER GET.
THAT EVEN WITH THE UNCERTAINTY, AND NO FOOD AND NO GUARANTEE OF A SAFE PLACE TO SLEEP...
...I'M THE ONLY ONE WHO WOULD NEVER TRADE BACK.

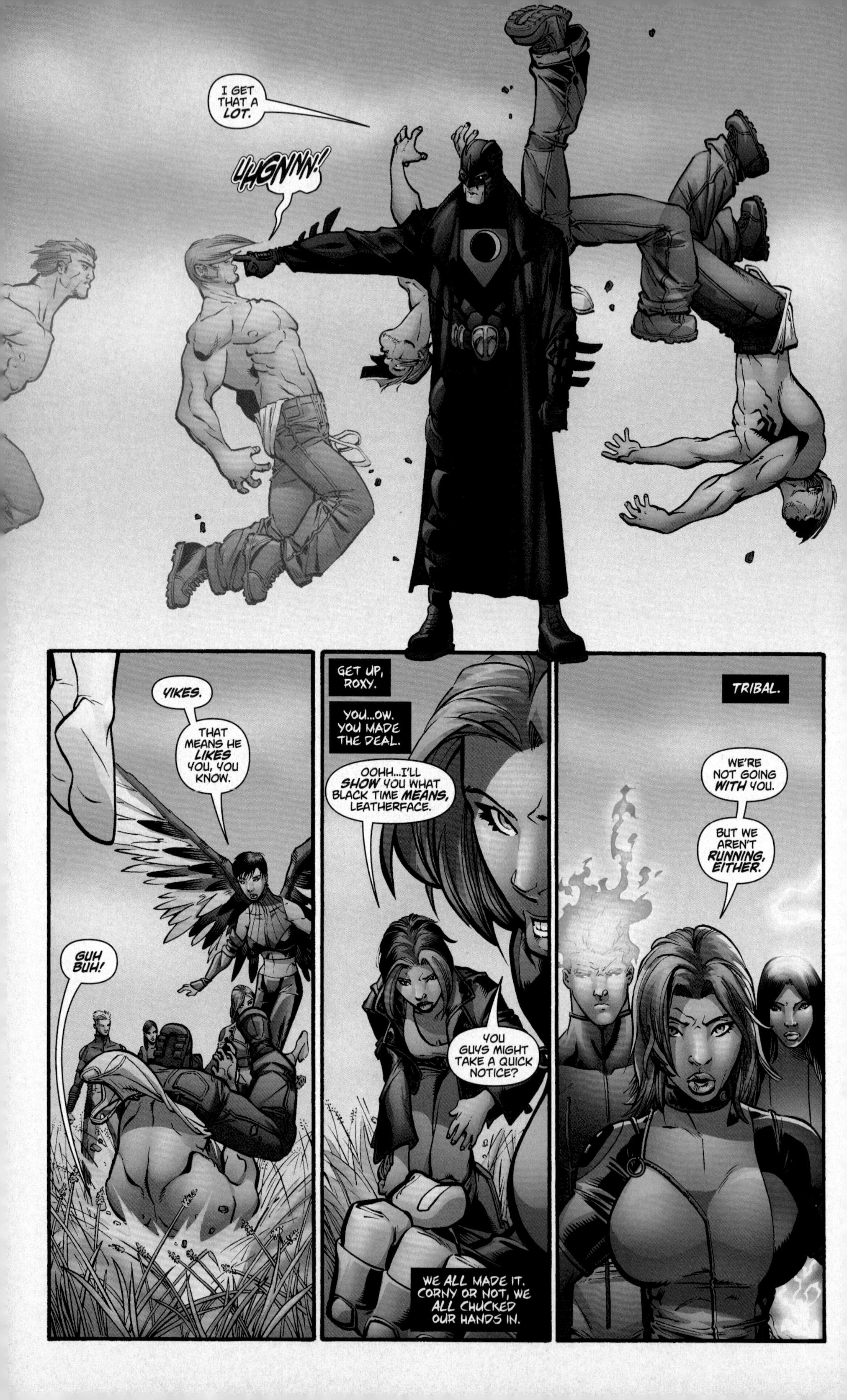
I GET THAT A LOT.
UHGNNN!
YIKES.
THAT MEANS HE LIKES YOU, YOU KNOW.
GUH BUH!
GET UP, ROXY.
YOU...OW. YOU MADE THE DEAL.
OOHH...I'LL SHOW YOU WHAT BLACK TIME MEANS, LEATHERFACE.
YOU GUYS MIGHT TAKE A QUICK NOTICE?
WE ALL MADE IT. CORNY OR NOT, WE ALL CHUCKED OUR HANDS IN.
TRIBAL.
WE'RE NOT GOING WITH YOU.
BUT WE AREN'T RUNNING, EITHER.

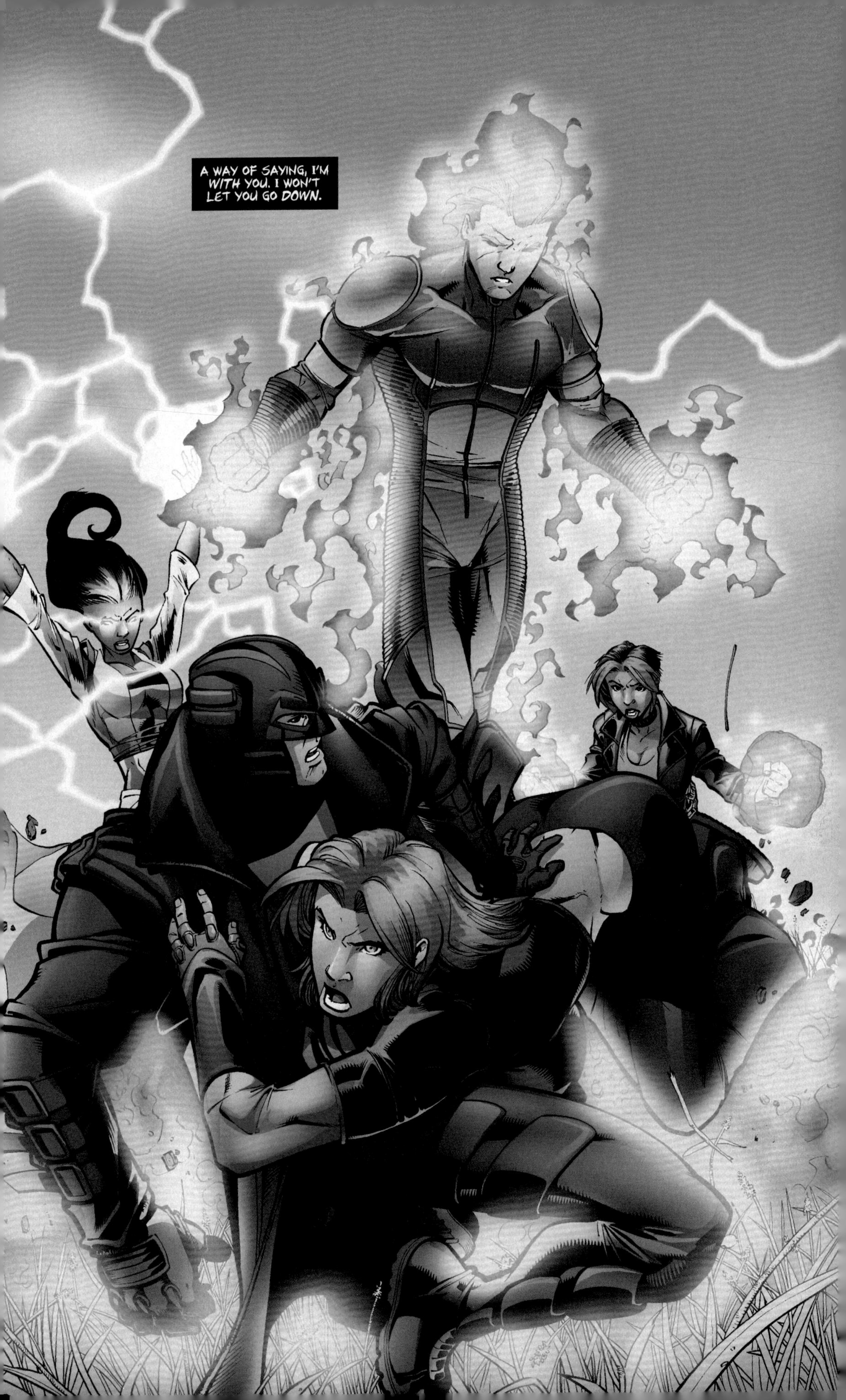
A WAY OF SAYING, I'M WITH YOU. I WON'T LET YOU GO DOWN.

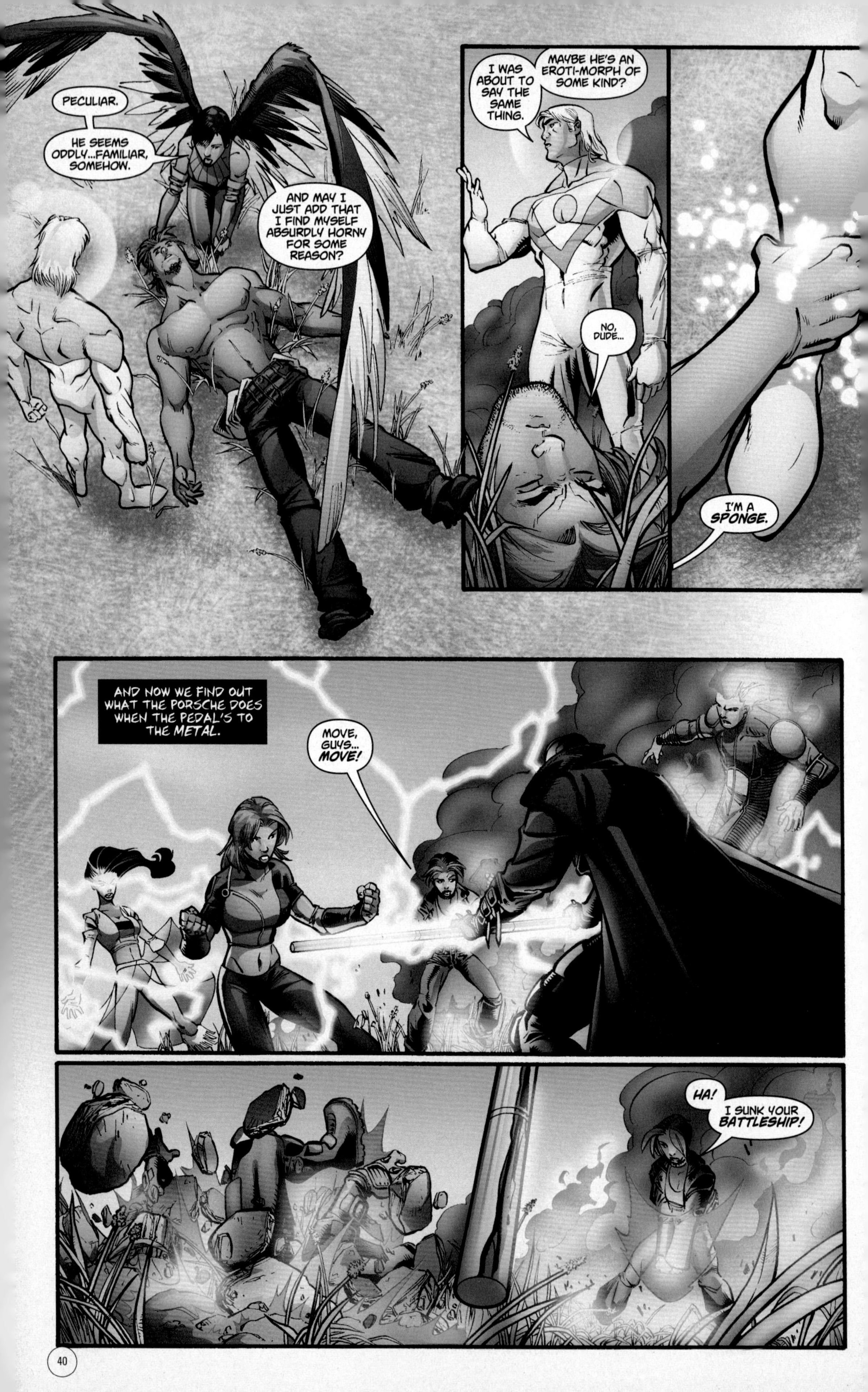
PECULIAR.
HE SEEMS ODDLY...FAMILIAR, SOMEHOW.
AND MAY I JUST ADD THAT I FIND MYSELF ABSURDLY HORNY FOR SOME REASON?
I WAS ABOUT TO SAY THE SAME THING.
MAYBE HE'S AN EROTI-MORPH OF SOME KIND?
NO, DUDE...
I'M A SPONGE.
AND NOW WE FIND OUT WHAT THE PORSCHE DOES WHEN THE PEDAL'S TO THE METAL.
MOVE, GUYS... MOVE!
HA!
I SUNK YOUR BATTLESHIP!

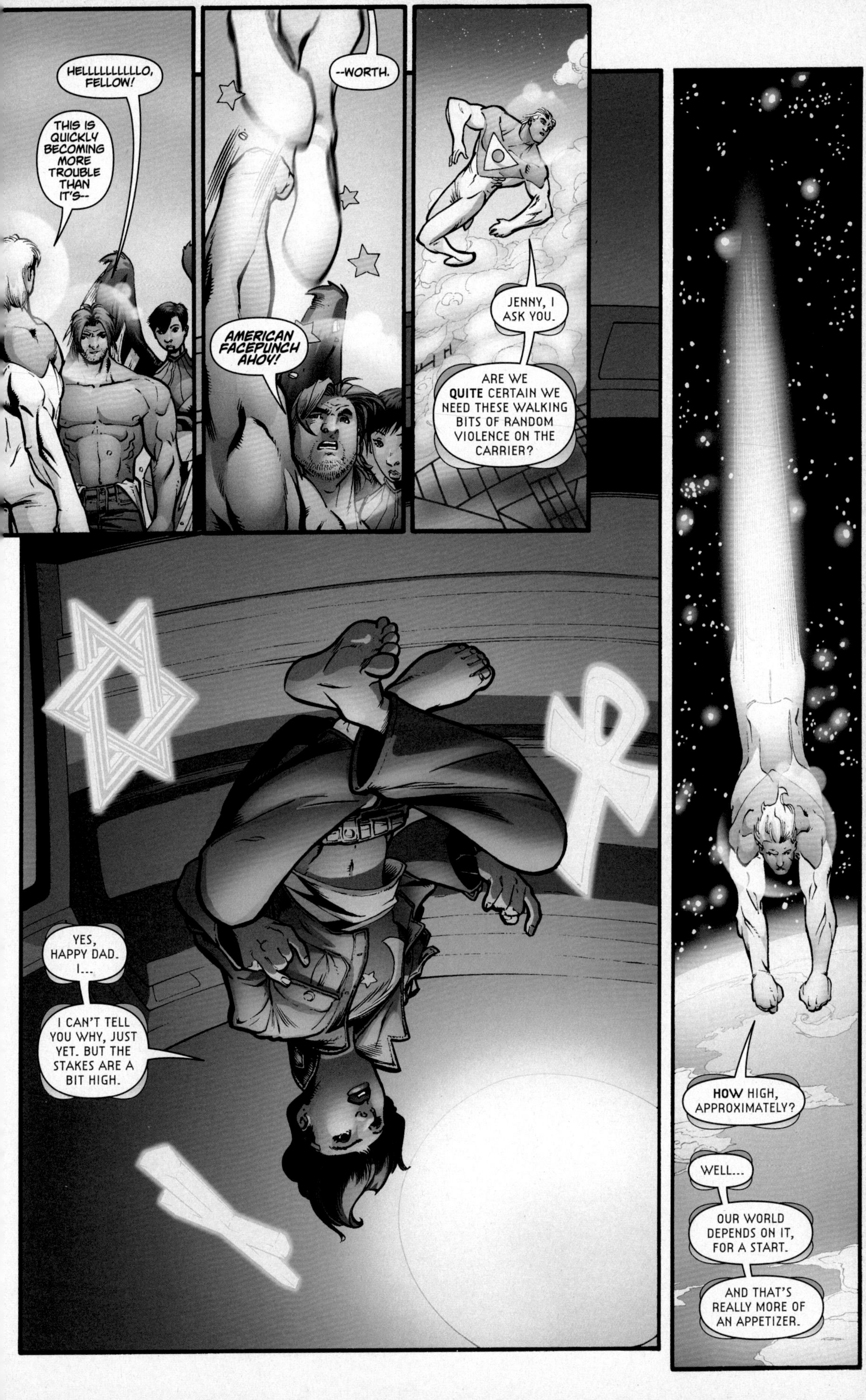
HELLLLLLLLLLO, FELLOW!
THIS IS QUICKLY BECOMING MORE TROUBLE THAN IT'S--
--WORTH.
AMERICAN FACEPUNCH AHOY!
JENNY, I ASK YOU.
ARE WE QUITE CERTAIN WE NEED THESE WALKING BITS OF RANDOM VIOLENCE ON THE CARRIER?
YES, HAPPY DAD. I...
I CAN'T TELL YOU WHY, JUST YET. BUT THE STAKES ARE A BIT HIGH.
HOW HIGH, APPROXIMATELY?
WELL...
OUR WORLD DEPENDS ON IT, FOR A START.
AND THAT'S REALLY MORE OF AN APPETIZER.

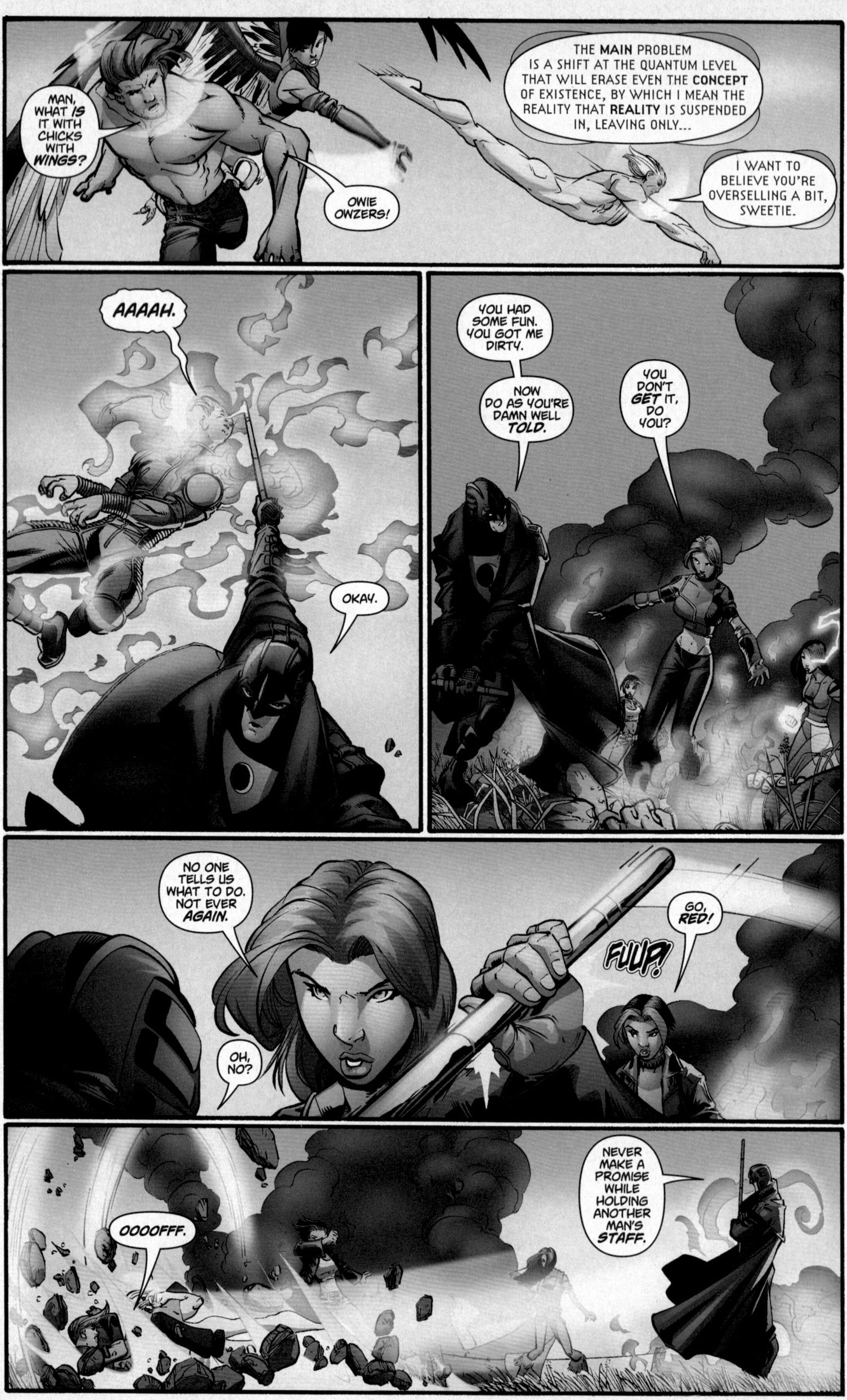
MAN, WHAT IS IT WITH CHICKS WITH WINGS?
OWIE OWZERS!
THE MAIN PROBLEM IS A SHIFT AT THE QUANTUM LEVEL THAT WILL ERASE EVEN THE CONCEPT OF EXISTENCE, BY WHICH I MEAN THE REALITY THAT REALITY IS SUSPENDED IN, LEAVING ONLY...
I WANT TO BELIEVE YOU'RE OVERSELLING A BIT, SWEETIE.
AAAAH.
OKAY.
YOU HAD SOME FUN. YOU GOT ME DIRTY.
NOW DO AS YOU'RE DAMN WELL TOLD.
YOU DON'T GET IT, DO YOU?
NO ONE TELLS US WHAT TO DO. NOT EVER AGAIN.
OH, NO?
FUUP!
GO, RED!
OOOOFFF.
NEVER MAKE A PROMISE WHILE HOLDING ANOTHER MAN'S STAFF.

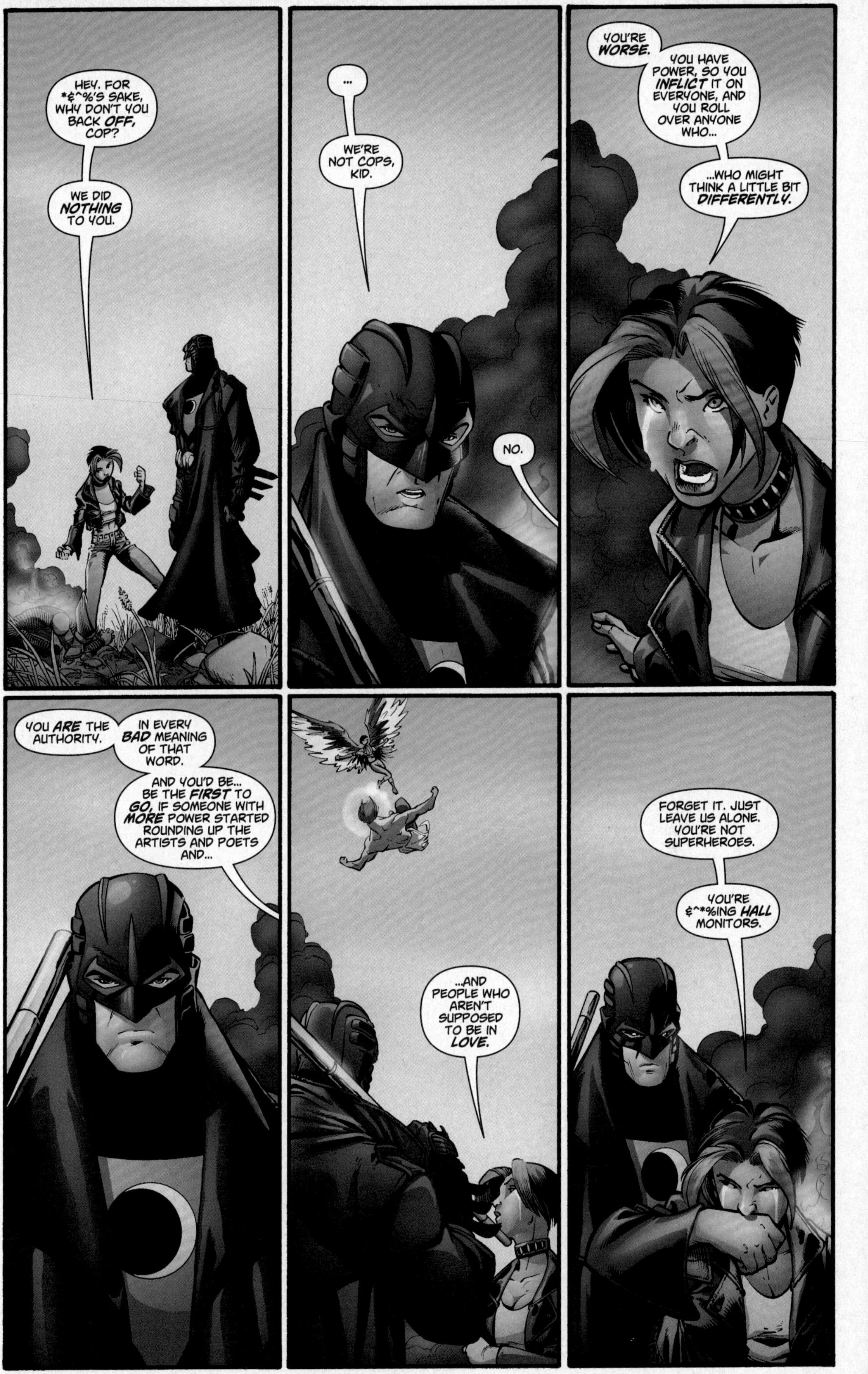
HEY. FOR *&^%'S SAKE, WHY DON'T YOU BACK OFF, COP?
WE DID NOTHING TO YOU.
...
WE'RE NOT COPS, KID.
NO.
YOU'RE WORSE.
YOU HAVE POWER, SO YOU INFLICT IT ON EVERYONE, AND YOU ROLL OVER ANYONE WHO...
...WHO MIGHT THINK A LITTLE BIT DIFFERENTLY.
YOU ARE THE AUTHORITY.
IN EVERY BAD MEANING OF THAT WORD.
AND YOU'D BE... BE THE FIRST TO GO, IF SOMEONE WITH MORE POWER STARTED ROUNDING UP THE ARTISTS AND POETS AND...
...AND PEOPLE WHO AREN'T SUPPOSED TO BE IN LOVE.
FORGET IT. JUST LEAVE US ALONE. YOU'RE NOT SUPERHEROES.
YOU'RE &^*%ING HALL MONITORS.

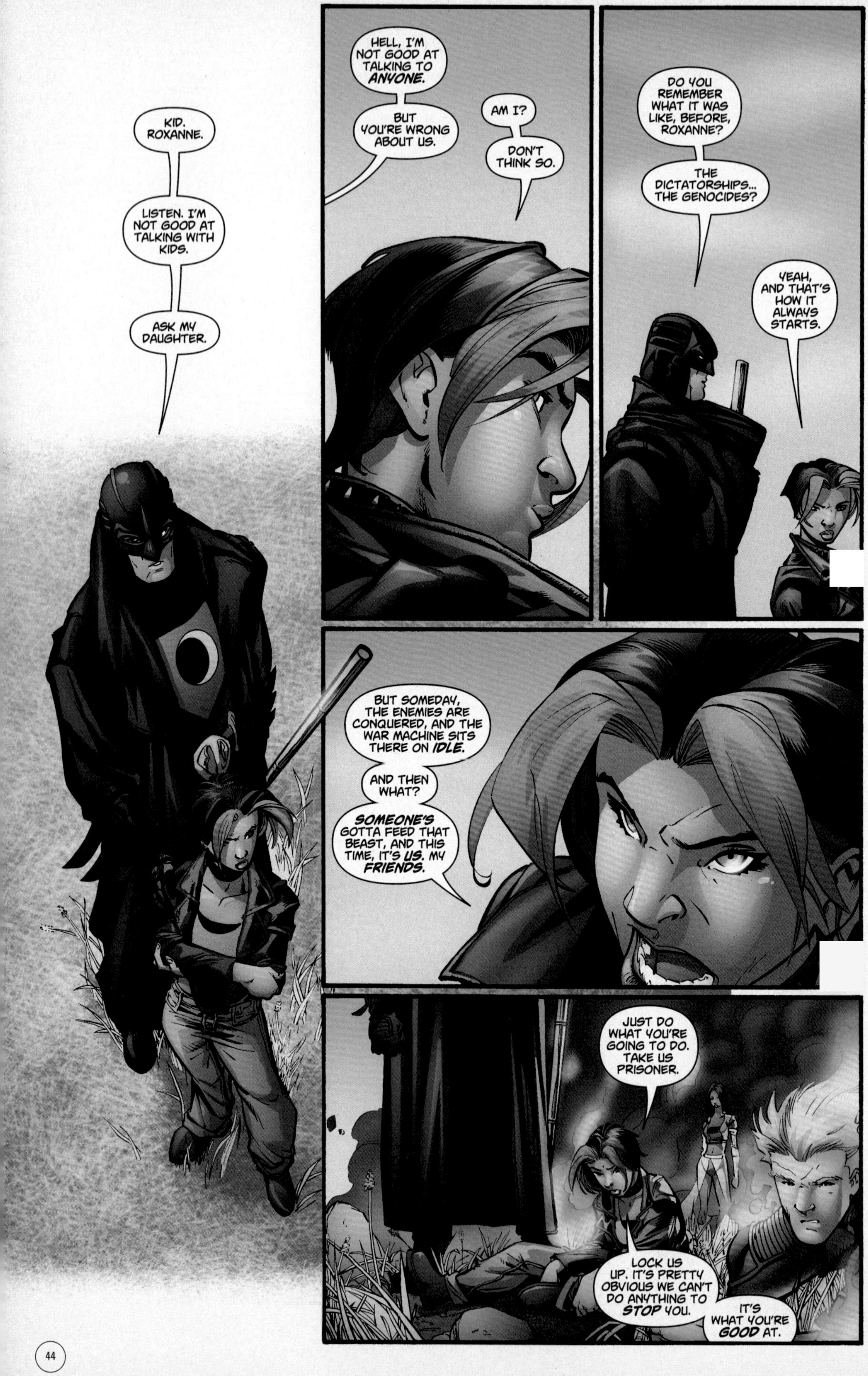
KID. ROXANNE.
LISTEN. I'M NOT GOOD AT TALKING WITH KIDS.
ASK MY DAUGHTER.
HELL, I'M NOT GOOD AT TALKING TO ANYONE.
BUT YOU'RE WRONG ABOUT US.
AM I?
DON'T THINK SO.
DO YOU REMEMBER WHAT IT WAS LIKE, BEFORE, ROXANNE?
THE DICTATORSHIPS... THE GENOCIDES?
YEAH, AND THAT'S HOW IT ALWAYS STARTS.
BUT SOMEDAY, THE ENEMIES ARE CONQUERED, AND THE WAR MACHINE SITS THERE ON IDLE.
AND THEN WHAT?
SOMEONE'S GOTTA FEED THAT BEAST, AND THIS TIME, IT'S US. MY FRIENDS.
JUST DO WHAT YOU'RE GOING TO DO. TAKE US PRISONER.
LOCK US UP. IT'S PRETTY OBVIOUS WE CAN'T DO ANYTHING TO STOP YOU.
IT'S WHAT YOU'RE GOOD AT.

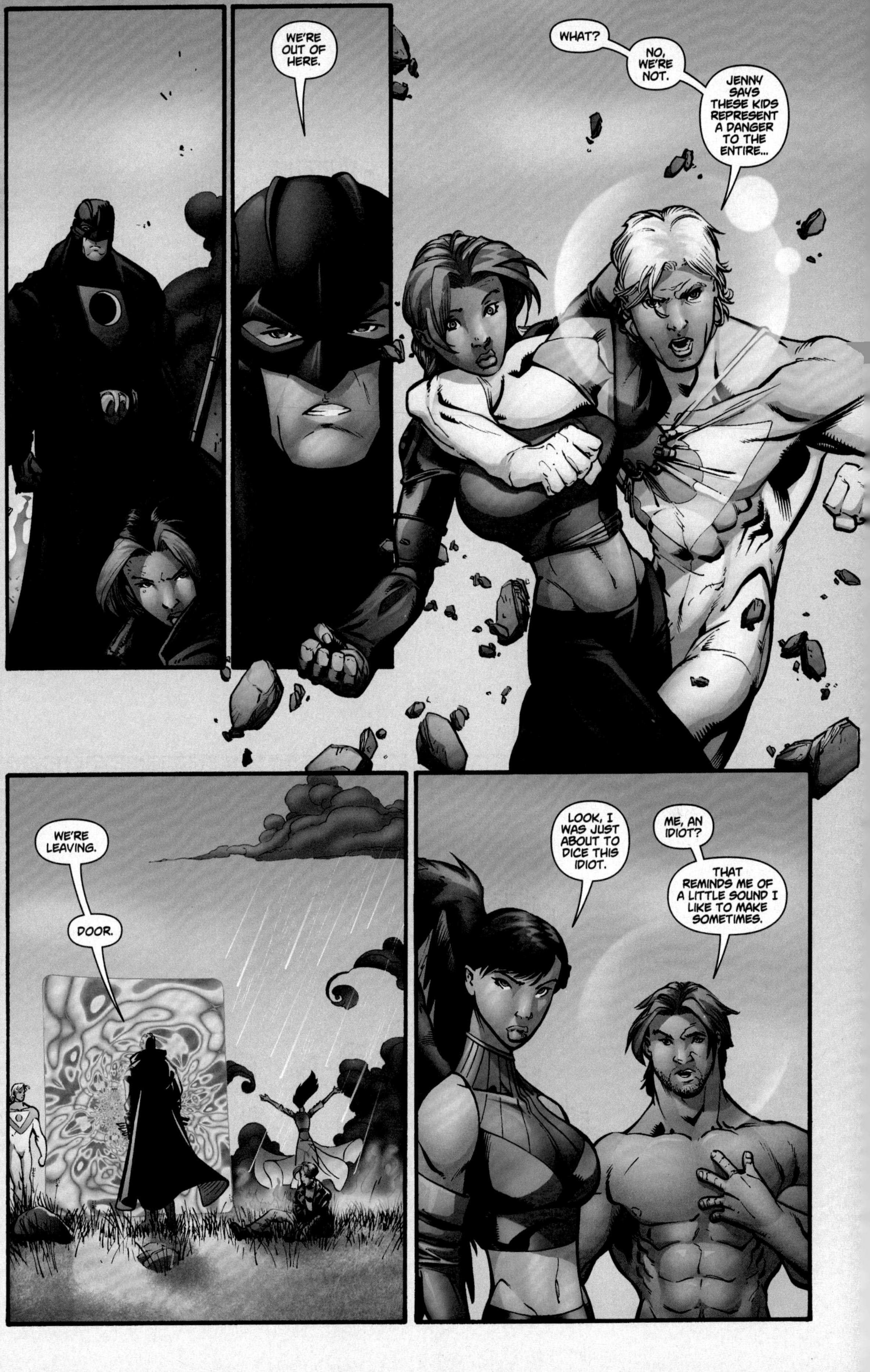

WE'RE OUT OF HERE.
WHAT?
NO, WE'RE NOT.
JENNY SAYS THESE KIDS REPRESENT A DANGER TO THE ENTIRE...
WE'RE LEAVING.
DOOR.
LOOK, I WAS JUST ABOUT TO DICE THIS IDIOT.
ME, AN IDIOT?
THAT REMINDS ME OF A LITTLE SOUND I LIKE TO MAKE SOMETIMES.

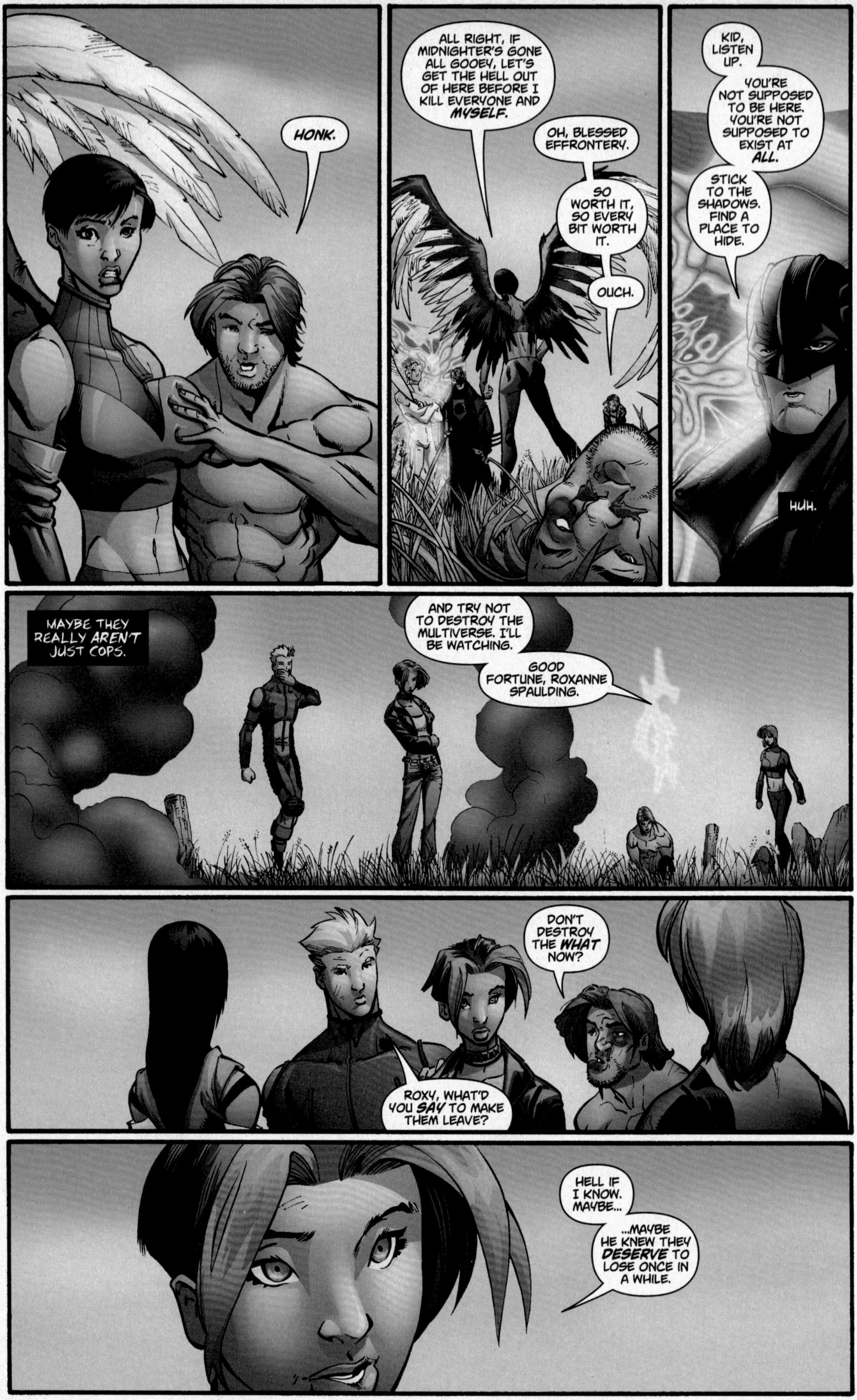
HONK.
ALL RIGHT, IF MIDNIGHTER'S GONE ALL GOOEY, LET'S GET THE HELL OUT OF HERE BEFORE I KILL EVERYONE AND MYSELF.
OH, BLESSED EFFRONTERY.
SO WORTH IT, SO EVERY BIT WORTH IT.
OUCH.
KID, LISTEN UP.
YOU'RE NOT SUPPOSED TO BE HERE. YOU'RE NOT SUPPOSED TO EXIST AT ALL.
STICK TO THE SHADOWS. FIND A PLACE TO HIDE.
HUH.
MAYBE THEY REALLY AREN'T JUST COPS.
AND TRY NOT TO DESTROY THE MULTIVERSE. I'LL BE WATCHING.
GOOD FORTUNE, ROXANNE SPAULDING.
DON'T DESTROY THE WHAT NOW?
ROXY, WHAT'D YOU SAY TO MAKE THEM LEAVE?
HELL IF I KNOW. MAYBE...
...MAYBE HE KNEW THEY DESERVE TO LOSE ONCE IN A WHILE.

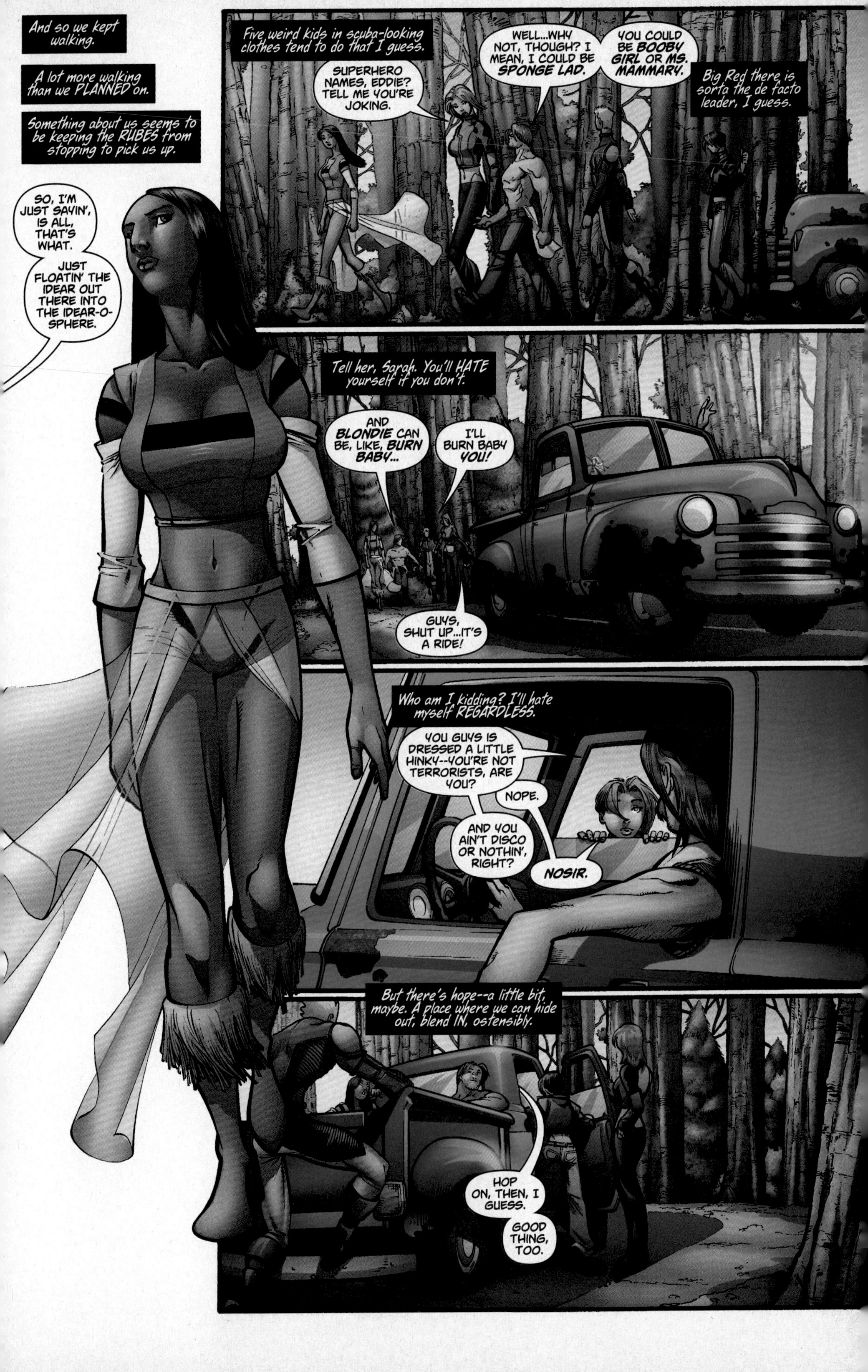

And so we kept walking.
A lot more walking than we PLANNED on.
Something about us seems to be keeping the RUBES from stopping to pick us up.
Five weird kids in scuba-looking clothes tend to do that I guess.
SUPERHERO NAMES, EDDIE? TELL ME YOU'RE JOKING.
WELL...WHY NOT, THOUGH? I MEAN, I COULD BE SPONGE LAD.
YOU COULD BE BOOBY GIRL OR MS. MAMMARY.
Big Red there is sorta the de facto leader, I guess.
SO, I'M JUST SAYIN', IS ALL, THAT'S WHAT.
JUST FLOATIN' THE IDEAR OUT THERE INTO THE IDEAR-O-SPHERE.
Tell her, Sarah. You'll HATE yourself if you don't.
AND BLONDIE CAN BE, LIKE, BURN BABY...
I'LL BURN BABY YOU!
GUYS, SHUT UP...IT'S A RIDE!
Who am I kidding? I'll hate myself REGARDLESS.
YOU GUYS IS DRESSED A LITTLE HINKY--YOU'RE NOT TERRORISTS, ARE YOU?
NOPE.
AND YOU AIN'T DISCO OR NOTHIN', RIGHT?
NOSIR.
But there's hope--a little bit, maybe. A place where we can hide out, blend IN, ostensibly.
HOP ON, THEN, I GUESS.
GOOD THING, TOO.

ONE SHOT OF A LONG, DARK ROAD
'CAUSE I HAVE TO SAY, I CAN'T ABIDE NO DISCO.
AND ROXY CAN BE BRAT GIRL AND SARAH CAN BE SEXSTORM AND...
TRANQUILITY 32 MILES
A better place, the others are saying.
I'll believe it when I SEE it.

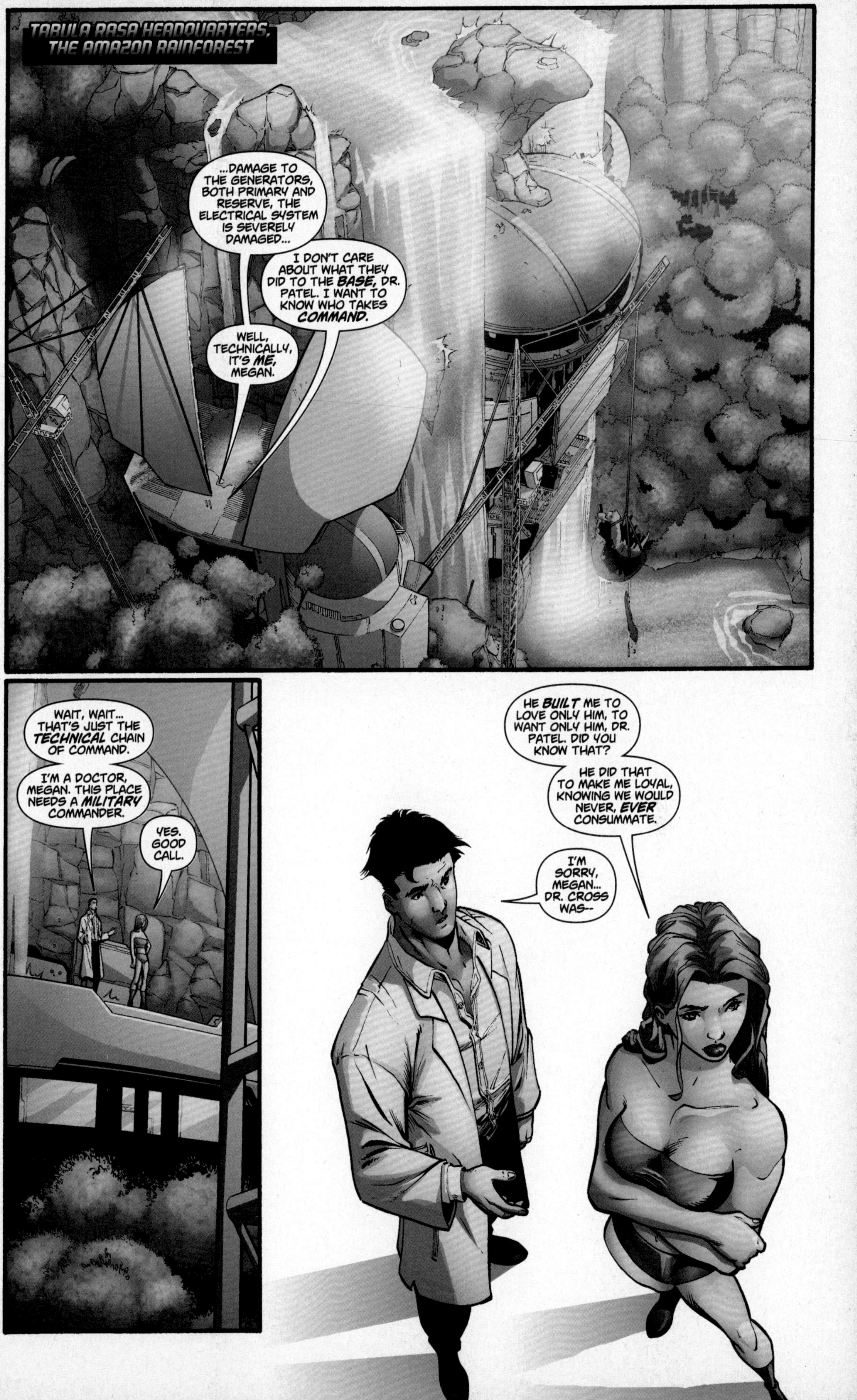
TABULA RASA HEADQUARTERS, THE AMAZON RAINFOREST
...DAMAGE TO THE GENERATORS, BOTH PRIMARY AND RESERVE, THE ELECTRICAL SYSTEM IS SEVERELY DAMAGED...
I DON'T CARE ABOUT WHAT THEY DID TO THE BASE, DR. PATEL. I WANT TO KNOW WHO TAKES COMMAND.
WELL, TECHNICALLY, IT'S ME, MEGAN.
WAIT, WAIT... THAT'S JUST THE TECHNICAL CHAIN OF COMMAND.
I'M A DOCTOR, MEGAN. THIS PLACE NEEDS A MILITARY COMMANDER.
YES. GOOD CALL.
HE BUILT ME TO LOVE ONLY HIM, TO WANT ONLY HIM, DR. PATEL. DID YOU KNOW THAT?
HE DID THAT TO MAKE ME LOYAL, KNOWING WE WOULD NEVER, EVER CONSUMMATE.
I'M SORRY, MEGAN... DR. CROSS WAS--

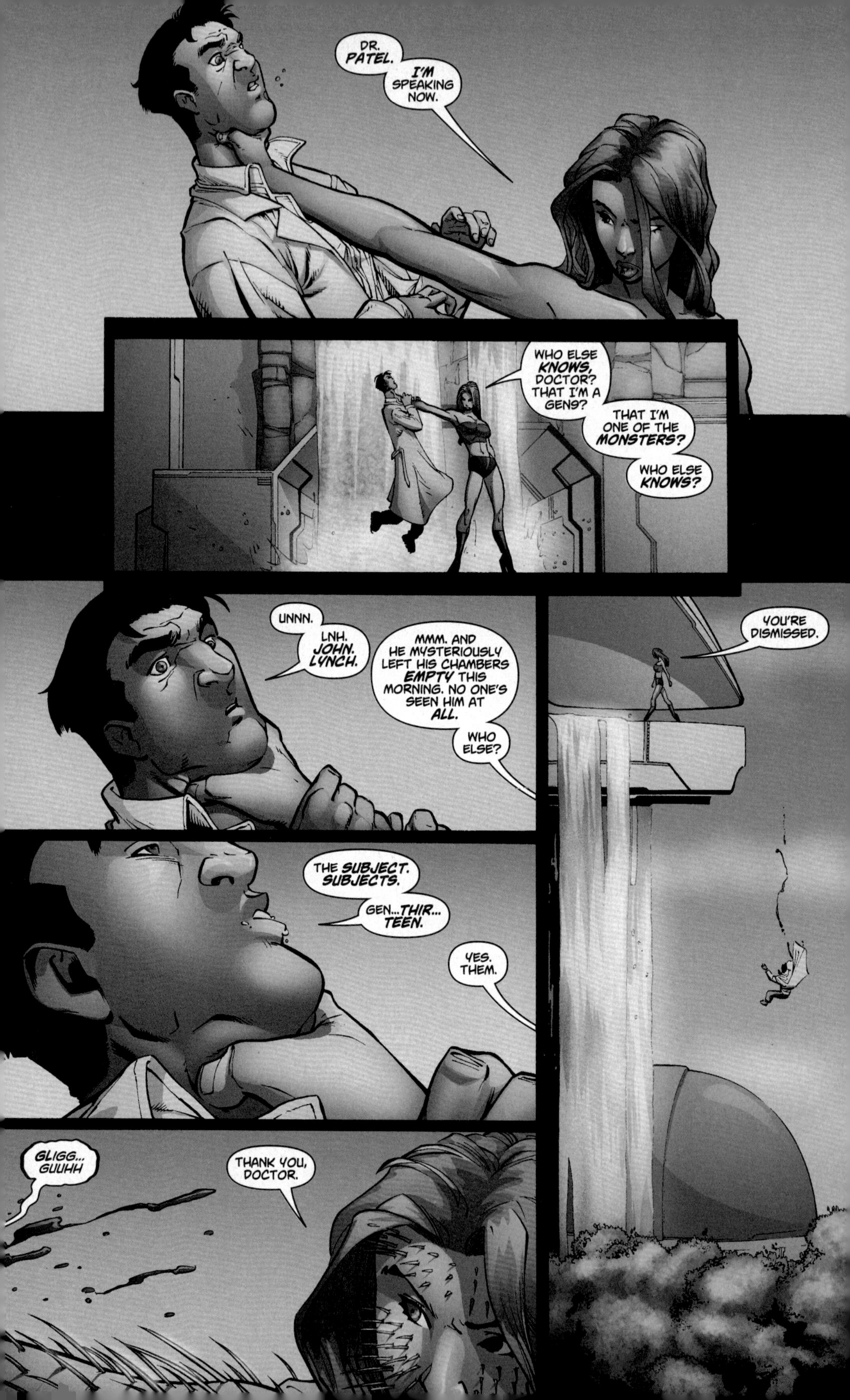
DR. PATEL. I'M SPEAKING NOW.
WHO ELSE KNOWS, DOCTOR? THAT I'M A GEN9?
THAT I'M ONE OF THE MONSTERS?
WHO ELSE KNOWS?
UNNN. LNH. JOHN. LYNCH.
MMM. AND HE MYSTERIOUSLY LEFT HIS CHAMBERS EMPTY THIS MORNING. NO ONE'S SEEN HIM AT ALL.
WHO ELSE?
THE SUBJECT. SUBJECTS.
GEN...THIR... TEEN.
YES. THEM.
GLIGG... GUUHH
THANK YOU, DOCTOR.
YOU'RE DISMISSED.

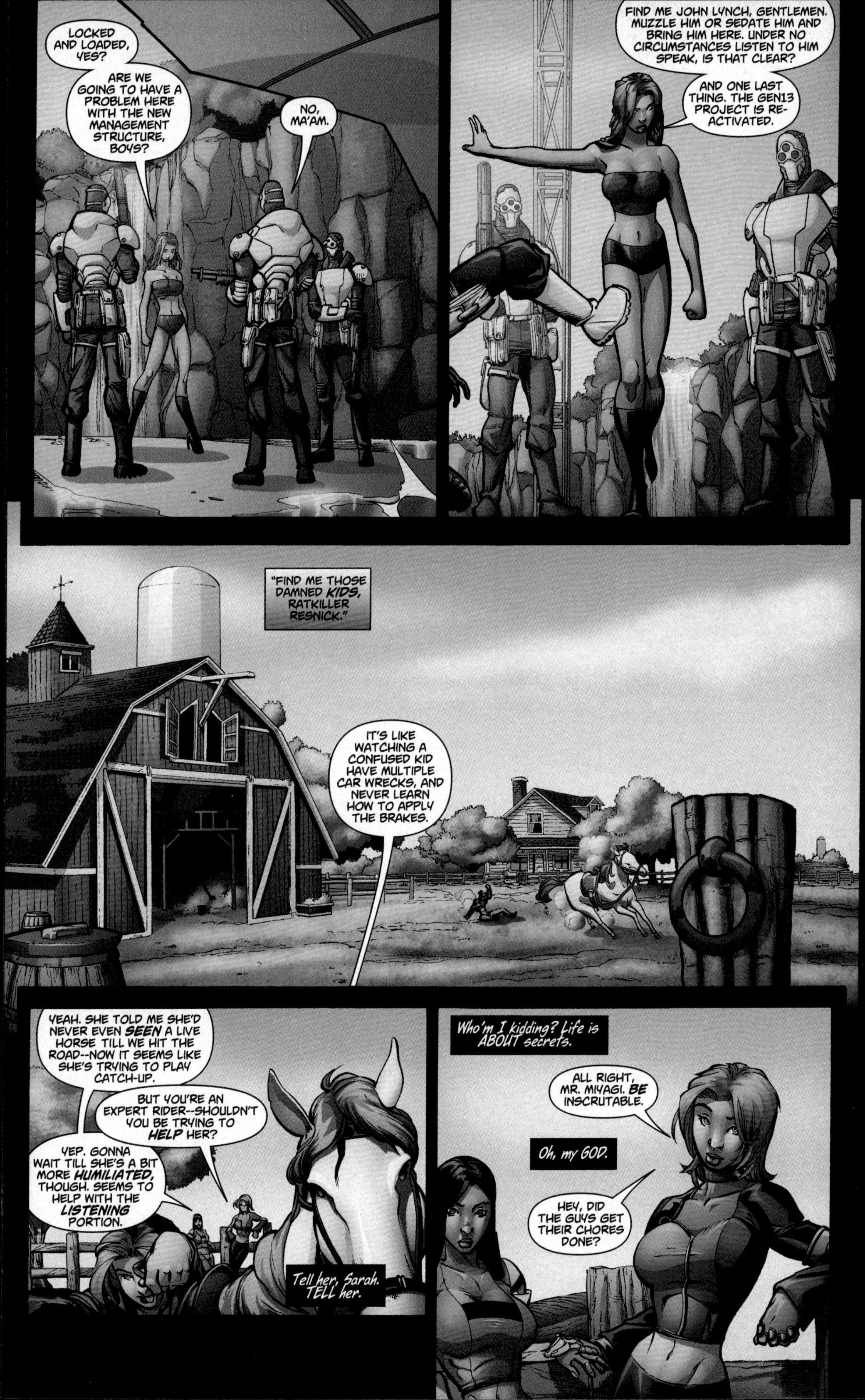
LOCKED AND LOADED, YES?
ARE WE GOING TO HAVE A PROBLEM HERE WITH THE NEW MANAGEMENT STRUCTURE, BOYS?
NO, MA'AM.
FIND ME JOHN LYNCH, GENTLEMEN. MUZZLE HIM OR SEDATE HIM AND BRING HIM HERE. UNDER NO CIRCUMSTANCES LISTEN TO HIM SPEAK, IS THAT CLEAR?
AND ONE LAST THING. THE GEN13 PROJECT IS RE-ACTIVATED.
"FIND ME THOSE DAMNED KIDS, RATKILLER RESNICK."
IT'S LIKE WATCHING A CONFUSED KID HAVE MULTIPLE CAR WRECKS, AND NEVER LEARN HOW TO APPLY THE BRAKES.
YEAH. SHE TOLD ME SHE'D NEVER EVEN SEEN A LIVE HORSE TILL WE HIT THE ROAD--NOW IT SEEMS LIKE SHE'S TRYING TO PLAY CATCH-UP.
BUT YOU'RE AN EXPERT RIDER--SHOULDN'T YOU BE TRYING TO HELP HER?
YEP. GONNA WAIT TILL SHE'S A BIT MORE HUMILIATED, THOUGH. SEEMS TO HELP WITH THE LISTENING PORTION.
Tell her, Sarah. TELL her.
Who'm I kidding? Life is ABOUT secrets.
ALL RIGHT, MR. MIYAGI. BE INSCRUTABLE.
Oh, my GOD.
HEY, DID THE GUYS GET THEIR CHORES DONE?

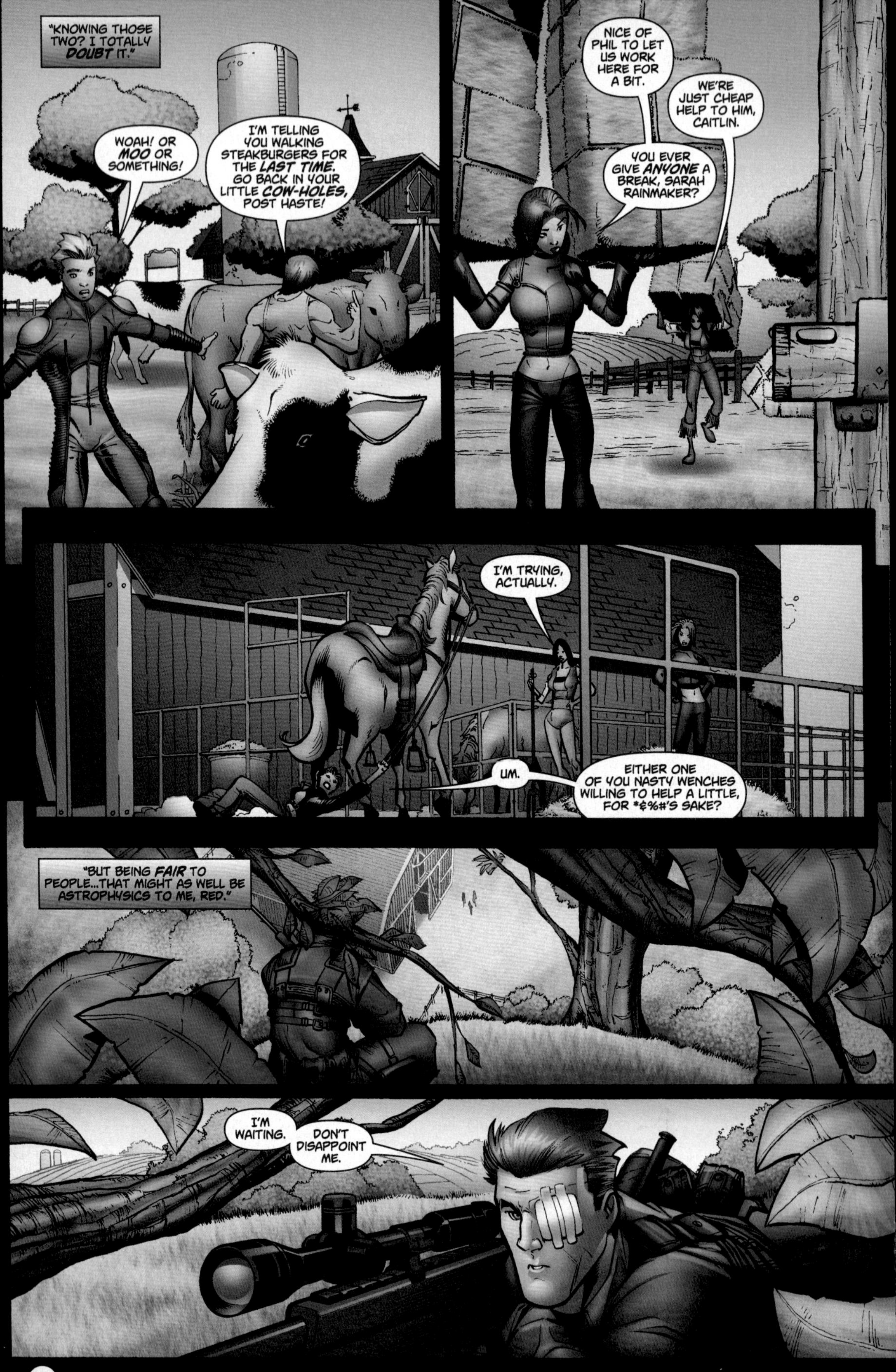

"KNOWING THOSE TWO? I TOTALLY DOUBT IT."
WOAH! OR MOO OR SOMETHING!
I'M TELLING YOU WALKING STEAKBURGERS FOR THE LAST TIME. GO BACK IN YOUR LITTLE COW-HOLES, POST HASTE!
NICE OF PHIL TO LET US WORK HERE FOR A BIT.
WE'RE JUST CHEAP HELP TO HIM, CAITLIN.
YOU EVER GIVE ANYONE A BREAK, SARAH RAINMAKER?
I'M TRYING, ACTUALLY.
UM.
EITHER ONE OF YOU NASTY WENCHES WILLING TO HELP A LITTLE, FOR *&%#'S SAKE?
"BUT BEING FAIR TO PEOPLE...THAT MIGHT AS WELL BE ASTROPHYSICS TO ME, RED."
I'M WAITING.
DON'T DISAPPOINT ME.

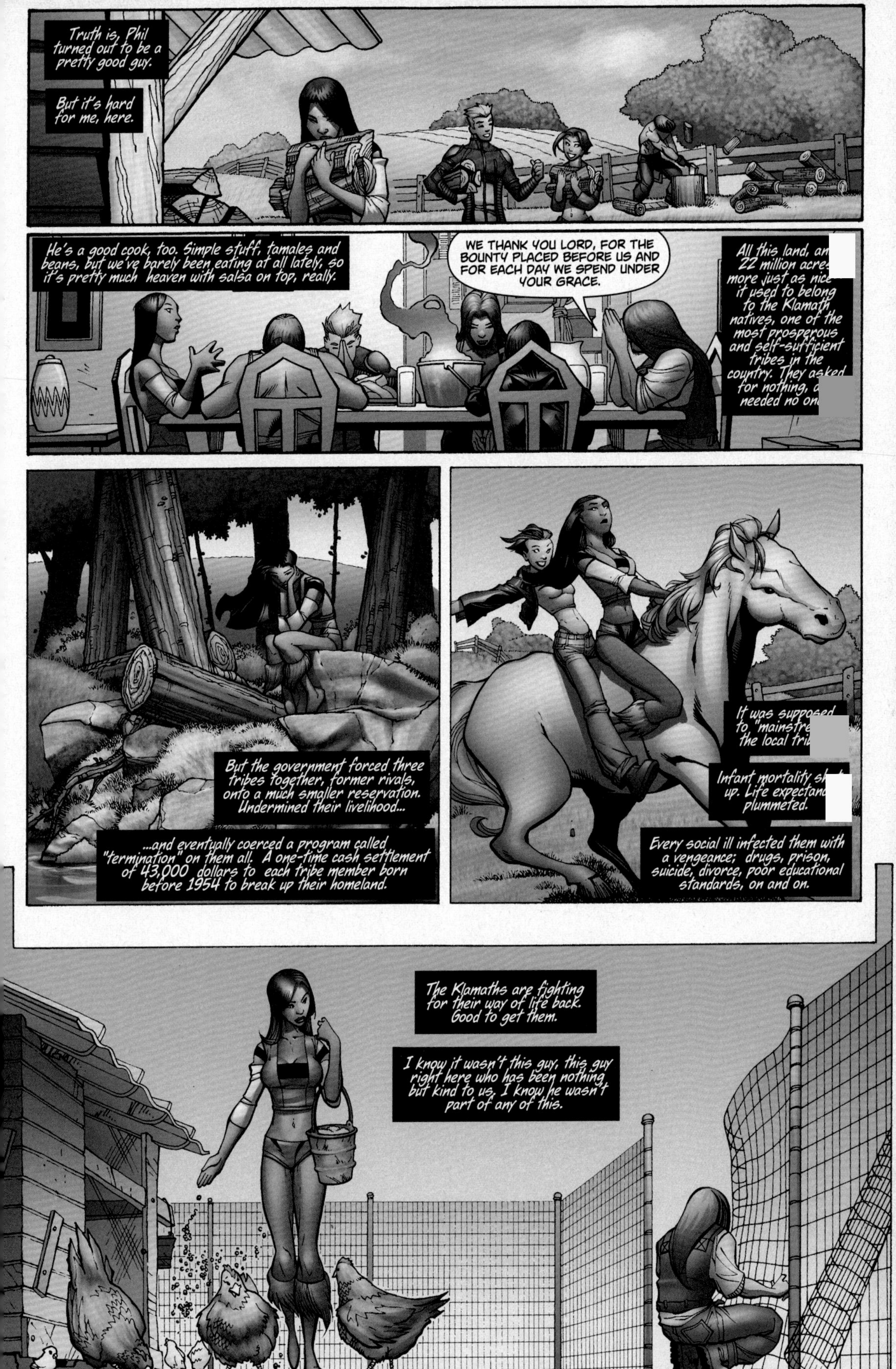

Truth is, Phil turned out to be a pretty good guy.
But it's hard for me, here.
He's a good cook, too. Simple stuff, tamales and beans, but we've barely been eating at all lately, so it's pretty much heaven with salsa on top, really.
WE THANK YOU LORD, FOR THE BOUNTY PLACED BEFORE US AND FOR EACH DAY WE SPEND UNDER YOUR GRACE.
All this land, an 22 million acres more just as nice it used to belong to the Klamath natives, one of the most prosperous and self-sufficient tribes in the country. They asked for nothing, a needed no on
But the government forced three tribes together, former rivals, onto a much smaller reservation. Undermined their livelihood...
...and eventually coerced a program called "termination" on them all. A one-time cash settlement of 43,000 dollars to each tribe member born before 1954 to break up their homeland.
It was supposed to "mainstre the local tri
Infant mortality sh up. Life expectan plummeted.
Every social ill infected them with a vengeance; drugs, prison, suicide, divorce, poor educational standards, on and on.
The Klamaths are fighting for their way of life back. Good to get them.
I know it wasn't this guy, this guy right here who has been nothing but kind to us, I know he wasn't part of any of this.

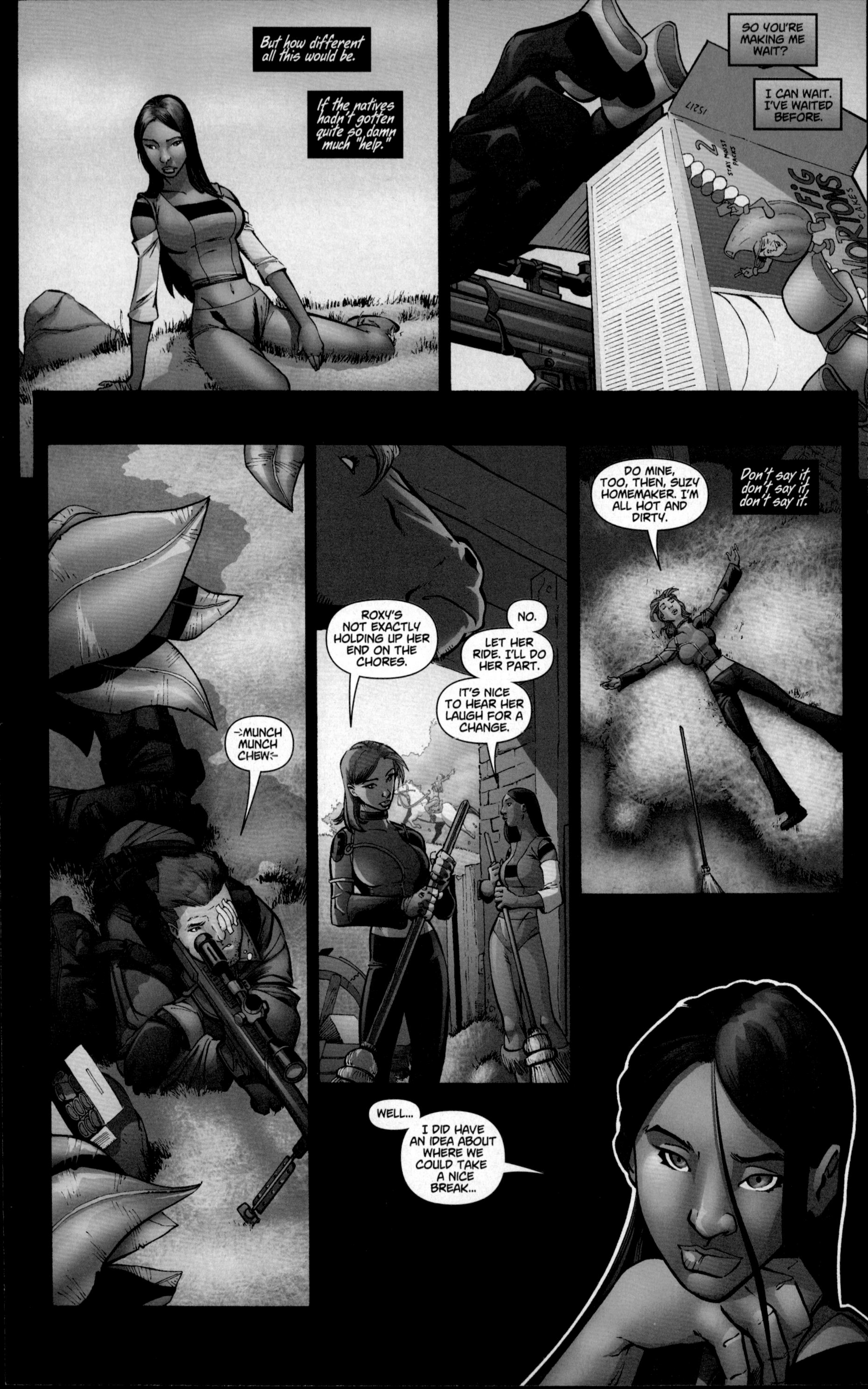
But how different all this would be.
If the natives hadn't gotten quite so damn much "help."
SO YOU'RE MAKING ME WAIT?
I CAN WAIT. I'VE WAITED BEFORE.
FIG NORTONS CAKES
STAY MOIST PACKS
-MUNCH MUNCH CHEW-
ROXY'S NOT EXACTLY HOLDING UP HER END ON THE CHORES.
NO.
LET HER RIDE. I'LL DO HER PART.
IT'S NICE TO HEAR HER LAUGH FOR A CHANGE.
DO MINE, TOO, THEN, SUZY HOMEMAKER. I'M ALL HOT AND DIRTY.
Don't say it, don't say it, don't say it.
WELL...
I DID HAVE AN IDEA ABOUT WHERE WE COULD TAKE A NICE BREAK...

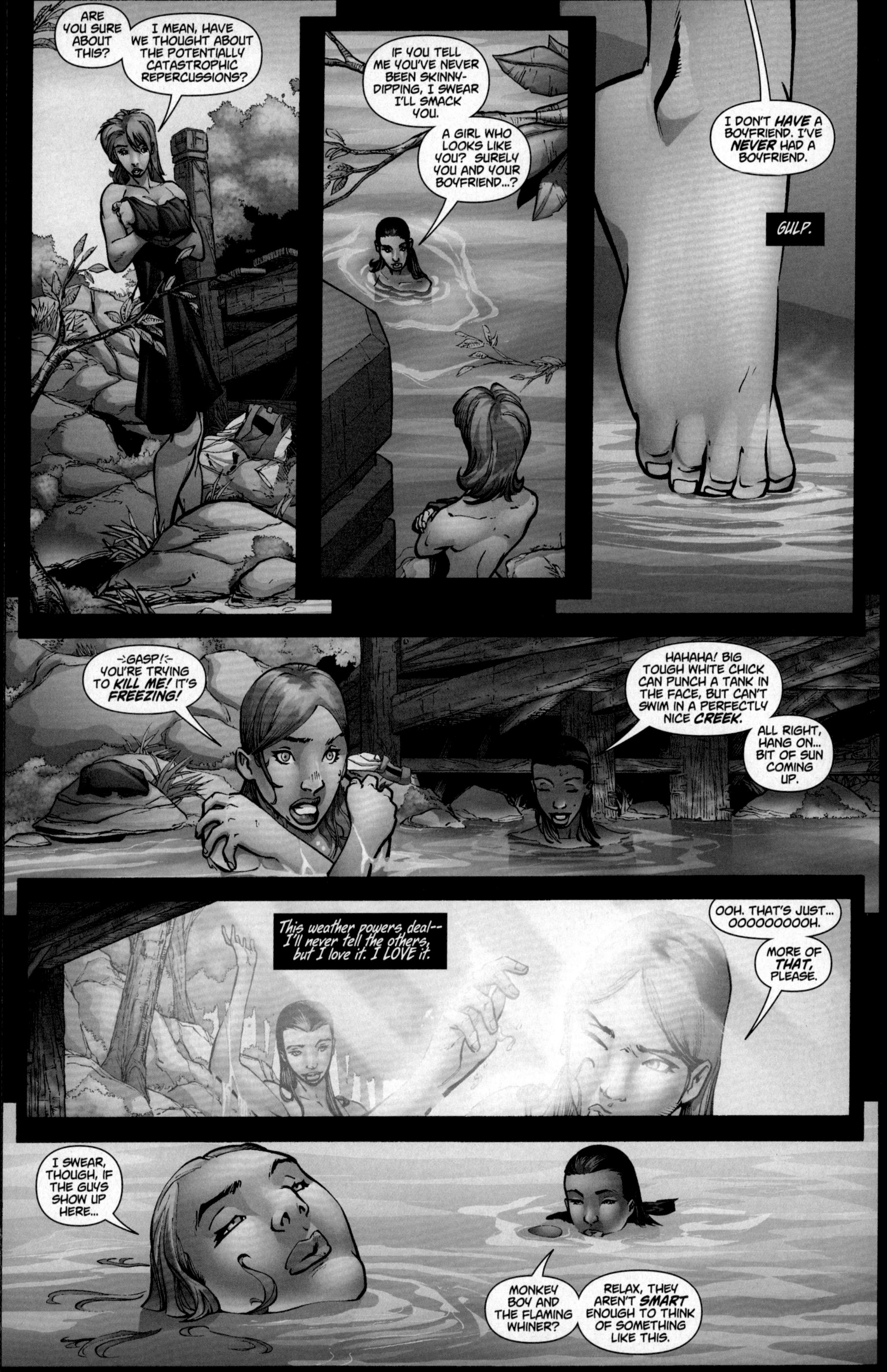
ARE YOU SURE ABOUT THIS?
I MEAN, HAVE WE THOUGHT ABOUT THE POTENTIALLY CATASTROPHIC REPERCUSSIONS?
IF YOU TELL ME YOU'VE NEVER BEEN SKINNY-DIPPING, I SWEAR I'LL SMACK YOU.
A GIRL WHO LOOKS LIKE YOU? SURELY YOU AND YOUR BOYFRIEND...?
I DON'T HAVE A BOYFRIEND. I'VE NEVER HAD A BOYFRIEND.
GULP.
-GASP!- YOU'RE TRYING TO KILL ME! IT'S FREEZING!
HAHAHA! BIG TOUGH WHITE CHICK CAN PUNCH A TANK IN THE FACE, BUT CAN'T SWIM IN A PERFECTLY NICE CREEK.
ALL RIGHT, HANG ON... BIT OF SUN COMING UP.
This weather powers deal-- I'll never tell the others, but I love it. I LOVE it.
OOH. THAT'S JUST... OOOOOOOOOH.
MORE OF THAT, PLEASE.
I SWEAR, THOUGH, IF THE GUYS SHOW UP HERE...
MONKEY BOY AND THE FLAMING WHINER?
RELAX, THEY AREN'T SMART ENOUGH TO THINK OF SOMETHING LIKE THIS.

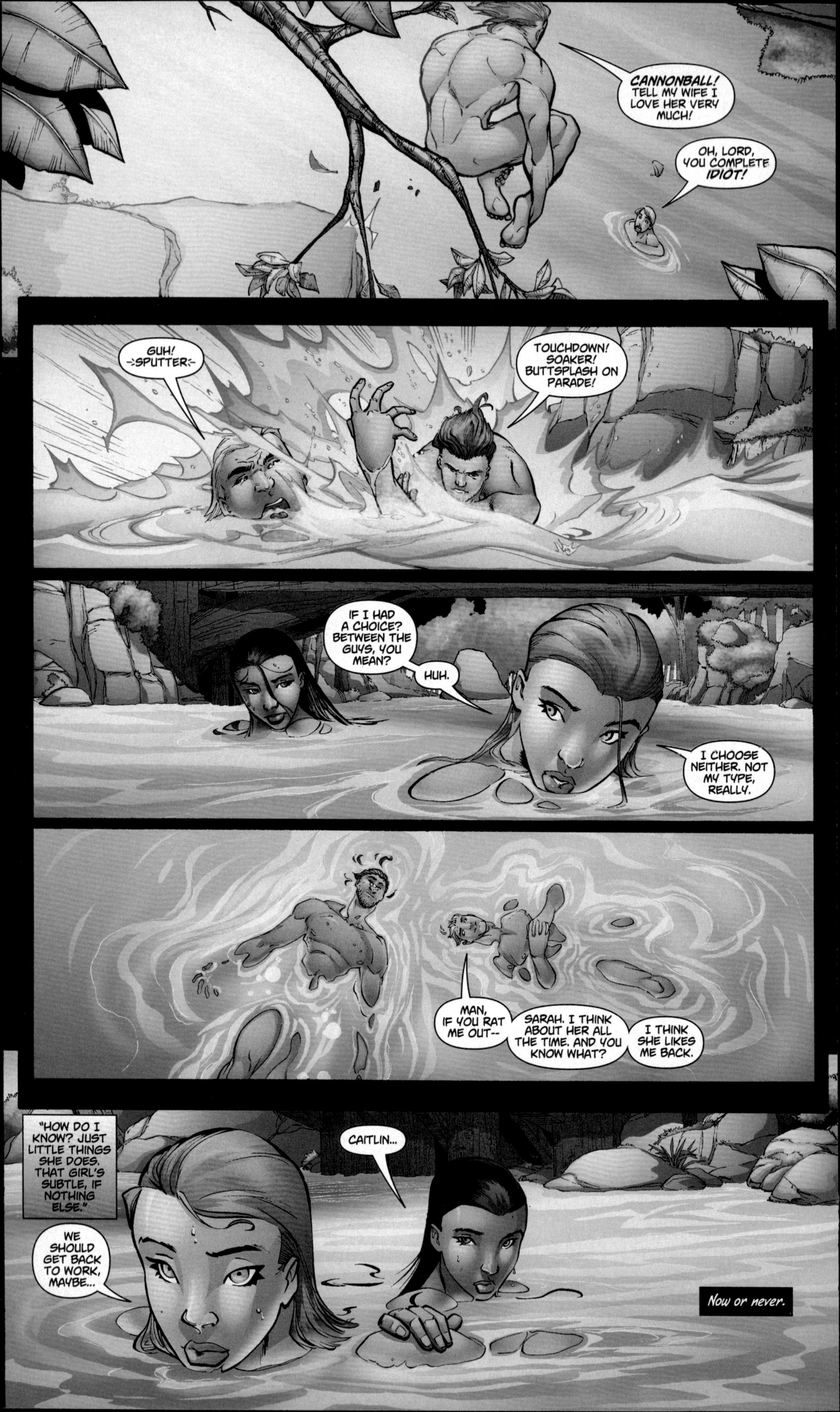
CANNONBALL! TELL MY WIFE I LOVE HER VERY MUCH!
OH, LORD, YOU COMPLETE IDIOT!
GUH! -SPUTTER-
TOUCHDOWN! SOAKER! BUTTSPLASH ON PARADE!
IF I HAD A CHOICE? BETWEEN THE GUYS, YOU MEAN?
HUH.
I CHOOSE NEITHER. NOT MY TYPE, REALLY.
MAN, IF YOU RAT ME OUT--
SARAH. I THINK ABOUT HER ALL THE TIME. AND YOU KNOW WHAT?
I THINK SHE LIKES ME BACK.
"HOW DO I KNOW? JUST LITTLE THINGS SHE DOES. THAT GIRL'S SUBTLE, IF NOTHING ELSE."
CAITLIN...
WE SHOULD GET BACK TO WORK, MAYBE...
Now or never.

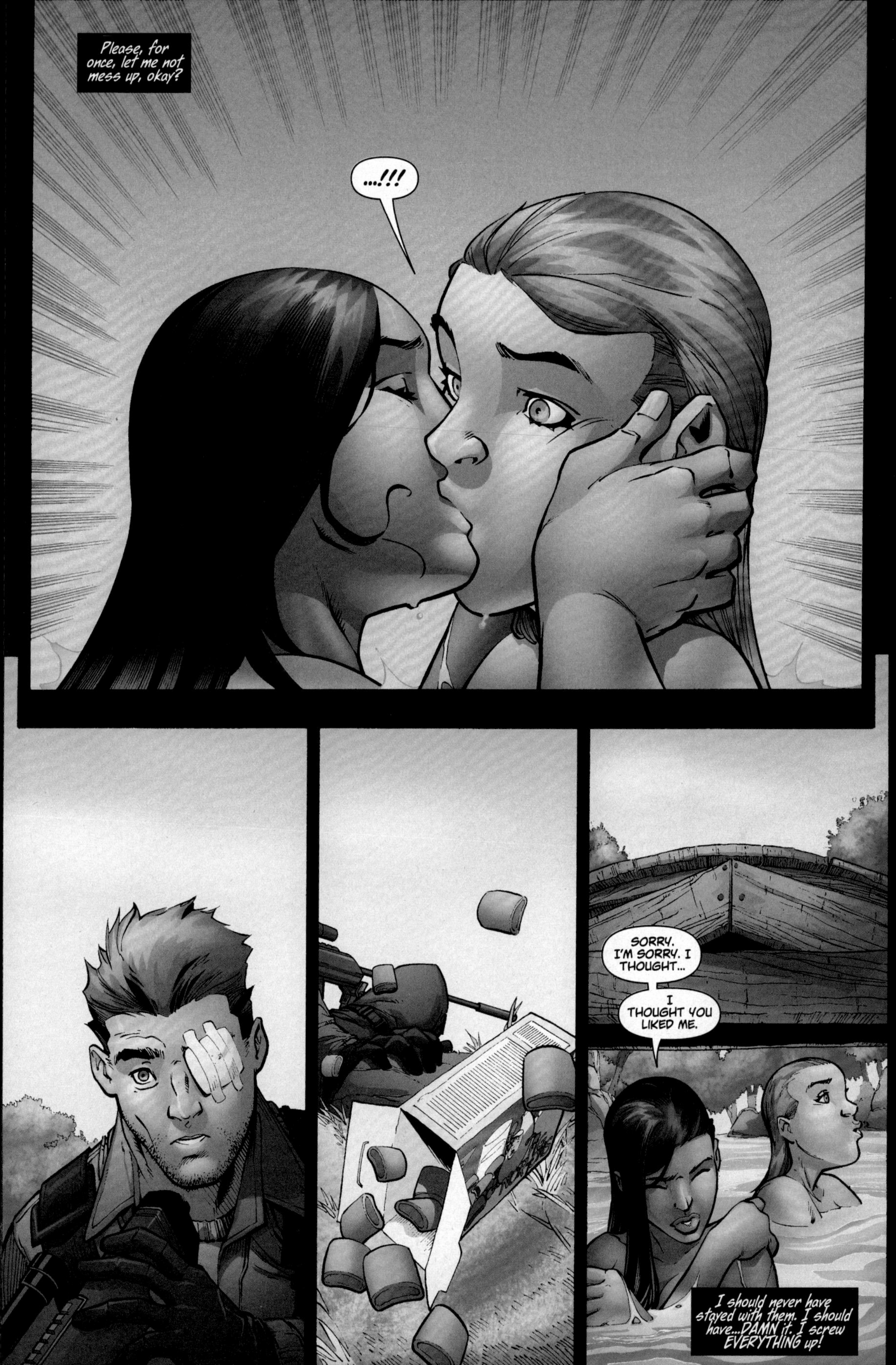
Please, for once, let me not mess up, okay?
...!!!
SORRY. I'M SORRY. I THOUGHT...
I THOUGHT YOU LIKED ME.
I should never have stayed with them. I should have...DAMN it. I screw EVERYTHING up!

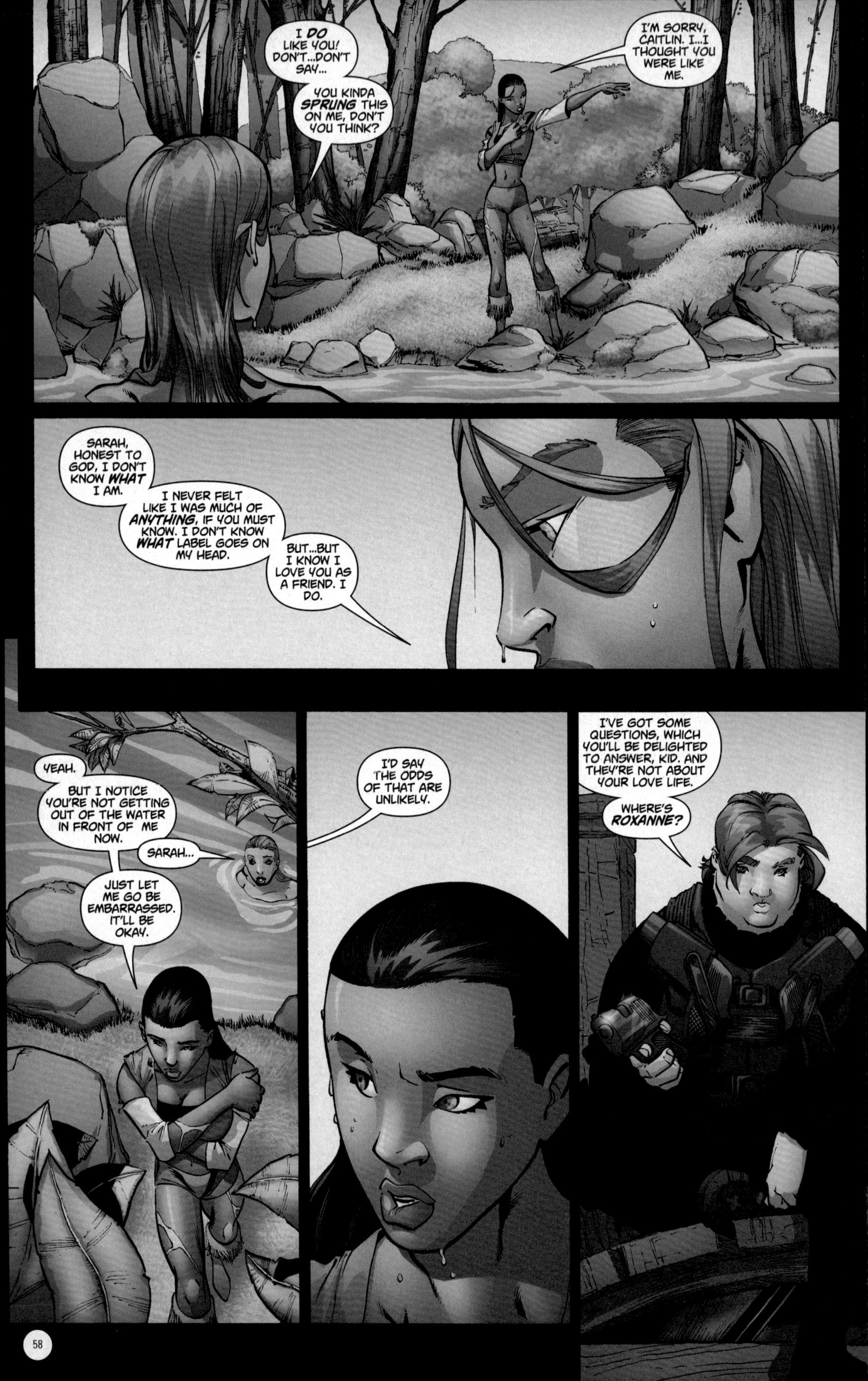
I DO LIKE YOU! DON'T...DON'T SAY...
YOU KINDA SPRUNG THIS ON ME, DON'T YOU THINK?
I'M SORRY, CAITLIN. I...I THOUGHT YOU WERE LIKE ME.
SARAH, HONEST TO GOD, I DON'T KNOW WHAT I AM.
I NEVER FELT LIKE I WAS MUCH OF ANYTHING, IF YOU MUST KNOW. I DON'T KNOW WHAT LABEL GOES ON MY HEAD.
BUT...BUT I KNOW I LOVE YOU AS A FRIEND. I DO.
YEAH.
BUT I NOTICE YOU'RE NOT GETTING OUT OF THE WATER IN FRONT OF ME NOW.
SARAH...
JUST LET ME GO BE EMBARRASSED. IT'LL BE OKAY.
I'D SAY THE ODDS OF THAT ARE UNLIKELY.
I'VE GOT SOME QUESTIONS, WHICH YOU'LL BE DELIGHTED TO ANSWER, KID. AND THEY'RE NOT ABOUT YOUR LOVE LIFE.
WHERE'S ROXANNE?

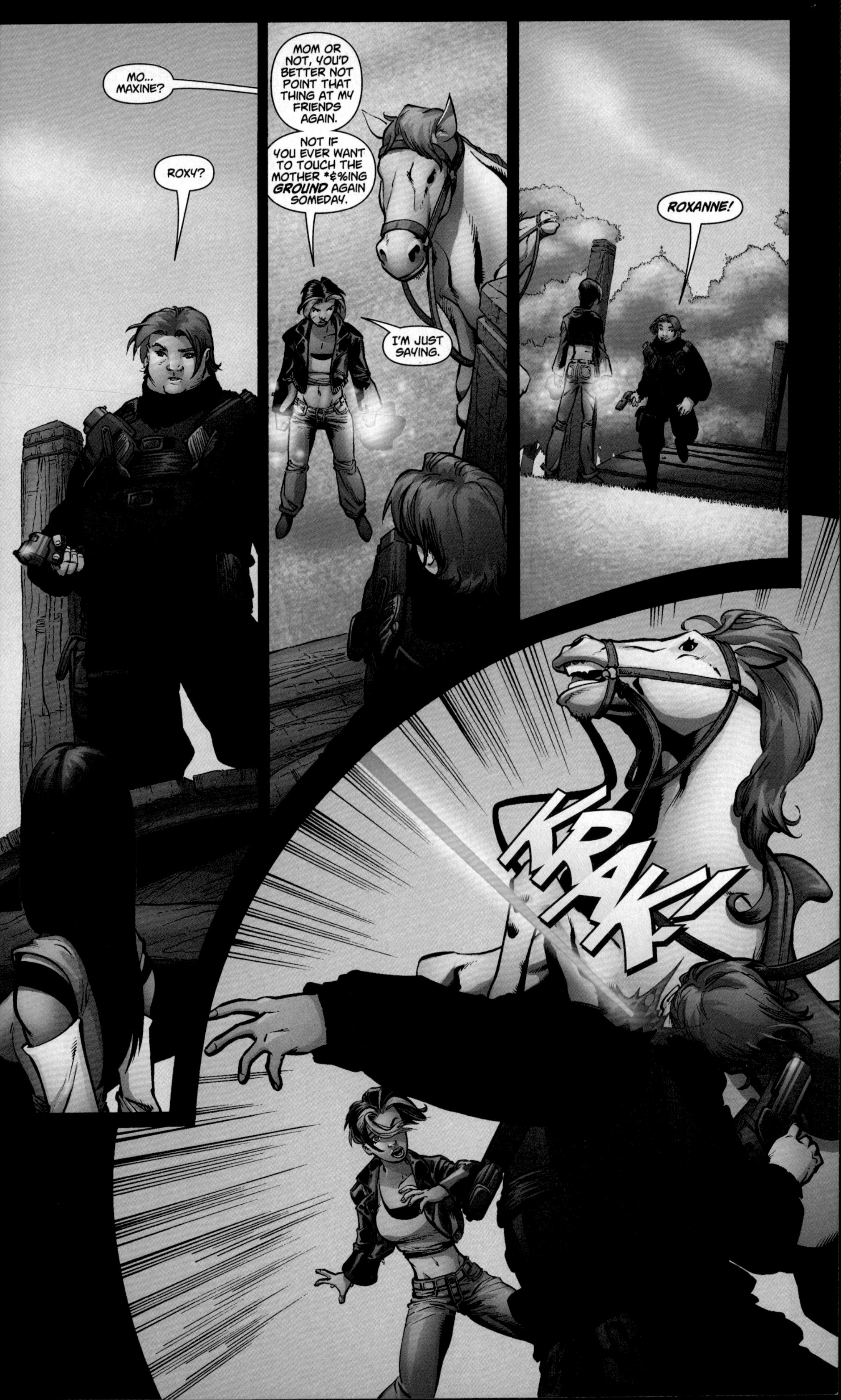
MO... MAXINE?
ROXY?
MOM OR NOT, YOU'D BETTER NOT POINT THAT THING AT MY FRIENDS AGAIN.
NOT IF YOU EVER WANT TO TOUCH THE MOTHER *&%ING GROUND AGAIN SOMEDAY.
I'M JUST SAYING.
ROXANNE!
KRAK!

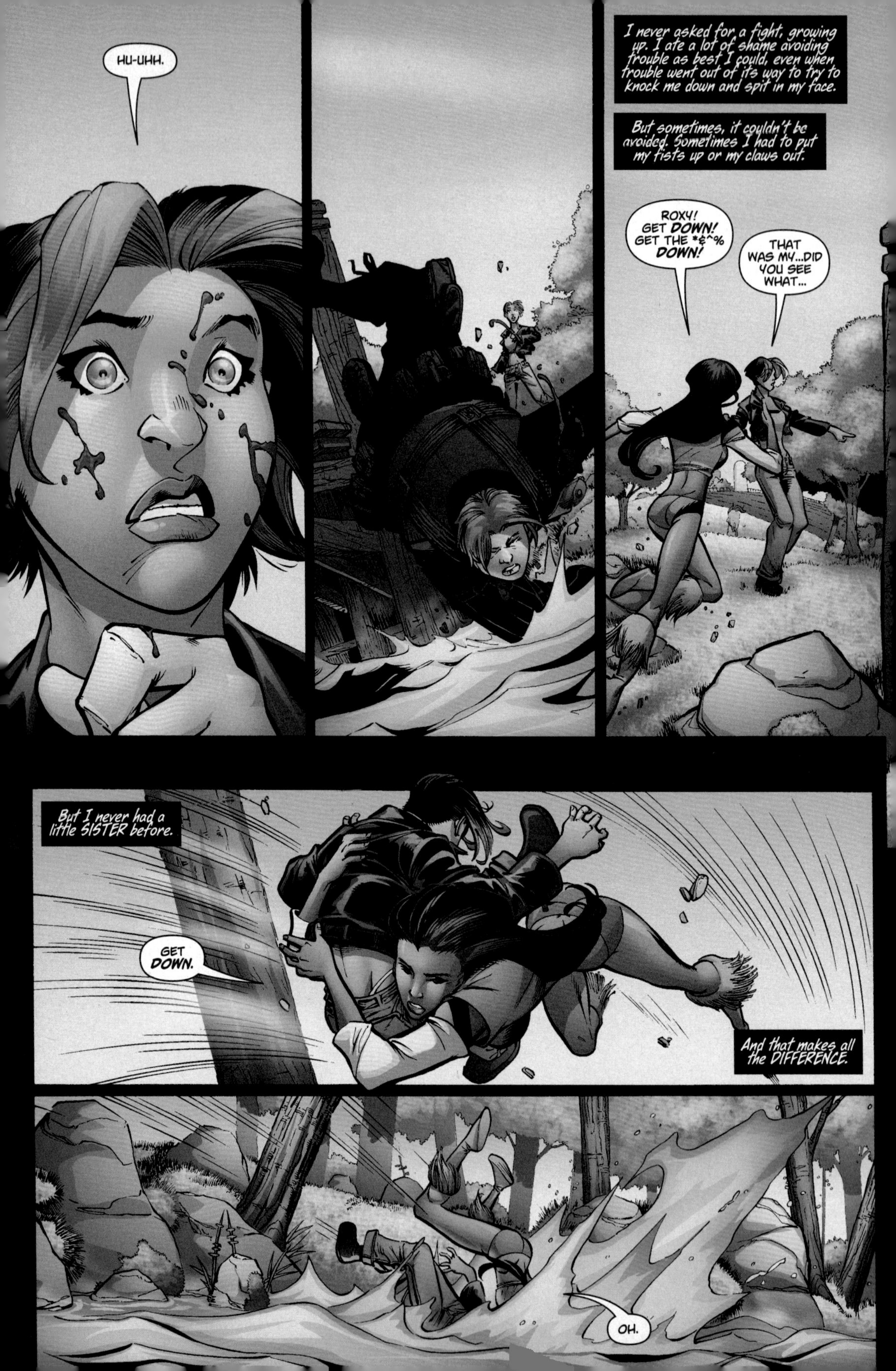
HU-UHH.
I never asked for a fight, growing up. I ate a lot of shame avoiding trouble as best I could, even when trouble went out of its way to try to knock me down and spit in my face.
But sometimes, it couldn't be avoided. Sometimes I had to put my fists up or my claws out.
ROXY! GET DOWN! GET THE *&^% DOWN!
THAT WAS MY...DID YOU SEE WHAT...
But I never had a little SISTER before.
GET DOWN.
And that makes all the DIFFERENCE.
OH.

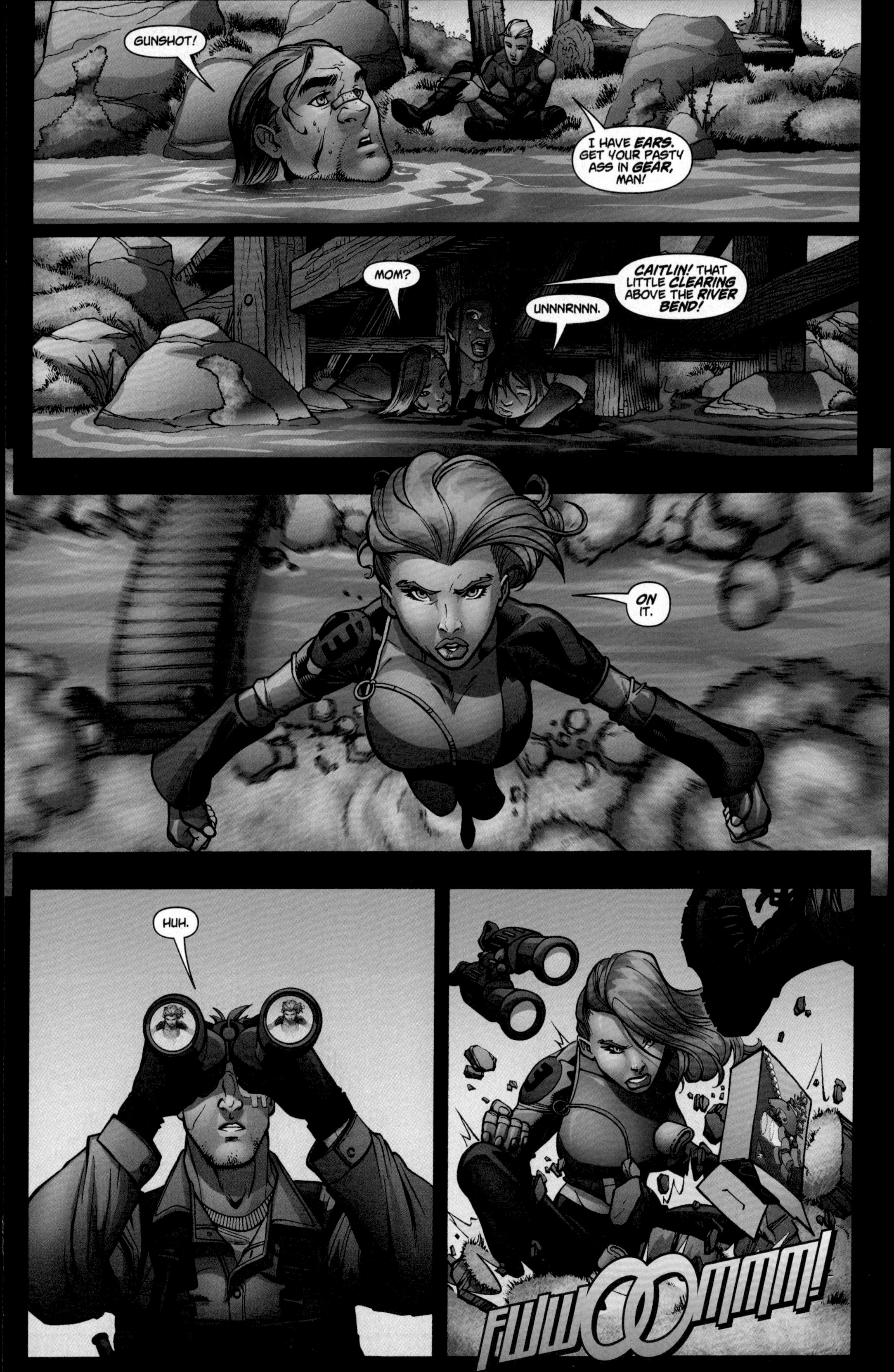
GUNSHOT!
I HAVE EARS. GET YOUR PASTY ASS IN GEAR, MAN!
MOM?
CAITLIN! THAT LITTLE CLEARING ABOVE THE RIVER BEND!
UNNNRNNN.
ON IT.
HUH.
FWWOOMMMM!

MISTER, THAT'S THE *SECOND* TIME YOU'VE TRIED TO KILL MY FRIEND ROXANNE. WON'T BE A THIRD.

WAIT. WHAT? NO. BACK *OFF*, COTTONTAIL.

I SAID *BACK OFF*.

DAMN *SPIRAL* IMPACT GRENADE...

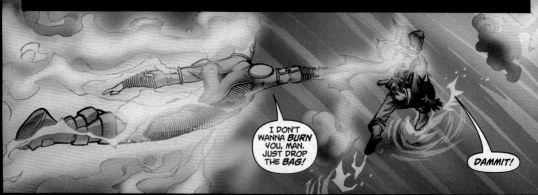

I DON'T WANNA *BURN* YOU, MAN. JUST DROP THE *BAG*!

DAMMIT!

62

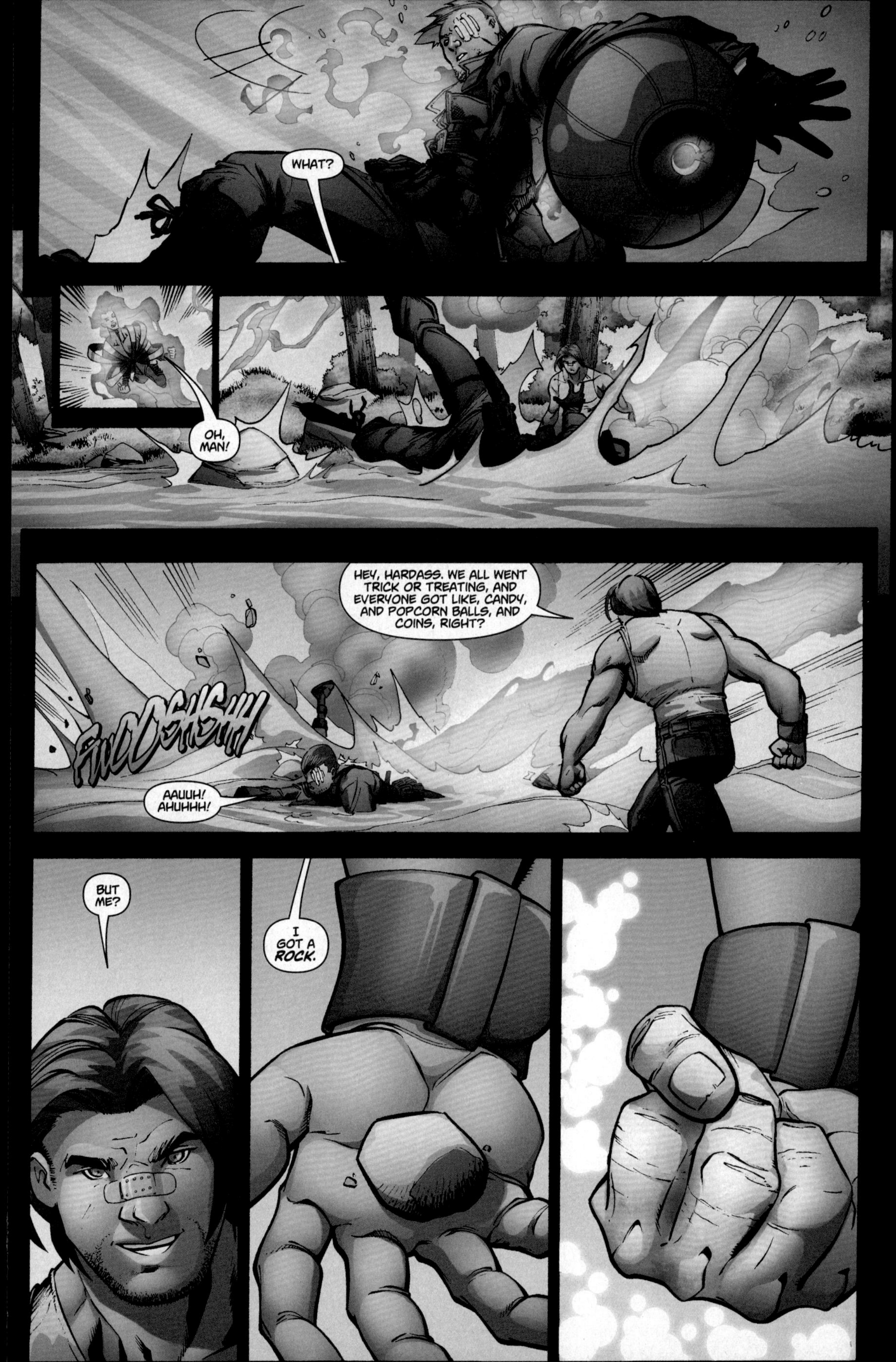
WHAT?
OH, MAN!
HEY, HARDASS. WE ALL WENT TRICK OR TREATING, AND EVERYONE GOT LIKE, CANDY, AND POPCORN BALLS, AND COINS, RIGHT?
FWOOSHSHH
AAUUH! AHUHHH!
BUT ME?
I GOT A ROCK.

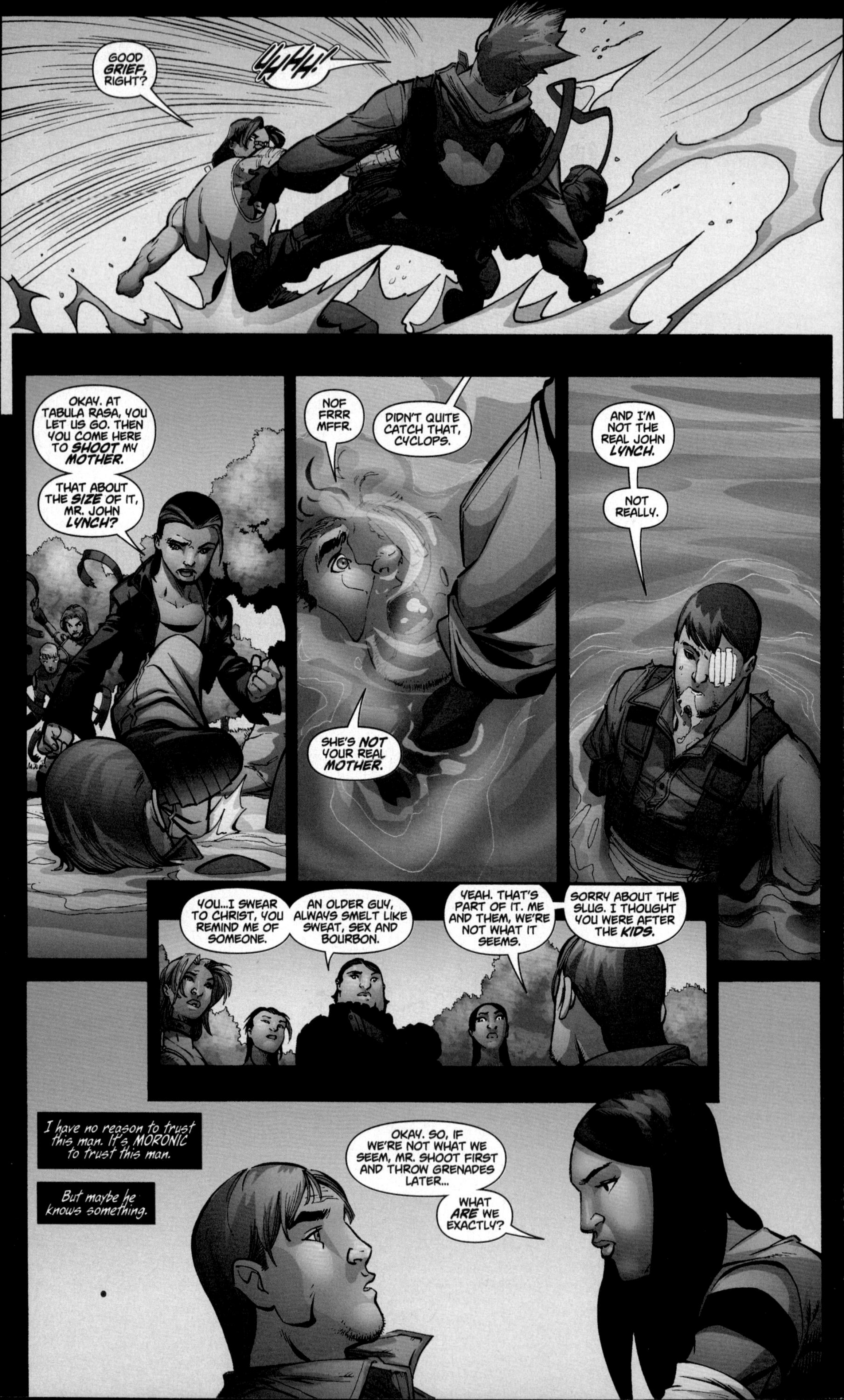
GOOD GRIEF, RIGHT?
UHH!
OKAY. AT TABULA RASA, YOU LET US GO. THEN YOU COME HERE TO SHOOT MY MOTHER.
THAT ABOUT THE SIZE OF IT, MR. JOHN LYNCH?
NOF FRRR MFFR.
DIDN'T QUITE CATCH THAT, CYCLOPS.
SHE'S NOT YOUR REAL MOTHER.
AND I'M NOT THE REAL JOHN LYNCH.
NOT REALLY.
YOU...I SWEAR TO CHRIST, YOU REMIND ME OF SOMEONE.
AN OLDER GUY, ALWAYS SMELT LIKE SWEAT, SEX AND BOURBON.
YEAH. THAT'S PART OF IT. ME AND THEM, WE'RE NOT WHAT IT SEEMS.
SORRY ABOUT THE SLUG. I THOUGHT YOU WERE AFTER THE KIDS.
I have no reason to trust this man. It's MORONIC to trust this man.
But maybe he knows something.
OKAY. SO, IF WE'RE NOT WHAT WE SEEM, MR. SHOOT FIRST AND THROW GRENADES LATER...
WHAT ARE WE EXACTLY?

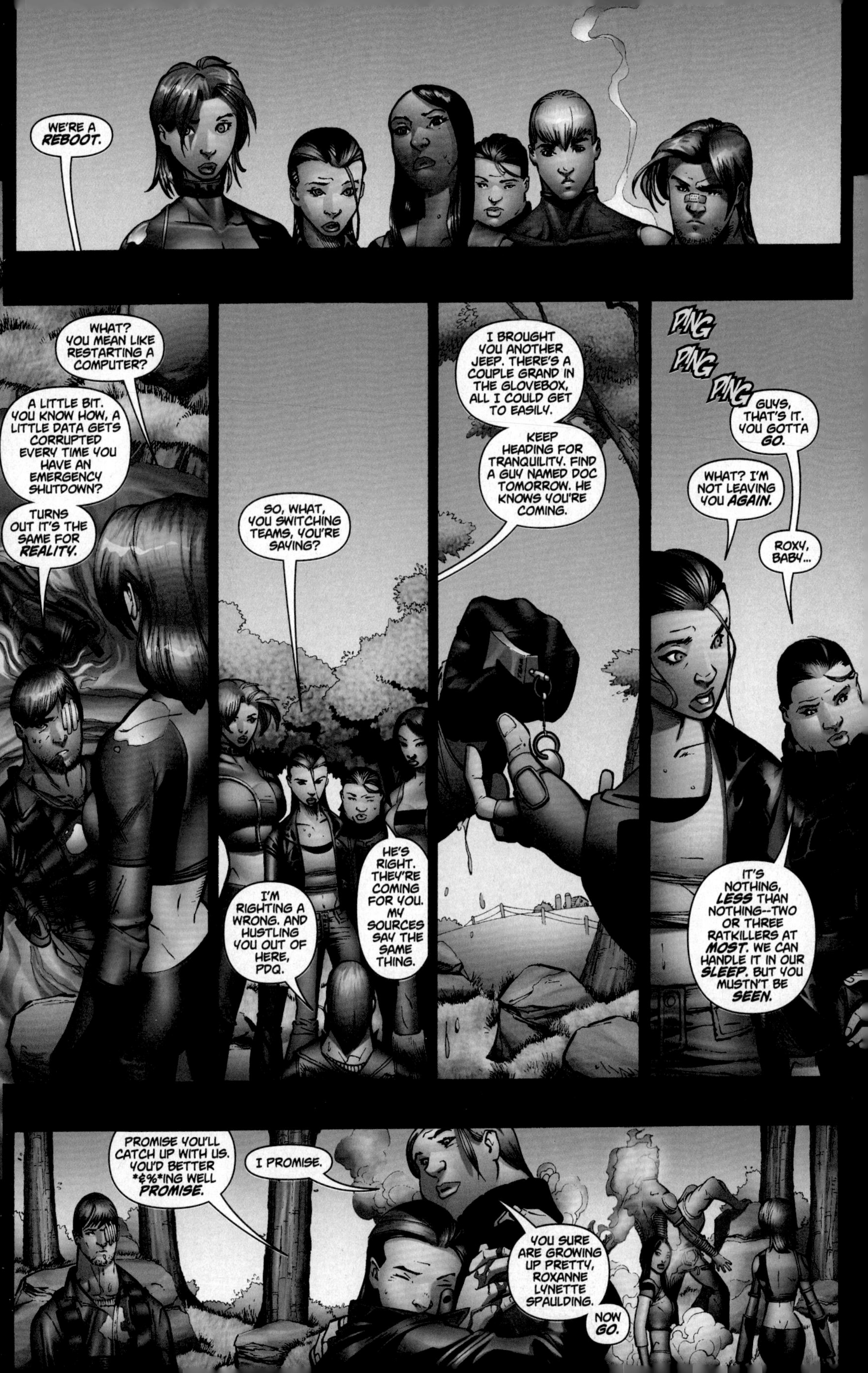
WE'RE A REBOOT.
WHAT? YOU MEAN LIKE RESTARTING A COMPUTER?
A LITTLE BIT. YOU KNOW HOW, A LITTLE DATA GETS CORRUPTED EVERY TIME YOU HAVE AN EMERGENCY SHUTDOWN?
TURNS OUT IT'S THE SAME FOR REALITY.
SO, WHAT, YOU SWITCHING TEAMS, YOU'RE SAYING?
I'M RIGHTING A WRONG. AND HUSTLING YOU OUT OF HERE, PDQ.
HE'S RIGHT. THEY'RE COMING FOR YOU. MY SOURCES SAY THE SAME THING.
I BROUGHT YOU ANOTHER JEEP. THERE'S A COUPLE GRAND IN THE GLOVEBOX, ALL I COULD GET TO EASILY.
KEEP HEADING FOR TRANQUILITY. FIND A GUY NAMED DOC TOMORROW. HE KNOWS YOU'RE COMING.
PING
PING
PING
GUYS, THAT'S IT. YOU GOTTA GO.
WHAT? I'M NOT LEAVING YOU AGAIN.
ROXY, BABY...
IT'S NOTHING, LESS THAN NOTHING--TWO OR THREE RATKILLERS AT MOST. WE CAN HANDLE IT IN OUR SLEEP. BUT YOU MUSTN'T BE SEEN.
PROMISE YOU'LL CATCH UP WITH US. YOU'D BETTER *&%*ING WELL PROMISE.
I PROMISE.
YOU SURE ARE GROWING UP PRETTY, ROXANNE LYNETTE SPAULDING.
NOW GO.

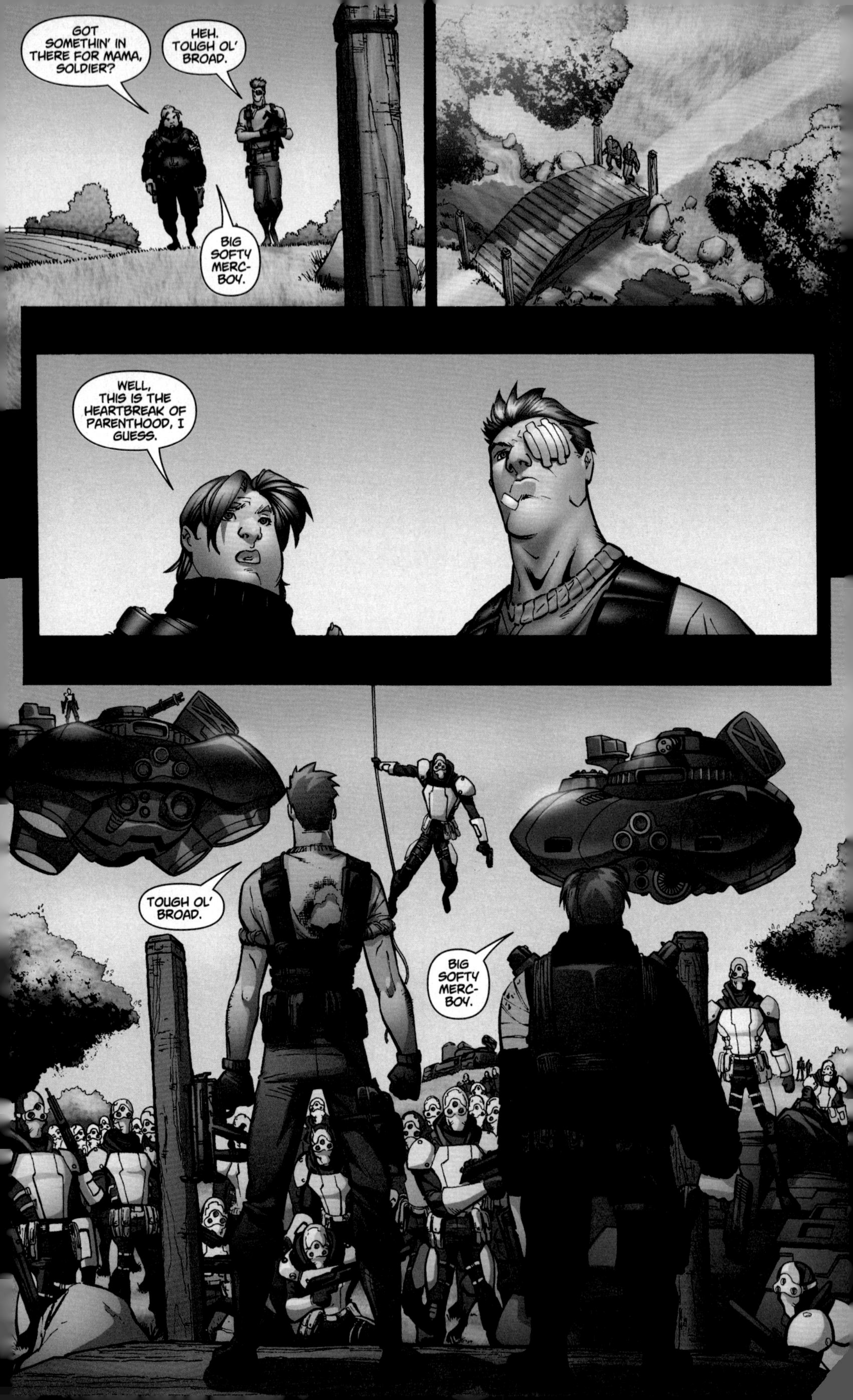
GOT SOMETHIN' IN THERE FOR MAMA, SOLDIER?
HEH. TOUGH OL' BROAD.
BIG SOFTY MERC-BOY.
WELL, THIS IS THE HEARTBREAK OF PARENTHOOD, I GUESS.
TOUGH OL' BROAD.
BIG SOFTY MERC-BOY.

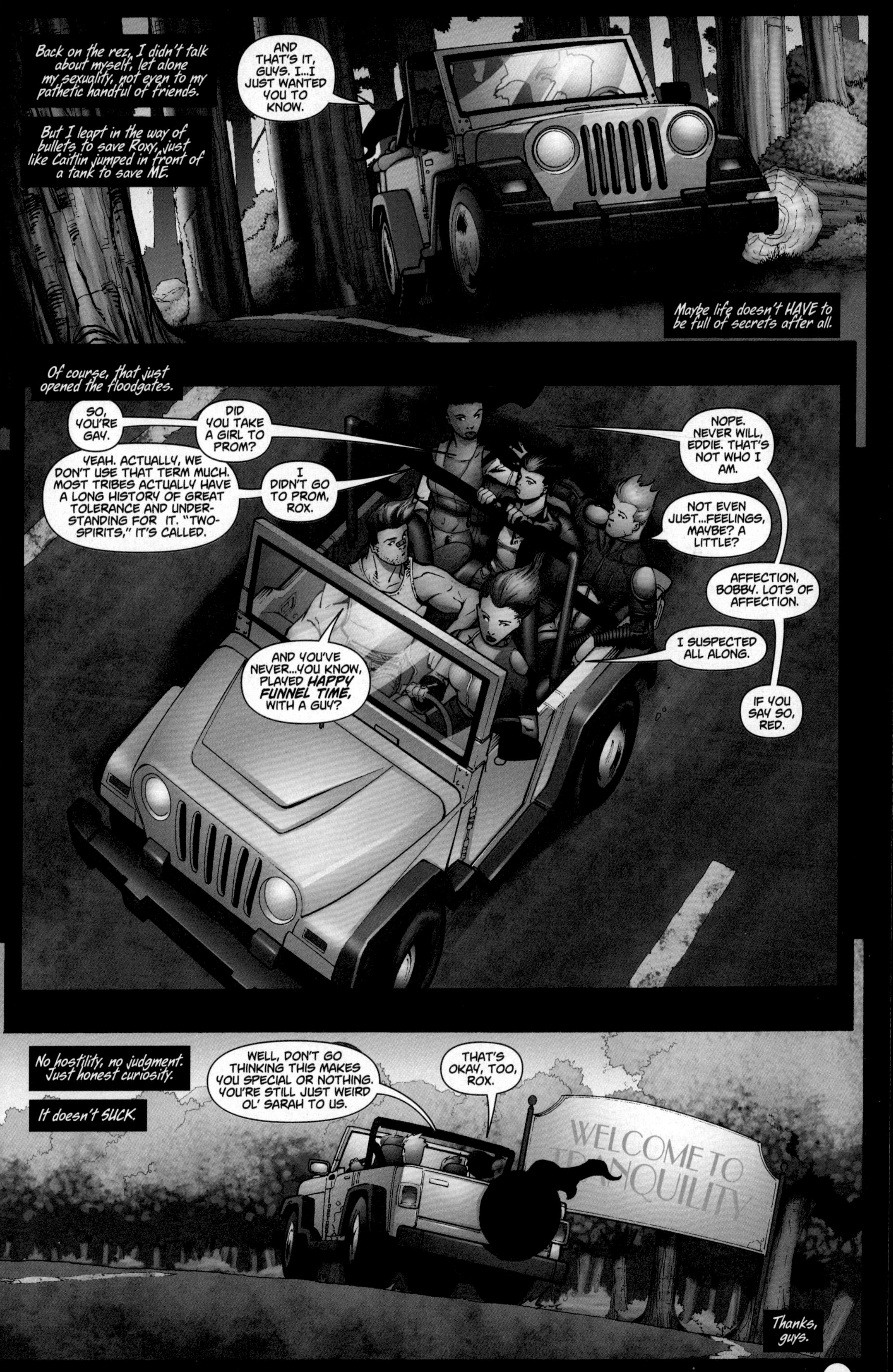
Back on the rez, I didn't talk about myself, let alone my sexuality, not even to my pathetic handful of friends.
AND THAT'S IT, GUYS. I...I JUST WANTED YOU TO KNOW.
But I leapt in the way of bullets to save Roxy, just like Caitlin jumped in front of a tank to save ME.
Maybe life doesn't HAVE to be full of secrets after all.
Of course, that just opened the floodgates.
SO, YOU'RE GAY.
DID YOU TAKE A GIRL TO PROM?
YEAH. ACTUALLY, WE DON'T USE THAT TERM MUCH. MOST TRIBES ACTUALLY HAVE A LONG HISTORY OF GREAT TOLERANCE AND UNDERSTANDING FOR IT. "TWO-SPIRITS," IT'S CALLED.
I DIDN'T GO TO PROM, ROX.
NOPE. NEVER WILL, EDDIE. THAT'S NOT WHO I AM.
NOT EVEN JUST...FEELINGS, MAYBE? A LITTLE?
AFFECTION, BOBBY. LOTS OF AFFECTION.
AND YOU'VE NEVER...YOU KNOW, PLAYED HAPPY FUNNEL TIME, WITH A GUY?
I SUSPECTED ALL ALONG.
IF YOU SAY SO, RED.
No hostility, no judgment. Just honest curiosity.
It doesn't SUCK.
WELL, DON'T GO THINKING THIS MAKES YOU SPECIAL OR NOTHING. YOU'RE STILL JUST WEIRD OL' SARAH TO US.
THAT'S OKAY, TOO, ROX.
WELCOME TO TRANQUILITY
Thanks, guys.

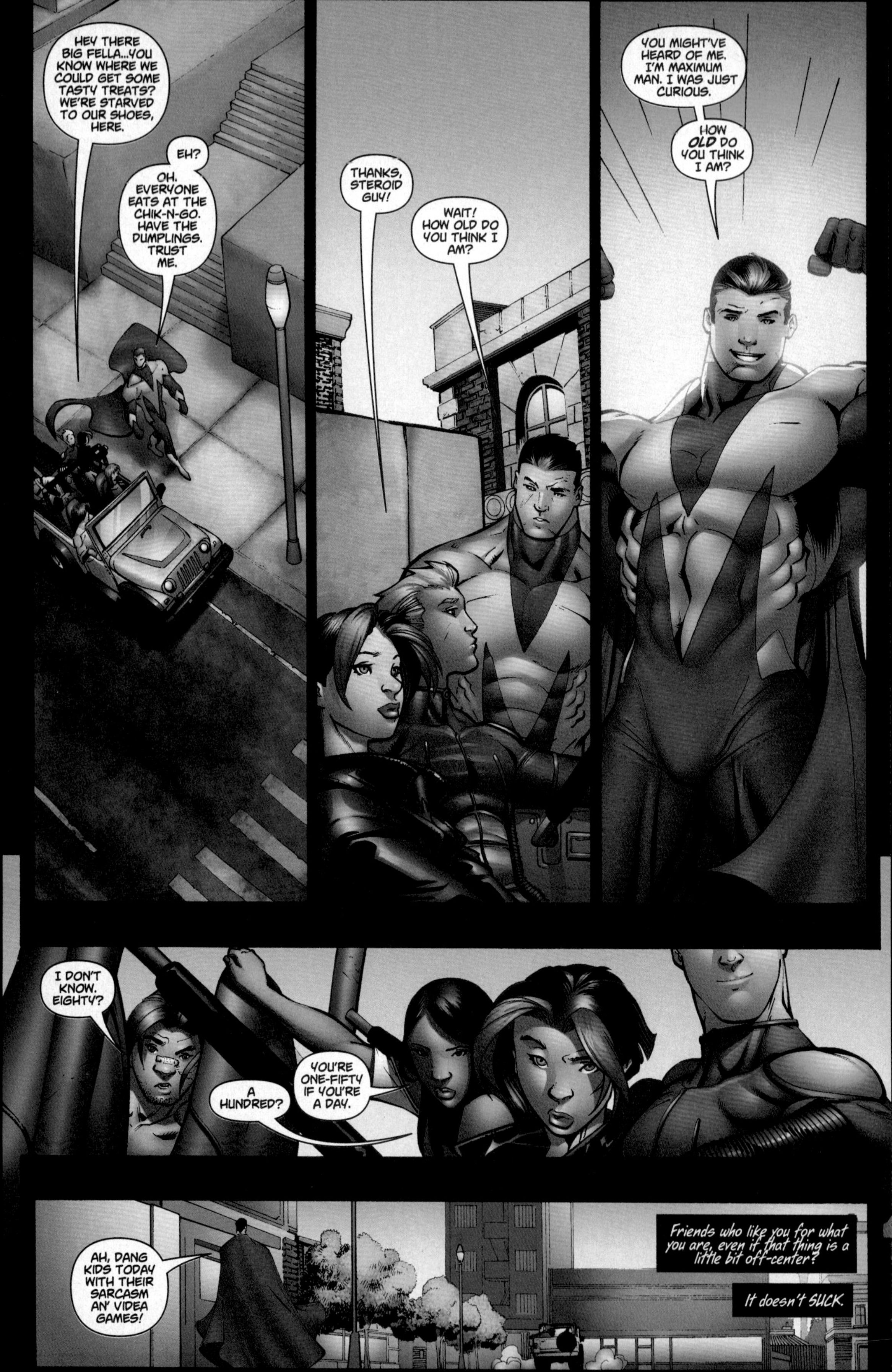

HEY THERE BIG FELLA...YOU KNOW WHERE WE COULD GET SOME TASTY TREATS? WE'RE STARVED TO OUR SHOES, HERE.
EH?
OH. EVERYONE EATS AT THE CHIK-N-GO. HAVE THE DUMPLINGS. TRUST ME.
THANKS, STEROID GUY!
WAIT! HOW OLD DO YOU THINK I AM?
YOU MIGHT'VE HEARD OF ME. I'M MAXIMUM MAN. I WAS JUST CURIOUS.
HOW OLD DO YOU THINK I AM?
I DON'T KNOW. EIGHTY?
A HUNDRED?
YOU'RE ONE-FIFTY IF YOU'RE A DAY.
AH, DANG KIDS TODAY WITH THEIR SARCASM AN' VIDEA GAMES!
Friends who like you for what you are, even if that thing is a little bit off-center?
It doesn't SUCK.

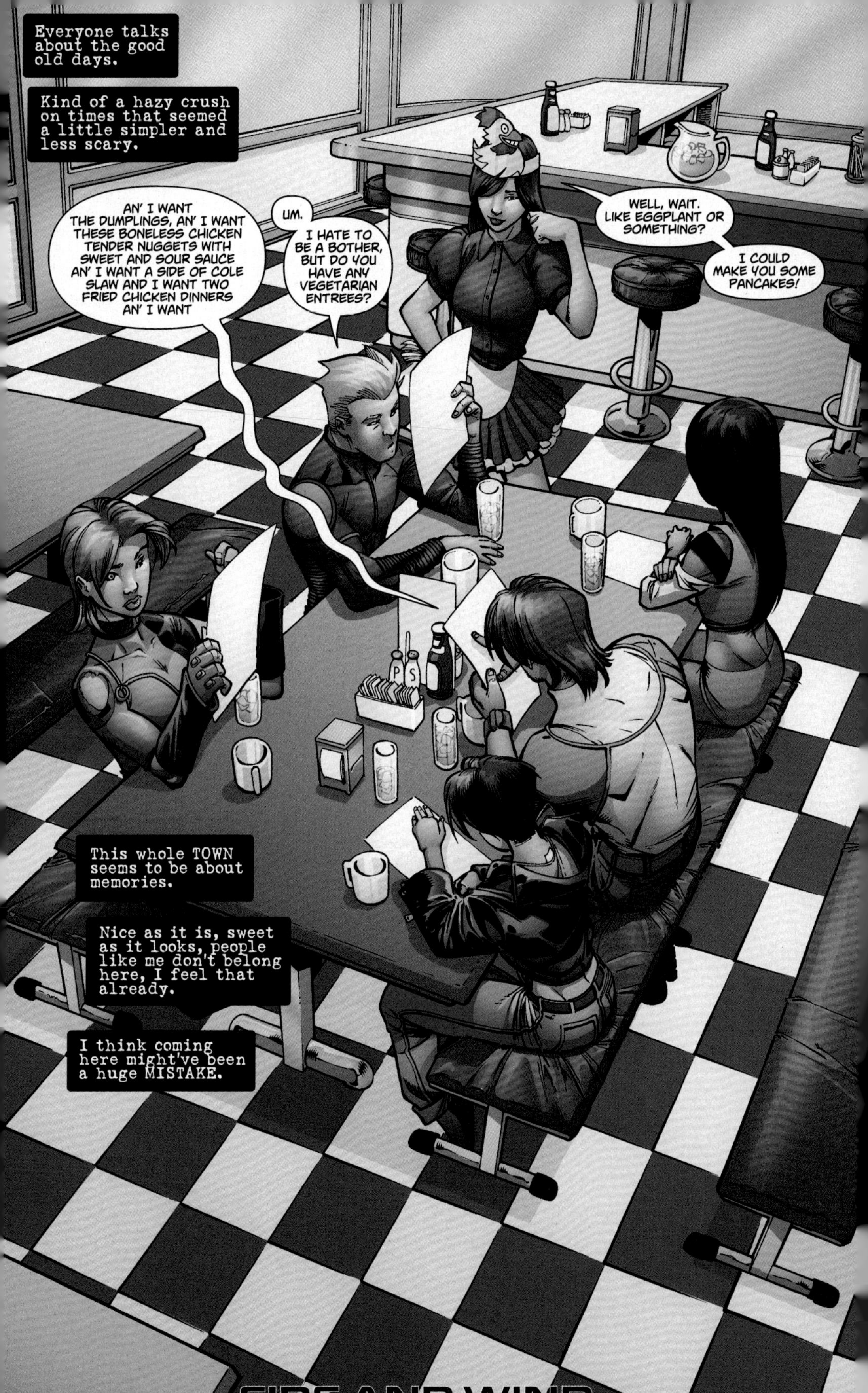

Everyone talks about the good old days.
Kind of a hazy crush on times that seemed a little simpler and less scary.
AN' I WANT THE DUMPLINGS, AN' I WANT THESE BONELESS CHICKEN TENDER NUGGETS WITH SWEET AND SOUR SAUCE AN' I WANT A SIDE OF COLE SLAW AND I WANT TWO FRIED CHICKEN DINNERS AN' I WANT
UM.
I HATE TO BE A BOTHER, BUT DO YOU HAVE ANY VEGETARIAN ENTREES?
WELL, WAIT. LIKE EGGPLANT OR SOMETHING?
I COULD MAKE YOU SOME PANCAKES!
This whole TOWN seems to be about memories.
Nice as it is, sweet as it looks, people like me don't belong here, I feel that already.
I think coming here might've been a huge MISTAKE.

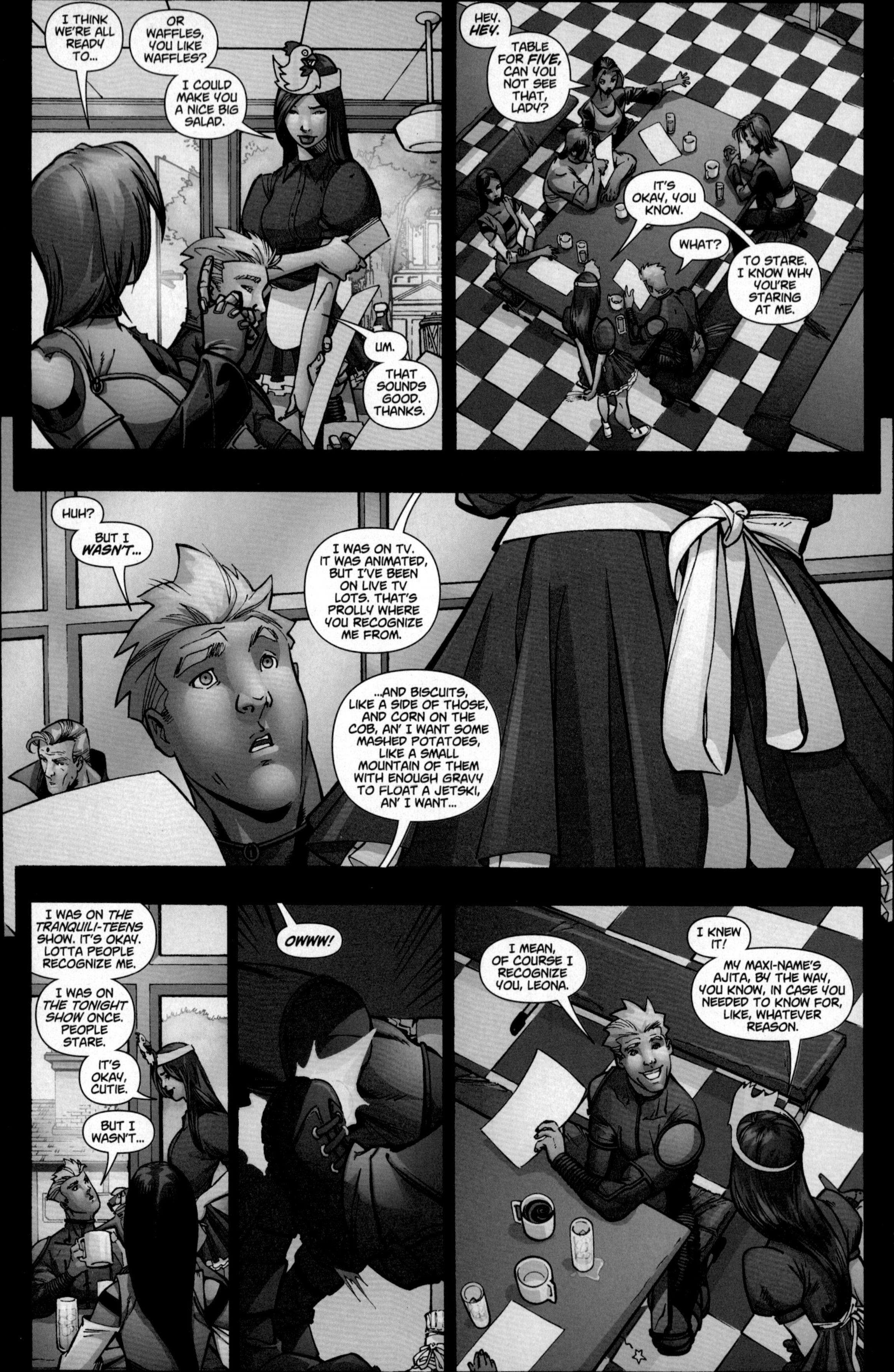

I THINK WE'RE ALL READY TO...
OR WAFFLES, YOU LIKE WAFFLES?
I COULD MAKE YOU A NICE BIG SALAD.
UM.
THAT SOUNDS GOOD. THANKS.
HEY. *HEY.*
TABLE FOR *FIVE*, CAN YOU NOT SEE THAT, LADY?
IT'S OKAY, YOU KNOW.
WHAT?
TO STARE. I KNOW WHY YOU'RE STARING AT ME.
HUH? BUT I *WASN'T*...
I WAS ON TV. IT WAS ANIMATED, BUT I'VE BEEN ON LIVE TV LOTS. THAT'S PROLLY WHERE YOU RECOGNIZE ME FROM.
...AND BISCUITS, LIKE A SIDE OF THOSE, AND CORN ON THE COB, AN' I WANT SOME MASHED POTATOES, LIKE A SMALL MOUNTAIN OF THEM WITH ENOUGH GRAVY TO FLOAT A JETSKI, AN' I WANT...
I WAS ON *THE TRANQUILI-TEENS* SHOW. IT'S OKAY. LOTTA PEOPLE RECOGNIZE ME.
I WAS ON *THE TONIGHT SHOW* ONCE. PEOPLE STARE.
IT'S OKAY, CUTIE.
BUT I WASN'T...
OWWW!
I MEAN, OF COURSE I RECOGNIZE YOU, LEONA.
I KNEW IT!
MY MAXI-NAME'S AJITA, BY THE WAY, YOU KNOW, IN CASE YOU NEEDED TO KNOW FOR, LIKE, WHATEVER REASON.

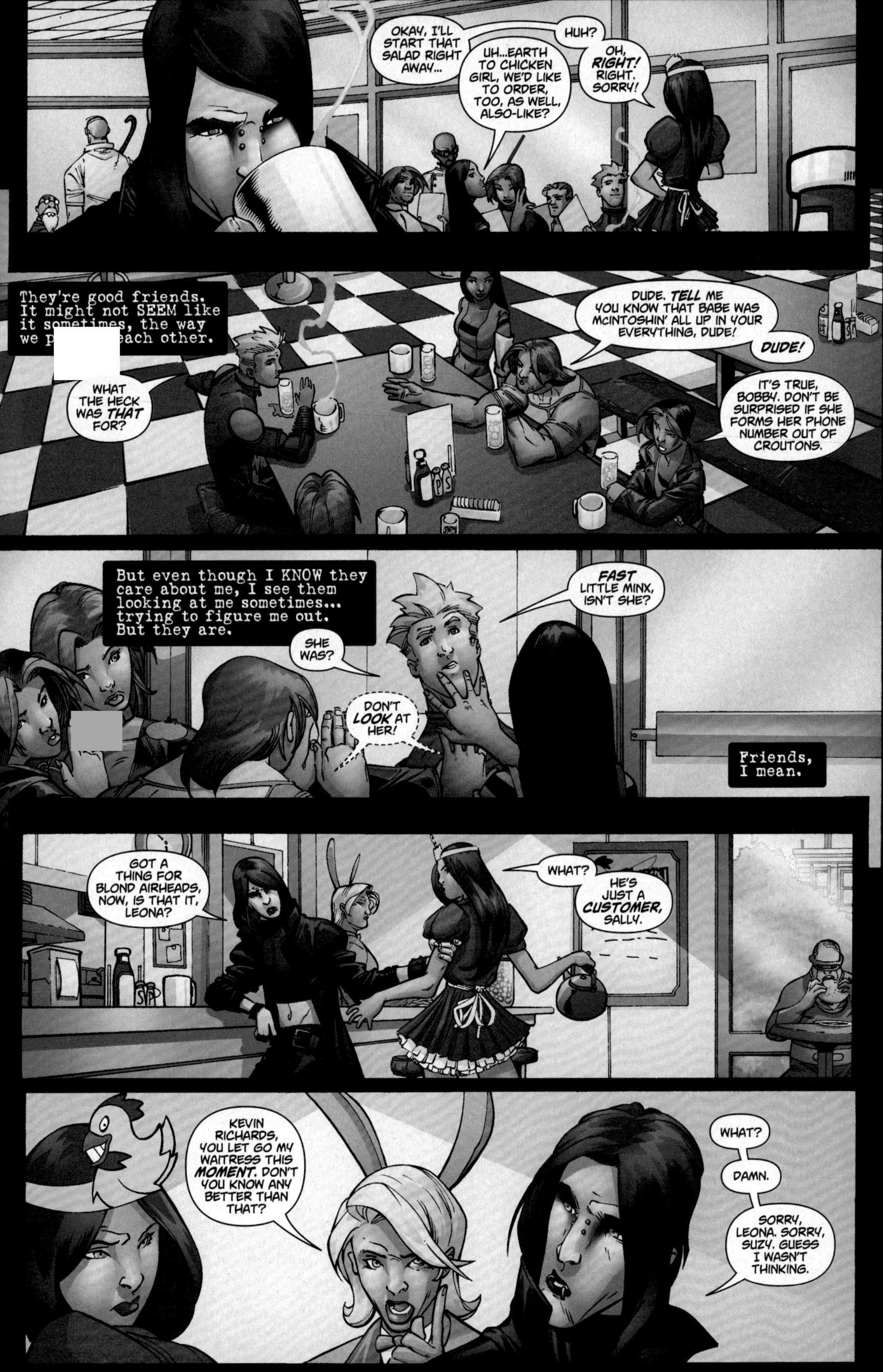
OKAY, I'LL START THAT SALAD RIGHT AWAY...
HUH?
UH...EARTH TO CHICKEN GIRL, WE'D LIKE TO ORDER, TOO, AS WELL, ALSO-LIKE?
OH, RIGHT! RIGHT. SORRY!
They're good friends. It might not SEEM like it sometimes, the way we p each other.
WHAT THE HECK WAS THAT FOR?
DUDE. TELL ME YOU KNOW THAT BABE WAS McINTOSHIN' ALL UP IN YOUR EVERYTHING, DUDE!
DUDE!
IT'S TRUE, BOBBY. DON'T BE SURPRISED IF SHE FORMS HER PHONE NUMBER OUT OF CROUTONS.
But even though I KNOW they care about me, I see them looking at me sometimes... trying to figure me out. But they are.
FAST LITTLE MINX, ISN'T SHE?
SHE WAS?
DON'T LOOK AT HER!
Friends, I mean.
GOT A THING FOR BLOND AIRHEADS, NOW, IS THAT IT, LEONA?
WHAT?
HE'S JUST A CUSTOMER, SALLY.
KEVIN RICHARDS, YOU LET GO MY WAITRESS THIS MOMENT. DON'T YOU KNOW ANY BETTER THAN THAT?
WHAT?
DAMN.
SORRY, LEONA. SORRY, SUZY. GUESS I WASN'T THINKING.

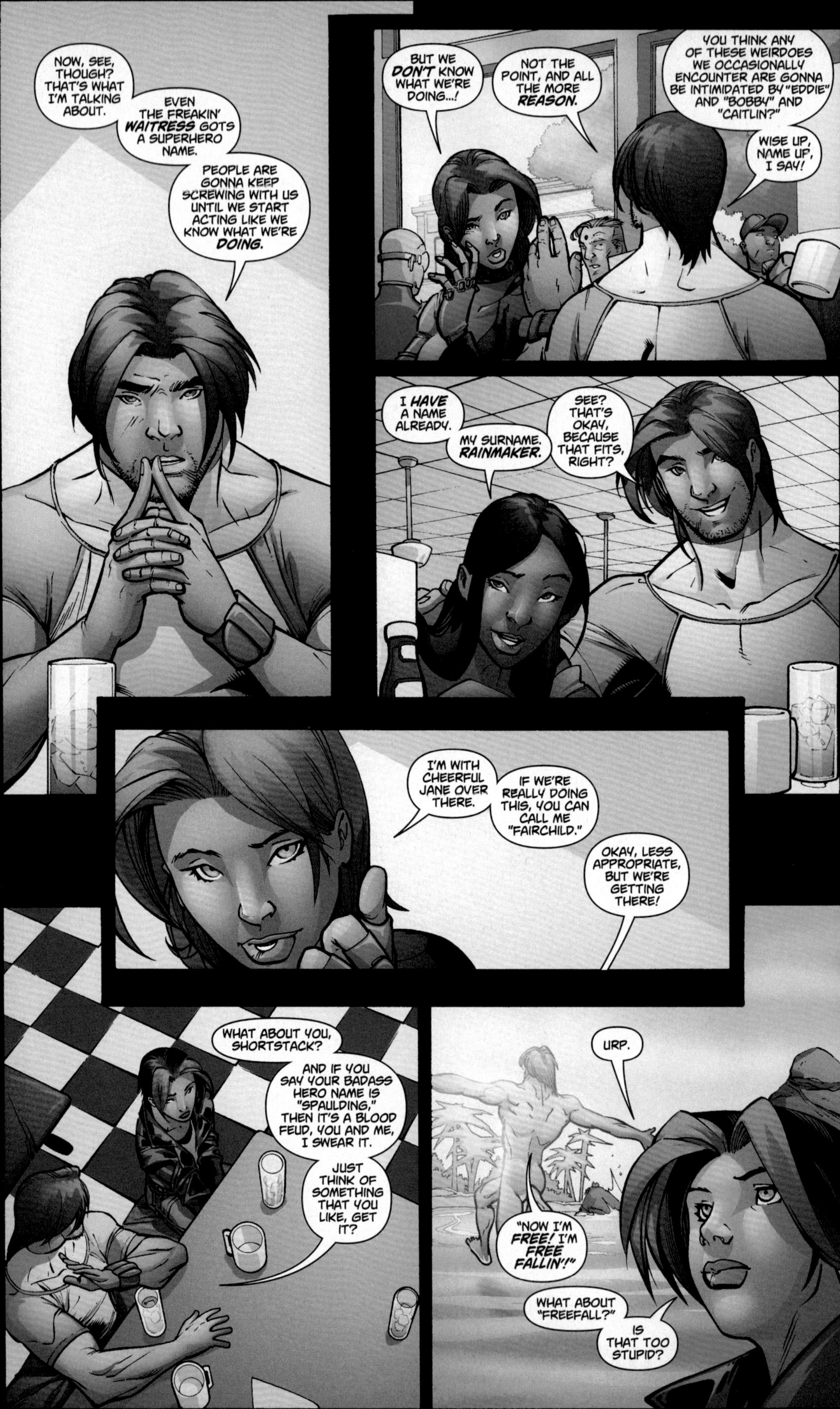
NOW, SEE, THOUGH? THAT'S WHAT I'M TALKING ABOUT.
EVEN THE FREAKIN' WAITRESS GOTS A SUPERHERO NAME.
PEOPLE ARE GONNA KEEP SCREWING WITH US UNTIL WE START ACTING LIKE WE KNOW WHAT WE'RE DOING.
BUT WE DON'T KNOW WHAT WE'RE DOING...!
NOT THE POINT, AND ALL THE MORE REASON.
YOU THINK ANY OF THESE WEIRDOES WE OCCASIONALLY ENCOUNTER ARE GONNA BE INTIMIDATED BY "EDDIE" AND "BOBBY" AND "CAITLIN?"
WISE UP, NAME UP, I SAY!
I HAVE A NAME ALREADY.
MY SURNAME. RAINMAKER.
SEE? THAT'S OKAY, BECAUSE THAT FITS, RIGHT?
I'M WITH CHEERFUL JANE OVER THERE.
IF WE'RE REALLY DOING THIS, YOU CAN CALL ME "FAIRCHILD."
OKAY, LESS APPROPRIATE, BUT WE'RE GETTING THERE!
WHAT ABOUT YOU, SHORTSTACK?
AND IF YOU SAY YOUR BADASS HERO NAME IS "SPAULDING," THEN IT'S A BLOOD FEUD, YOU AND ME, I SWEAR IT.
JUST THINK OF SOMETHING THAT YOU LIKE, GET IT?
URP.
"NOW I'M FREE! I'M FREE FALLIN'!"
WHAT ABOUT "FREEFALL?"
IS THAT TOO STUPID?

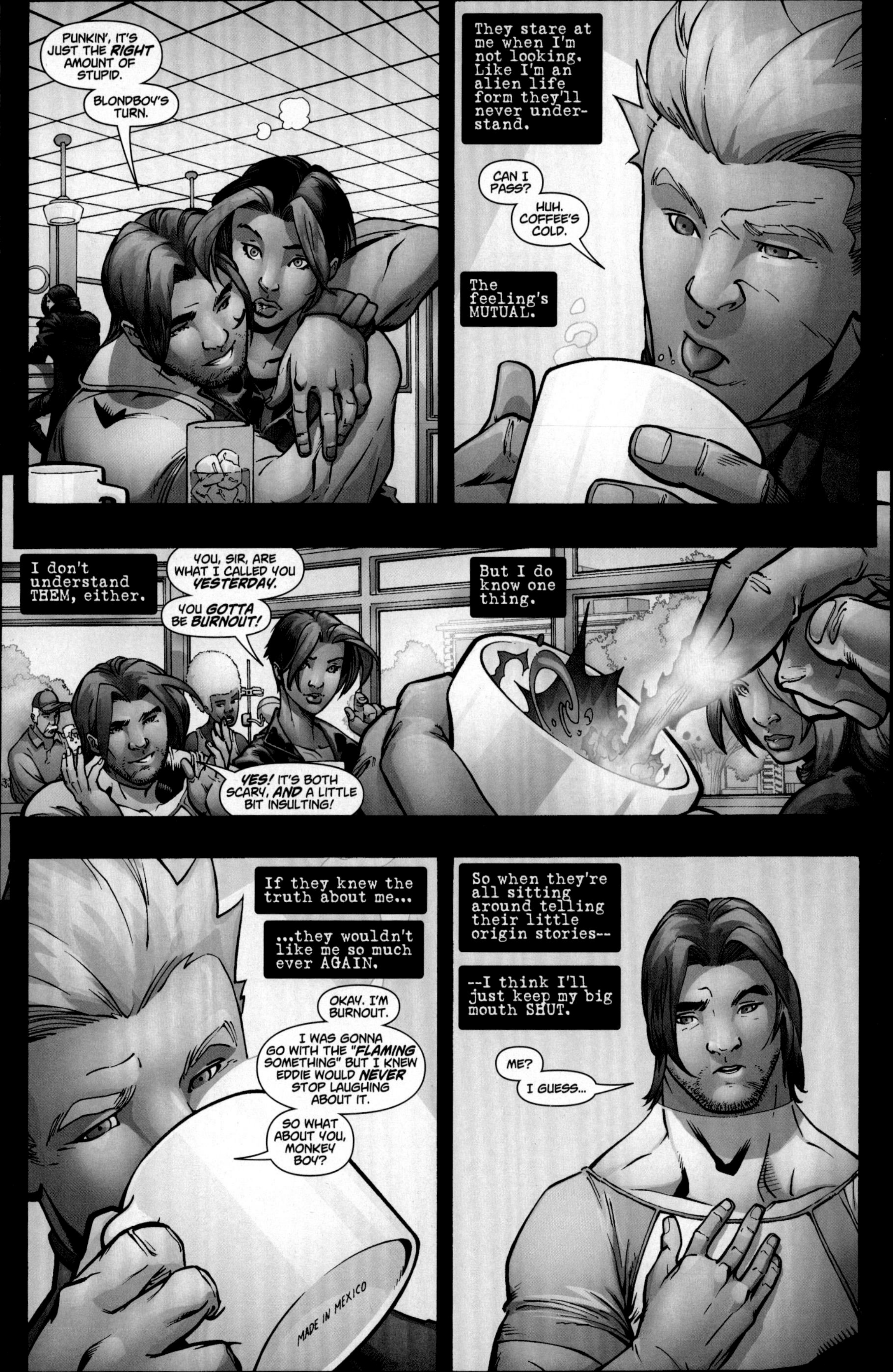
PUNKIN', IT'S JUST THE RIGHT AMOUNT OF STUPID.
BLONDBOY'S TURN.
They stare at me when I'm not looking. Like I'm an alien life form they'll never under-stand.
CAN I PASS?
HUH. COFFEE'S COLD.
The feeling's MUTUAL.
I don't understand THEM, either.
YOU, SIR, ARE WHAT I CALLED YOU YESTERDAY.
YOU GOTTA BE BURNOUT!
YES! IT'S BOTH SCARY, AND A LITTLE BIT INSULTING!
But I do know one thing.
If they knew the truth about me...
...they wouldn't like me so much ever AGAIN.
OKAY. I'M BURNOUT.
I WAS GONNA GO WITH THE "FLAMING SOMETHING" BUT I KNEW EDDIE WOULD NEVER STOP LAUGHING ABOUT IT.
SO WHAT ABOUT YOU, MONKEY BOY?
MADE IN MEXICO
So when they're all sitting around telling their little origin stories--
--I think I'll just keep my big mouth SHUT.
ME?
I GUESS...

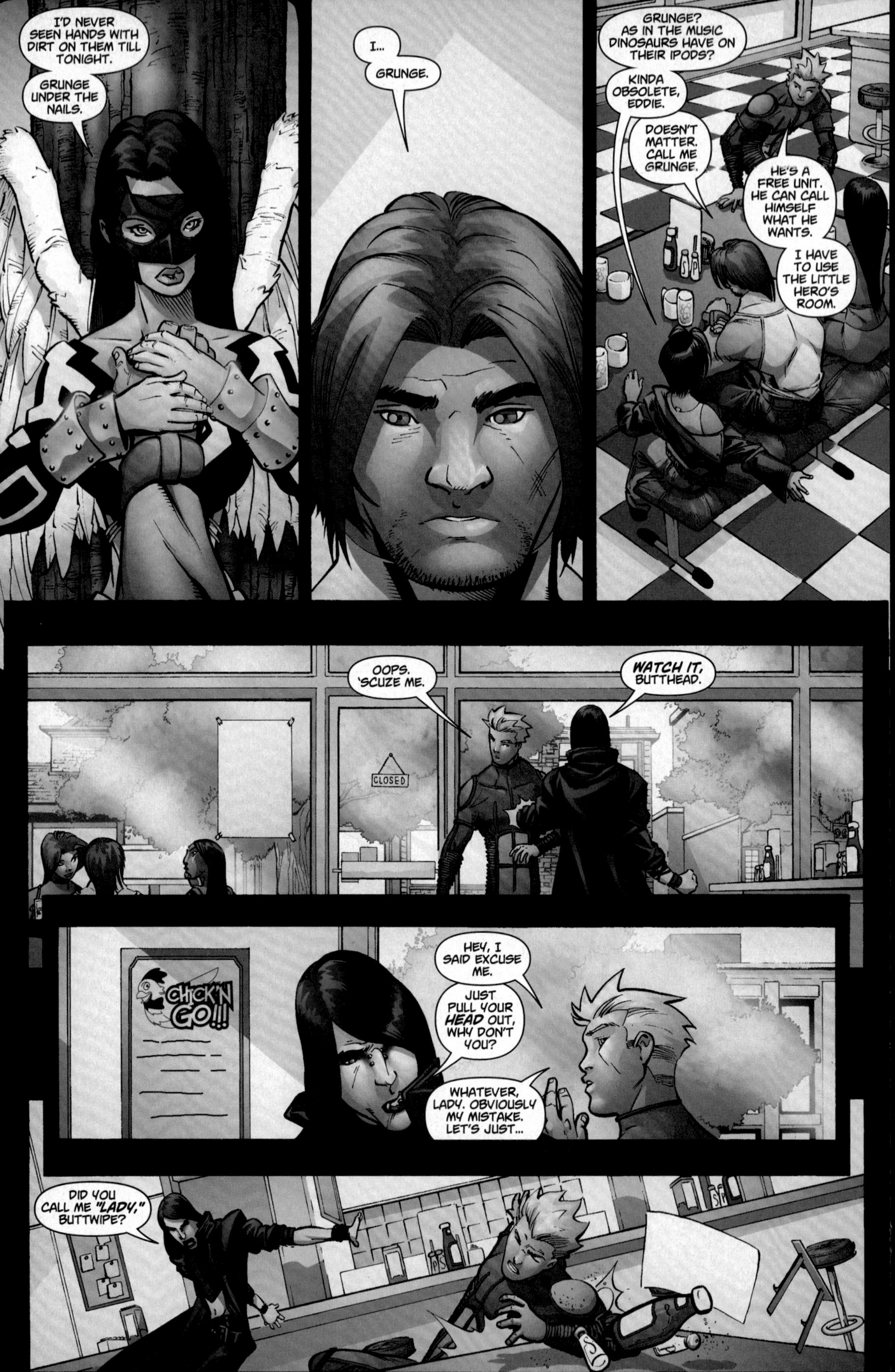
I'D NEVER SEEN HANDS WITH DIRT ON THEM TILL TONIGHT.
GRUNGE UNDER THE NAILS.
I...
GRUNGE.
GRUNGE? AS IN THE MUSIC DINOSAURS HAVE ON THEIR IPODS?
KINDA OBSOLETE, EDDIE.
DOESN'T MATTER. CALL ME GRUNGE.
HE'S A FREE UNIT. HE CAN CALL HIMSELF WHAT HE WANTS.
I HAVE TO USE THE LITTLE HERO'S ROOM.
OOPS. 'SCUZE ME.
WATCH IT, BUTTHEAD.
CLOSED
CHICK'N GO!!!
HEY, I SAID EXCUSE ME.
JUST PULL YOUR HEAD OUT, WHY DON'T YOU?
WHATEVER, LADY. OBVIOUSLY MY MISTAKE. LET'S JUST...
DID YOU CALL ME "LADY," BUTTWIPE?

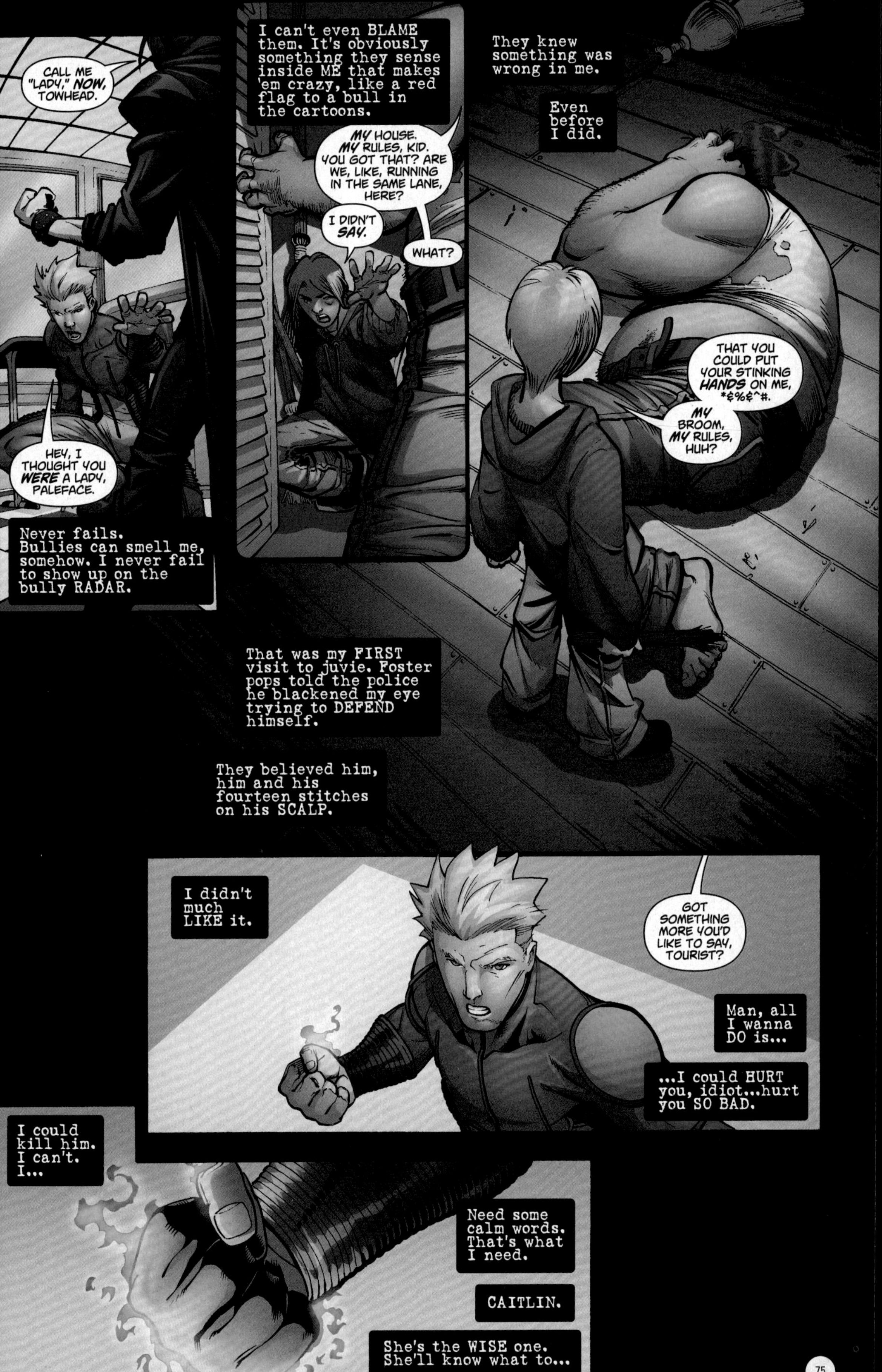

CALL ME "LADY," NOW, TOWHEAD.
HEY, I THOUGHT YOU WERE A LADY, PALEFACE.
Never fails. Bullies can smell me, somehow. I never fail to show up on the bully RADAR.
I can't even BLAME them. It's obviously something they sense inside ME that makes 'em crazy, like a red flag to a bull in the cartoons.
MY HOUSE. MY RULES, KID. YOU GOT THAT? ARE WE, LIKE, RUNNING IN THE SAME LANE, HERE?
I DIDN'T SAY.
WHAT?
They knew something was wrong in me.
Even before I did.
THAT YOU COULD PUT YOUR STINKING HANDS ON ME, *¢%¢^#.
MY BROOM, MY RULES, HUH?
That was my FIRST visit to juvie. Foster pops told the police he blackened my eye trying to DEFEND himself.
They believed him, him and his fourteen stitches on his SCALP.
I didn't much LIKE it.
GOT SOMETHING MORE YOU'D LIKE TO SAY, TOURIST?
Man, all I wanna DO is...
...I could HURT you, idiot...hurt you SO BAD.
I could kill him. I can't. I...
Need some calm words. That's what I need.
CAITLIN.
She's the WISE one. She'll know what to...

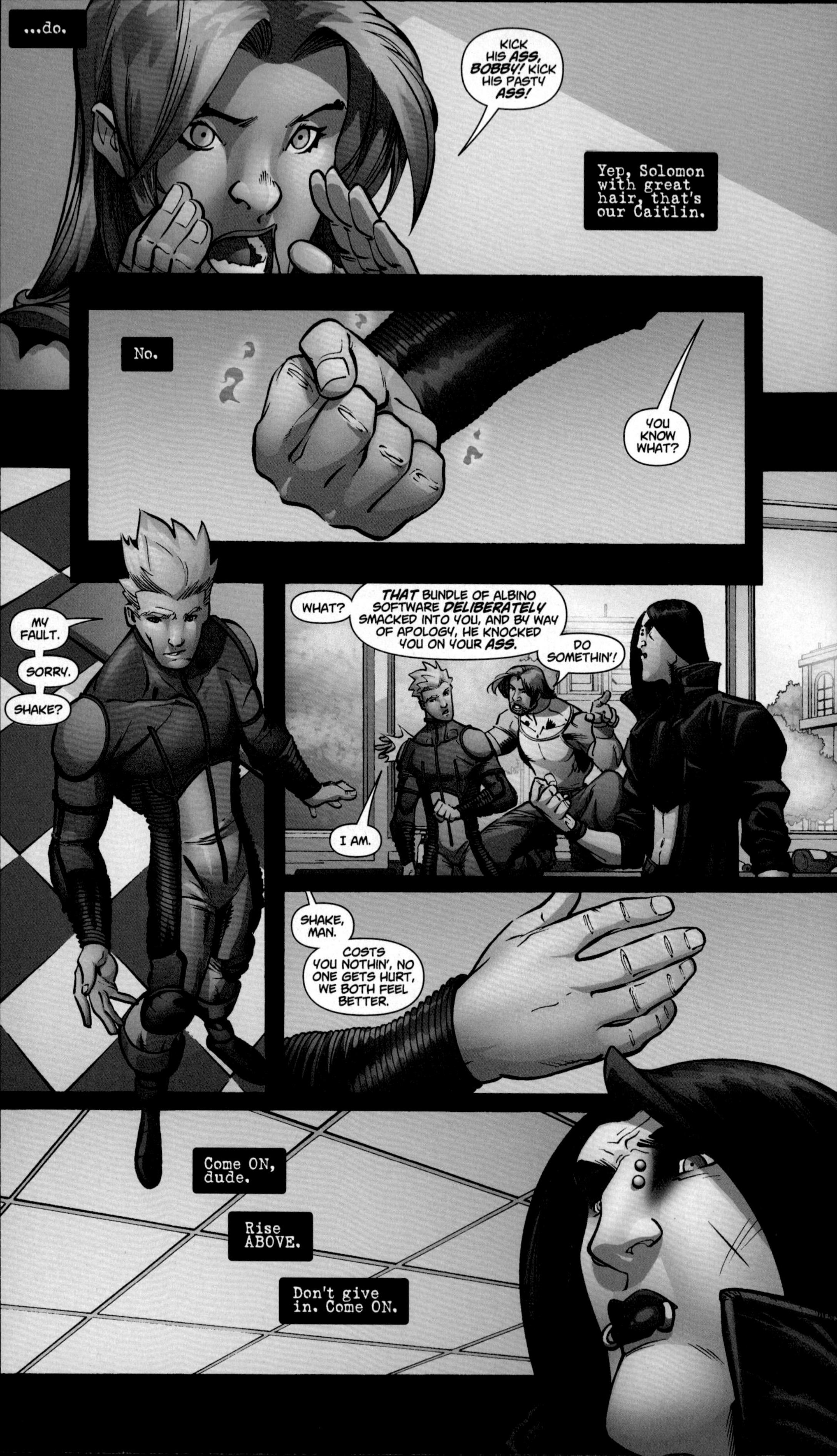
...do.
KICK HIS ASS, BOBBY! KICK HIS PASTY ASS!
Yep, Solomon with great hair, that's our Caitlin.
No.
YOU KNOW WHAT?
MY FAULT.
SORRY.
SHAKE?
WHAT?
THAT BUNDLE OF ALBINO SOFTWARE DELIBERATELY SMACKED INTO YOU, AND BY WAY OF APOLOGY, HE KNOCKED YOU ON YOUR ASS.
DO SOMETHIN'!
I AM.
SHAKE, MAN.
COSTS YOU NOTHIN', NO ONE GETS HURT, WE BOTH FEEL BETTER.
Come ON, dude.
Rise ABOVE.
Don't give in. Come ON.

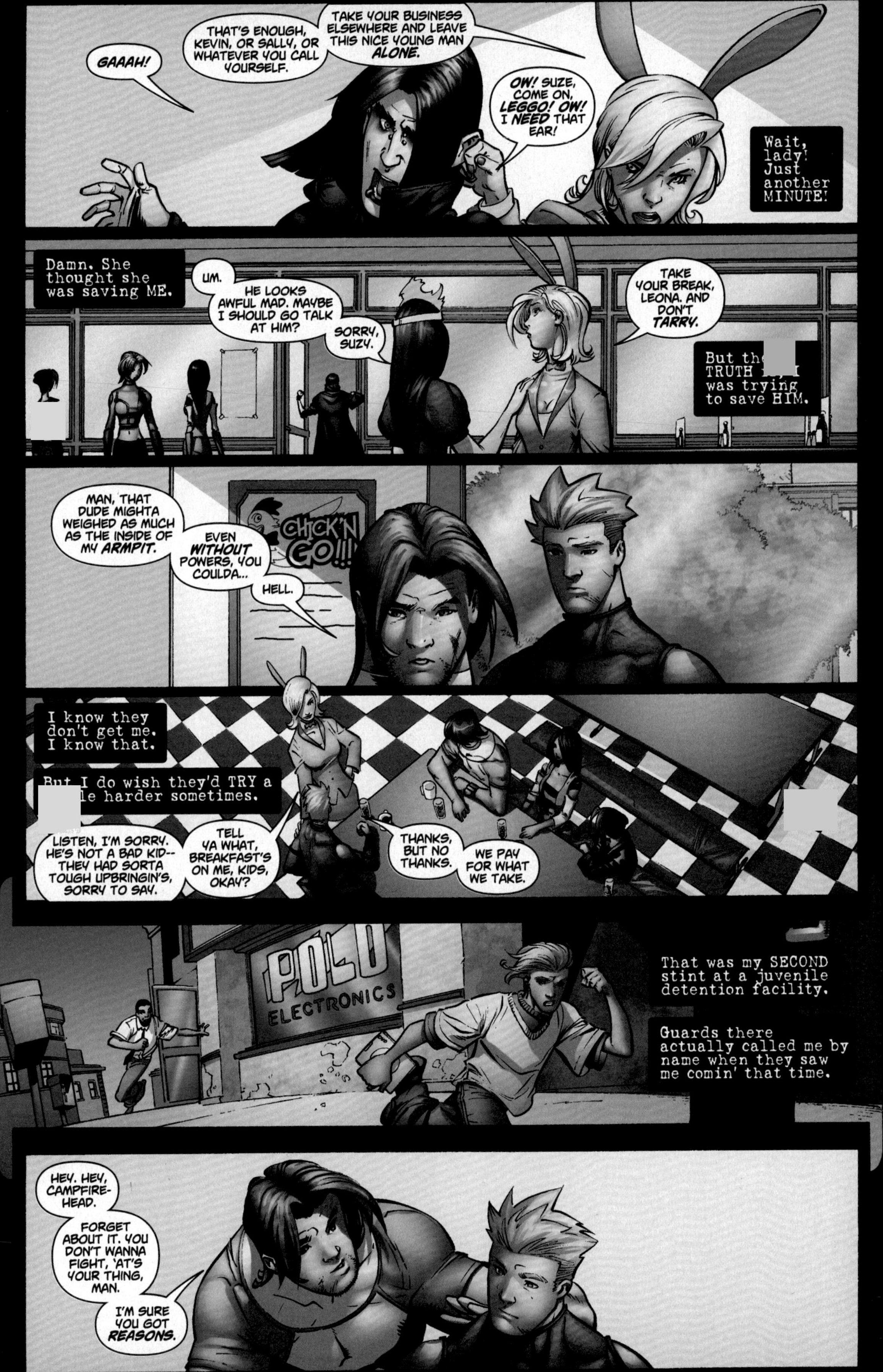
GAAAH!
THAT'S ENOUGH, KEVIN, OR SALLY, OR WHATEVER YOU CALL YOURSELF.
TAKE YOUR BUSINESS ELSEWHERE AND LEAVE THIS NICE YOUNG MAN ALONE.
OW! SUZE, COME ON, LEGGO! OW! I NEED THAT EAR!
Wait, lady! Just another MINUTE!
Damn. She thought she was saving ME.
UM.
HE LOOKS AWFUL MAD. MAYBE I SHOULD GO TALK AT HIM?
SORRY, SUZY.
TAKE YOUR BREAK, LEONA. AND DON'T TARRY.
But the
TRUTH
I was trying to save HIM.
MAN, THAT DUDE MIGHTA WEIGHED AS MUCH AS THE INSIDE OF MY ARMPIT.
EVEN WITHOUT POWERS, YOU COULDA...
HELL.
CHICK'N GO!!!
I know they don't get me. I know that.
But I do wish they'd TRY a
le harder sometimes.
LISTEN, I'M SORRY. HE'S NOT A BAD KID-- THEY HAD SORTA TOUGH UPBRINGIN'S, SORRY TO SAY.
TELL YA WHAT, BREAKFAST'S ON ME, KIDS, OKAY?
THANKS, BUT NO THANKS.
WE PAY FOR WHAT WE TAKE.
POLO ELECTRONICS
That was my SECOND stint at a juvenile detention facility.
Guards there actually called me by name when they saw me comin' that time.
HEY. HEY, CAMPFIRE-HEAD.
FORGET ABOUT IT. YOU DON'T WANNA FIGHT, 'AT'S YOUR THING, MAN.
I'M SURE YOU GOT REASONS.

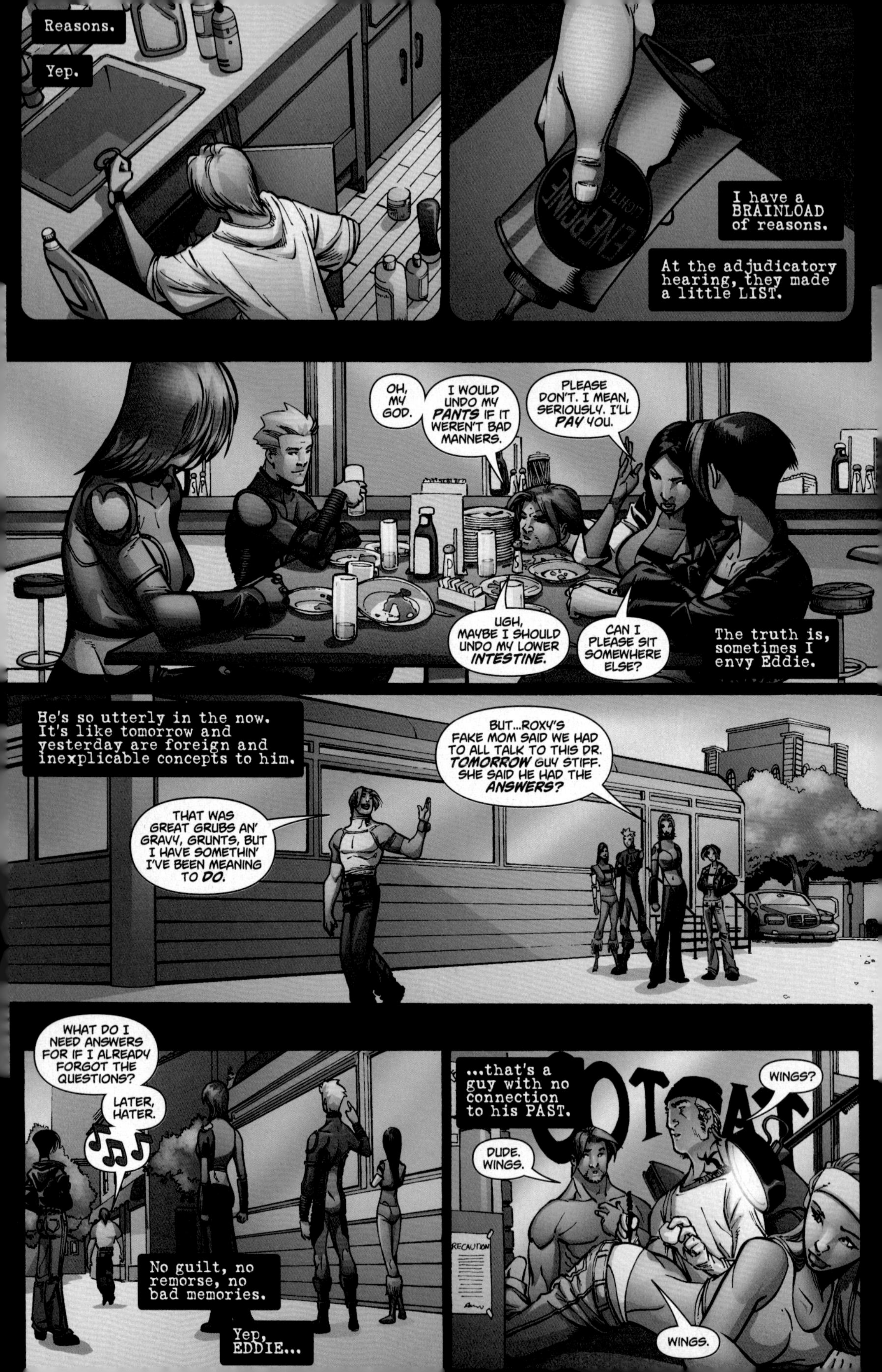

Reasons.
Yep.
I have a BRAINLOAD of reasons.
At the adjudicatory hearing, they made a little LIST.
OH, MY GOD.
I WOULD UNDO MY PANTS IF IT WEREN'T BAD MANNERS.
PLEASE DON'T. I MEAN, SERIOUSLY. I'LL PAY YOU.
UGH, MAYBE I SHOULD UNDO MY LOWER INTESTINE.
CAN I PLEASE SIT SOMEWHERE ELSE?
The truth is, sometimes I envy Eddie.
He's so utterly in the now. It's like tomorrow and yesterday are foreign and inexplicable concepts to him.
BUT...ROXY'S FAKE MOM SAID WE HAD TO ALL TALK TO THIS DR. TOMORROW GUY STIFF. SHE SAID HE HAD THE ANSWERS?
THAT WAS GREAT GRUBS AN' GRAVY, GRUNTS, BUT I HAVE SOMETHIN' I'VE BEEN MEANING TO DO.
WHAT DO I NEED ANSWERS FOR IF I ALREADY FORGOT THE QUESTIONS?
LATER, HATER.
No guilt, no remorse, no bad memories.
Yep, EDDIE...
...that's a guy with no connection to his PAST.
WINGS?
DUDE. WINGS.
WINGS.

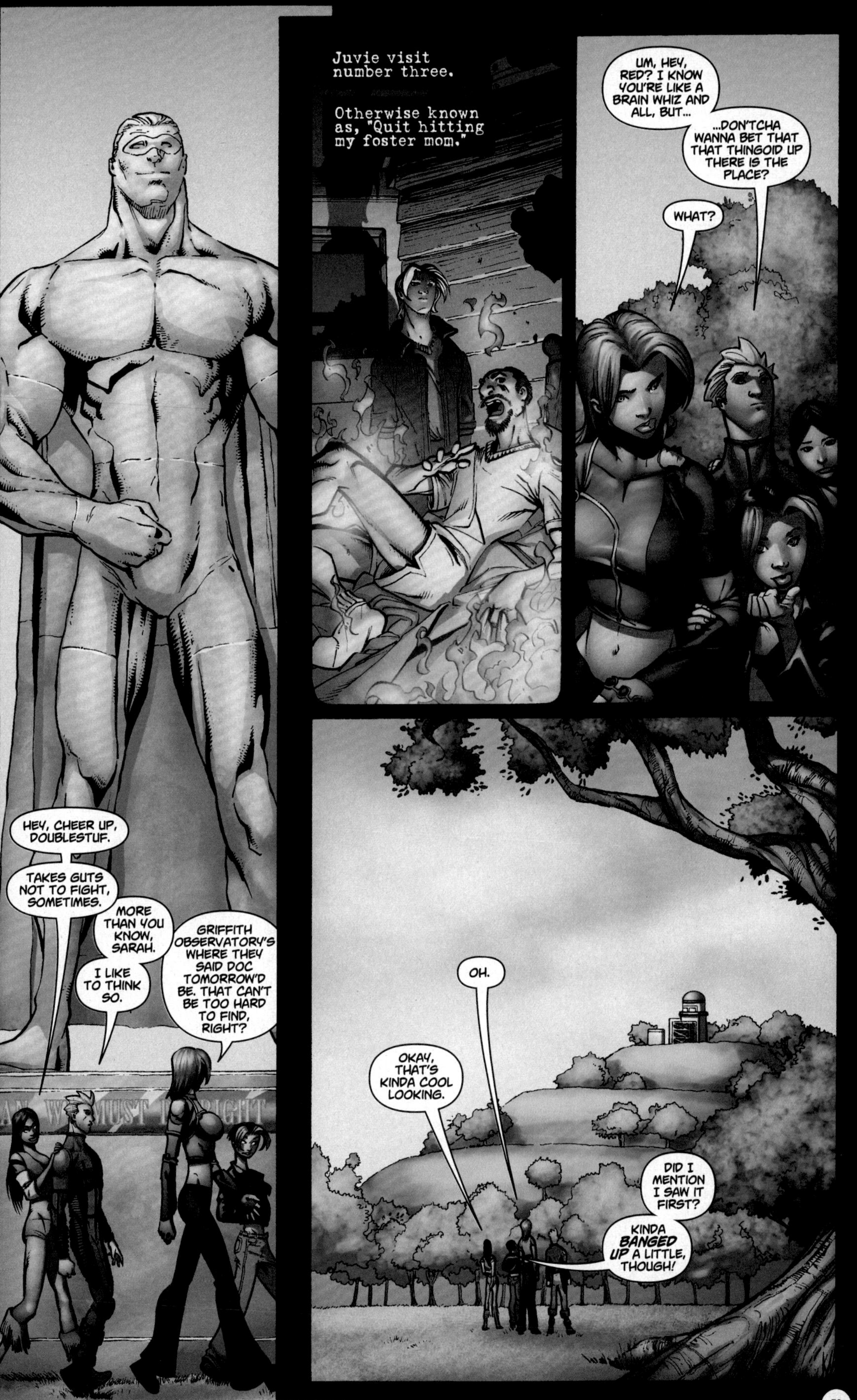
Juvie visit number three.
Otherwise known as, "Quit hitting my foster mom."
UM, HEY, RED? I KNOW YOU'RE LIKE A BRAIN WHIZ AND ALL, BUT...
...DON'TCHA WANNA BET THAT THAT THINGOID UP THERE IS THE PLACE?
WHAT?
HEY, CHEER UP, DOUBLESTUF.
TAKES GUTS NOT TO FIGHT, SOMETIMES.
MORE THAN YOU KNOW, SARAH.
I LIKE TO THINK SO.
GRIFFITH OBSERVATORY'S WHERE THEY SAID DOC TOMORROW'D BE. THAT CAN'T BE TOO HARD TO FIND, RIGHT?
OH.
OKAY, THAT'S KINDA COOL LOOKING.
DID I MENTION I SAW IT FIRST?
KINDA **BANGED UP** A LITTLE, THOUGH!

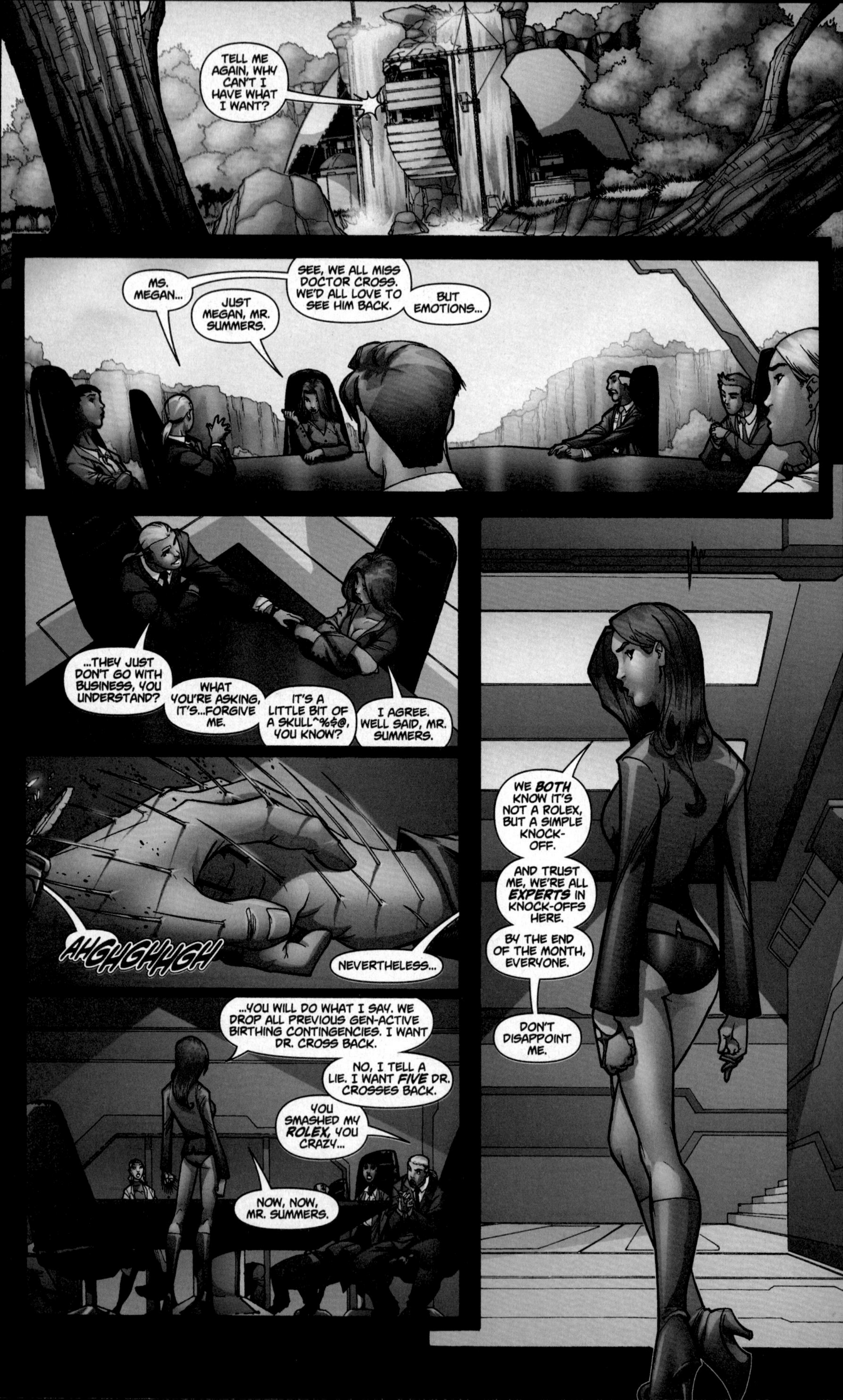
TELL ME AGAIN, WHY CAN'T I HAVE WHAT I WANT?
MS. MEGAN...
JUST MEGAN, MR. SUMMERS.
SEE, WE ALL MISS DOCTOR CROSS. WE'D ALL LOVE TO SEE HIM BACK.
BUT EMOTIONS...
...THEY JUST DON'T GO WITH BUSINESS, YOU UNDERSTAND?
WHAT YOU'RE ASKING, IT'S...FORGIVE ME.
IT'S A LITTLE BIT OF A SKULL^%$@, YOU KNOW?
I AGREE. WELL SAID, MR. SUMMERS.
AHGHGHHGH
NEVERTHELESS...
...YOU WILL DO WHAT I SAY. WE DROP ALL PREVIOUS GEN-ACTIVE BIRTHING CONTINGENCIES. I WANT DR. CROSS BACK.
NO, I TELL A LIE. I WANT FIVE DR. CROSSES BACK.
YOU SMASHED MY ROLEX, YOU CRAZY...
NOW, NOW, MR. SUMMERS.
WE BOTH KNOW IT'S NOT A ROLEX, BUT A SIMPLE KNOCK-OFF.
AND TRUST ME, WE'RE ALL EXPERTS IN KNOCK-OFFS HERE.
BY THE END OF THE MONTH, EVERYONE.
DON'T DISAPPOINT ME.

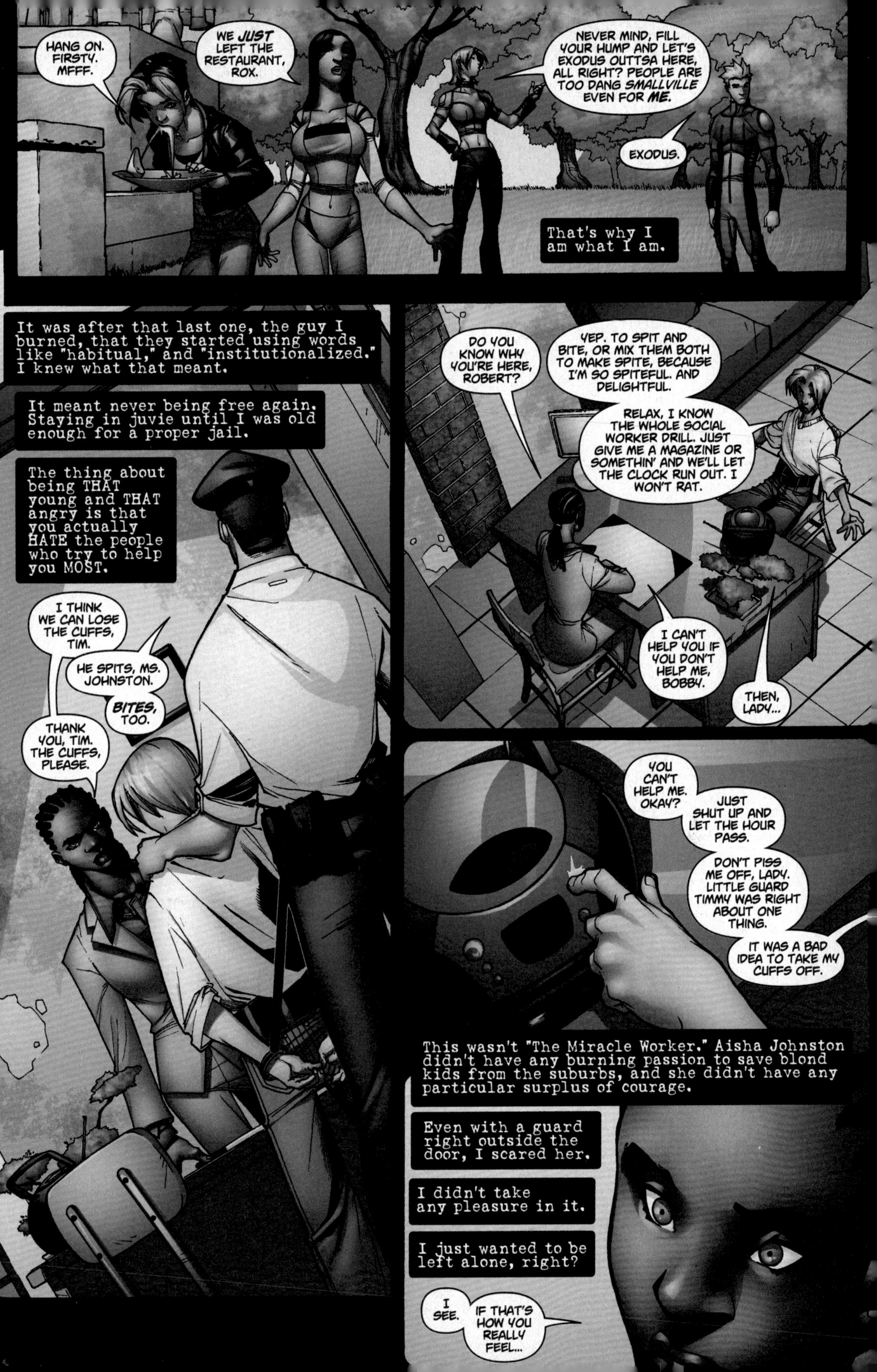
HANG ON. FIRSTY. MFFF.
WE JUST LEFT THE RESTAURANT, ROX.
NEVER MIND, FILL YOUR HUMP AND LET'S EXODUS OUTTSA HERE, ALL RIGHT? PEOPLE ARE TOO DANG SMALLVILLE EVEN FOR ME.
EXODUS.
That's why I am what I am.
It was after that last one, the guy I burned, that they started using words like "habitual," and "institutionalized." I knew what that meant.
It meant never being free again. Staying in juvie until I was old enough for a proper jail.
The thing about being THAT young and THAT angry is that you actually HATE the people who try to help you MOST.
I THINK WE CAN LOSE THE CUFFS, TIM.
HE SPITS, MS. JOHNSTON.
BITES, TOO.
THANK YOU, TIM. THE CUFFS, PLEASE.
DO YOU KNOW WHY YOU'RE HERE, ROBERT?
YEP. TO SPIT AND BITE, OR MIX THEM BOTH TO MAKE SPITE, BECAUSE I'M SO SPITEFUL. AND DELIGHTFUL.
RELAX, I KNOW THE WHOLE SOCIAL WORKER DRILL. JUST GIVE ME A MAGAZINE OR SOMETHIN' AND WE'LL LET THE CLOCK RUN OUT. I WON'T RAT.
I CAN'T HELP YOU IF YOU DON'T HELP ME, BOBBY.
THEN, LADY...
YOU CAN'T HELP ME. OKAY?
JUST SHUT UP AND LET THE HOUR PASS.
DON'T PISS ME OFF, LADY. LITTLE GUARD TIMMY WAS RIGHT ABOUT ONE THING.
IT WAS A BAD IDEA TO TAKE MY CUFFS OFF.
This wasn't "The Miracle Worker." Aisha Johnston didn't have any burning passion to save blond kids from the suburbs, and she didn't have any particular surplus of courage.
Even with a guard right outside the door, I scared her.
I didn't take any pleasure in it.
I just wanted to be left alone, right?
I SEE.
IF THAT'S HOW YOU REALLY FEEL...

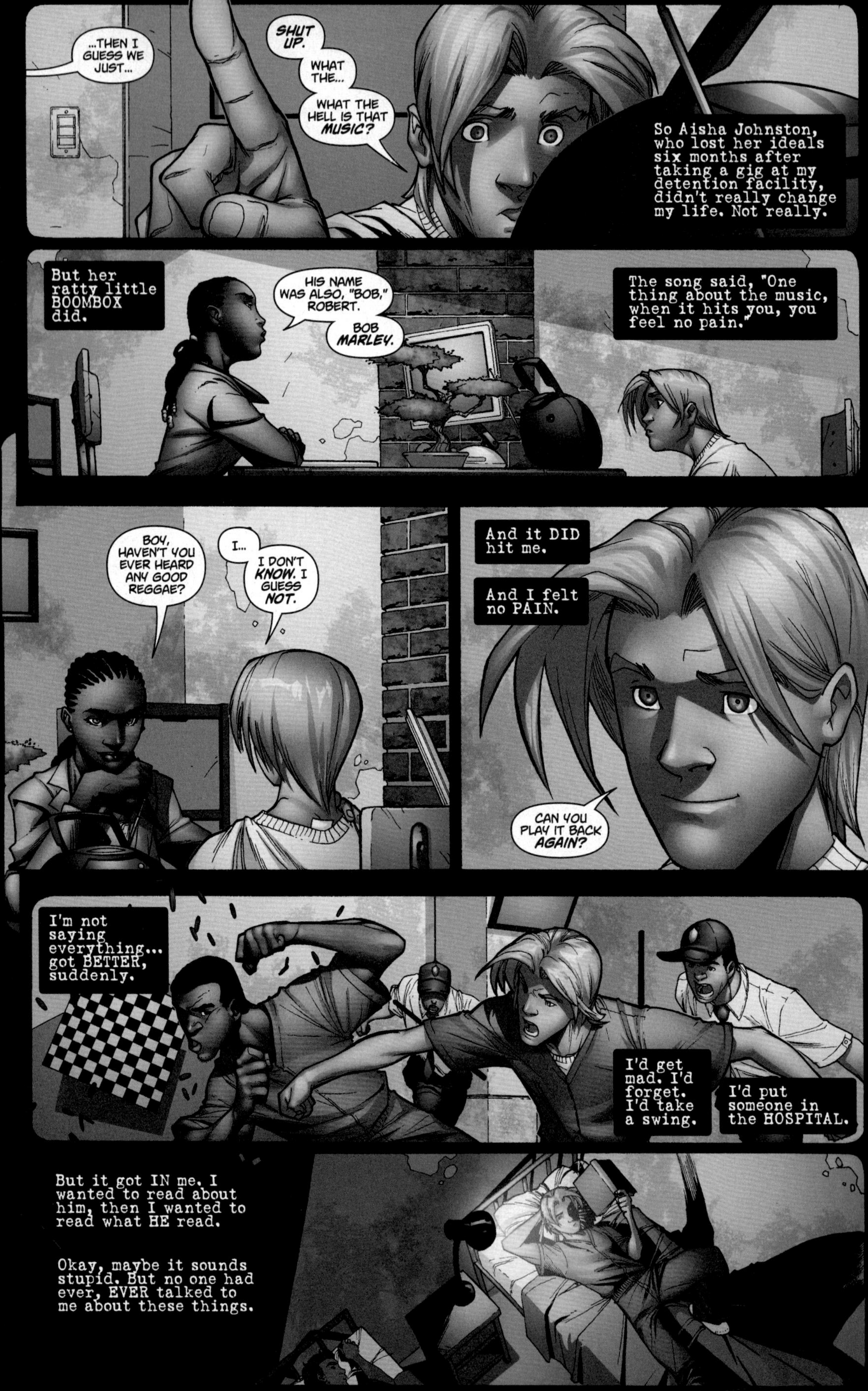
...THEN I GUESS WE JUST...
SHUT UP.
WHAT THE...
WHAT THE HELL IS THAT MUSIC?
So Aisha Johnston, who lost her ideals six months after taking a gig at my detention facility, didn't really change my life. Not really.
But her ratty little BOOMBOX did.
HIS NAME WAS ALSO, "BOB," ROBERT.
BOB MARLEY.
The song said, "One thing about the music, when it hits you, you feel no pain."
BOY, HAVEN'T YOU EVER HEARD ANY GOOD REGGAE?
I...
I DON'T KNOW. I GUESS NOT.
And it DID hit me.
And I felt no PAIN.
CAN YOU PLAY IT BACK AGAIN?
I'm not saying everything... got BETTER, suddenly.
I'd get mad. I'd forget. I'd take a swing.
I'd put someone in the HOSPITAL.
But it got IN me. I wanted to read about him, then I wanted to read what HE read.
Okay, maybe it sounds stupid. But no one had ever, EVER talked to me about these things.

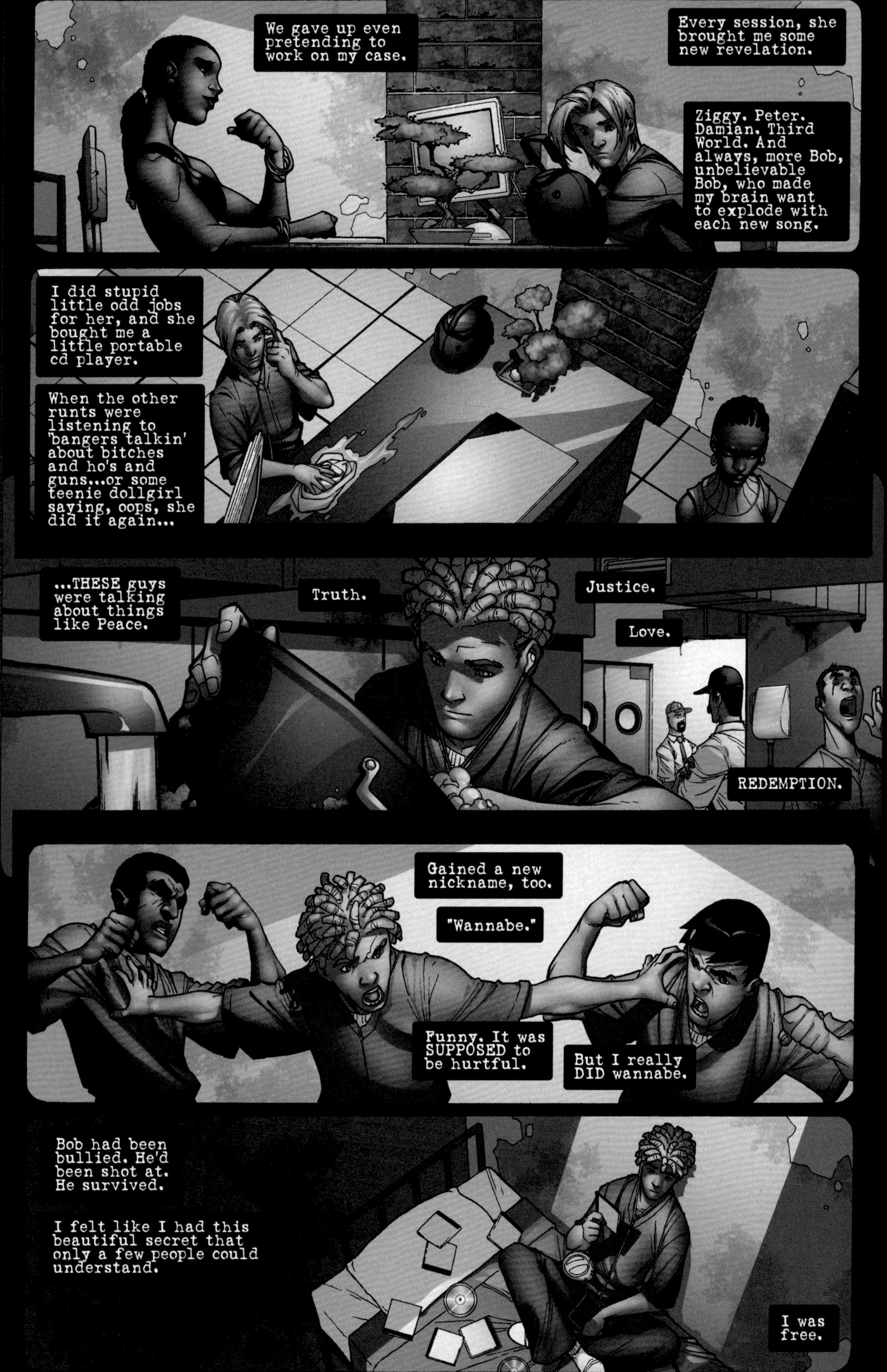
We gave up even pretending to work on my case.
Every session, she brought me some new revelation.
Ziggy. Peter. Damian. Third World. And always, more Bob, unbelievable Bob, who made my brain want to explode with each new song.
I did stupid little odd jobs for her, and she bought me a little portable cd player.
When the other runts were listening to 'bangers talkin' about bitches and ho's and guns...or some teenie dollgirl saying, oops, she did it again...
...THESE guys were talking about things like Peace.
Truth.
Justice.
Love.
REDEMPTION.
Gained a new nickname, too.
"Wannabe."
Funny. It was SUPPOSED to be hurtful.
But I really DID wannabe.
Bob had been bullied. He'd been shot at. He survived.
I felt like I had this beautiful secret that only a few people could understand.
I was free.

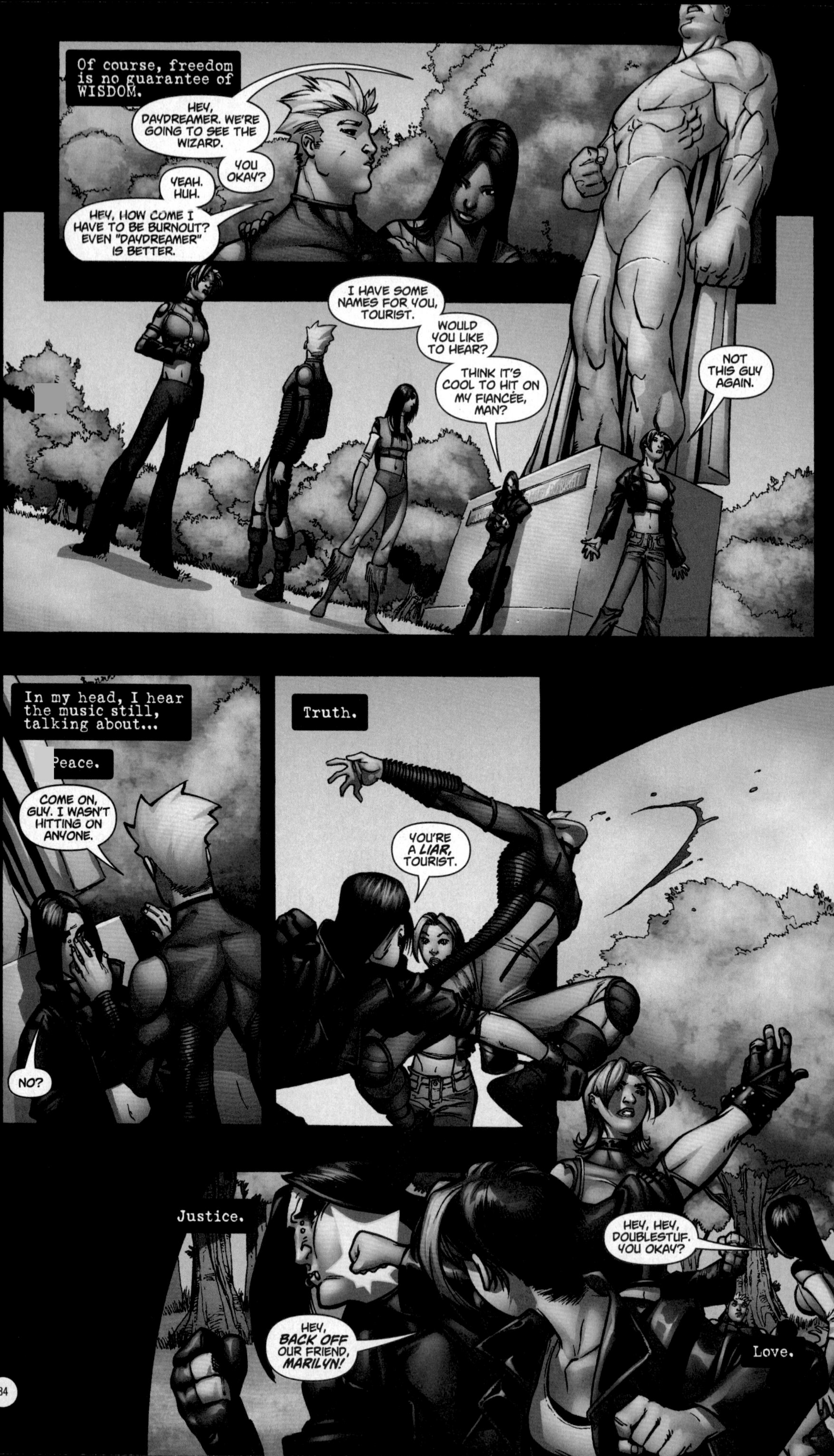
Of course, freedom is no guarantee of WISDOM.
HEY, DAYDREAMER. WE'RE GOING TO SEE THE WIZARD.
YOU OKAY?
YEAH. HUH.
HEY, HOW COME I HAVE TO BE BURNOUT? EVEN "DAYDREAMER" IS BETTER.
I HAVE SOME NAMES FOR YOU, TOURIST.
WOULD YOU LIKE TO HEAR?
THINK IT'S COOL TO HIT ON MY FIANCÉE, MAN?
NOT THIS GUY AGAIN.
In my head, I hear the music still, talking about...
Peace.
COME ON, GUY. I WASN'T HITTING ON ANYONE.
NO?
Truth.
YOU'RE A *LIAR*, TOURIST.
Justice.
HEY, HEY, DOUBLESTUF. YOU OKAY?
HEY, *BACK OFF* OUR FRIEND, *MARILYN!*
Love.

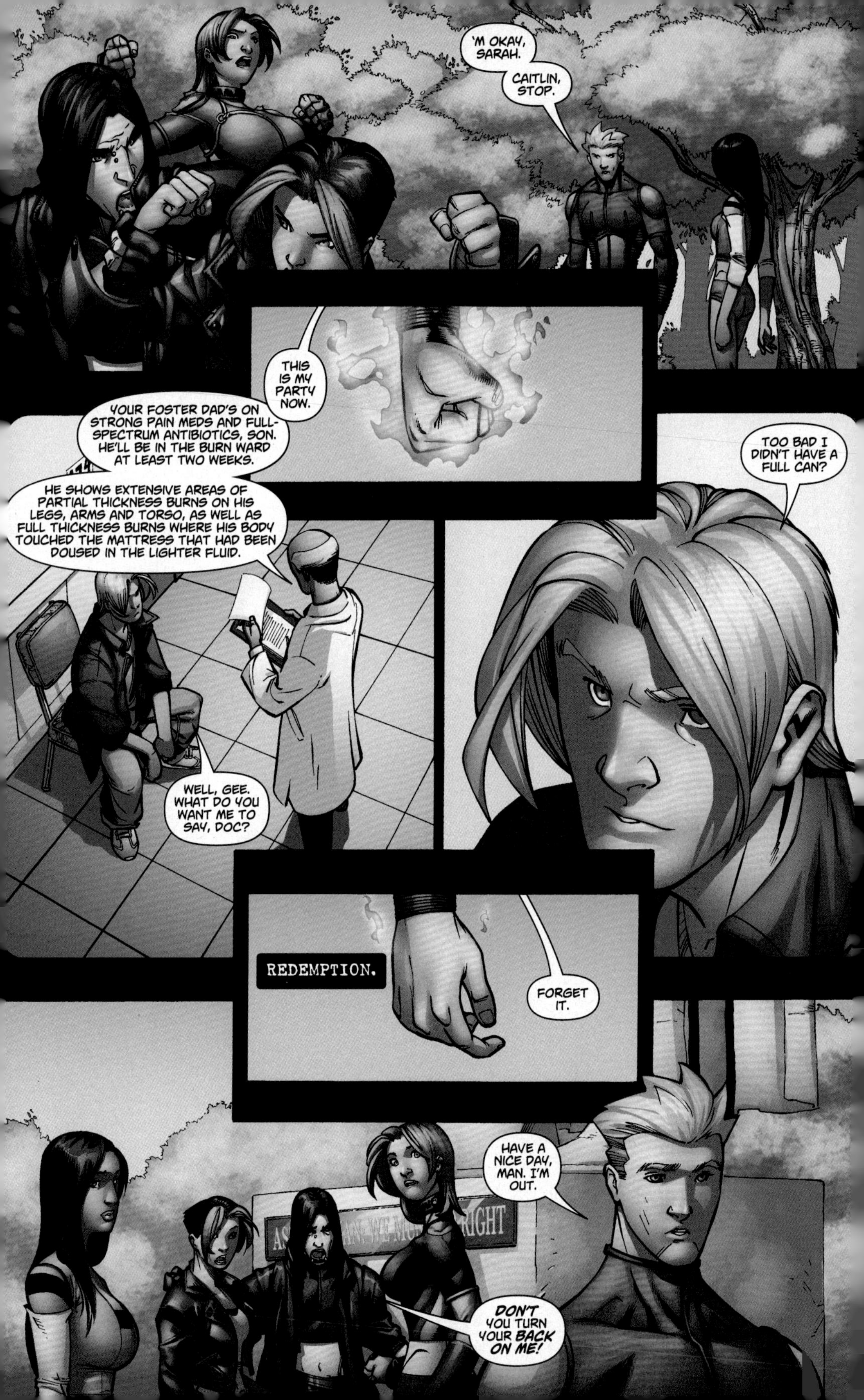
'M OKAY, SARAH.
CAITLIN, STOP.
THIS IS MY PARTY NOW.
YOUR FOSTER DAD'S ON STRONG PAIN MEDS AND FULL-SPECTRUM ANTIBIOTICS, SON. HE'LL BE IN THE BURN WARD AT LEAST TWO WEEKS.
HE SHOWS EXTENSIVE AREAS OF PARTIAL THICKNESS BURNS ON HIS LEGS, ARMS AND TORSO, AS WELL AS FULL THICKNESS BURNS WHERE HIS BODY TOUCHED THE MATTRESS THAT HAD BEEN DOUSED IN THE LIGHTER FLUID.
WELL, GEE. WHAT DO YOU WANT ME TO SAY, DOC?
TOO BAD I DIDN'T HAVE A FULL CAN?
REDEMPTION.
FORGET IT.
HAVE A NICE DAY, MAN. I'M OUT.
DON'T YOU TURN YOUR BACK ON ME!

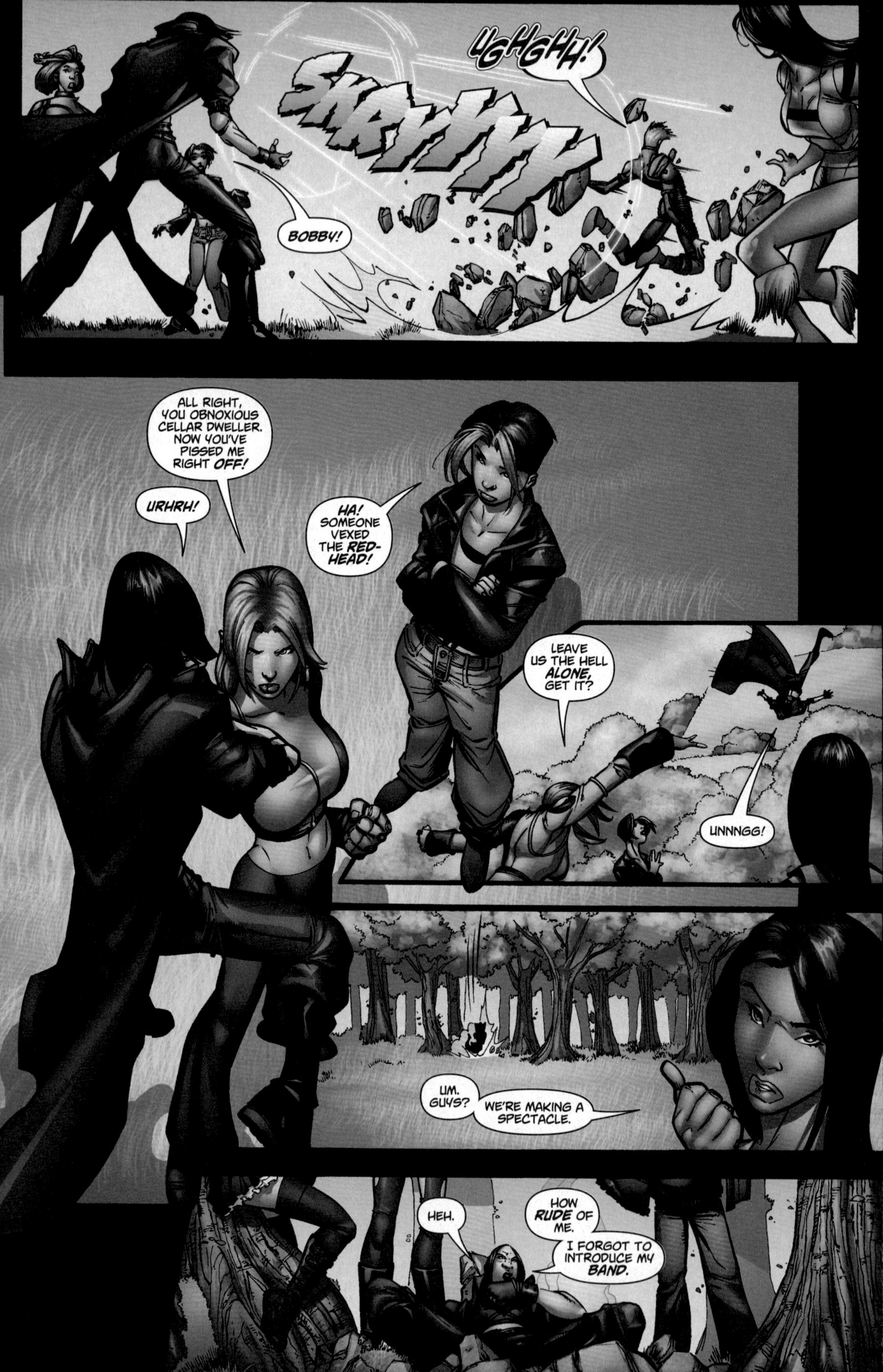
SKRYYYYY
UGHGHH!
BOBBY!
ALL RIGHT, YOU OBNOXIOUS CELLAR DWELLER. NOW YOU'VE PISSED ME RIGHT OFF!
URHRH!
HA! SOMEONE VEXED THE RED-HEAD!
LEAVE US THE HELL ALONE, GET IT?
UNNNGG!
UM. GUYS?
WE'RE MAKING A SPECTACLE.
HEH.
HOW RUDE OF ME.
I FORGOT TO INTRODUCE MY BAND.

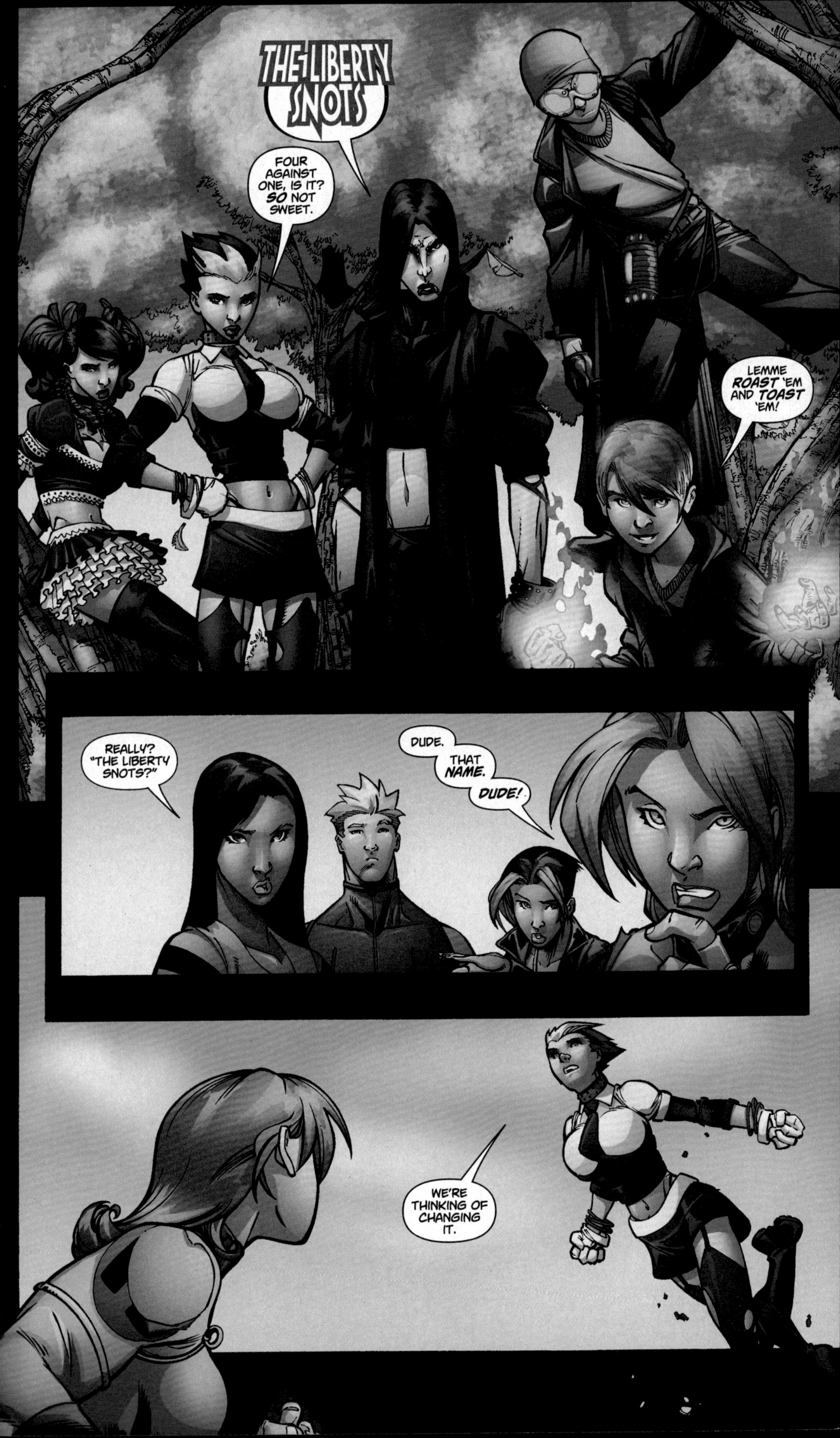
THE LIBERTY SNOTS
FOUR AGAINST ONE, IS IT? SO NOT SWEET.
LEMME ROAST 'EM AND TOAST 'EM!
REALLY? "THE LIBERTY SNOTS?"
DUDE. THAT NAME. DUDE!
WE'RE THINKING OF CHANGING IT.

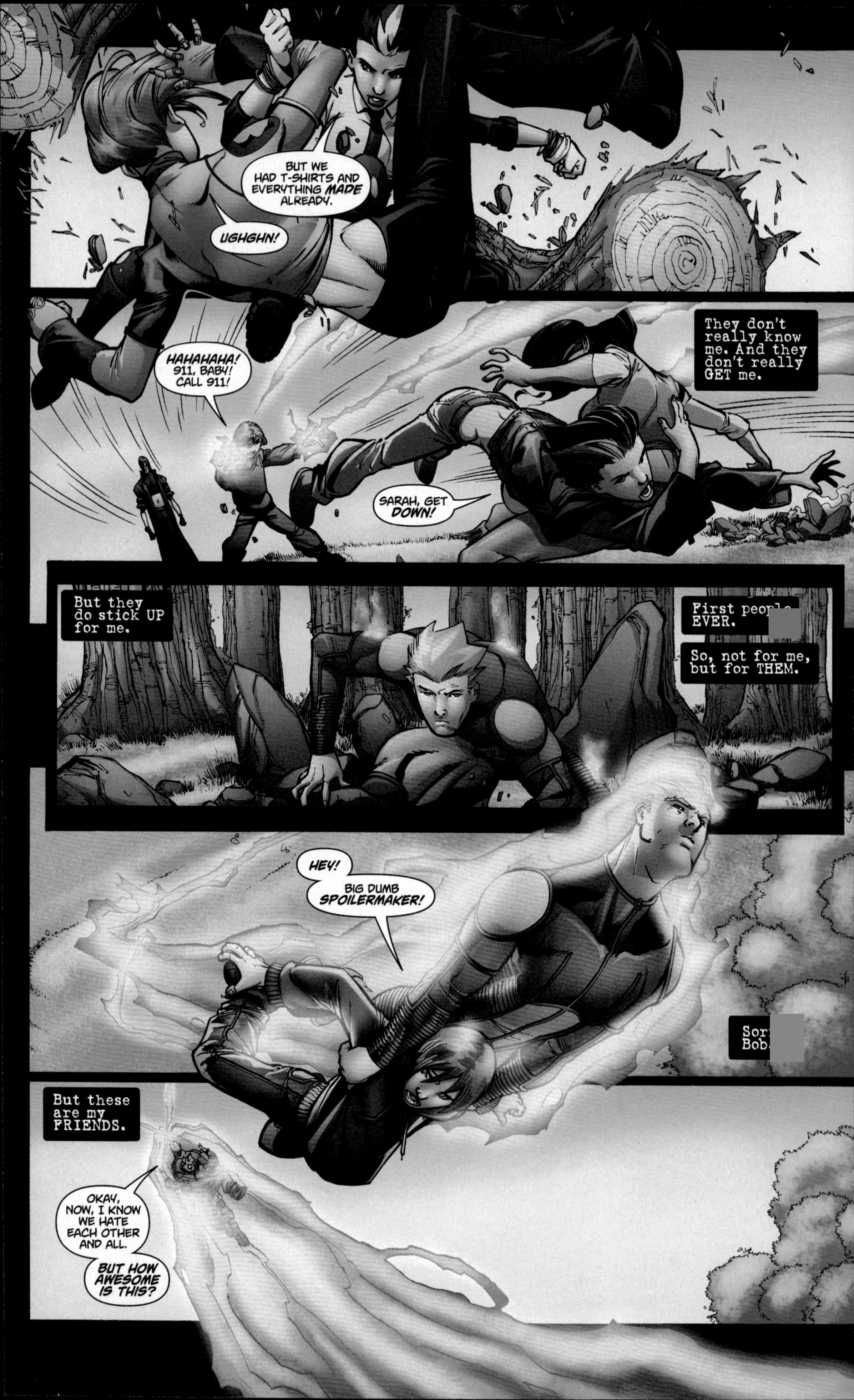
BUT WE HAD T-SHIRTS AND EVERYTHING *MADE* ALREADY.
UGHGHN!
They don't really know me. And they don't really GET me.
HAHAHAHA! 911, BABY! CALL 911!
SARAH, GET *DOWN!*
But they do stick UP for me.
First peop
EVER.
So, not for me, but for THEM.
HEY!
BIG DUMB *SPOILERMAKER!*
Sor
Bob
But these are my FRIENDS.
OKAY, NOW, I KNOW WE HATE EACH OTHER AND ALL.
BUT HOW AWESOME IS THIS?

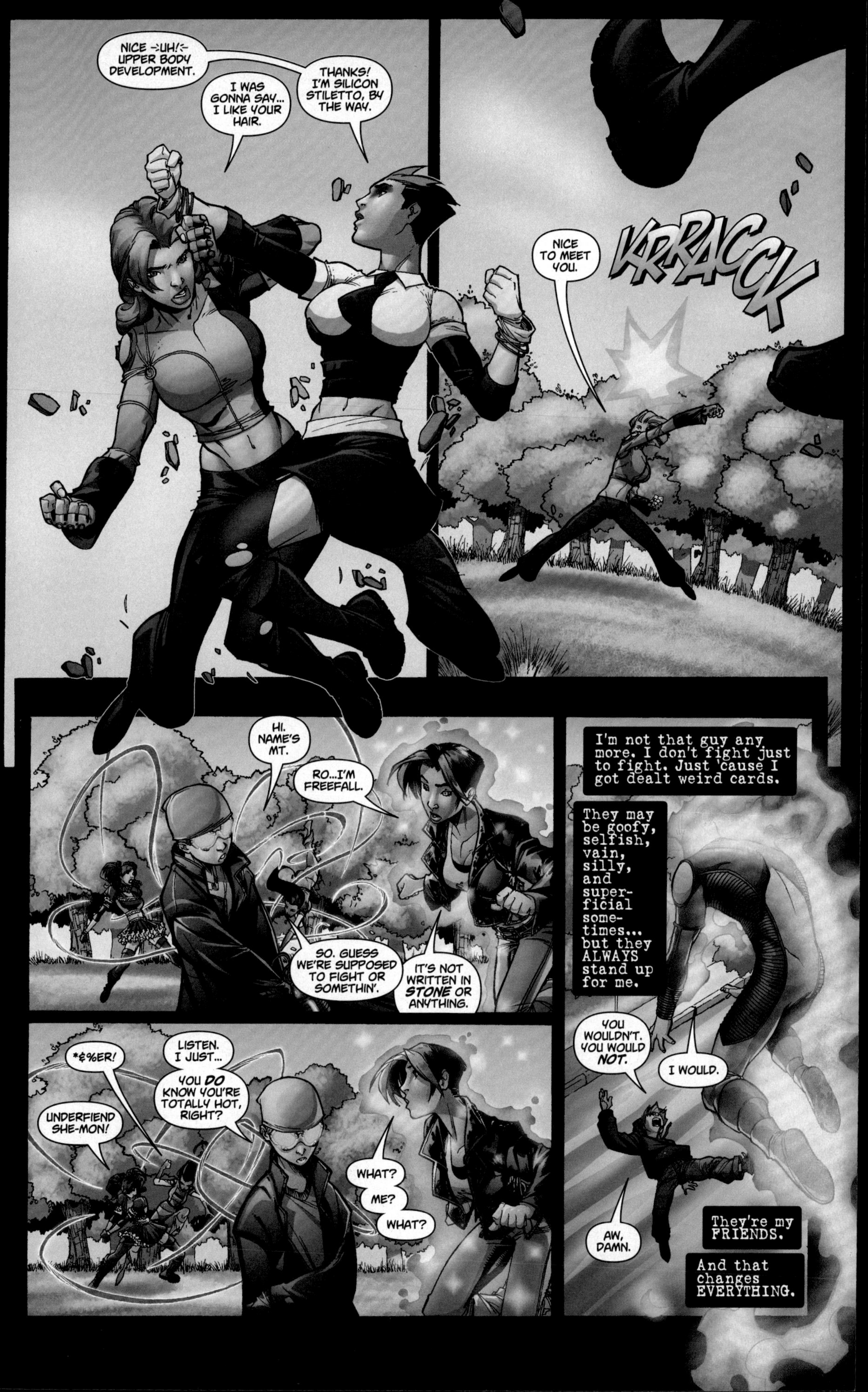
NICE -UH!- UPPER BODY DEVELOPMENT.
I WAS GONNA SAY... I LIKE YOUR HAIR.
THANKS! I'M SILICON STILETTO, BY THE WAY.
NICE TO MEET YOU.
KRRRACCK
HI. NAME'S MT.
RO...I'M FREEFALL.
SO. GUESS WE'RE SUPPOSED TO FIGHT OR SOMETHIN'.
IT'S NOT WRITTEN IN STONE OR ANYTHING.
*$%ER!
UNDERFIEND SHE-MON!
LISTEN. I JUST...
YOU DO KNOW YOU'RE TOTALLY HOT, RIGHT?
WHAT?
ME?
WHAT?
I'm not that guy any more. I don't fight just to fight. Just 'cause I got dealt weird cards.
They may be goofy, selfish, vain, silly, and super-ficial some-times... but they ALWAYS stand up for me.
YOU WOULDN'T. YOU WOULD NOT.
I WOULD.
AW, DAMN.
They're my FRIENDS.
And that changes EVERYTHING.

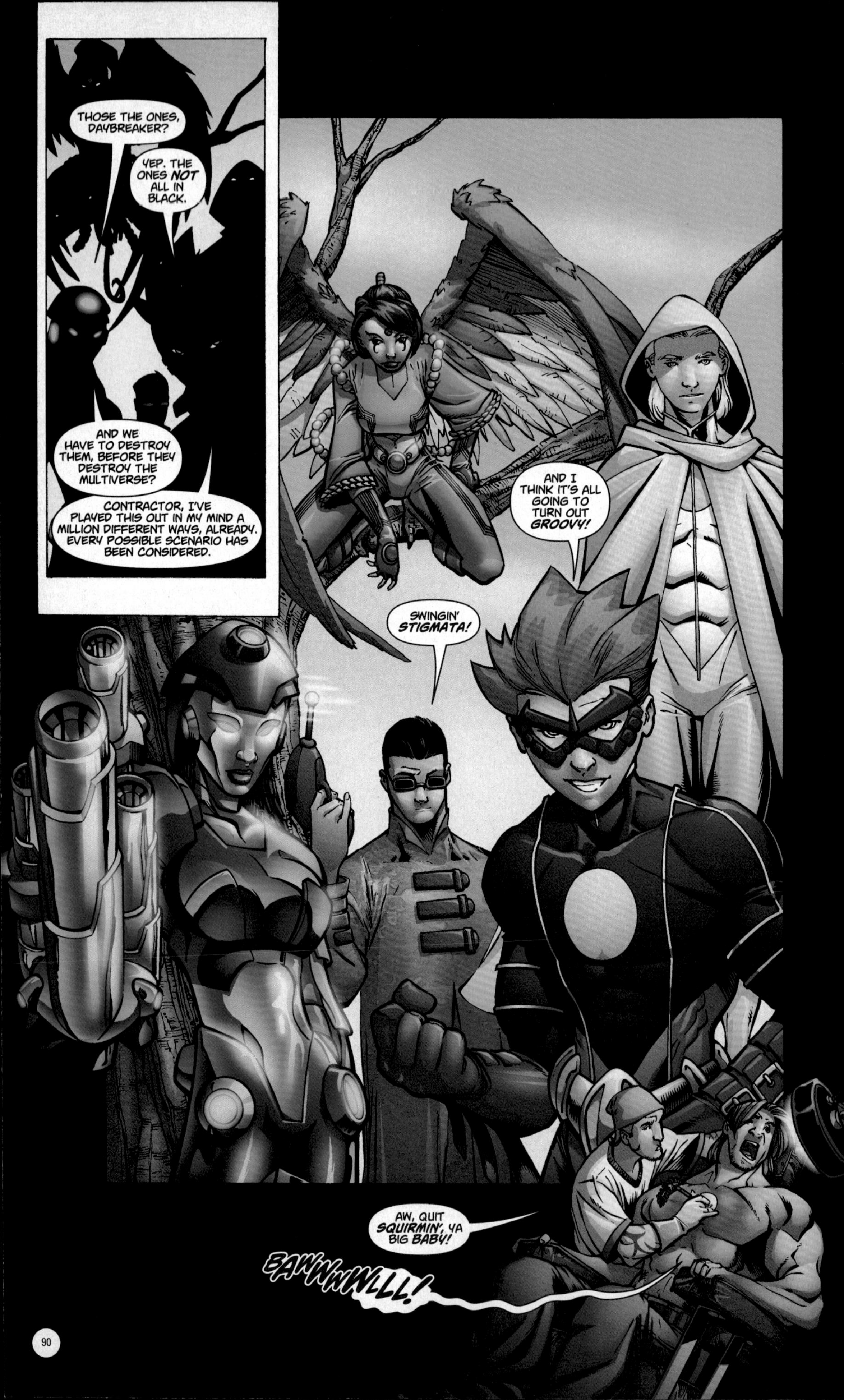
THOSE THE ONES, DAYBREAKER?
YEP. THE ONES NOT ALL IN BLACK.
AND WE HAVE TO DESTROY THEM, BEFORE THEY DESTROY THE MULTIVERSE?
CONTRACTOR, I'VE PLAYED THIS OUT IN MY MIND A MILLION DIFFERENT WAYS, ALREADY. EVERY POSSIBLE SCENARIO HAS BEEN CONSIDERED.
AND I THINK IT'S ALL GOING TO TURN OUT GROOVY!
SWINGIN' STIGMATA!
AW, QUIT SQUIRMIN', YA BIG BABY!
BAWWWWLLL!

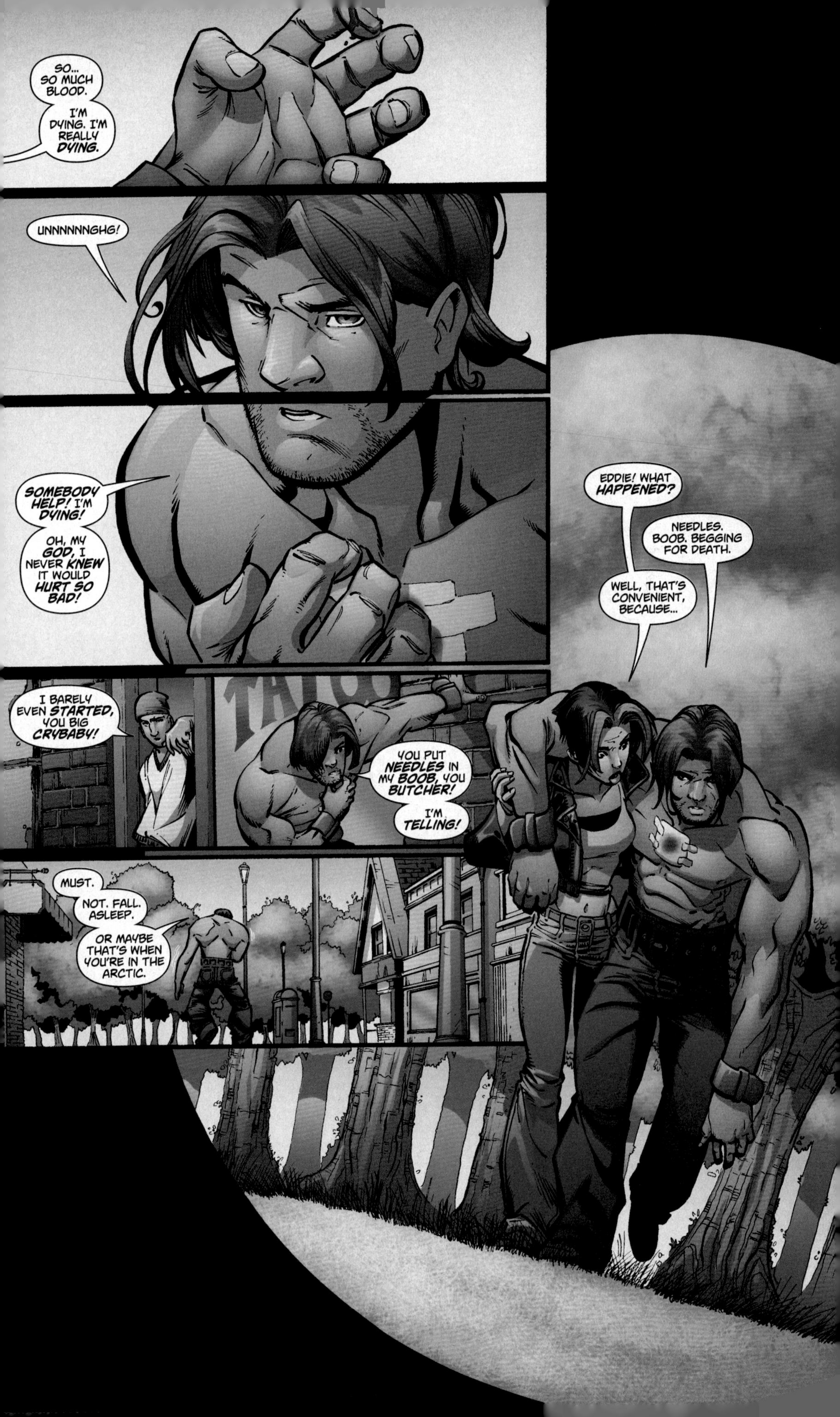
SO... SO MUCH BLOOD.
I'M DYING. I'M REALLY DYING.
UNNNNNNGHG!
SOMEBODY HELP! I'M DYING!
OH, MY GOD, I NEVER KNEW IT WOULD HURT SO BAD!
I BARELY EVEN STARTED, YOU BIG CRYBABY!
YOU PUT NEEDLES IN MY BOOB, YOU BUTCHER!
I'M TELLING!
MUST.
NOT. FALL. ASLEEP.
OR MAYBE THAT'S WHEN YOU'RE IN THE ARCTIC.
EDDIE! WHAT HAPPENED?
NEEDLES. BOOB. BEGGING FOR DEATH.
WELL, THAT'S CONVENIENT, BECAUSE...

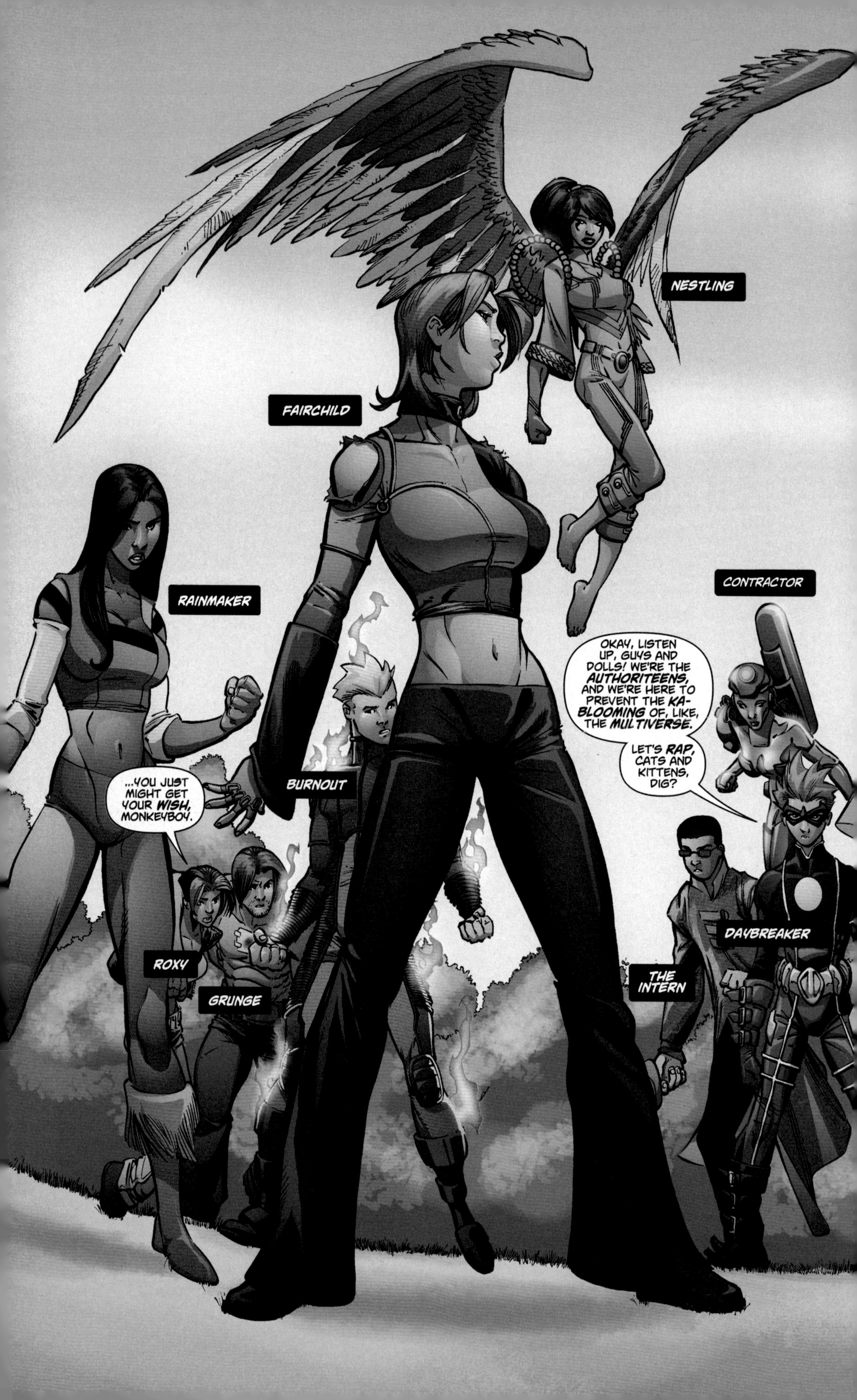
NESTLING
FAIRCHILD
RAINMAKER
CONTRACTOR
OKAY, LISTEN UP, GUYS AND DOLLS! WE'RE THE AUTHORITEENS, AND WE'RE HERE TO PREVENT THE KA-BLOOMING OF, LIKE, THE MULTIVERSE.
LET'S RAP, CATS AND KITTENS, DIG?
...YOU JUST MIGHT GET YOUR WISH, MONKEYBOY.
BURNOUT
ROXY
GRUNGE
THE INTERN
DAYBREAKER

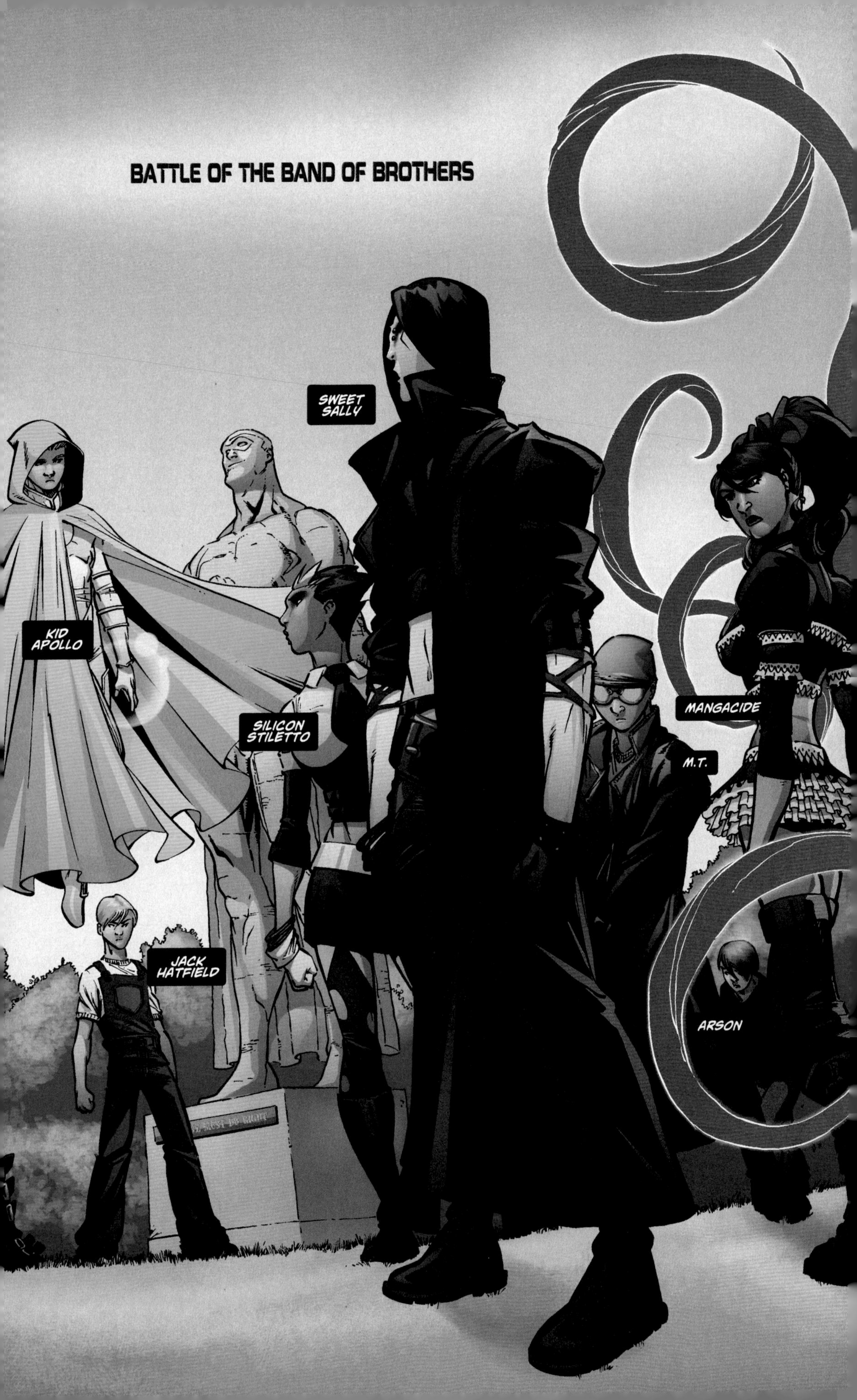
BATTLE OF THE BAND OF BROTHERS
SWEET SALLY
KID APOLLO
SILICON STILETTO
MANGACIDE
M.T.
JACK HATFIELD
ARSON

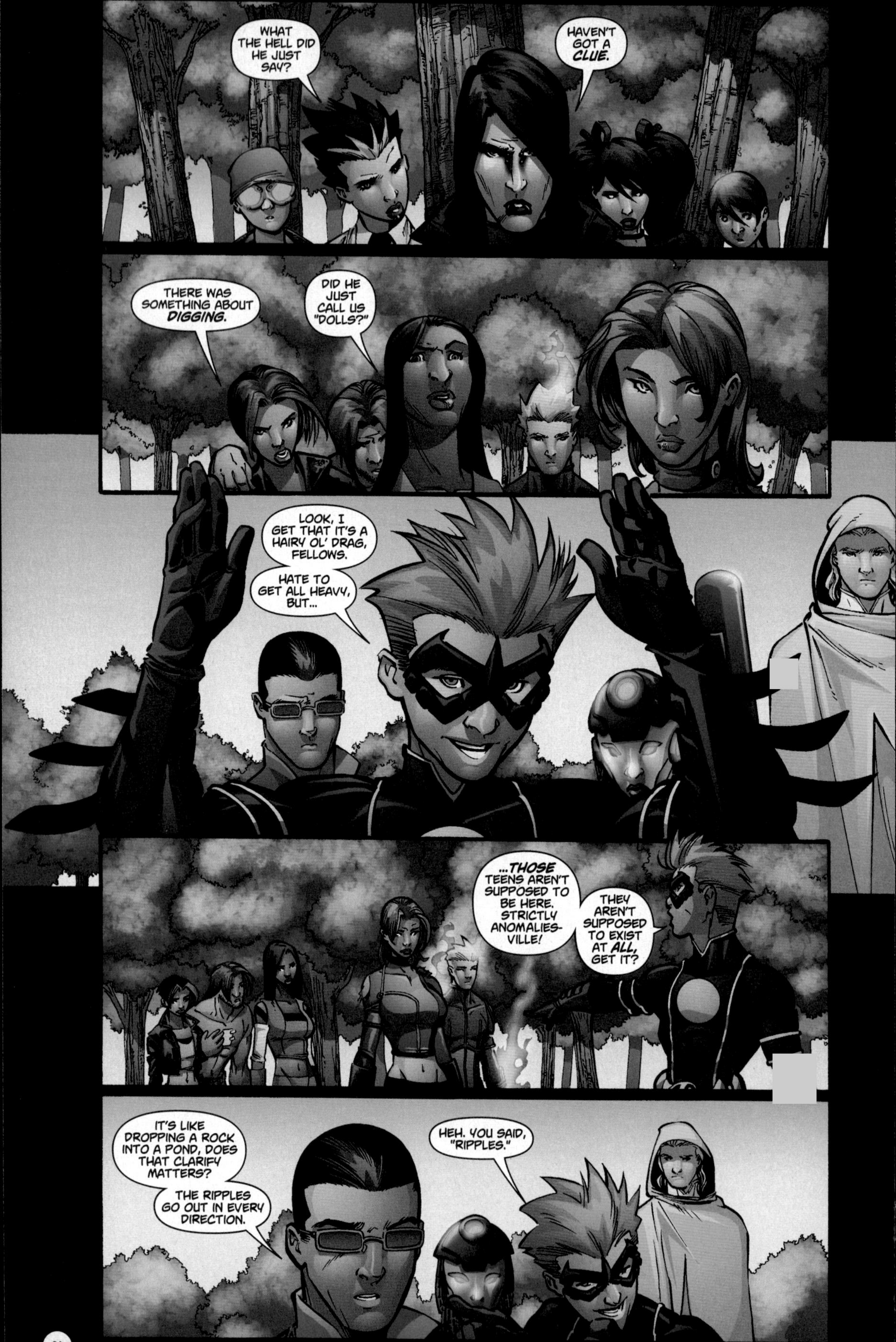
WHAT THE HELL DID HE JUST SAY?
HAVEN'T GOT A CLUE.
THERE WAS SOMETHING ABOUT DIGGING.
DID HE JUST CALL US "DOLLS?"
LOOK, I GET THAT IT'S A HAIRY OL' DRAG, FELLOWS.
HATE TO GET ALL HEAVY, BUT...
...THOSE TEENS AREN'T SUPPOSED TO BE HERE. STRICTLY ANOMALIES-VILLE!
THEY AREN'T SUPPOSED TO EXIST AT ALL, GET IT?
IT'S LIKE DROPPING A ROCK INTO A POND, DOES THAT CLARIFY MATTERS?
THE RIPPLES GO OUT IN EVERY DIRECTION.
HEH. YOU SAID, "RIPPLES."

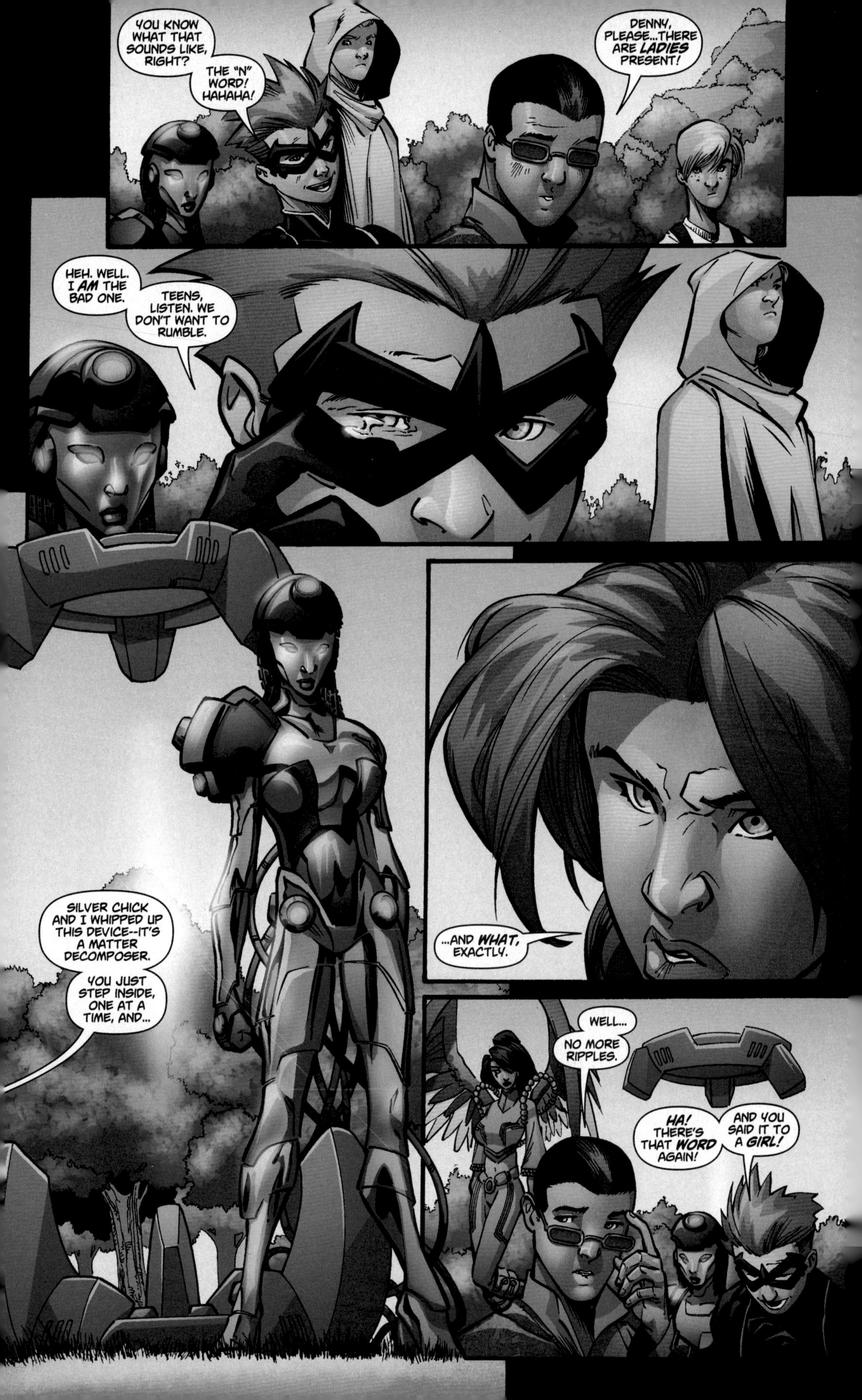
YOU KNOW WHAT THAT SOUNDS LIKE, RIGHT?
THE "N" WORD! HAHAHA!
DENNY, PLEASE...THERE ARE LADIES PRESENT!
HEH. WELL. I AM THE BAD ONE.
TEENS, LISTEN. WE DON'T WANT TO RUMBLE.
SILVER CHICK AND I WHIPPED UP THIS DEVICE--IT'S A MATTER DECOMPOSER.
YOU JUST STEP INSIDE, ONE AT A TIME, AND...
...AND WHAT, EXACTLY.
WELL...
NO MORE RIPPLES.
HA! THERE'S THAT WORD AGAIN!
AND YOU SAID IT TO A GIRL!

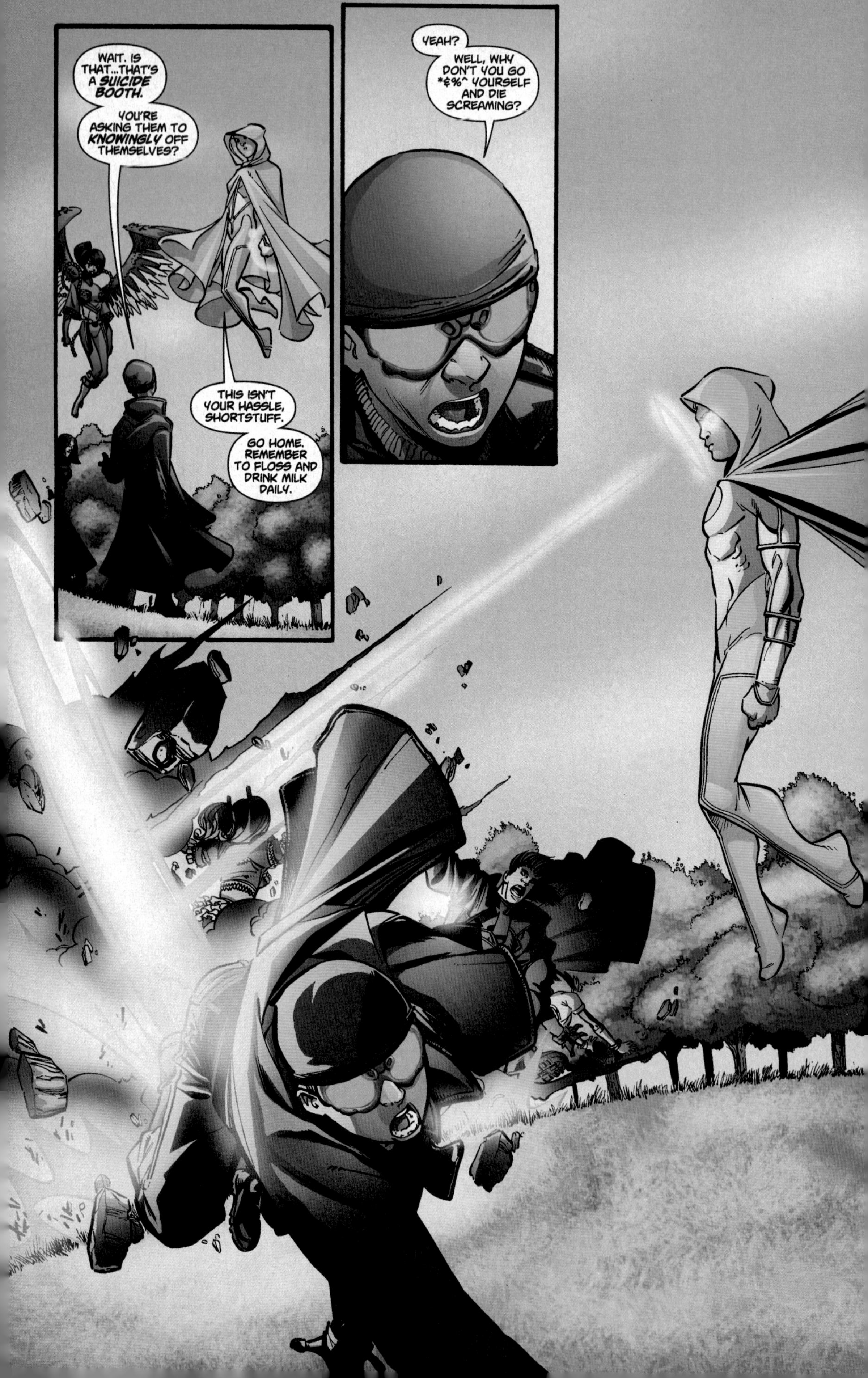
WAIT. IS THAT...THAT'S A SUICIDE BOOTH.
YOU'RE ASKING THEM TO KNOWINGLY OFF THEMSELVES?
THIS ISN'T YOUR HASSLE, SHORTSTUFF.
GO HOME. REMEMBER TO FLOSS AND DRINK MILK DAILY.
YEAH?
WELL, WHY DON'T YOU GO *¢%^ YOURSELF AND DIE SCREAMING?

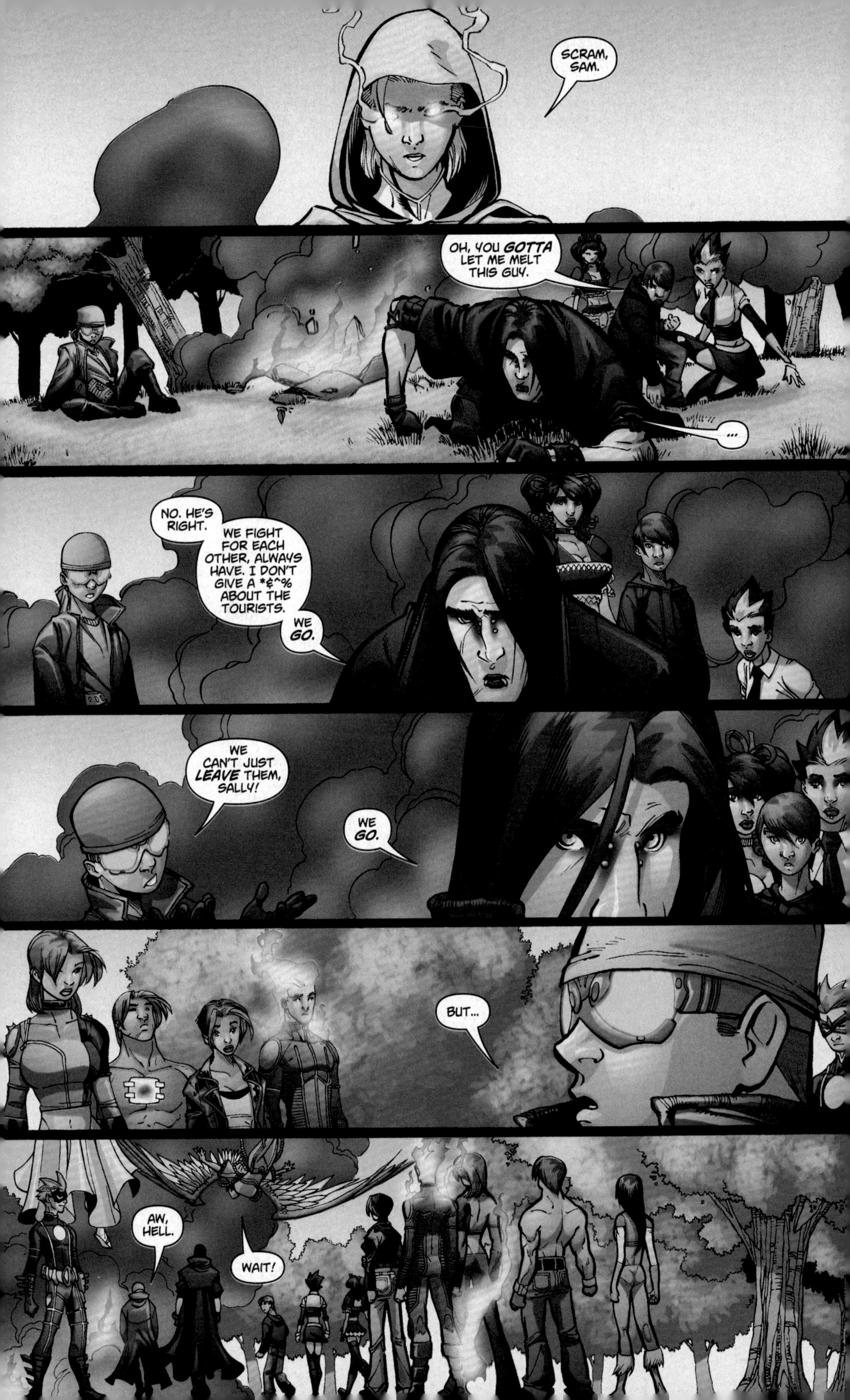
SCRAM, SAM.
OH, YOU GOTTA LET ME MELT THIS GUY.
...
NO. HE'S RIGHT.
WE FIGHT FOR EACH OTHER, ALWAYS HAVE. I DON'T GIVE A *&^% ABOUT THE TOURISTS.
WE GO.
WE CAN'T JUST LEAVE THEM, SALLY!
WE GO.
BUT...
AW, HELL.
WAIT!

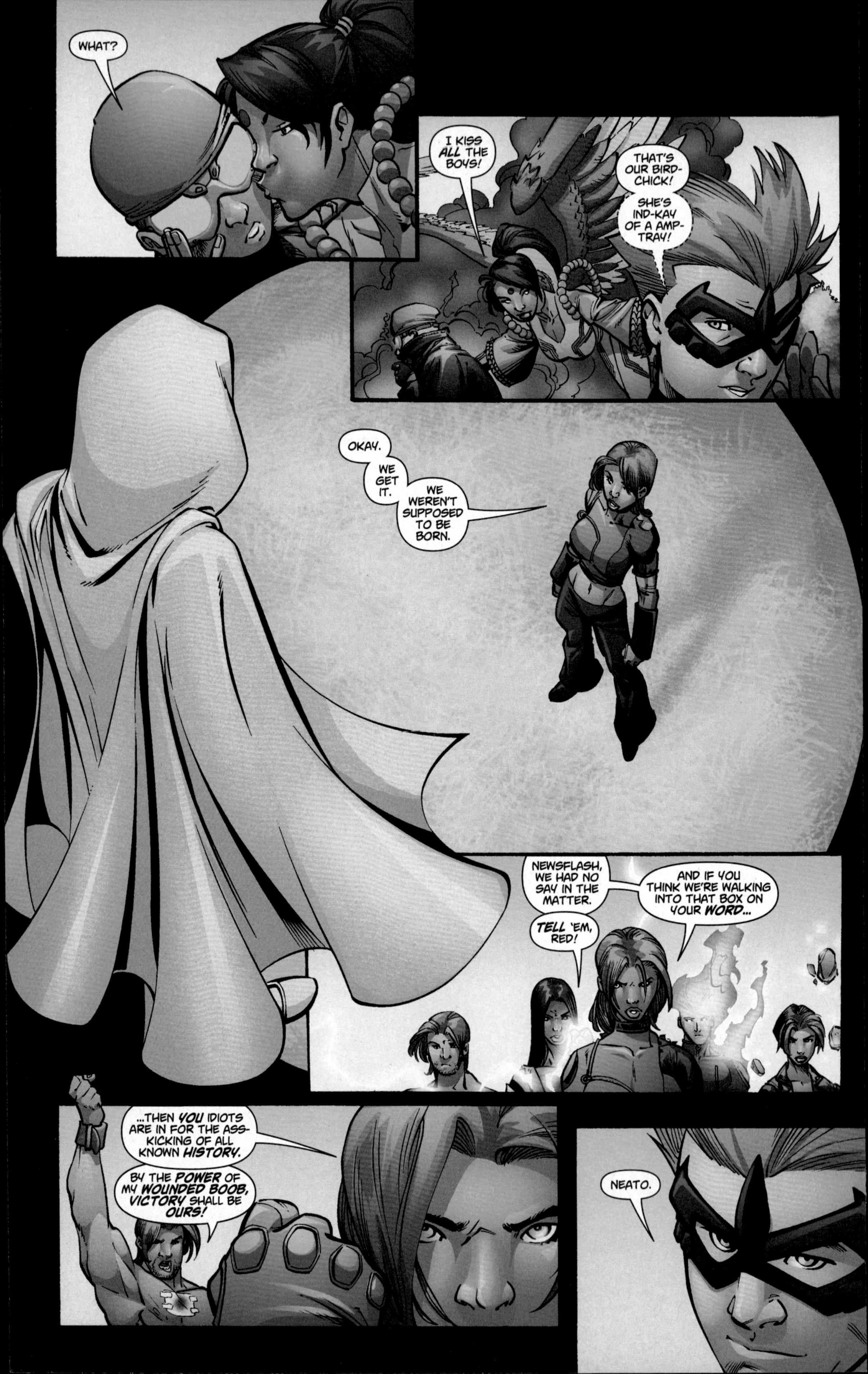
WHAT?
I KISS ALL THE BOYS!
THAT'S OUR BIRD-CHICK!
SHE'S IND-KAY OF A AMP-TRAY!
OKAY.
WE GET IT.
WE WEREN'T SUPPOSED TO BE BORN.
NEWSFLASH, WE HAD NO SAY IN THE MATTER.
TELL 'EM, RED!
AND IF YOU THINK WE'RE WALKING INTO THAT BOX ON YOUR WORD...
...THEN YOU IDIOTS ARE IN FOR THE ASS-KICKING OF ALL KNOWN HISTORY.
BY THE POWER OF MY WOUNDED BOOB, VICTORY SHALL BE OURS!
NEATO.

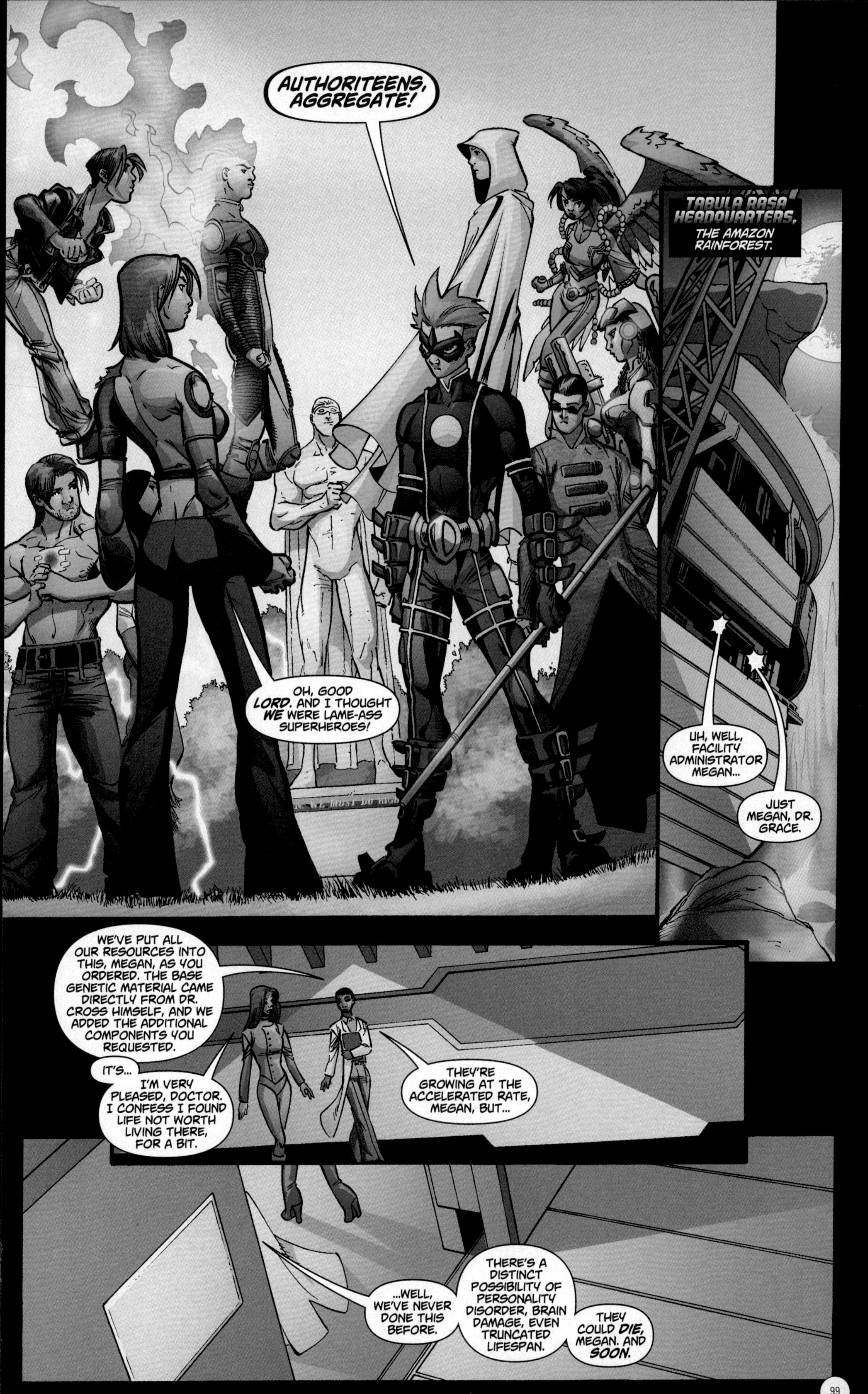
AUTHORITEENS, AGGREGATE!
TABULA RASA HEADQUARTERS, THE AMAZON RAINFOREST.
OH, GOOD LORD. AND I THOUGHT WE WERE LAME-ASS SUPERHEROES!
UH, WELL, FACILITY ADMINISTRATOR MEGAN...
JUST MEGAN, DR. GRACE.
WE'VE PUT ALL OUR RESOURCES INTO THIS, MEGAN, AS YOU ORDERED. THE BASE GENETIC MATERIAL CAME DIRECTLY FROM DR. CROSS HIMSELF, AND WE ADDED THE ADDITIONAL COMPONENTS YOU REQUESTED.
IT'S...
I'M VERY PLEASED, DOCTOR. I CONFESS I FOUND LIFE NOT WORTH LIVING THERE, FOR A BIT.
THEY'RE GROWING AT THE ACCELERATED RATE, MEGAN, BUT...
...WELL, WE'VE NEVER DONE THIS BEFORE.
THERE'S A DISTINCT POSSIBILITY OF PERSONALITY DISORDER, BRAIN DAMAGE, EVEN TRUNCATED LIFESPAN.
THEY COULD DIE, MEGAN. AND SOON.

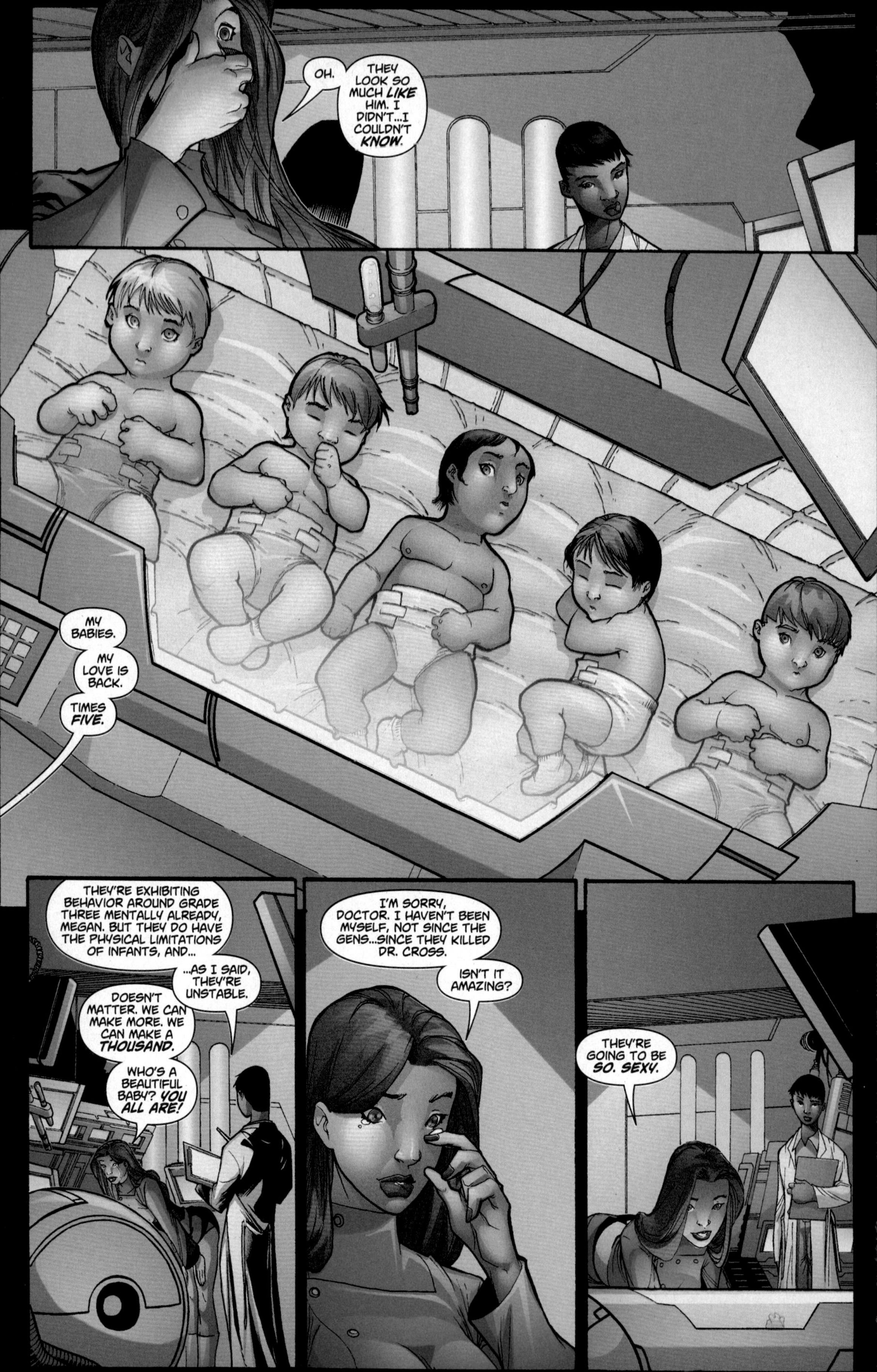
OH.
THEY LOOK SO MUCH **LIKE** HIM. I DIDN'T...I COULDN'T **KNOW**.
MY BABIES.
MY LOVE IS BACK.
TIMES **FIVE**.
THEY'RE EXHIBITING BEHAVIOR AROUND GRADE THREE MENTALLY ALREADY, MEGAN. BUT THEY DO HAVE THE PHYSICAL LIMITATIONS OF INFANTS, AND...
...AS I SAID, THEY'RE UNSTABLE.
DOESN'T MATTER. WE CAN MAKE MORE. WE CAN MAKE A **THOUSAND**.
WHO'S A BEAUTIFUL BABY? **YOU ALL ARE!**
I'M SORRY, DOCTOR. I HAVEN'T BEEN MYSELF, NOT SINCE THE GENS...SINCE THEY KILLED DR. CROSS.
ISN'T IT AMAZING?
THEY'RE GOING TO BE **SO. SEXY.**

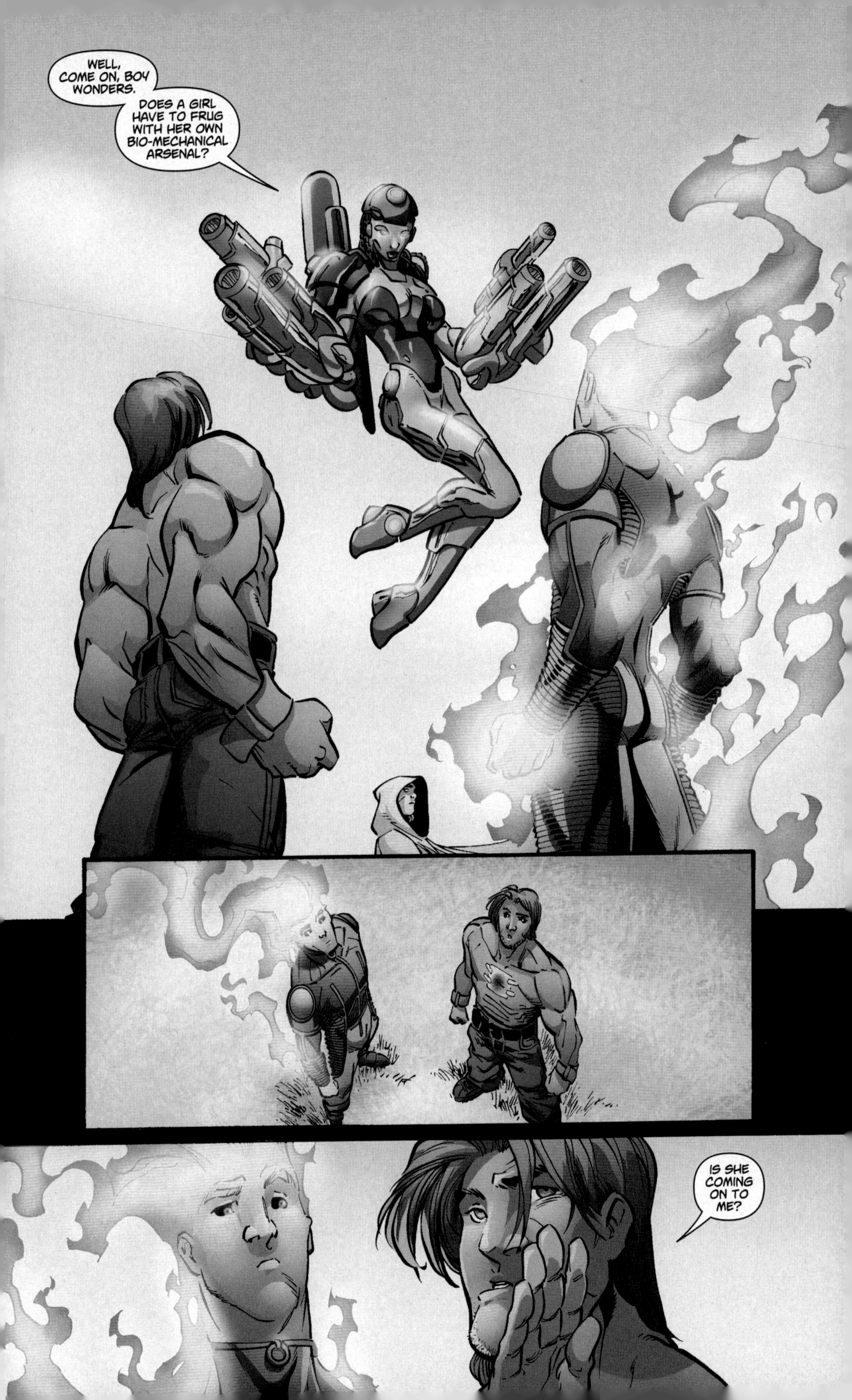
WELL, COME ON, BOY WONDERS.
DOES A GIRL HAVE TO FRUG WITH HER OWN BIO-MECHANICAL ARSENAL?
IS SHE COMING ON TO ME?

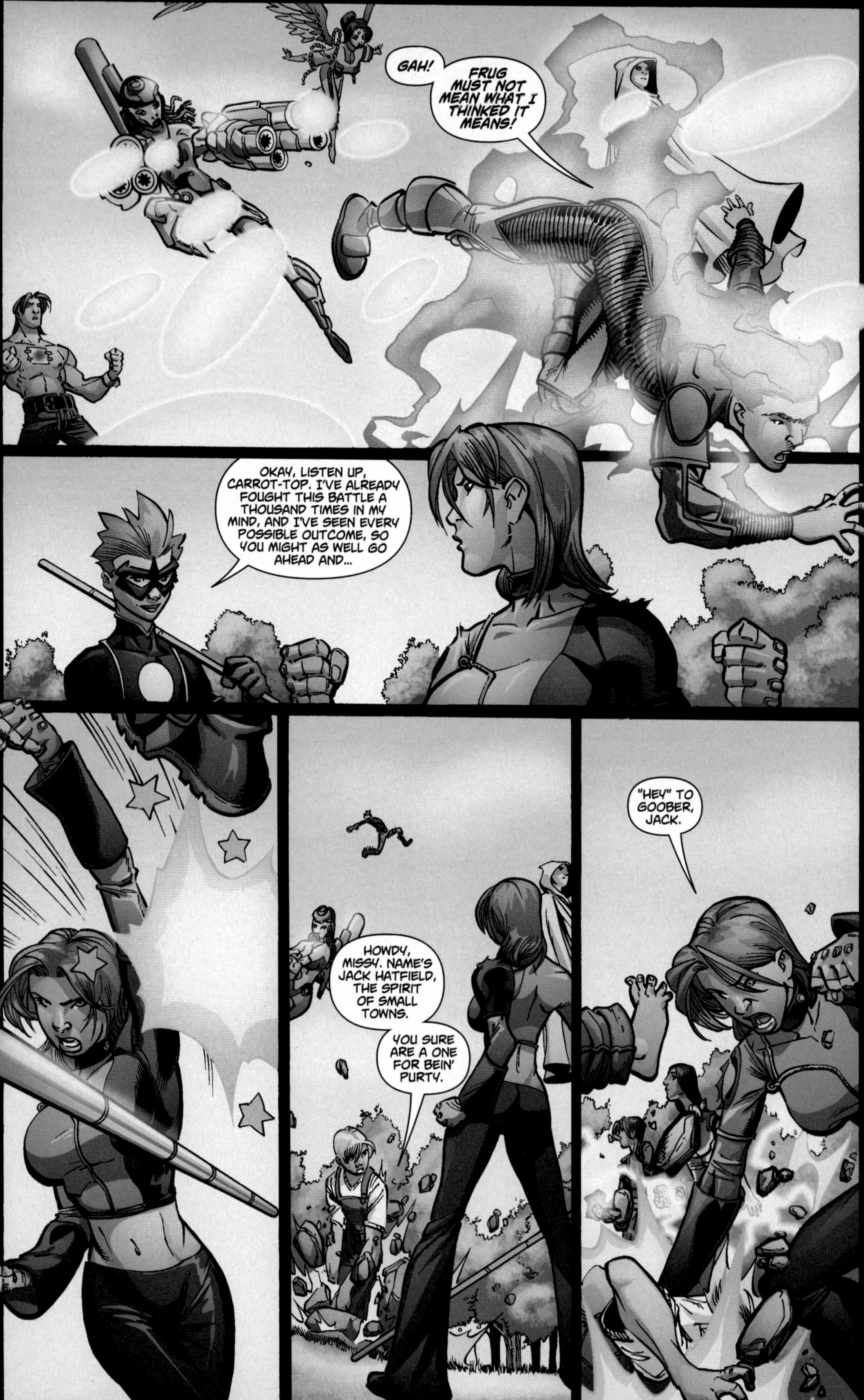
GAH!
FRUG MUST NOT MEAN WHAT I THINKED IT MEANS!
OKAY, LISTEN UP, CARROT-TOP. I'VE ALREADY FOUGHT THIS BATTLE A THOUSAND TIMES IN MY MIND, AND I'VE SEEN EVERY POSSIBLE OUTCOME, SO YOU MIGHT AS WELL GO AHEAD AND...
HOWDY, MISSY. NAME'S JACK HATFIELD, THE SPIRIT OF SMALL TOWNS.
YOU SURE ARE A ONE FOR BEIN' PURTY.
"HEY" TO GOOBER, JACK.

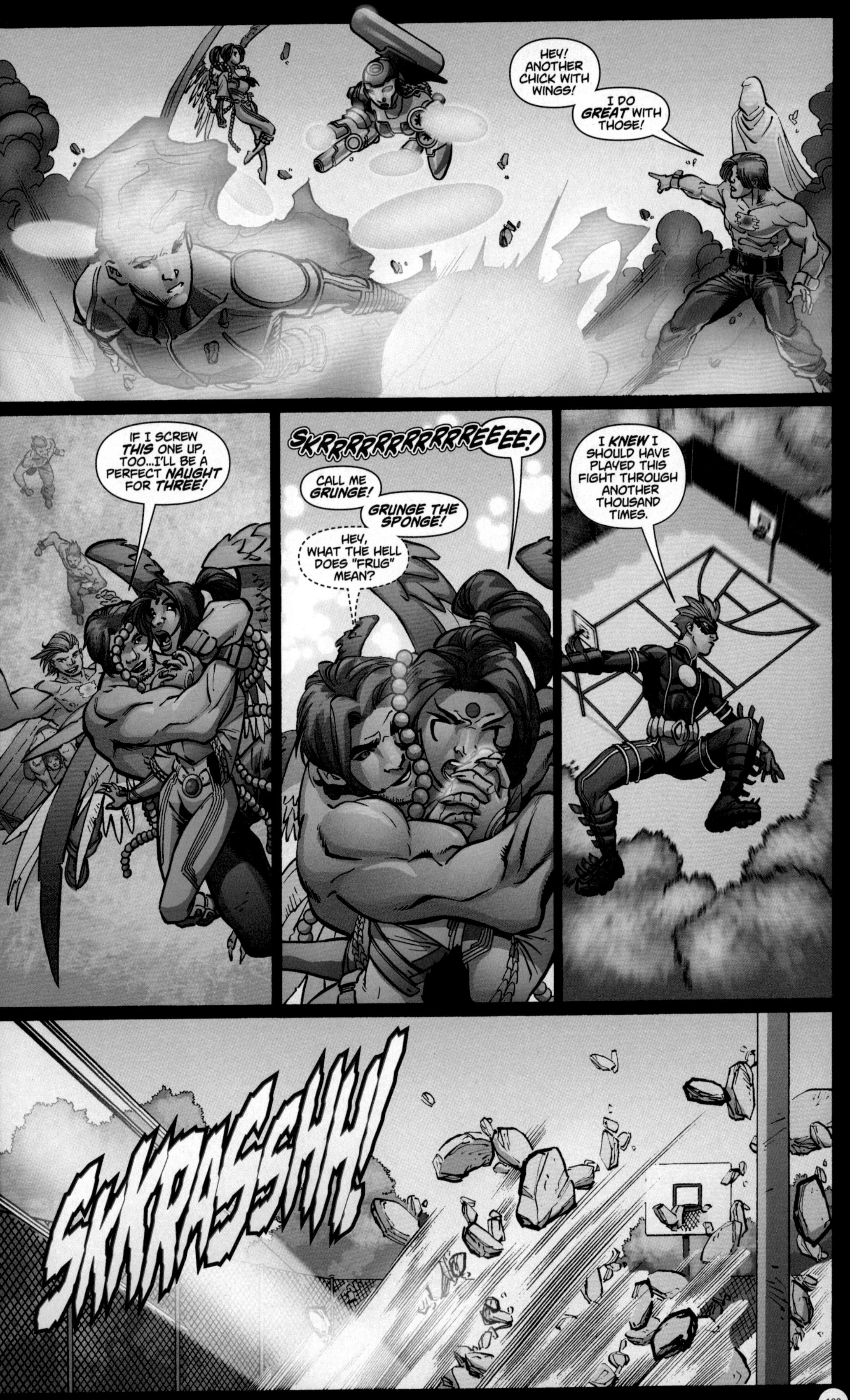
HEY! ANOTHER CHICK WITH WINGS!
I DO GREAT WITH THOSE!
IF I SCREW THIS ONE UP, TOO...I'LL BE A PERFECT NAUGHT FOR THREE!
SKRRRRRRRRRRREEEE!
CALL ME GRUNGE!
GRUNGE THE SPONGE!
HEY, WHAT THE HELL DOES "FRUG" MEAN?
I KNEW I SHOULD HAVE PLAYED THIS FIGHT THROUGH ANOTHER THOUSAND TIMES.
SKRASSHH!

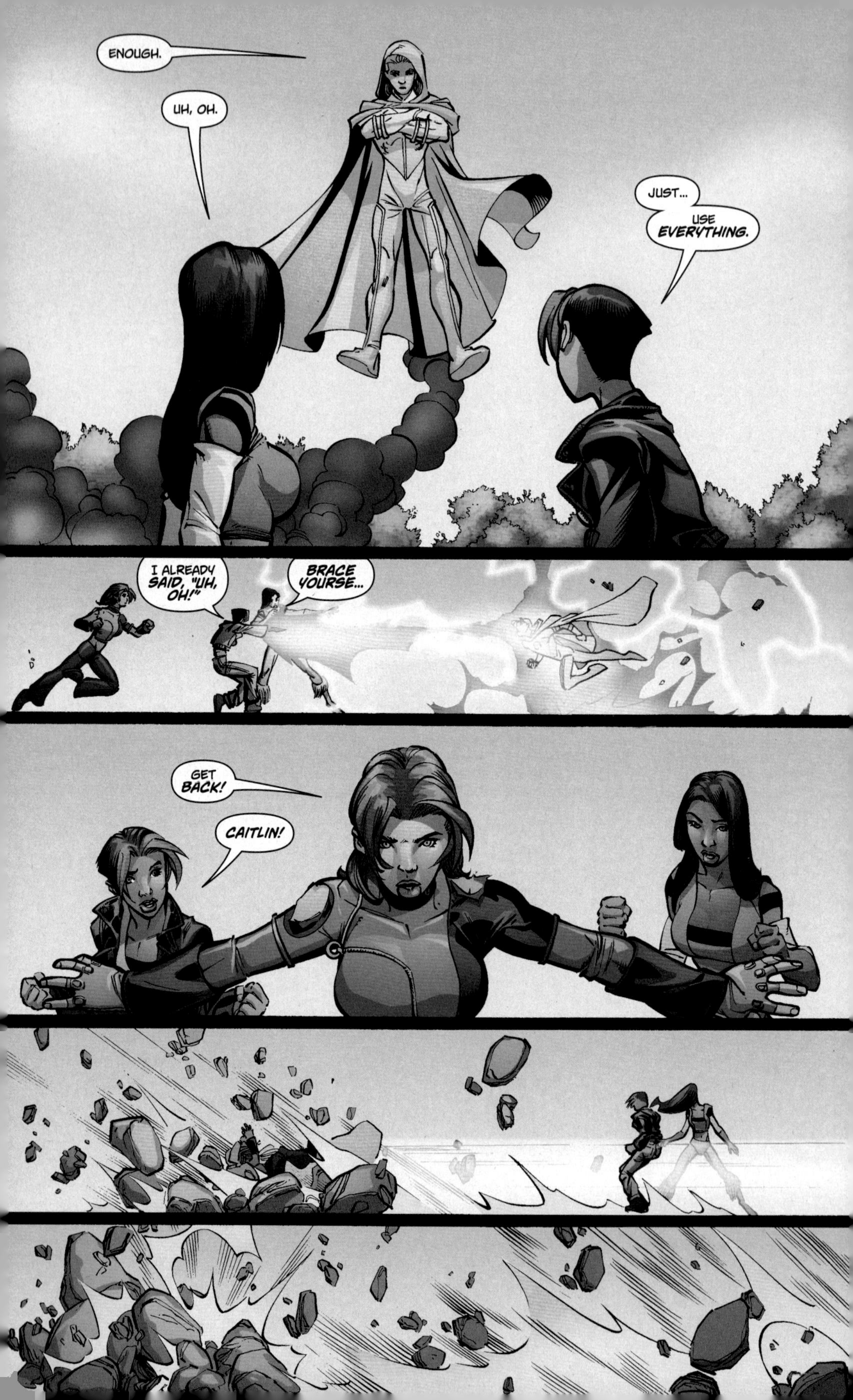
ENOUGH.
UH, OH.
JUST...
USE EVERYTHING.
I ALREADY SAID, "UH, OH!"
BRACE YOURSE...
GET BACK!
CAITLIN!

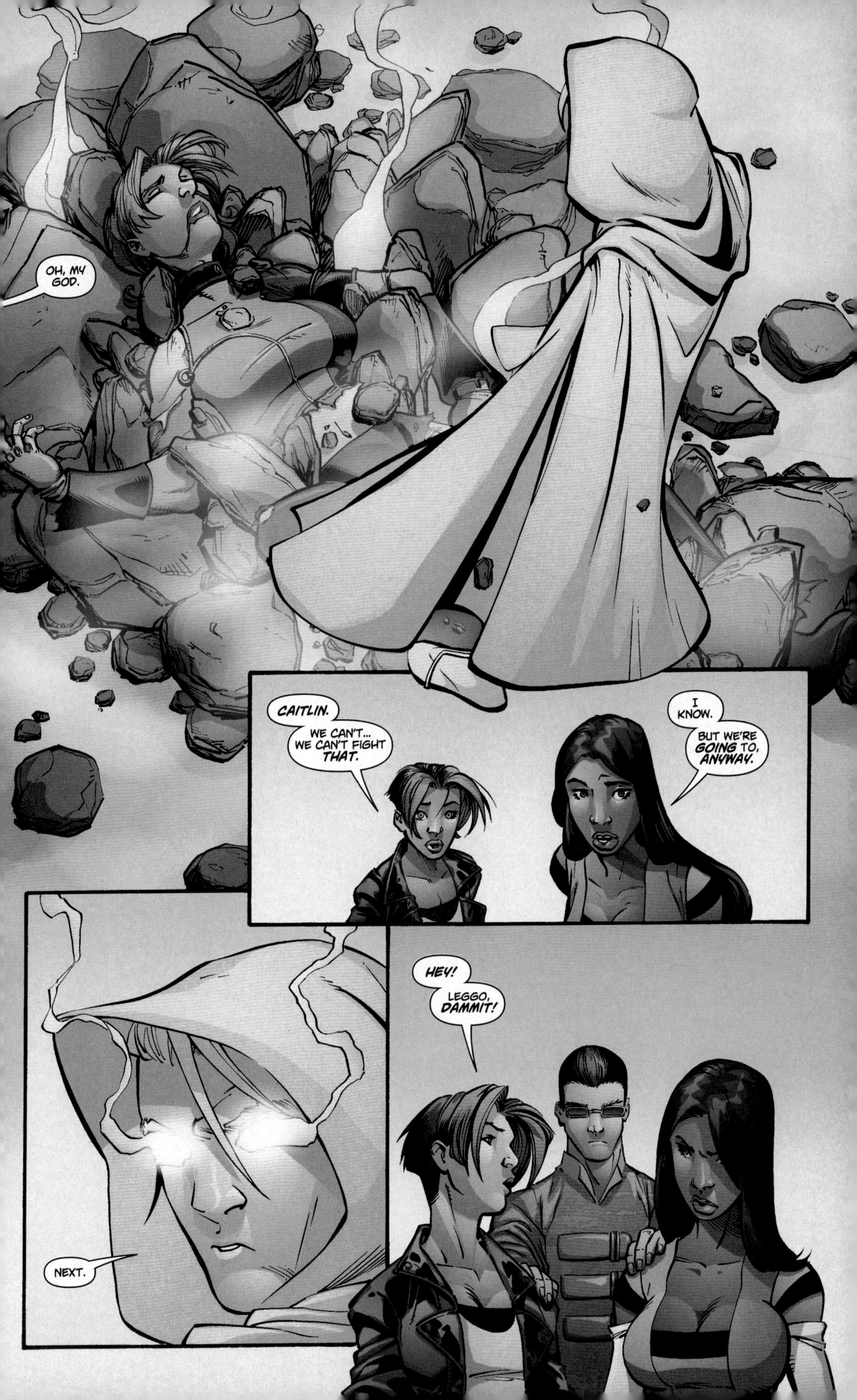
OH, MY GOD.
CAITLIN.
WE CAN'T... WE CAN'T FIGHT THAT.
I KNOW.
BUT WE'RE GOING TO, ANYWAY.
NEXT.
HEY!
LEGGO, DAMMIT!

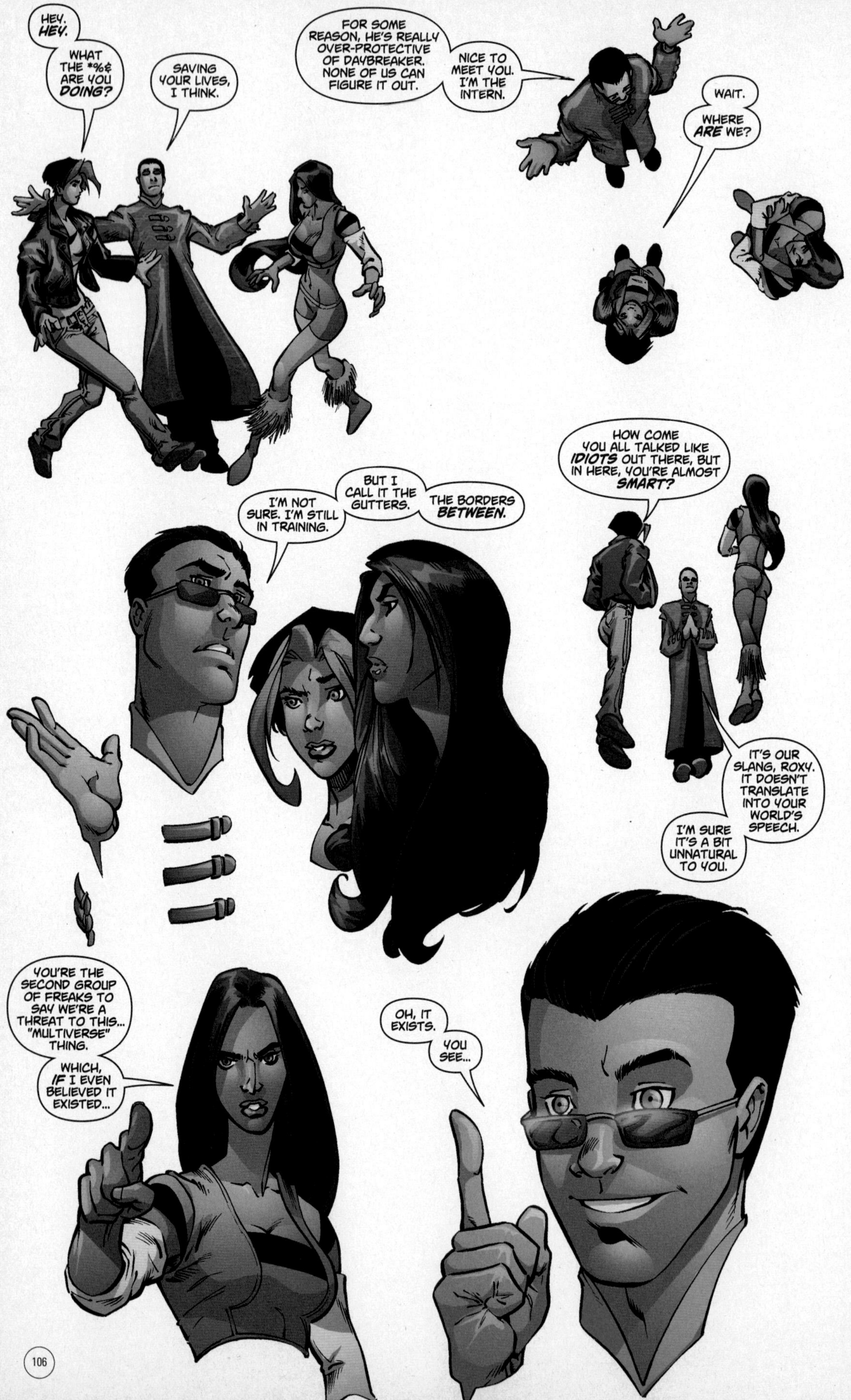
HEY. HEY.
WHAT THE *%$ ARE YOU DOING?
SAVING YOUR LIVES, I THINK.
FOR SOME REASON, HE'S REALLY OVER-PROTECTIVE OF DAYBREAKER. NONE OF US CAN FIGURE IT OUT.
NICE TO MEET YOU. I'M THE INTERN.
WAIT.
WHERE ARE WE?
I'M NOT SURE. I'M STILL IN TRAINING.
BUT I CALL IT THE GUTTERS.
THE BORDERS BETWEEN.
HOW COME YOU ALL TALKED LIKE IDIOTS OUT THERE, BUT IN HERE, YOU'RE ALMOST SMART?
IT'S OUR SLANG, ROXY. IT DOESN'T TRANSLATE INTO YOUR WORLD'S SPEECH.
I'M SURE IT'S A BIT UNNATURAL TO YOU.
YOU'RE THE SECOND GROUP OF FREAKS TO SAY WE'RE A THREAT TO THIS... "MULTIVERSE" THING.
WHICH, IF I EVEN BELIEVED IT EXISTED...
OH, IT EXISTS.
YOU SEE...

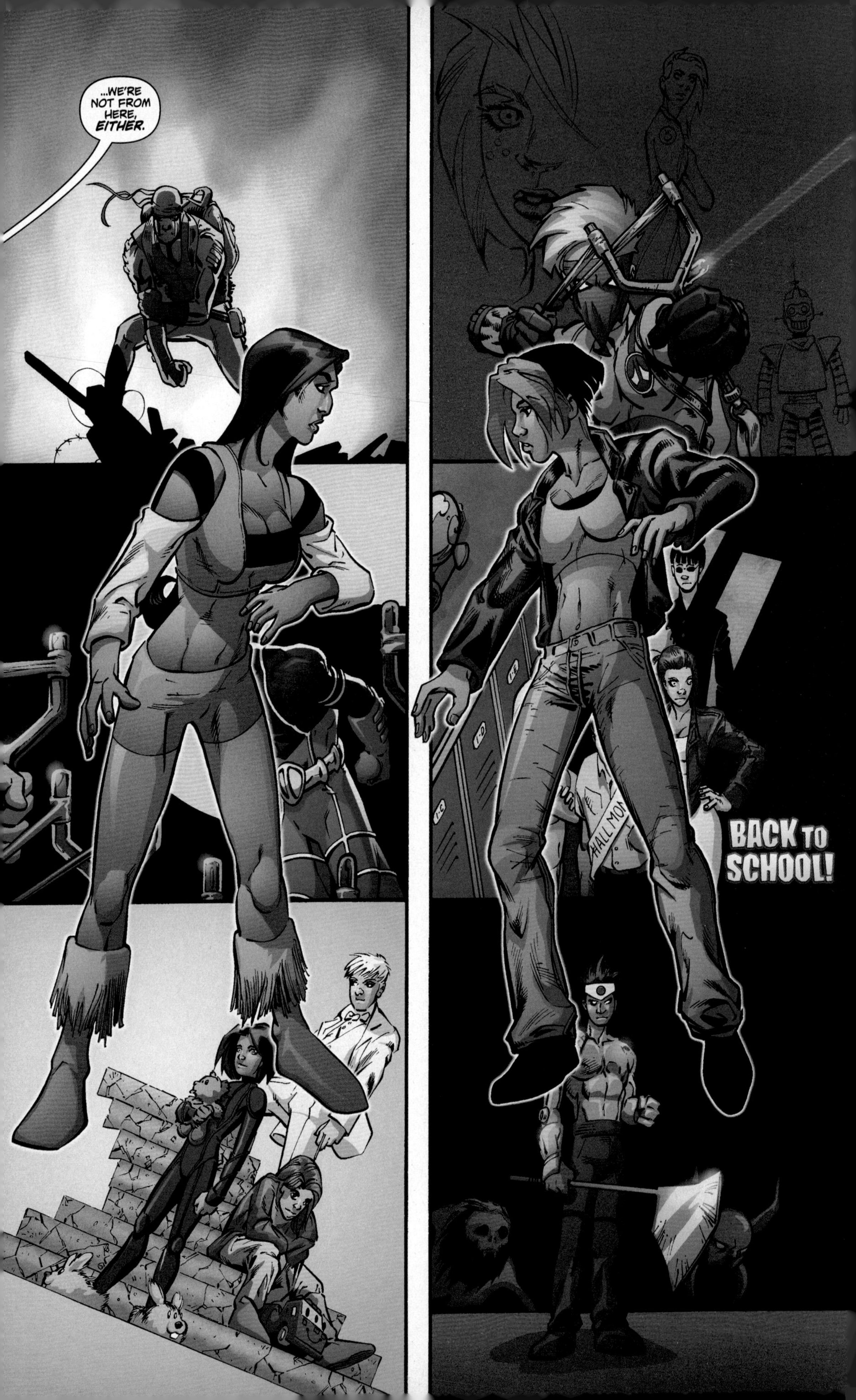
...WE'RE NOT FROM HERE, EITHER.
BACK TO SCHOOL!

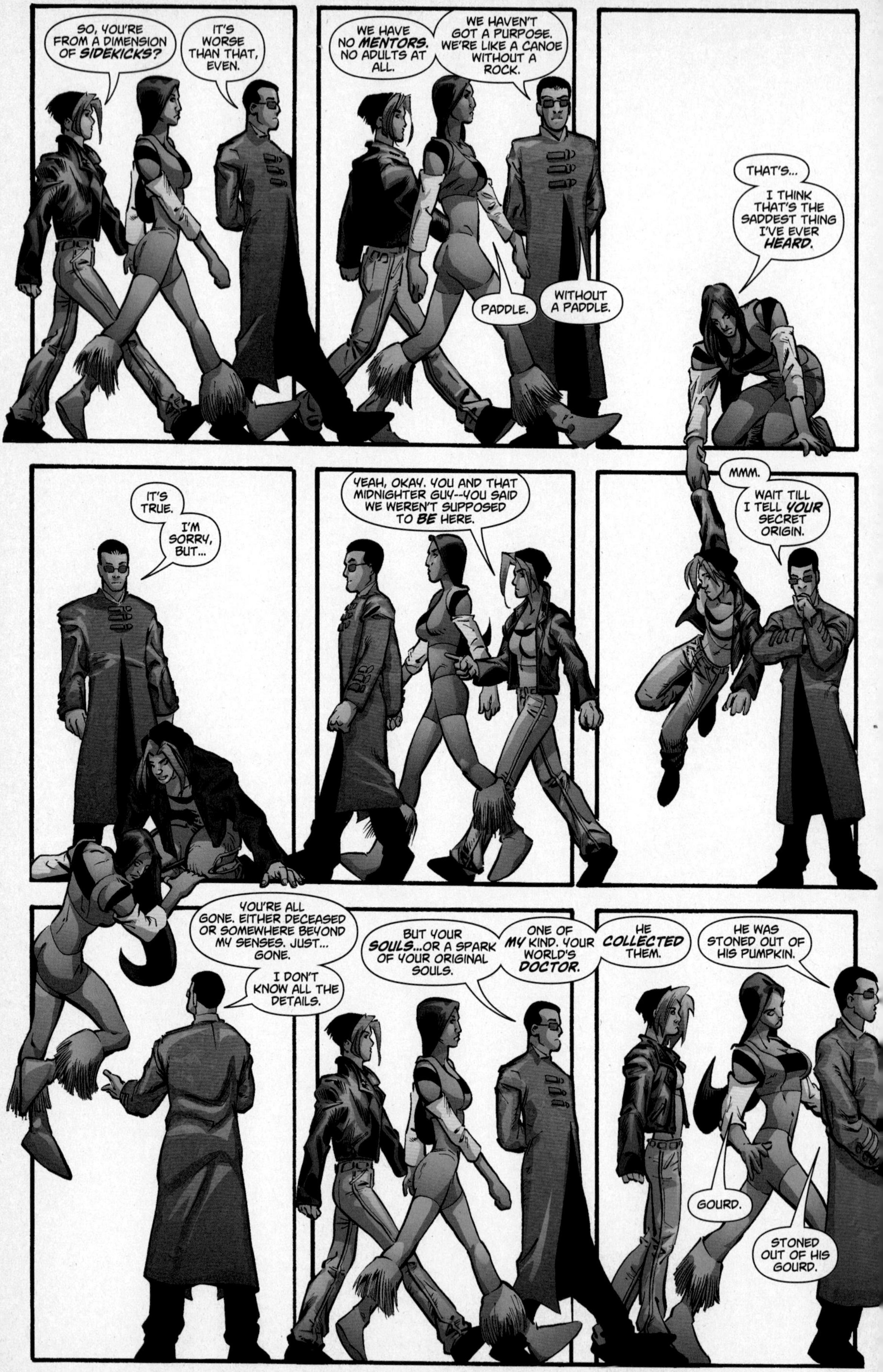
SO, YOU'RE FROM A DIMENSION OF SIDEKICKS?
IT'S WORSE THAN THAT, EVEN.
WE HAVE NO MENTORS. NO ADULTS AT ALL.
WE HAVEN'T GOT A PURPOSE. WE'RE LIKE A CANOE WITHOUT A ROCK.
PADDLE.
WITHOUT A PADDLE.
THAT'S...
I THINK THAT'S THE SADDEST THING I'VE EVER HEARD.
IT'S TRUE.
I'M SORRY, BUT...
YEAH, OKAY. YOU AND THAT MIDNIGHTER GUY--YOU SAID WE WEREN'T SUPPOSED TO BE HERE.
MMM.
WAIT TILL I TELL YOUR SECRET ORIGIN.
YOU'RE ALL GONE. EITHER DECEASED OR SOMEWHERE BEYOND MY SENSES. JUST... GONE.
I DON'T KNOW ALL THE DETAILS.
BUT YOUR SOULS...OR A SPARK OF YOUR ORIGINAL SOULS.
ONE OF MY KIND. YOUR WORLD'S DOCTOR.
HE COLLECTED THEM.
HE WAS STONED OUT OF HIS PUMPKIN.
GOURD.
STONED OUT OF HIS GOURD.

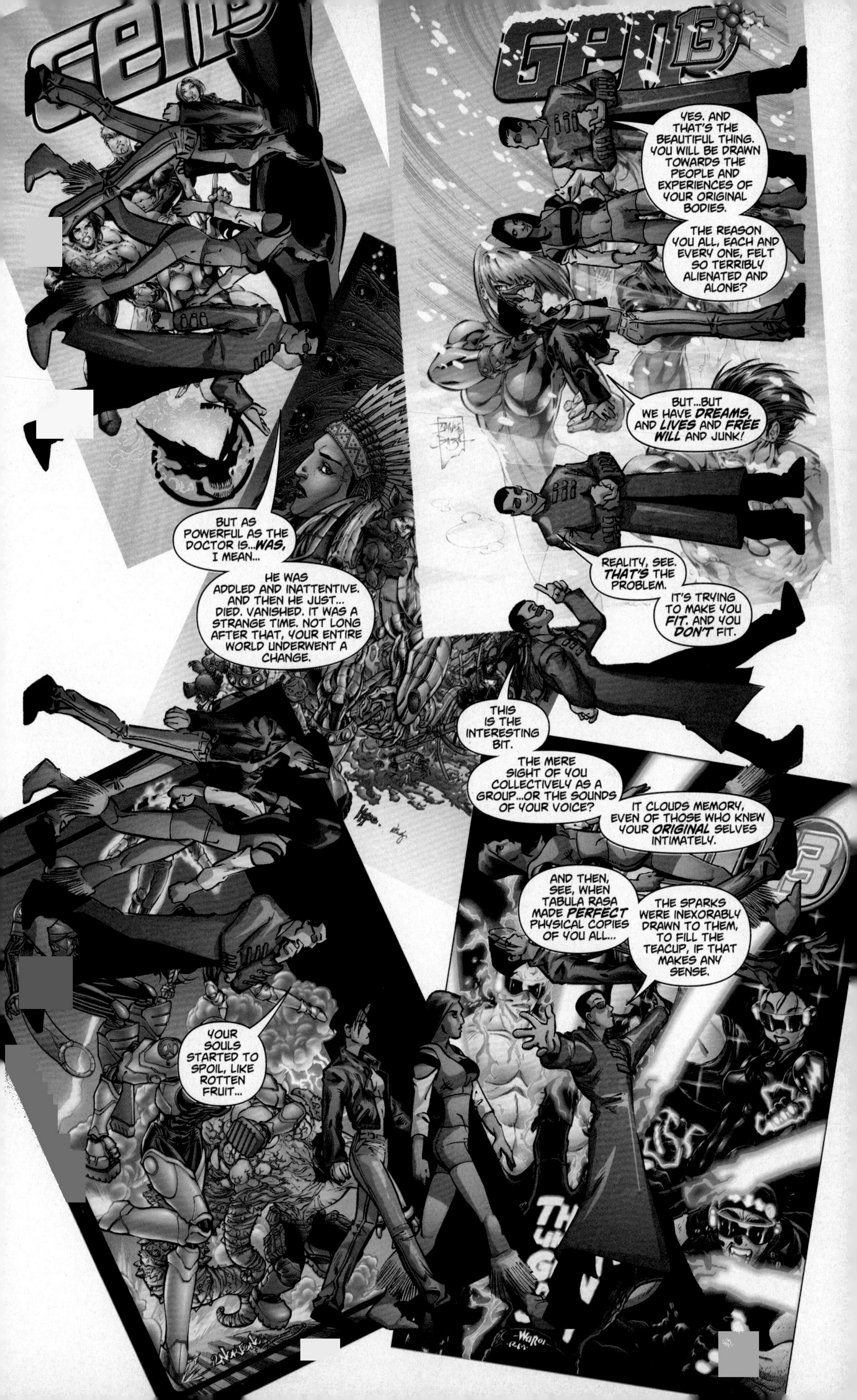
BUT AS POWERFUL AS THE DOCTOR IS...WAS, I MEAN...
HE WAS ADDLED AND INATTENTIVE. AND THEN HE JUST... DIED. VANISHED. IT WAS A STRANGE TIME. NOT LONG AFTER THAT, YOUR ENTIRE WORLD UNDERWENT A CHANGE.
YOUR SOULS STARTED TO SPOIL, LIKE ROTTEN FRUIT...
YES. AND THAT'S THE BEAUTIFUL THING. YOU WILL BE DRAWN TOWARDS THE PEOPLE AND EXPERIENCES OF YOUR ORIGINAL BODIES.
THE REASON YOU ALL, EACH AND EVERY ONE, FELT SO TERRIBLY ALIENATED AND ALONE?
BUT...BUT WE HAVE DREAMS, AND LIVES AND FREE WILL AND JUNK!
REALITY, SEE. THAT'S THE PROBLEM.
IT'S TRYING TO MAKE YOU FIT. AND YOU DON'T FIT.
THIS IS THE INTERESTING BIT.
THE MERE SIGHT OF YOU COLLECTIVELY AS A GROUP...OR THE SOUNDS OF YOUR VOICE?
IT CLOUDS MEMORY, EVEN OF THOSE WHO KNEW YOUR ORIGINAL SELVES INTIMATELY.
AND THEN, SEE, WHEN TABULA RASA MADE PERFECT PHYSICAL COPIES OF YOU ALL...
THE SPARKS WERE INEXORABLY DRAWN TO THEM, TO FILL THE TEACUP, IF THAT MAKES ANY SENSE.

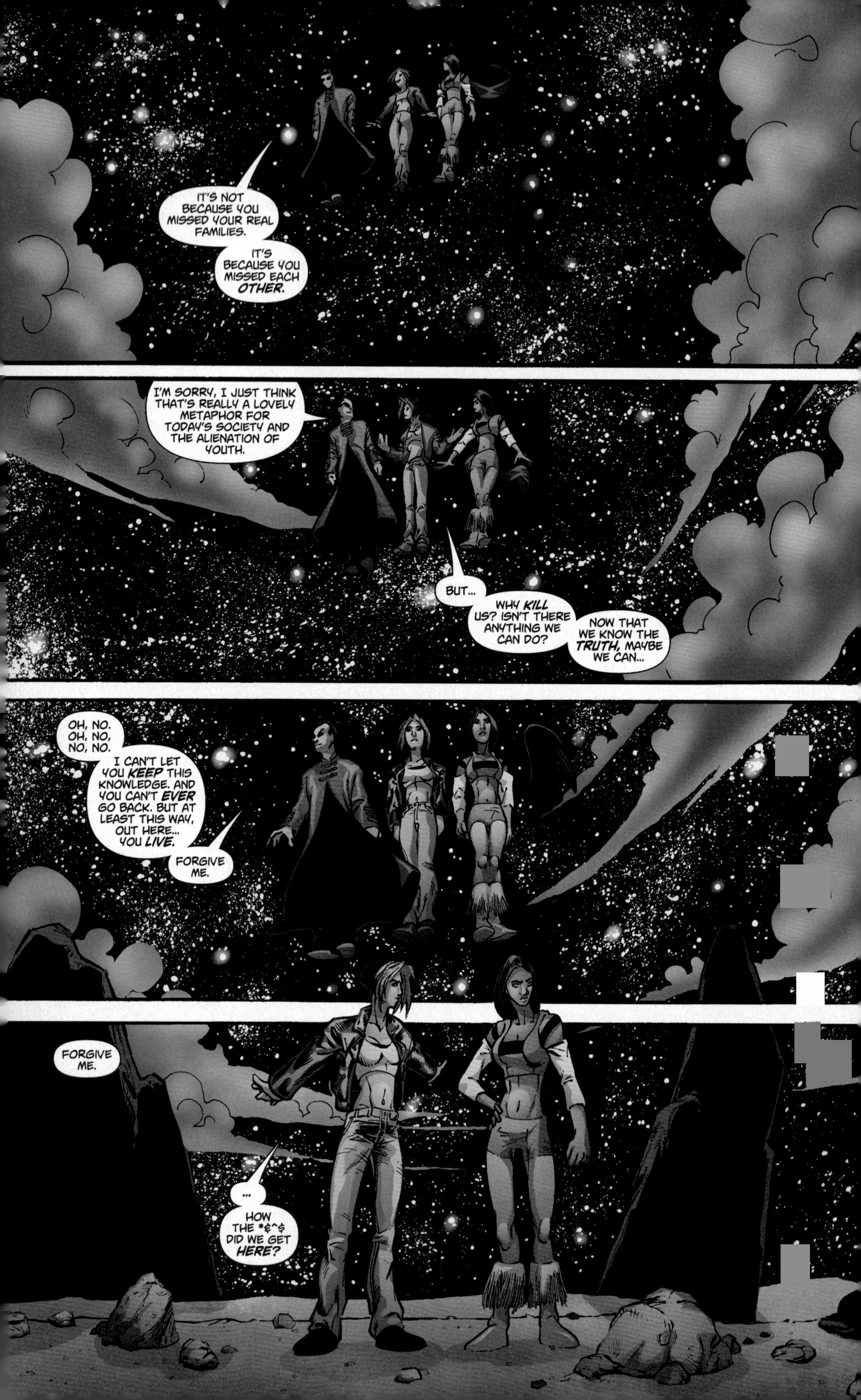
IT'S NOT BECAUSE YOU MISSED YOUR REAL FAMILIES.
IT'S BECAUSE YOU MISSED EACH OTHER.
I'M SORRY, I JUST THINK THAT'S REALLY A LOVELY METAPHOR FOR TODAY'S SOCIETY AND THE ALIENATION OF YOUTH.
BUT...
WHY KILL US? ISN'T THERE ANYTHING WE CAN DO?
NOW THAT WE KNOW THE TRUTH, MAYBE WE CAN...
OH, NO. OH, NO, NO, NO.
I CAN'T LET YOU KEEP THIS KNOWLEDGE. AND YOU CAN'T EVER GO BACK. BUT AT LEAST THIS WAY, OUT HERE... YOU LIVE.
FORGIVE ME.
FORGIVE ME.
...
HOW THE *$^$ DID WE GET HERE?

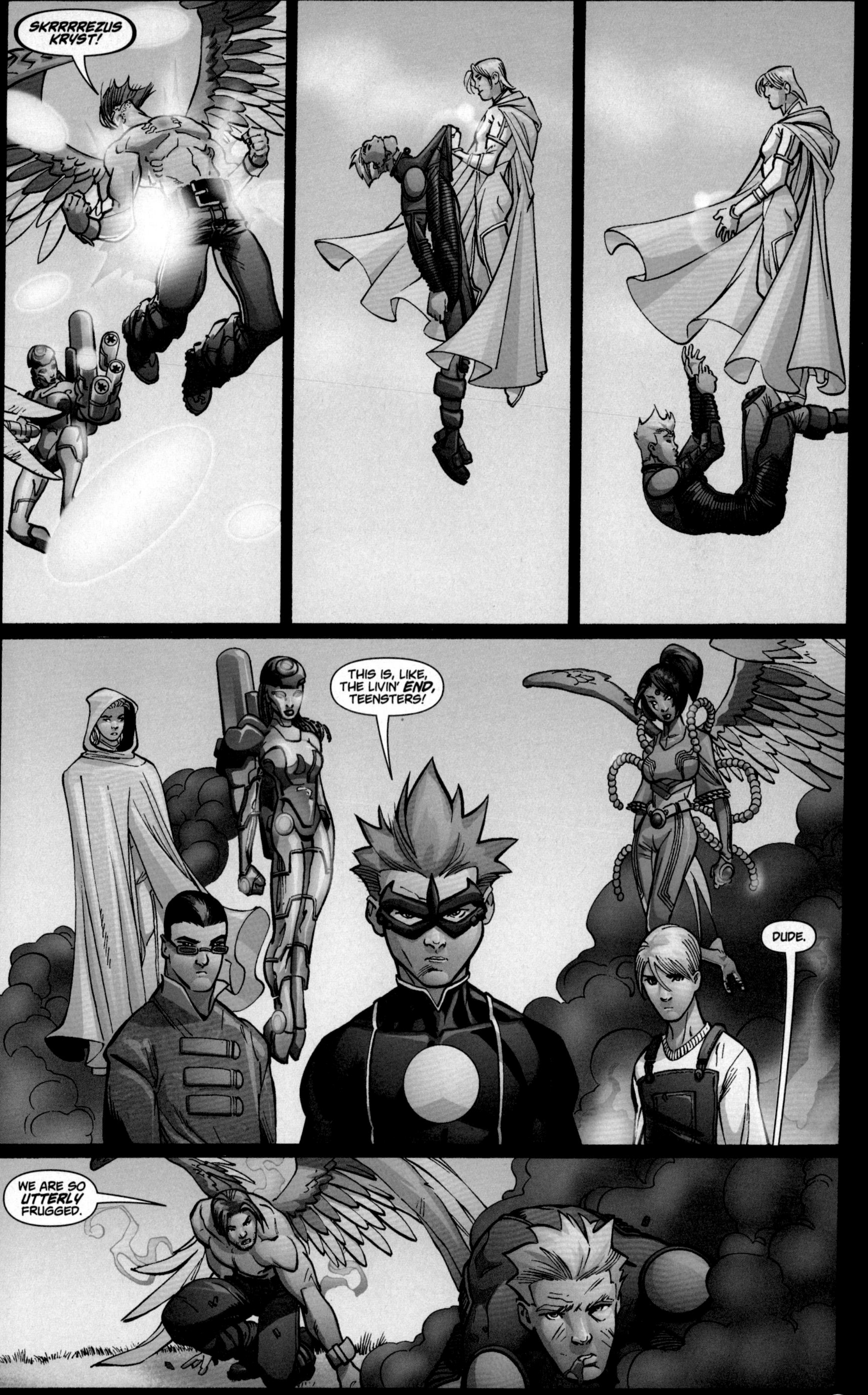
SKRRRREZUS KRYST!
THIS IS, LIKE, THE LIVIN' END, TEENSTERS!
DUDE.
WE ARE SO UTTERLY FRUGGED.

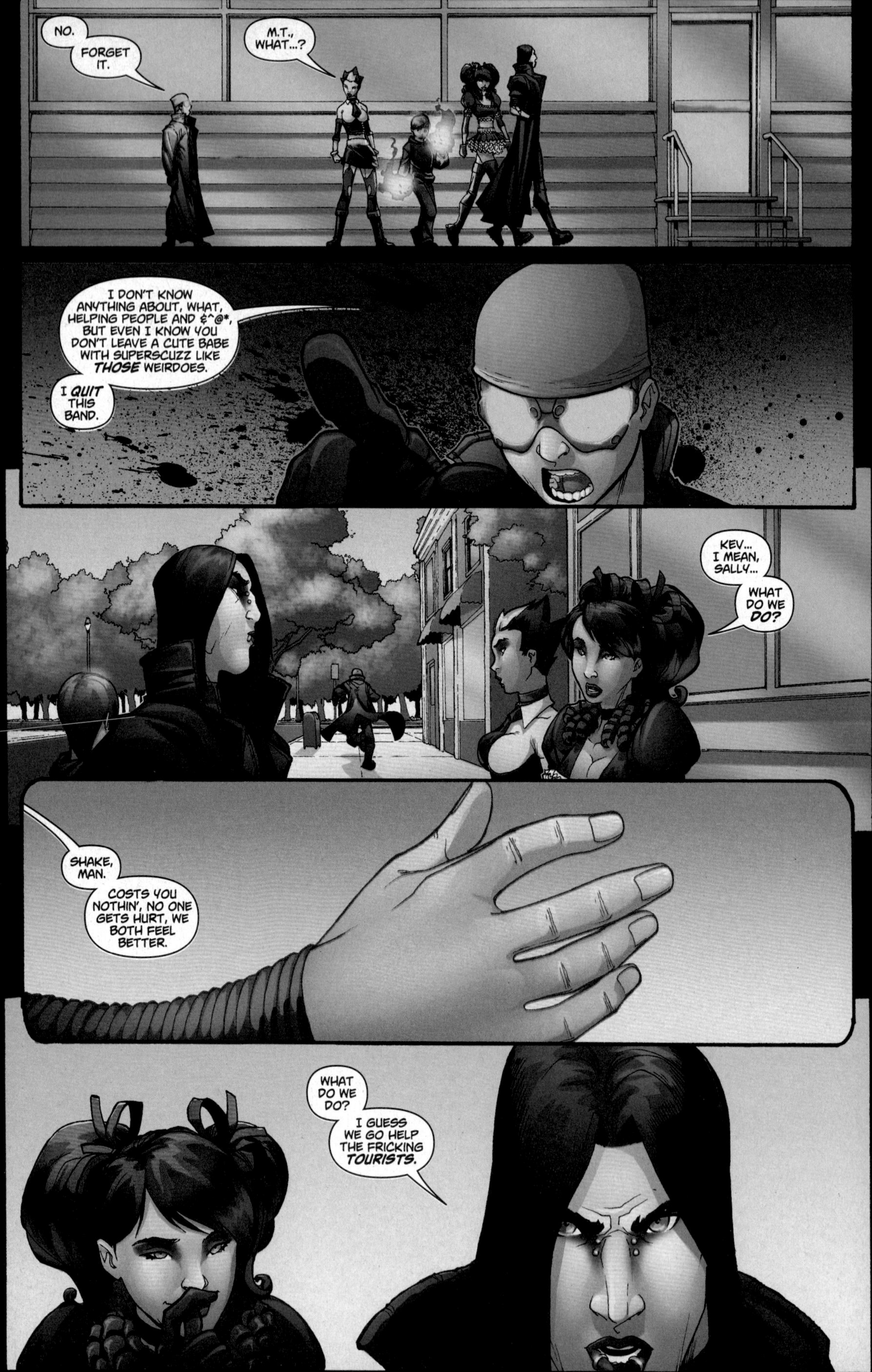
NO.
FORGET IT.
M.T., WHAT...?
I DON'T KNOW ANYTHING ABOUT, WHAT, HELPING PEOPLE AND &^@*, BUT EVEN I KNOW YOU DON'T LEAVE A CUTE BABE WITH SUPERSCUZZ LIKE THOSE WEIRDOES.
I QUIT THIS BAND.
KEV... I MEAN, SALLY...
WHAT DO WE DO?
SHAKE, MAN.
COSTS YOU NOTHIN', NO ONE GETS HURT, WE BOTH FEEL BETTER.
WHAT DO WE DO?
I GUESS WE GO HELP THE FRICKING TOURISTS.

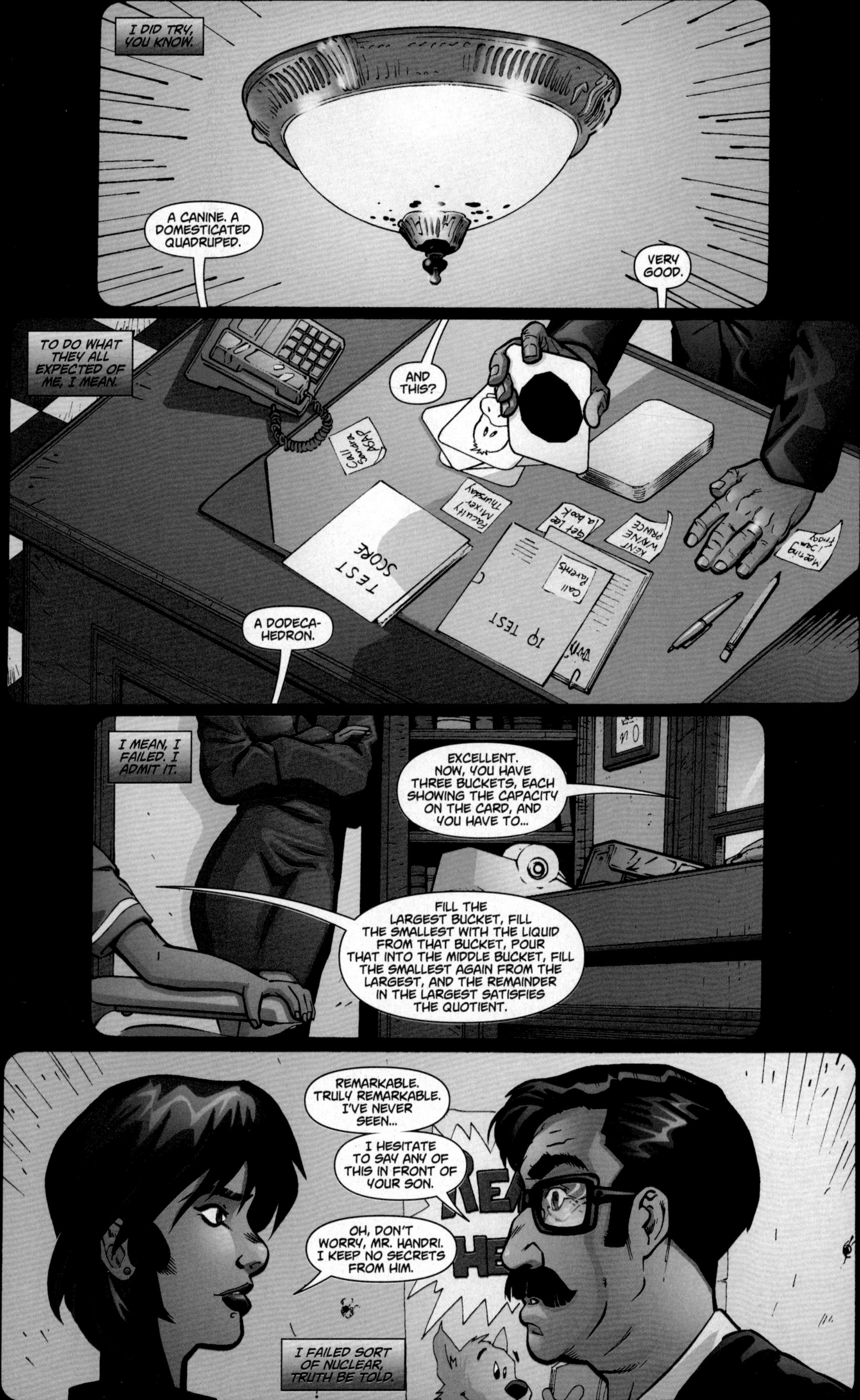
I DID TRY, YOU KNOW.
A CANINE. A DOMESTICATED QUADRUPED.
VERY GOOD.
TO DO WHAT THEY ALL EXPECTED OF ME, I MEAN.
AND THIS?
TEST SCORE
IQ TEST
Call Parents
KENT WAYNE PRINCE
Faculty Mixer Thursday
A DODECA-HEDRON.
I MEAN, I FAILED. I ADMIT IT.
EXCELLENT. NOW, YOU HAVE THREE BUCKETS, EACH SHOWING THE CAPACITY ON THE CARD, AND YOU HAVE TO...
FILL THE LARGEST BUCKET, FILL THE SMALLEST WITH THE LIQUID FROM THAT BUCKET, POUR THAT INTO THE MIDDLE BUCKET, FILL THE SMALLEST AGAIN FROM THE LARGEST, AND THE REMAINDER IN THE LARGEST SATISFIES THE QUOTIENT.
REMARKABLE. TRULY REMARKABLE. I'VE NEVER SEEN...
I HESITATE TO SAY ANY OF THIS IN FRONT OF YOUR SON.
OH, DON'T WORRY, MR. HANDRI. I KEEP NO SECRETS FROM HIM.
I FAILED SORT OF NUCLEAR, TRUTH BE TOLD.

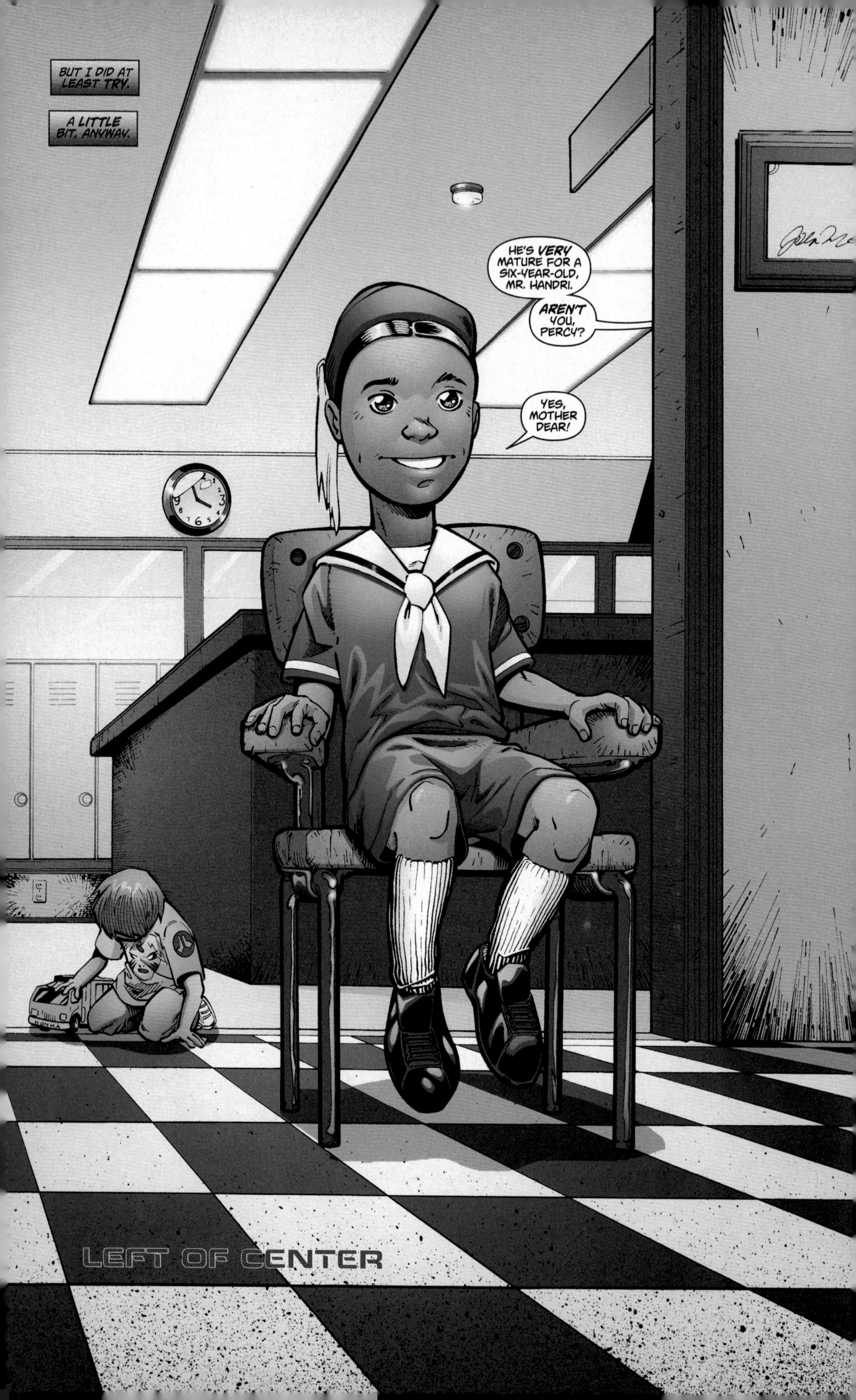

BUT I DID AT LEAST TRY.
A LITTLE BIT, ANYWAY.
HE'S VERY MATURE FOR A SIX-YEAR-OLD, MR. HANDRI.
AREN'T YOU, PERCY?
YES, MOTHER DEAR!
HONKA
LEFT OF CENTER

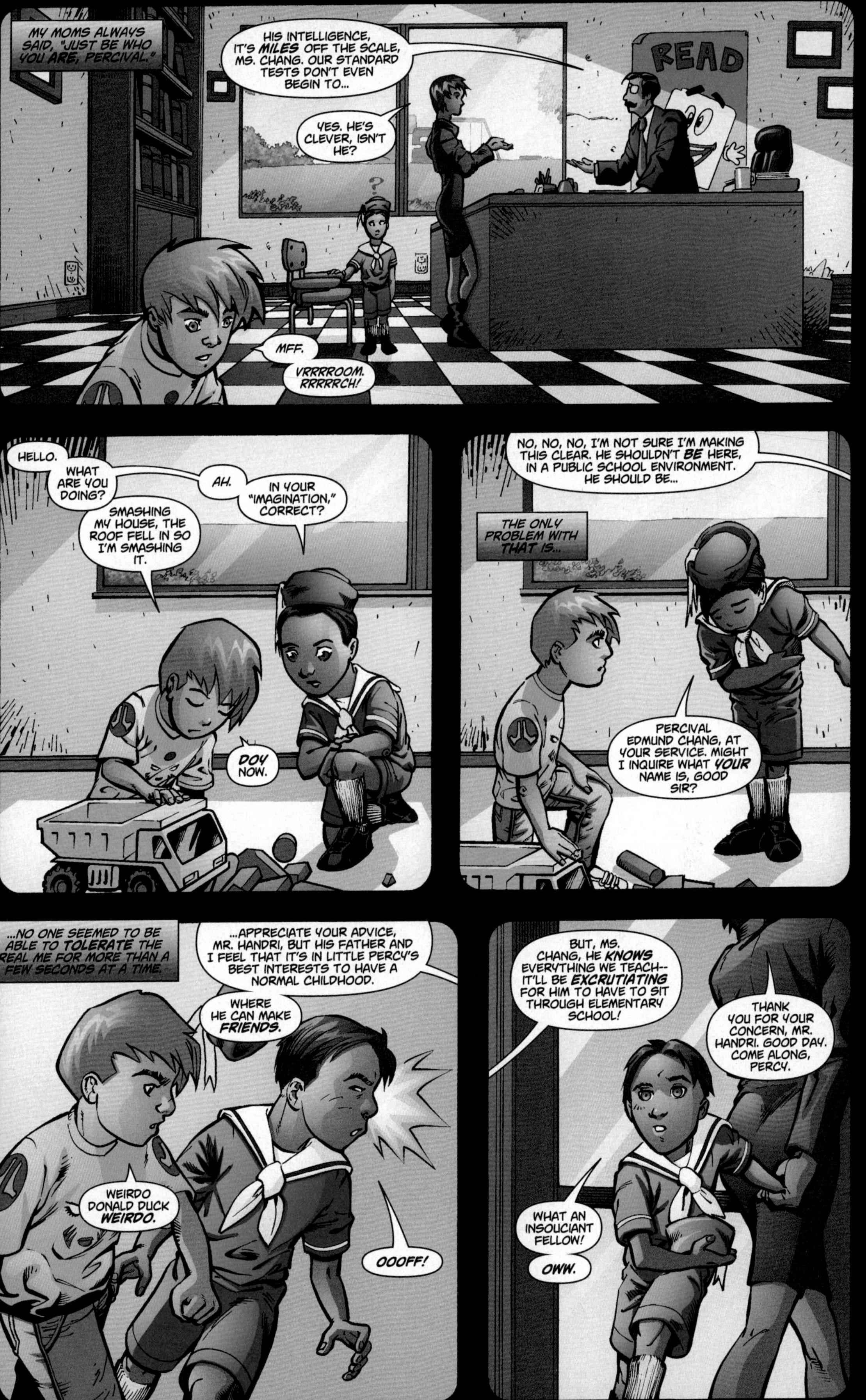

MY MOMS ALWAYS SAID, "JUST BE WHO YOU ARE, PERCIVAL."
HIS INTELLIGENCE, IT'S MILES OFF THE SCALE, MS. CHANG. OUR STANDARD TESTS DON'T EVEN BEGIN TO...
YES. HE'S CLEVER, ISN'T HE?
READ
?
MFF.
VRRRROOM. RRRRRCH!
HELLO.
WHAT ARE YOU DOING?
AH.
IN YOUR "IMAGINATION," CORRECT?
SMASHING MY HOUSE, THE ROOF FELL IN SO I'M SMASHING IT.
DOY NOW.
NO, NO, NO, I'M NOT SURE I'M MAKING THIS CLEAR. HE SHOULDN'T BE HERE, IN A PUBLIC SCHOOL ENVIRONMENT. HE SHOULD BE...
THE ONLY PROBLEM WITH THAT IS...
PERCIVAL EDMUND CHANG, AT YOUR SERVICE. MIGHT I INQUIRE WHAT YOUR NAME IS, GOOD SIR?
...NO ONE SEEMED TO BE ABLE TO TOLERATE THE REAL ME FOR MORE THAN A FEW SECONDS AT A TIME.
...APPRECIATE YOUR ADVICE, MR. HANDRI, BUT HIS FATHER AND I FEEL THAT IT'S IN LITTLE PERCY'S BEST INTERESTS TO HAVE A NORMAL CHILDHOOD.
WHERE HE CAN MAKE FRIENDS.
WEIRDO DONALD DUCK WEIRDO.
OOOFF!
BUT, MS. CHANG, HE KNOWS EVERYTHING WE TEACH--IT'LL BE EXCRUTIATING FOR HIM TO HAVE TO SIT THROUGH ELEMENTARY SCHOOL!
THANK YOU FOR YOUR CONCERN, MR. HANDRI. GOOD DAY. COME ALONG, PERCY.
WHAT AN INSOUCIANT FELLOW!
OWW.

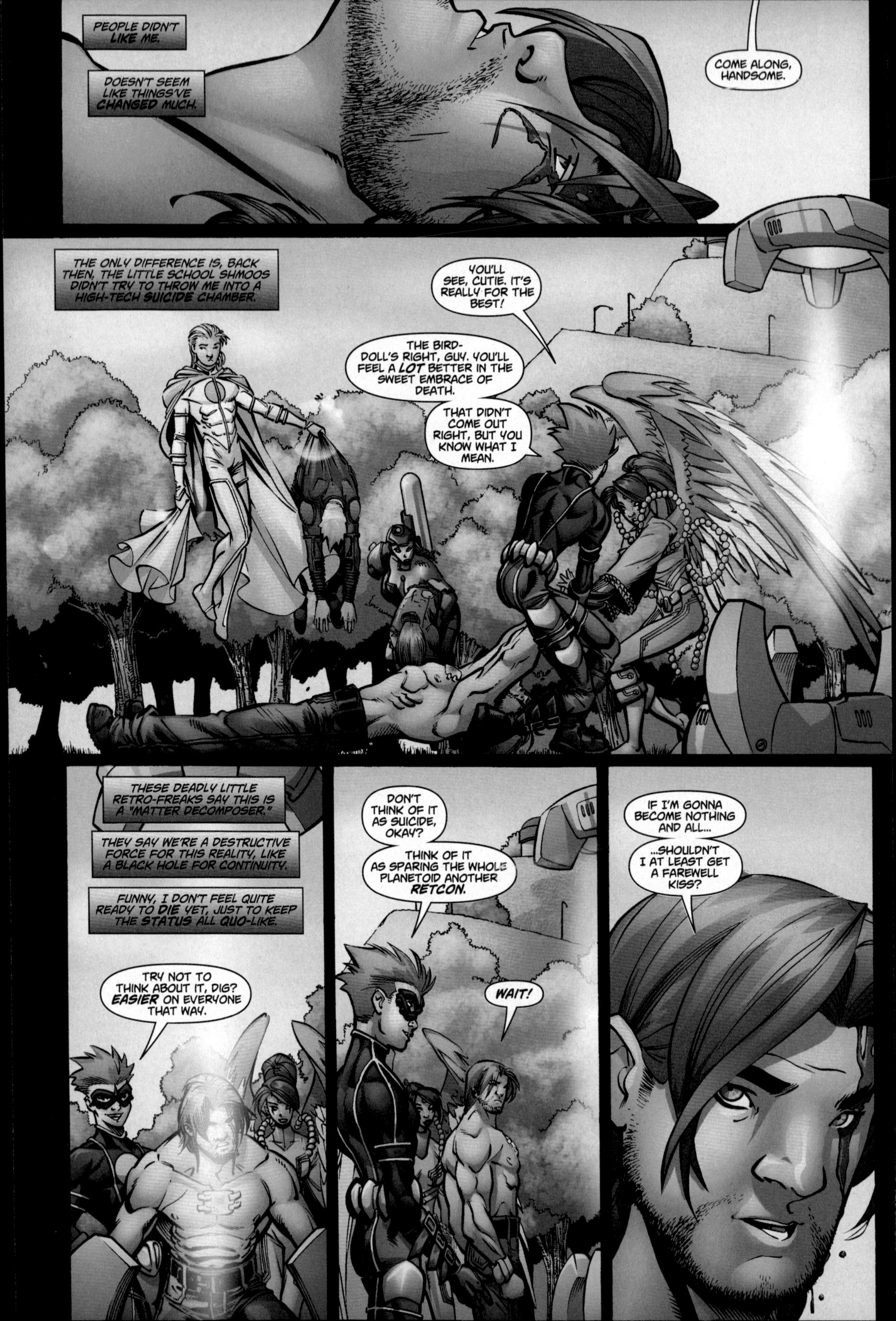
PEOPLE DIDN'T LIKE ME.
DOESN'T SEEM LIKE THINGS'VE CHANGED MUCH.
COME ALONG, HANDSOME.
THE ONLY DIFFERENCE IS, BACK THEN, THE LITTLE SCHOOL SHMOOS DIDN'T TRY TO THROW ME INTO A HIGH-TECH SUICIDE CHAMBER.
YOU'LL SEE, CUTIE. IT'S REALLY FOR THE BEST!
THE BIRD-DOLL'S RIGHT, GUY. YOU'LL FEEL A LOT BETTER IN THE SWEET EMBRACE OF DEATH.
THAT DIDN'T COME OUT RIGHT, BUT YOU KNOW WHAT I MEAN.
THESE DEADLY LITTLE RETRO-FREAKS SAY THIS IS A "MATTER DECOMPOSER."
THEY SAY WE'RE A DESTRUCTIVE FORCE FOR THIS REALITY, LIKE A BLACK HOLE FOR CONTINUITY.
FUNNY, I DON'T FEEL QUITE READY TO DIE YET, JUST TO KEEP THE STATUS ALL QUO-LIKE.
TRY NOT TO THINK ABOUT IT, DIG? EASIER ON EVERYONE THAT WAY.
DON'T THINK OF IT AS SUICIDE, OKAY?
THINK OF IT AS SPARING THE WHOLE PLANETOID ANOTHER RETCON.
WAIT!
IF I'M GONNA BECOME NOTHING AND ALL...
...SHOULDN'T I AT LEAST GET A FAREWELL KISS?

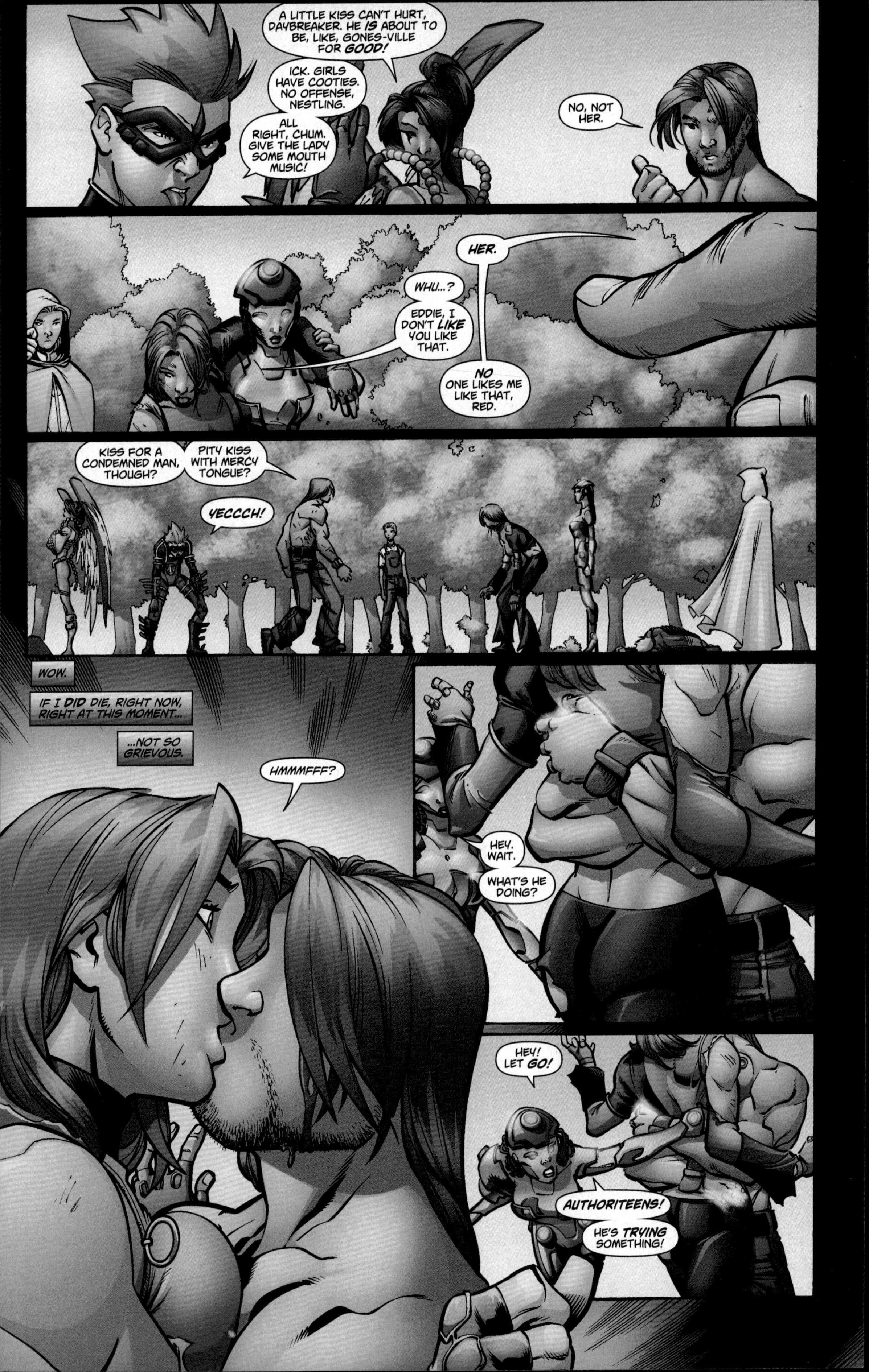
A LITTLE KISS CAN'T HURT, DAYBREAKER. HE IS ABOUT TO BE, LIKE, GONES-VILLE FOR GOOD!
ICK. GIRLS HAVE COOTIES. NO OFFENSE, NESTLING.
ALL RIGHT, CHUM. GIVE THE LADY SOME MOUTH MUSIC!
NO, NOT HER.
HER.
WHU...?
EDDIE, I DON'T LIKE YOU LIKE THAT.
NO ONE LIKES ME LIKE THAT, RED.
KISS FOR A CONDEMNED MAN, THOUGH?
PITY KISS WITH MERCY TONGUE?
YECCCH!
WOW.
IF I DID DIE, RIGHT NOW, RIGHT AT THIS MOMENT...
...NOT SO GRIEVOUS.
HMMMFFF?
HEY. WAIT.
WHAT'S HE DOING?
HEY! LET GO!
AUTHORITEENS!
HE'S TRYING SOMETHING!

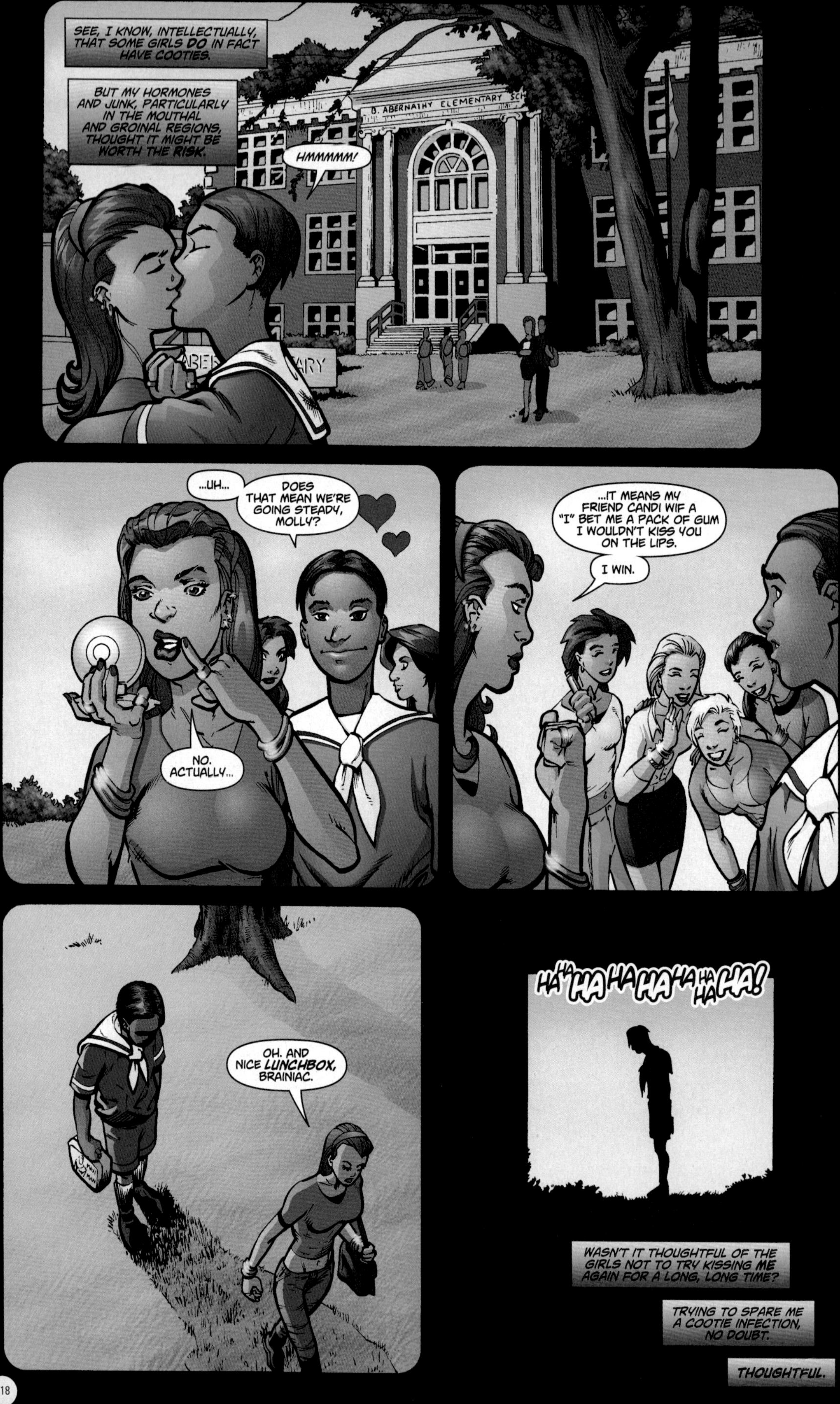

SEE, I KNOW, INTELLECTUALLY, THAT SOME GIRLS DO IN FACT HAVE COOTIES.
BUT MY HORMONES AND JUNK, PARTICULARLY IN THE MOUTHAL AND GROINAL REGIONS, THOUGHT IT MIGHT BE WORTH THE RISK.
B. ABERNATHY ELEMENTARY SCH
HMMMMM!
...UH...
DOES THAT MEAN WE'RE GOING STEADY, MOLLY?
NO. ACTUALLY...
...IT MEANS MY FRIEND CANDI WIF A "I" BET ME A PACK OF GUM I WOULDN'T KISS YOU ON THE LIPS.
I WIN.
OH. AND NICE LUNCHBOX, BRAINIAC.
HA HA HA HA HA HA HA HA HA HA!
WASN'T IT THOUGHTFUL OF THE GIRLS NOT TO TRY KISSING ME AGAIN FOR A LONG, LONG TIME?
TRYING TO SPARE ME A COOTIE INFECTION, NO DOUBT.
THOUGHTFUL.

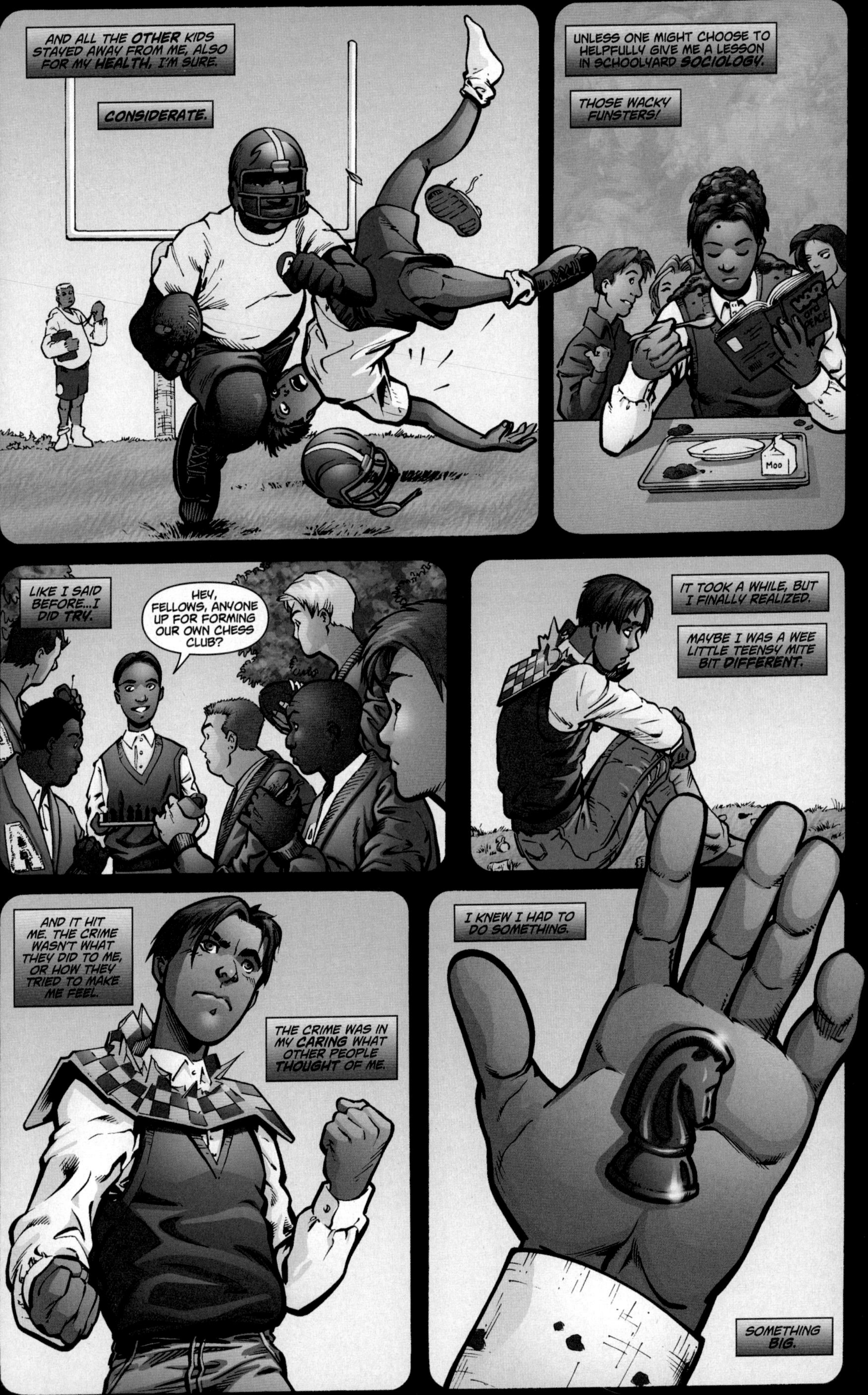
AND ALL THE OTHER KIDS STAYED AWAY FROM ME, ALSO FOR MY HEALTH, I'M SURE.
CONSIDERATE.
UNLESS ONE MIGHT CHOOSE TO HELPFULLY GIVE ME A LESSON IN SCHOOLYARD SOCIOLOGY.
THOSE WACKY FUNSTERS!
WAR and PEACE
MOO
LIKE I SAID BEFORE...I DID TRY.
HEY, FELLOWS, ANYONE UP FOR FORMING OUR OWN CHESS CLUB?
IT TOOK A WHILE, BUT I FINALLY REALIZED.
MAYBE I WAS A WEE LITTLE TEENSY MITE BIT DIFFERENT.
AND IT HIT ME. THE CRIME WASN'T WHAT THEY DID TO ME, OR HOW THEY TRIED TO MAKE ME FEEL.
THE CRIME WAS IN MY CARING WHAT OTHER PEOPLE THOUGHT OF ME.
I KNEW I HAD TO DO SOMETHING.
SOMETHING BIG.

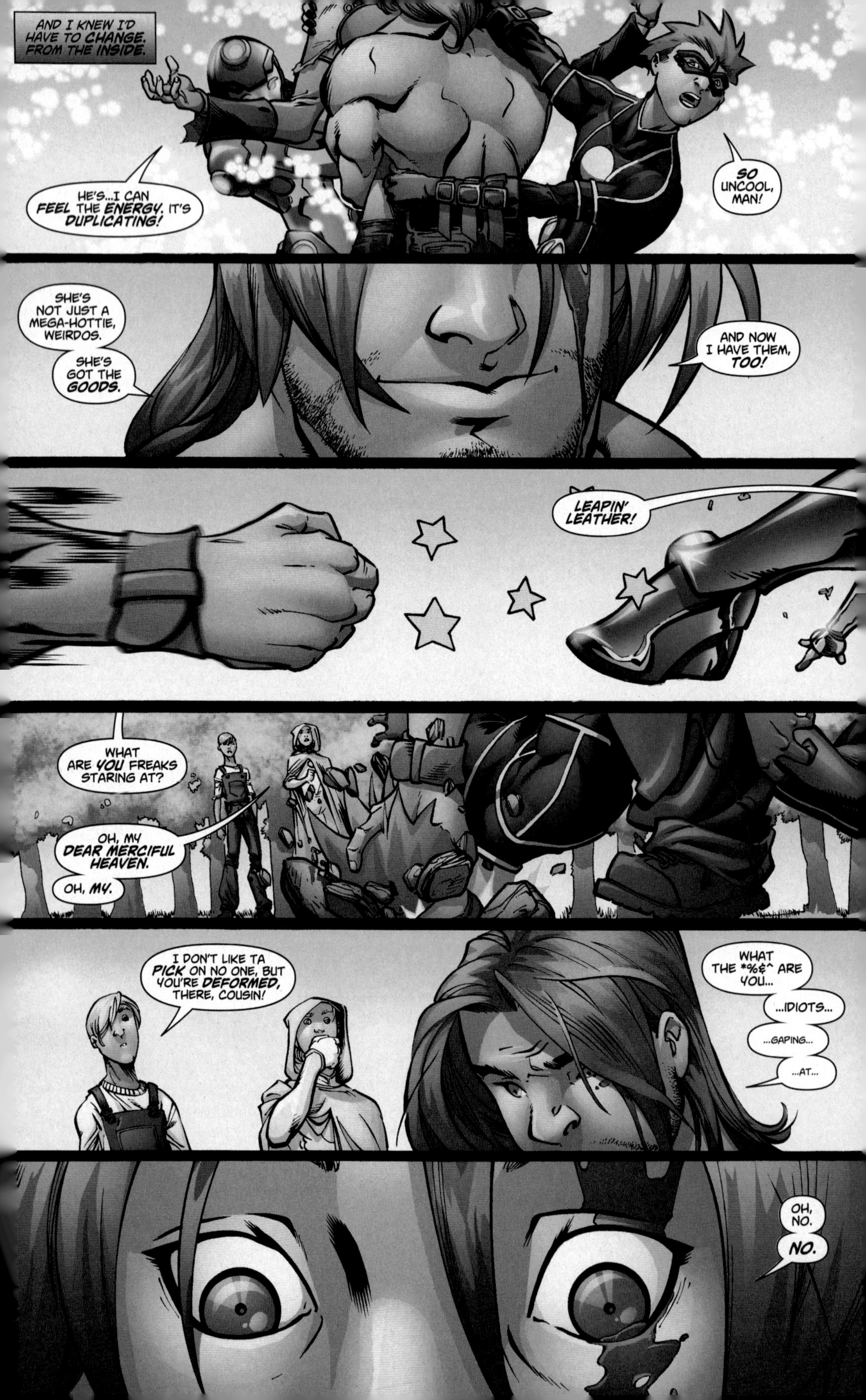
AND I KNEW I'D HAVE TO CHANGE. FROM THE INSIDE.
HE'S...I CAN FEEL THE ENERGY. IT'S DUPLICATING!
SO UNCOOL, MAN!
SHE'S NOT JUST A MEGA-HOTTIE, WEIRDOS.
SHE'S GOT THE GOODS.
AND NOW I HAVE THEM, TOO!
LEAPIN' LEATHER!
WHAT ARE YOU FREAKS STARING AT?
OH, MY DEAR MERCIFUL HEAVEN.
OH, MY.
I DON'T LIKE TA PICK ON NO ONE, BUT YOU'RE DEFORMED, THERE, COUSIN!
WHAT THE *%$^ ARE YOU...
...IDIOTS...
...GAPING...
...AT...
OH, NO.
NO.

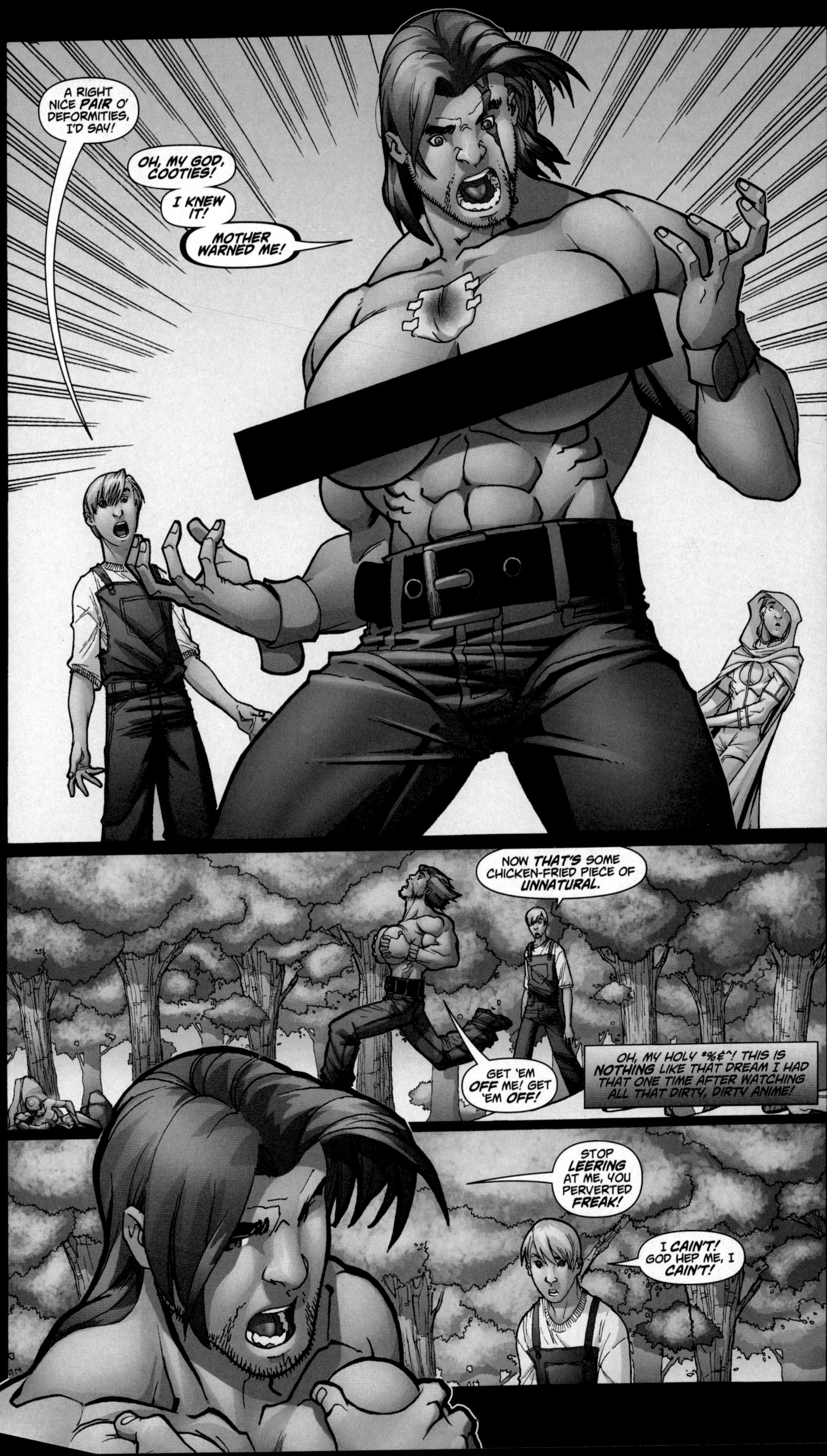
A RIGHT NICE PAIR O' DEFORMITIES, I'D SAY!
OH, MY GOD, COOTIES!
I KNEW IT!
MOTHER WARNED ME!
NOW THAT'S SOME CHICKEN-FRIED PIECE OF UNNATURAL.
GET 'EM OFF ME! GET 'EM OFF!
OH, MY HOLY *%&^! THIS IS NOTHING LIKE THAT DREAM I HAD THAT ONE TIME AFTER WATCHING ALL THAT DIRTY, DIRTY ANIME!
STOP LEERING AT ME, YOU PERVERTED FREAK!
I CAIN'T! GOD HEP ME, I CAIN'T!

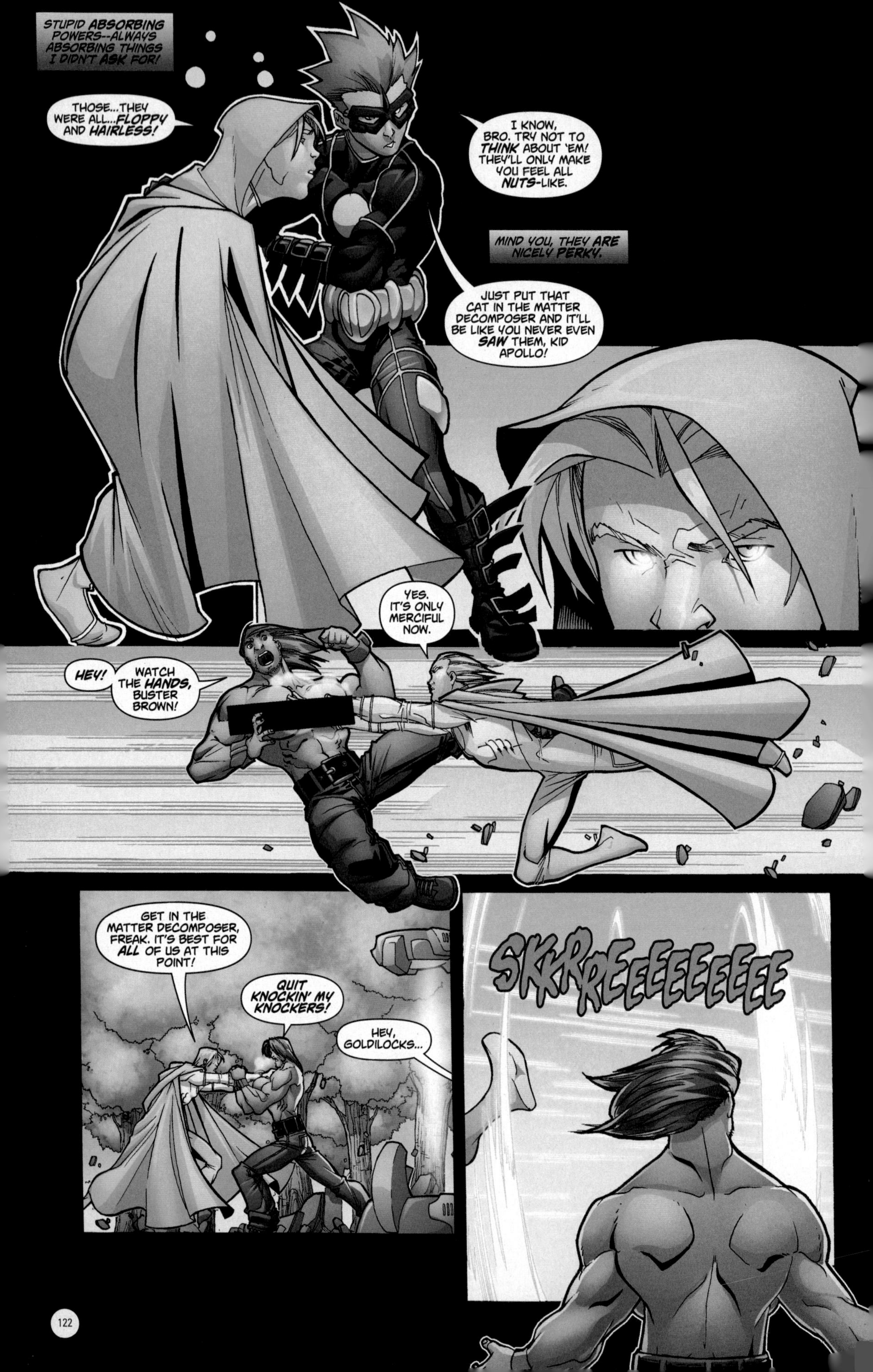
STUPID ABSORBING POWERS--ALWAYS ABSORBING THINGS I DIDN'T ASK FOR!
THOSE...THEY WERE ALL...FLOPPY AND HAIRLESS!
I KNOW, BRO. TRY NOT TO THINK ABOUT 'EM! THEY'LL ONLY MAKE YOU FEEL ALL NUTS-LIKE.
MIND YOU, THEY ARE NICELY PERKY.
JUST PUT THAT CAT IN THE MATTER DECOMPOSER AND IT'LL BE LIKE YOU NEVER EVEN SAW THEM, KID APOLLO!
YES. IT'S ONLY MERCIFUL NOW.
HEY!
WATCH THE HANDS, BUSTER BROWN!
GET IN THE MATTER DECOMPOSER, FREAK. IT'S BEST FOR ALL OF US AT THIS POINT!
QUIT KNOCKIN' MY KNOCKERS!
HEY, GOLDILOCKS...
SKKRREEEEEEEEEE

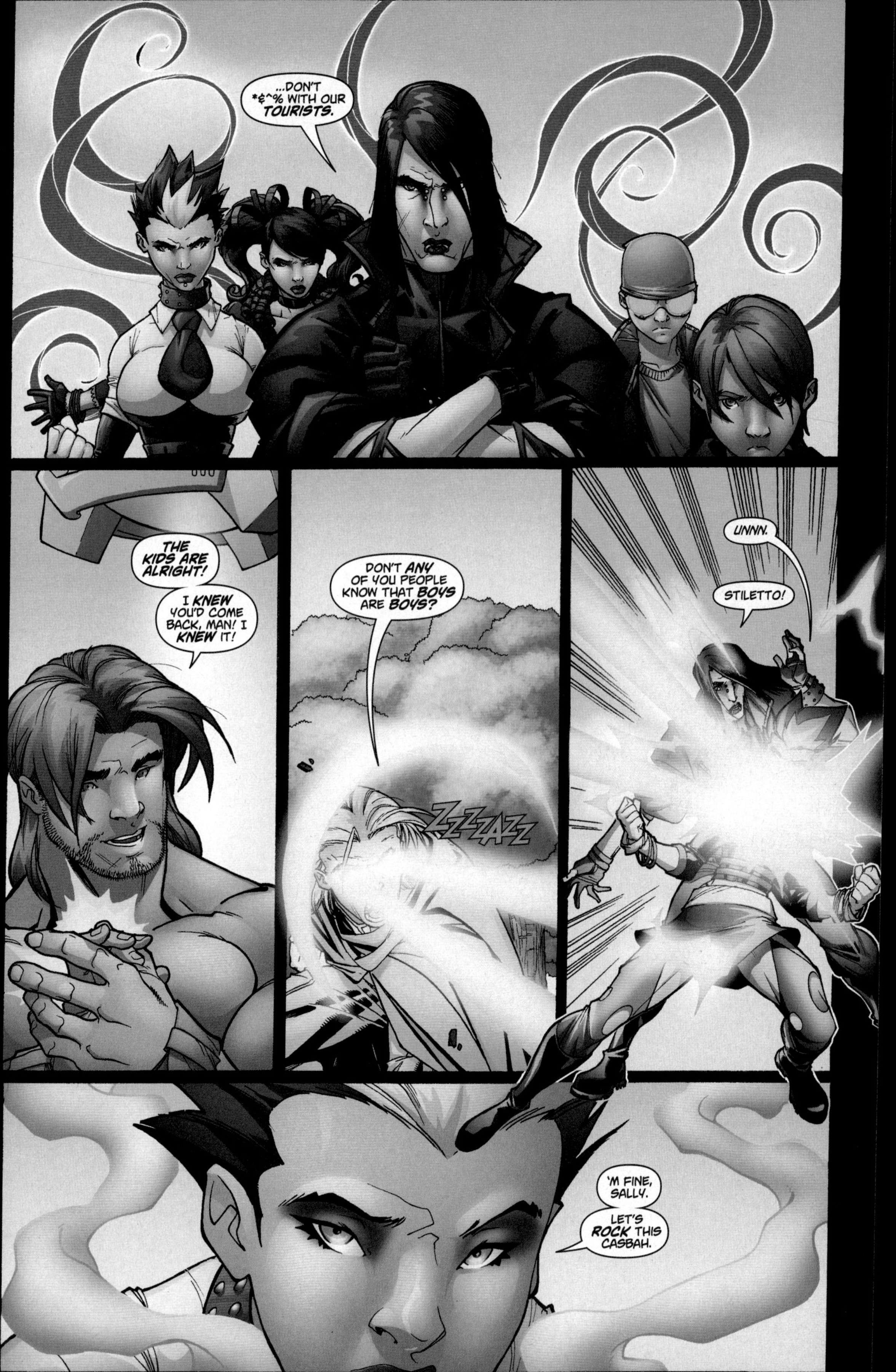
...DON'T *¢^% WITH OUR TOURISTS.
THE KIDS ARE ALRIGHT!
I KNEW YOU'D COME BACK, MAN! I KNEW IT!
DON'T ANY OF YOU PEOPLE KNOW THAT BOYS ARE BOYS?
ZZZZAZZ
UNNN.
STILETTO!
'M FINE, SALLY.
LET'S ROCK THIS CASBAH.

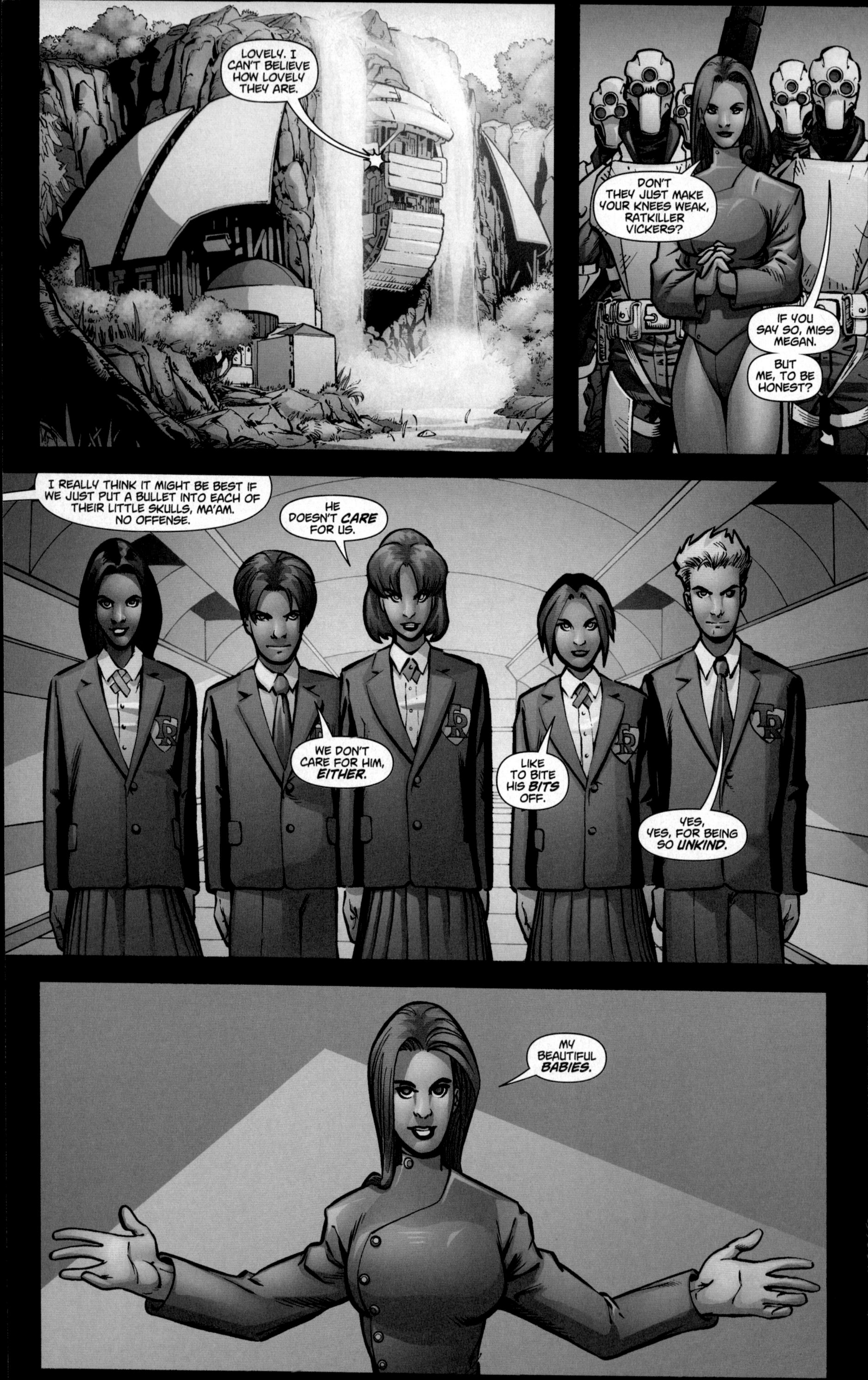
LOVELY. I CAN'T BELIEVE HOW LOVELY THEY ARE.
DON'T THEY JUST MAKE YOUR KNEES WEAK, RATKILLER VICKERS?
IF YOU SAY SO, MISS MEGAN.
BUT ME, TO BE HONEST?
I REALLY THINK IT MIGHT BE BEST IF WE JUST PUT A BULLET INTO EACH OF THEIR LITTLE SKULLS, MA'AM. NO OFFENSE.
HE DOESN'T CARE FOR US.
WE DON'T CARE FOR HIM, EITHER.
LIKE TO BITE HIS BITS OFF.
YES, YES, FOR BEING SO UNKIND.
MY BEAUTIFUL BABIES.

MOTHER!

WE *LOVE YOU,* MOTHER!

SO *HOT! SO HOT!*

I HEARD SHE HAD THEM *ALTERED* SO THAT THEY COULDN'T EVER FEEL ANY *LOVE* UNLESS IT WAS DIRECTED TOWARDS *HER.*

MAN, *SHUT UP.* DO YOU KNOW HOW MANY *TR* EMPLOYEES SHE'S *KILLED?*

FAR MORE THAN YOU COULD EVEN *GUESS,* RATKILLER VICKERS. *FAR* MORE.

NOW, DARLINGS, I HAVE SOMETHING FOR YOU. A GIFT.

IT'S A GROUP OF TRAITOROUS TEENAGERS I NEED YOU TO KILL.

BUT FIRST...

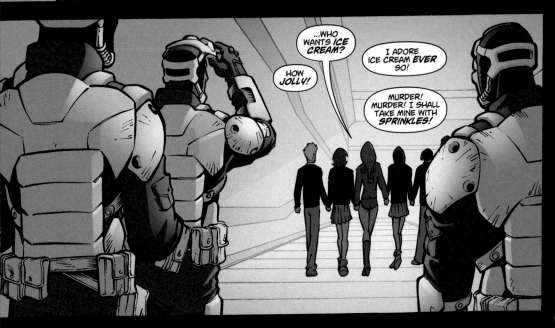

...WHO WANTS *ICE CREAM?*

HOW *JOLLY!*

I ADORE ICE CREAM *EVER* SO!

MURDER! MURDER! I SHALL TAKE MINE WITH *SPRINKLES!*

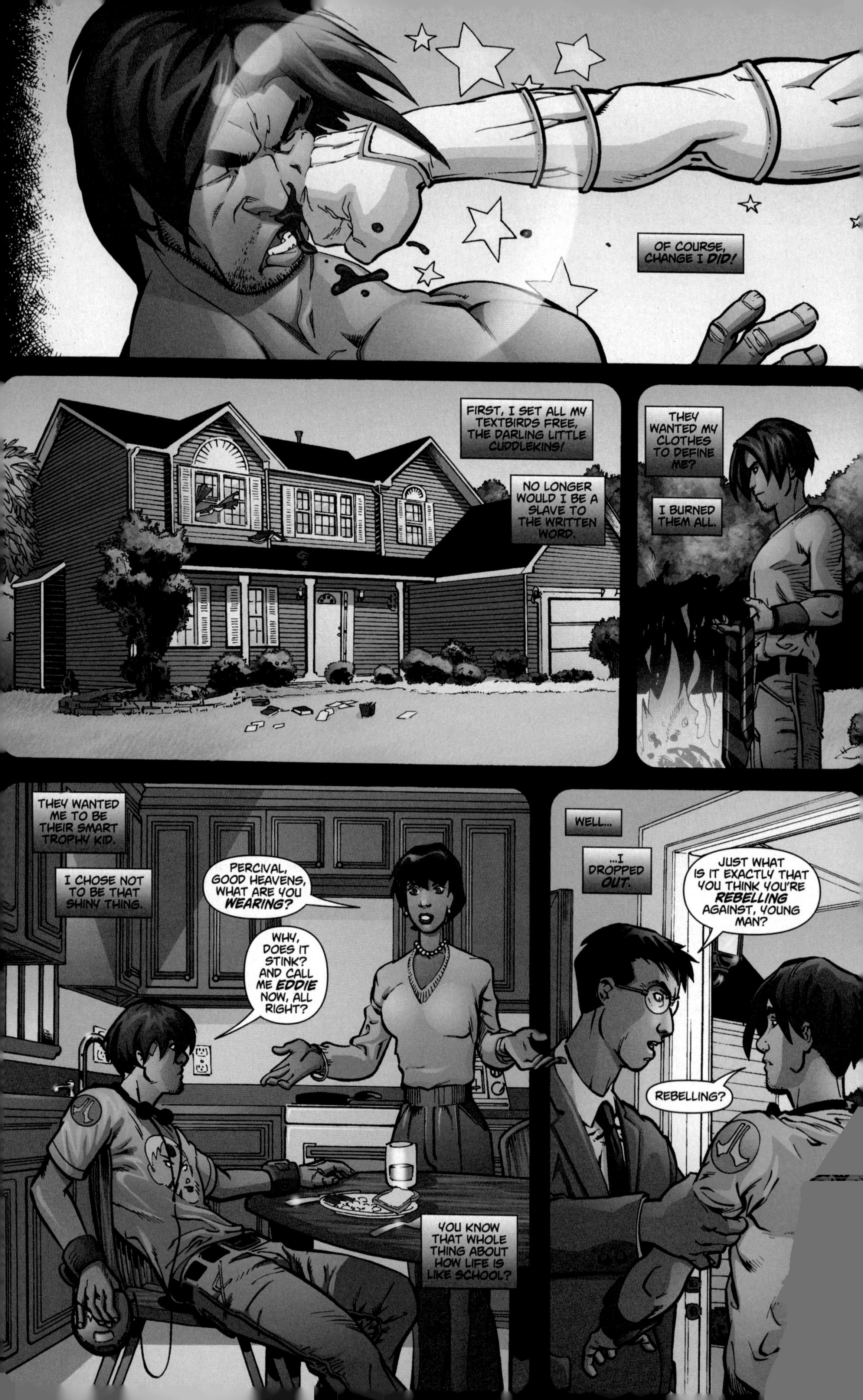
OF COURSE, CHANGE I DID!
FIRST, I SET ALL MY TEXTBIRDS FREE, THE DARLING LITTLE CUDDLEKINS!
NO LONGER WOULD I BE A SLAVE TO THE WRITTEN WORD.
THEY WANTED MY CLOTHES TO DEFINE ME?
I BURNED THEM ALL.
THEY WANTED ME TO BE THEIR SMART TROPHY KID.
I CHOSE NOT TO BE THAT SHINY THING.
PERCIVAL, GOOD HEAVENS, WHAT ARE YOU WEARING?
WHY, DOES IT STINK? AND CALL ME EDDIE NOW, ALL RIGHT?
YOU KNOW THAT WHOLE THING ABOUT HOW LIFE IS LIKE SCHOOL?
WELL...
...I DROPPED OUT.
JUST WHAT IS IT EXACTLY THAT YOU THINK YOU'RE REBELLING AGAINST, YOUNG MAN?
REBELLING?

SOUNDS TOO MUCH LIKE WORK, POPS.

SEEYA WHEN I SEEYA, I GUESS.

AND IT WAS TRUE. I REALLY HAD STOPPED CARING WHAT ANYONE ELSE THOUGHT OF ME.

DO YOU KNOW WHAT A GIFT THAT IS TO A KID LIKE ME? TO *ANYONE?*

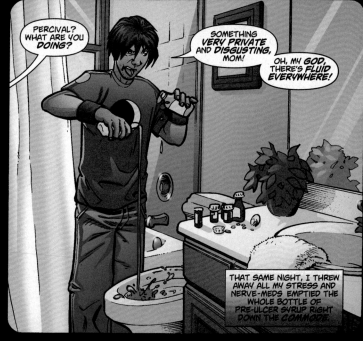

PERCIVAL? WHAT ARE YOU *DOING?*

SOMETHING *VERY PRIVATE* AND *DISGUSTING,* MOM!

OH, MY *GOD,* THERE'S *FLUID* EVERYWHERE!

THAT SAME NIGHT, I THREW AWAY ALL MY STRESS AND NERVE-MEDS EMPTIED THE WHOLE BOTTLE OF PRE-ULCER SYRUP RIGHT DOWN THE *COMMODE.*

OF COURSE, IT WAS A BIT OF A SHOCK TO EVERYONE *ELSE.*

EDDIE? ARE YOU... ARE YOU ALL RIGHT?

I'M JUST CHILLIN', MS. ORTIZ. NOT REALLY IN A HARD SCIENCE *MOOD,* YOU KNOW?

I SHOULD'VE EXPECTED IT.

EVERYONE FEARS THE MAN WHO CAN REMAKE HIMSELF.

HEY, THAT LOOKS KINDA...

CAN I TRY IT?

SURE, BRO. TAKE IT EASY FIRST TIME, THOUGH, OKAY?

I TOOK OFF HALF MY SKIN THAT DAY.

HALF THE *OLD EDDIE.*

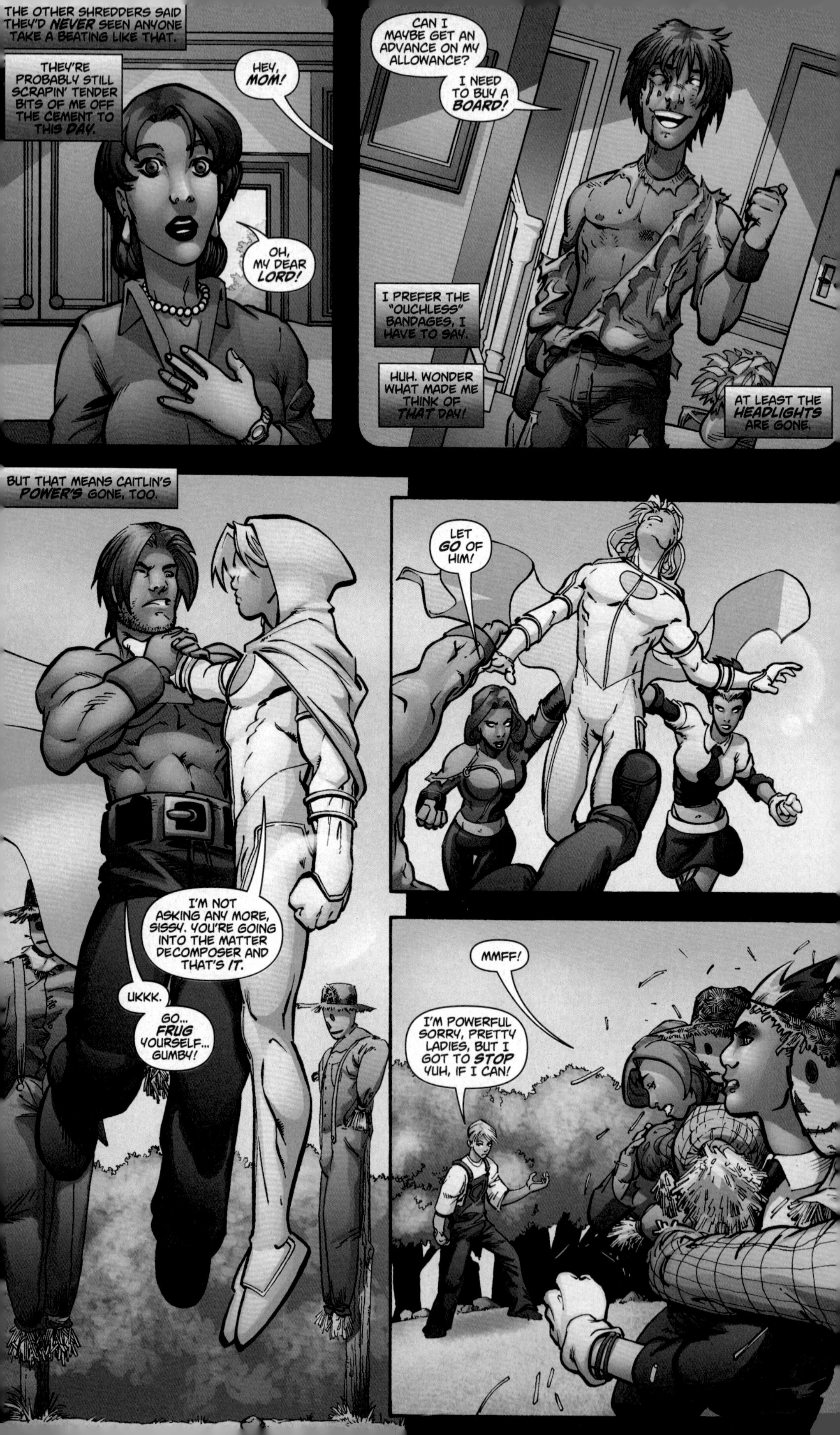
THE OTHER SHREDDERS SAID THEY'D NEVER SEEN ANYONE TAKE A BEATING LIKE THAT.
THEY'RE PROBABLY STILL SCRAPIN' TENDER BITS OF ME OFF THE CEMENT TO THIS DAY.
HEY, MOM!
OH, MY DEAR LORD!
CAN I MAYBE GET AN ADVANCE ON MY ALLOWANCE?
I NEED TO BUY A BOARD!
I PREFER THE "OUCHLESS" BANDAGES, I HAVE TO SAY.
HUH. WONDER WHAT MADE ME THINK OF THAT DAY!
AT LEAST THE HEADLIGHTS ARE GONE.
BUT THAT MEANS CAITLIN'S POWER'S GONE, TOO.
I'M NOT ASKING ANY MORE, SISSY. YOU'RE GOING INTO THE MATTER DECOMPOSER AND THAT'S IT.
UKKK.
GO... FRUG YOURSELF... GUMBY!
LET GO OF HIM!
MMFF!
I'M POWERFUL SORRY, PRETTY LADIES, BUT I GOT TO STOP YUH, IF I CAN!

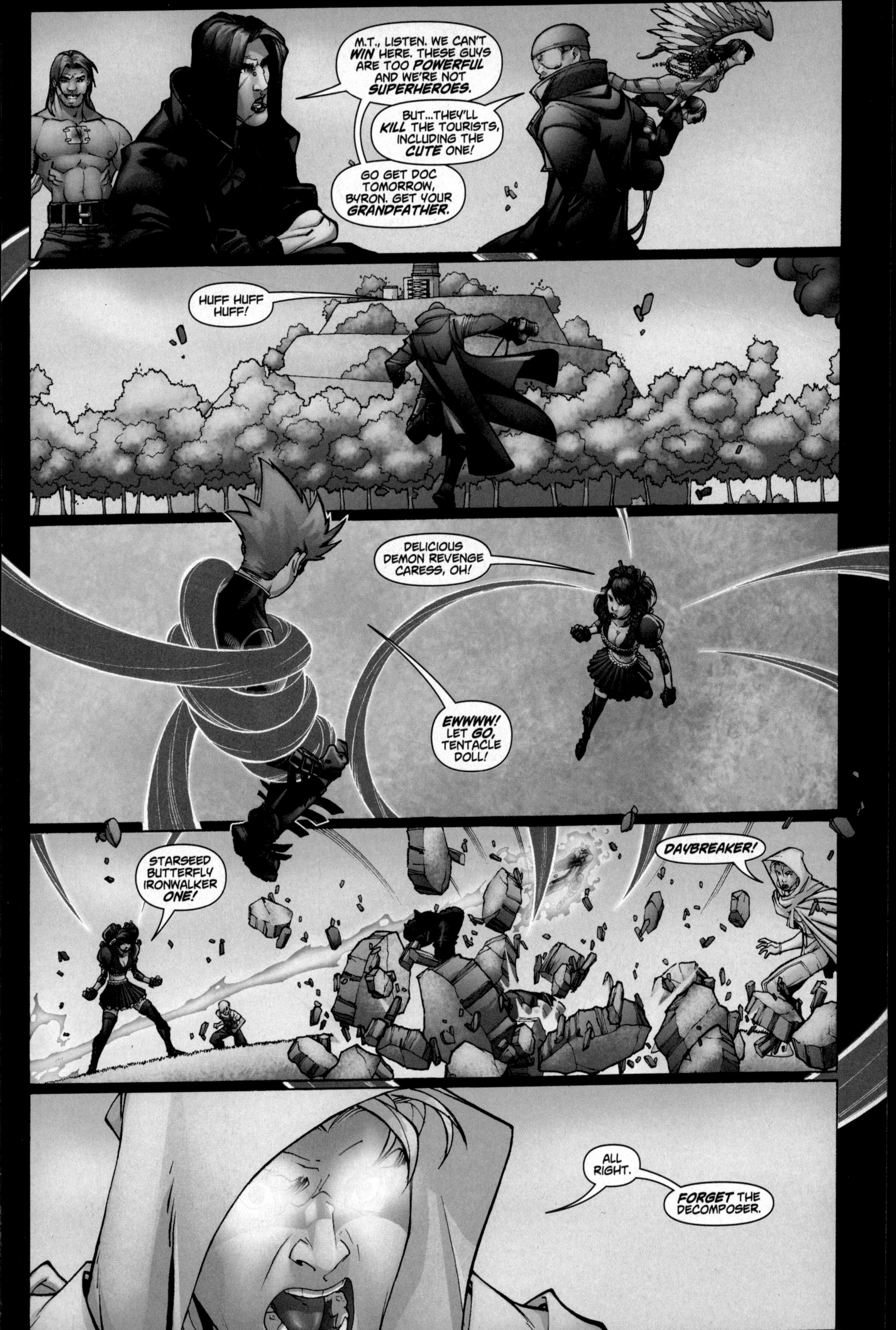
M.T., LISTEN. WE CAN'T WIN HERE. THESE GUYS ARE TOO POWERFUL AND WE'RE NOT SUPERHEROES.
BUT...THEY'LL KILL THE TOURISTS, INCLUDING THE CUTE ONE!
GO GET DOC TOMORROW, BYRON. GET YOUR GRANDFATHER.
HUFF HUFF HUFF!
DELICIOUS DEMON REVENGE CARESS, OH!
EWWWW! LET GO, TENTACLE DOLL!
STARSEED BUTTERFLY IRONWALKER ONE!
DAYBREAKER!
ALL RIGHT.
FORGET THE DECOMPOSER.

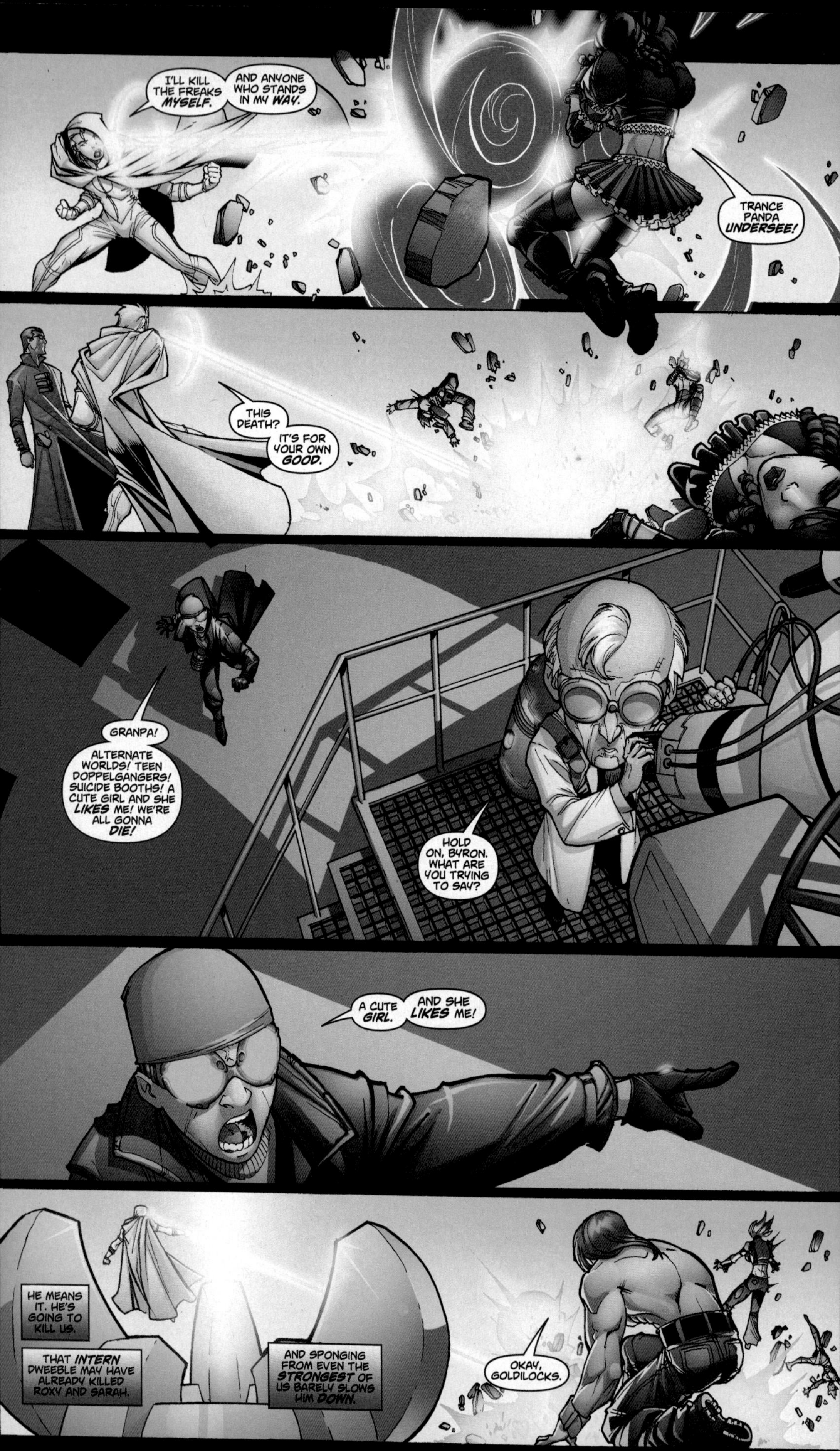
I'LL KILL THE FREAKS MYSELF.
AND ANYONE WHO STANDS IN MY WAY.
TRANCE PANDA UNDERSEE!
THIS DEATH?
IT'S FOR YOUR OWN GOOD.
GRANPA!
ALTERNATE WORLDS! TEEN DOPPELGANGERS! SUICIDE BOOTHS! A CUTE GIRL AND SHE LIKES ME! WE'RE ALL GONNA DIE!
HOLD ON, BYRON. WHAT ARE YOU TRYING TO SAY?
A CUTE GIRL.
AND SHE LIKES ME!
HE MEANS IT. HE'S GOING TO KILL US.
THAT INTERN DWEEBLE MAY HAVE ALREADY KILLED ROXY AND SARAH.
AND SPONGING FROM EVEN THE STRONGEST OF US BARELY SLOWS HIM DOWN.
OKAY, GOLDILOCKS.

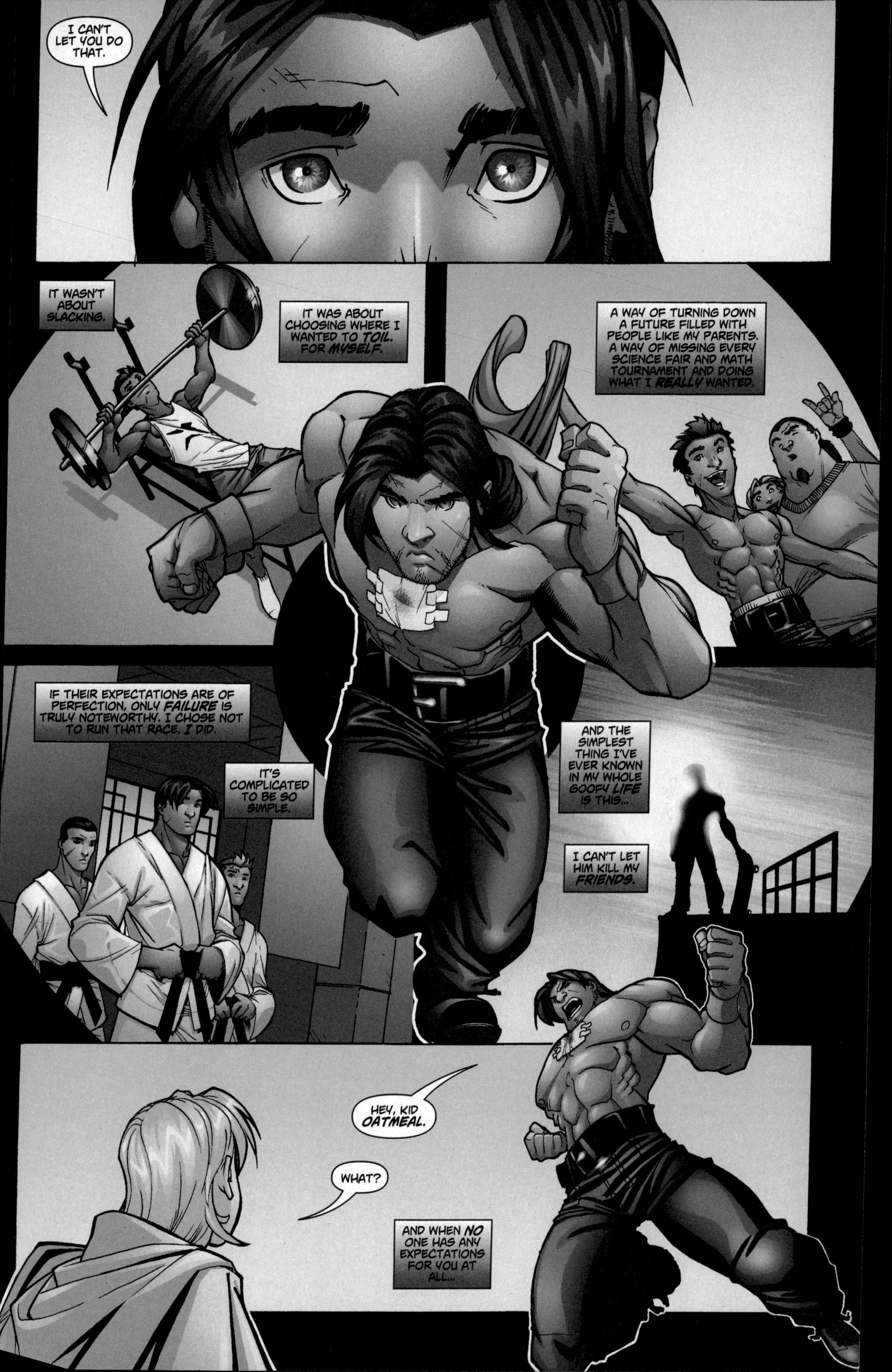

I CAN'T LET YOU DO THAT.
IT WASN'T ABOUT SLACKING.
IT WAS ABOUT CHOOSING WHERE I WANTED TO TOIL. FOR MYSELF.
A WAY OF TURNING DOWN A FUTURE FILLED WITH PEOPLE LIKE MY PARENTS. A WAY OF MISSING EVERY SCIENCE FAIR AND MATH TOURNAMENT AND DOING WHAT I REALLY WANTED.
IF THEIR EXPECTATIONS ARE OF PERFECTION, ONLY FAILURE IS TRULY NOTEWORTHY. I CHOSE NOT TO RUN THAT RACE. I DID.
IT'S COMPLICATED TO BE SO SIMPLE.
AND THE SIMPLEST THING I'VE EVER KNOWN IN MY WHOLE GOOFY LIFE IS THIS...
I CAN'T LET HIM KILL MY FRIENDS.
HEY, KID OATMEAL.
WHAT?
AND WHEN NO ONE HAS ANY EXPECTATIONS FOR YOU AT ALL...

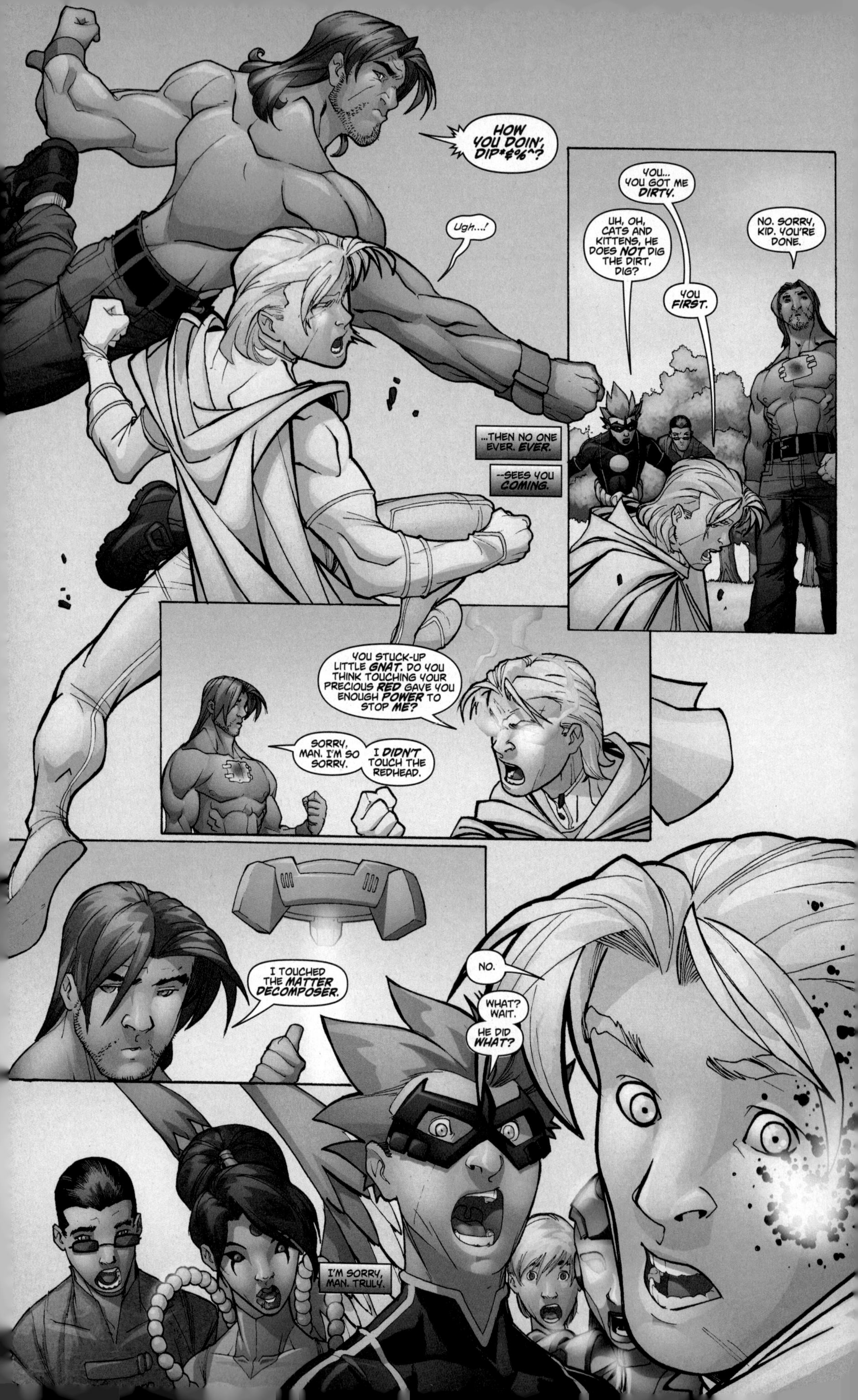
HOW YOU DOIN', DIP*$%^?
Ugh...!
...THEN NO ONE EVER. EVER.
--SEES YOU COMING.
YOU... YOU GOT ME DIRTY.
UH, OH, CATS AND KITTENS, HE DOES NOT DIG THE DIRT, DIG?
YOU FIRST.
NO. SORRY, KID. YOU'RE DONE.
YOU STUCK-UP LITTLE GNAT. DO YOU THINK TOUCHING YOUR PRECIOUS RED GAVE YOU ENOUGH POWER TO STOP ME?
SORRY, MAN. I'M SO SORRY.
I DIDN'T TOUCH THE REDHEAD.
I TOUCHED THE MATTER DECOMPOSER.
NO.
WHAT? WAIT.
HE DID WHAT?
I'M SORRY, MAN. TRULY.

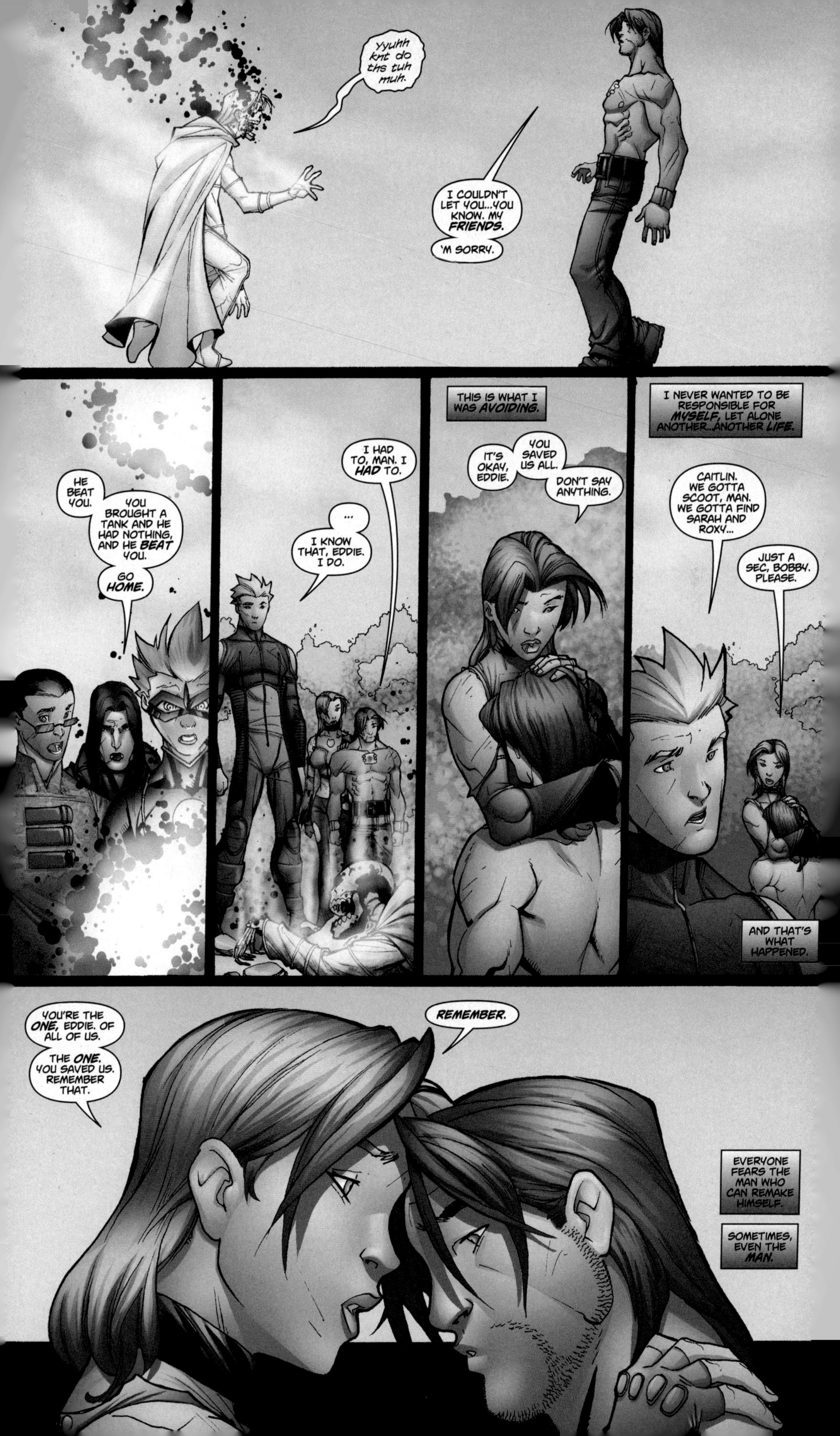

Yyuhh knt do ths tuh muh.
I COULDN'T LET YOU...YOU KNOW. MY FRIENDS.
'M SORRY.
HE BEAT YOU.
YOU BROUGHT A TANK AND HE HAD NOTHING, AND HE BEAT YOU.
GO HOME.
I HAD TO, MAN. I HAD TO.
...
I KNOW THAT, EDDIE. I DO.
THIS IS WHAT I WAS AVOIDING.
IT'S OKAY, EDDIE.
YOU SAVED US ALL.
DON'T SAY ANYTHING.
I NEVER WANTED TO BE RESPONSIBLE FOR MYSELF, LET ALONE ANOTHER...ANOTHER LIFE.
CAITLIN. WE GOTTA SCOOT, MAN. WE GOTTA FIND SARAH AND ROXY...
JUST A SEC, BOBBY. PLEASE.
AND THAT'S WHAT HAPPENED.
YOU'RE THE ONE, EDDIE. OF ALL OF US.
THE ONE. YOU SAVED US. REMEMBER THAT.
REMEMBER.
EVERYONE FEARS THE MAN WHO CAN REMAKE HIMSELF.
SOMETIMES, EVEN THE MAN.

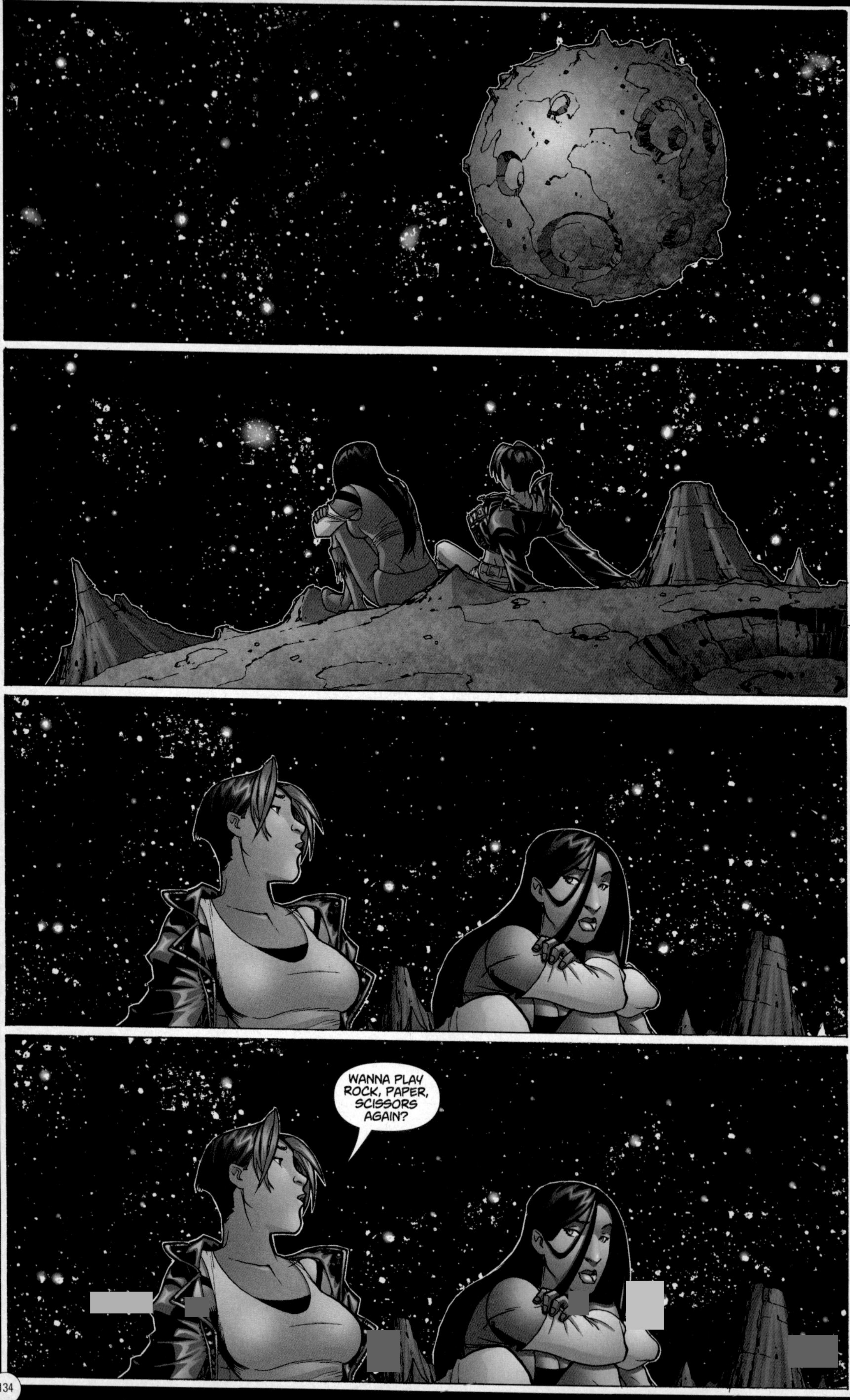
WANNA PLAY ROCK, PAPER, SCISSORS AGAIN?

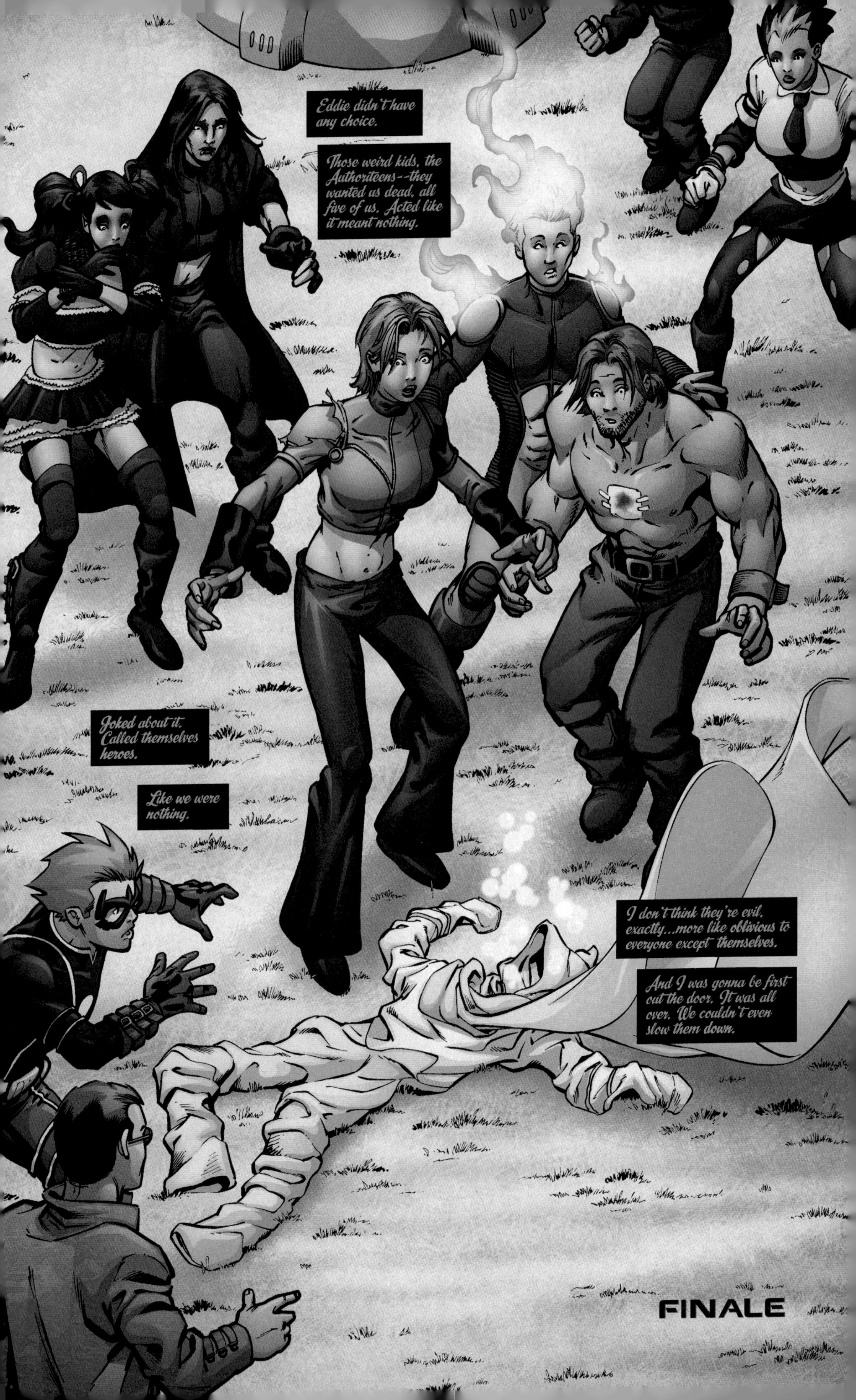
Eddie didn't have any choice.
Those weird kids, the Authoriteens--they wanted us dead, all five of us. Acted like it meant nothing.
Joked about it. Called themselves heroes.
Like we were nothing.
I don't think they're evil, exactly...more like oblivious to everyone except themselves.
And I was gonna be first out the door. It was all over. We couldn't even slow them down.
FINALE

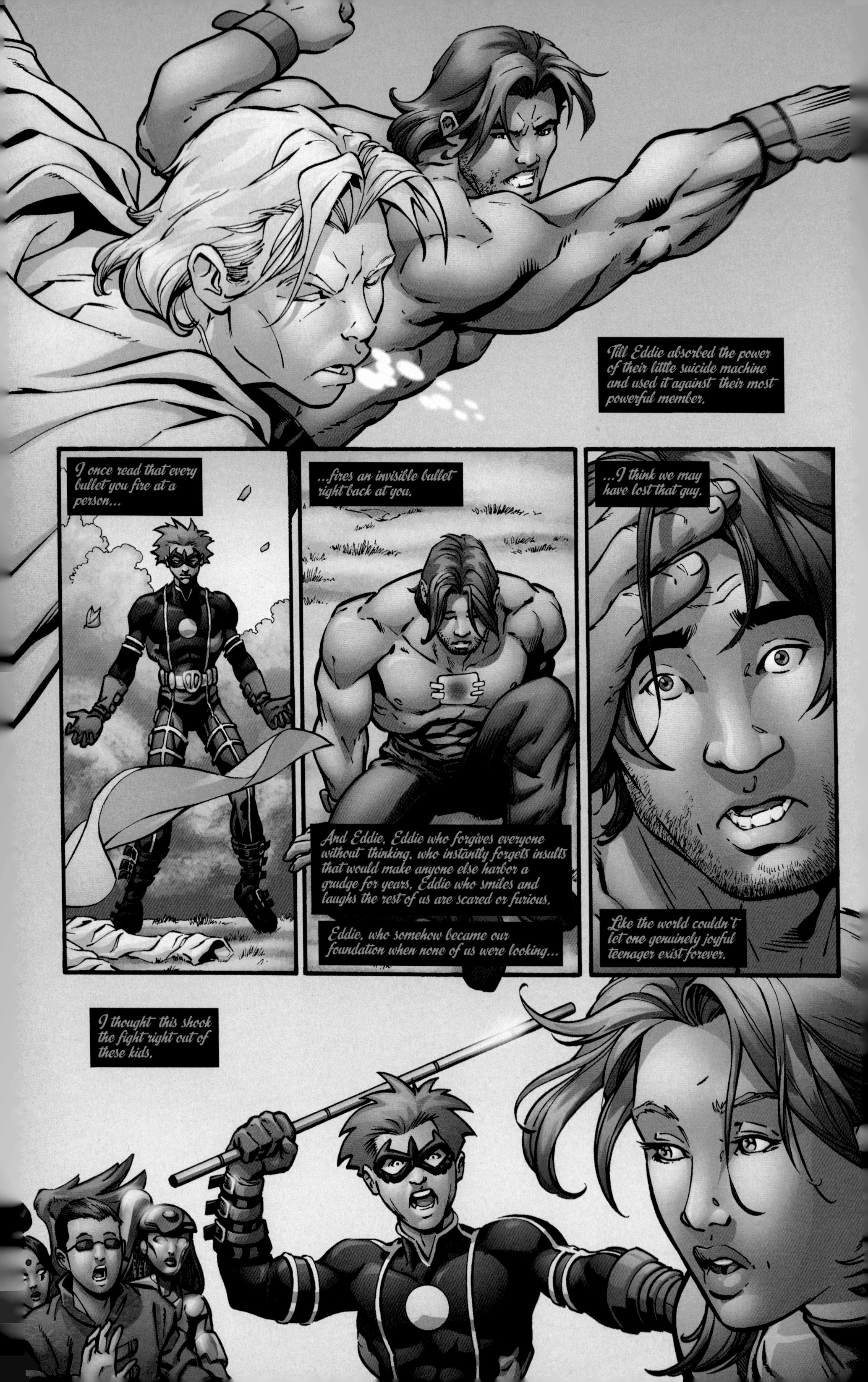
Till Eddie absorbed the power of their little suicide machine and used it against their most powerful member.
I once read that every bullet you fire at a person...
...fires an invisible bullet right back at you.
And Eddie, Eddie who forgives everyone without thinking, who instantly forgets insults that would make anyone else harbor a grudge for years, Eddie who smiles and laughs the rest of us are scared or furious.
Eddie, who somehow became our foundation when none of us were looking...
...I think we may have lost that guy.
Like the world couldn't let one genuinely joyful teenager exist forever.
I thought this shook the fight right out of these kids.

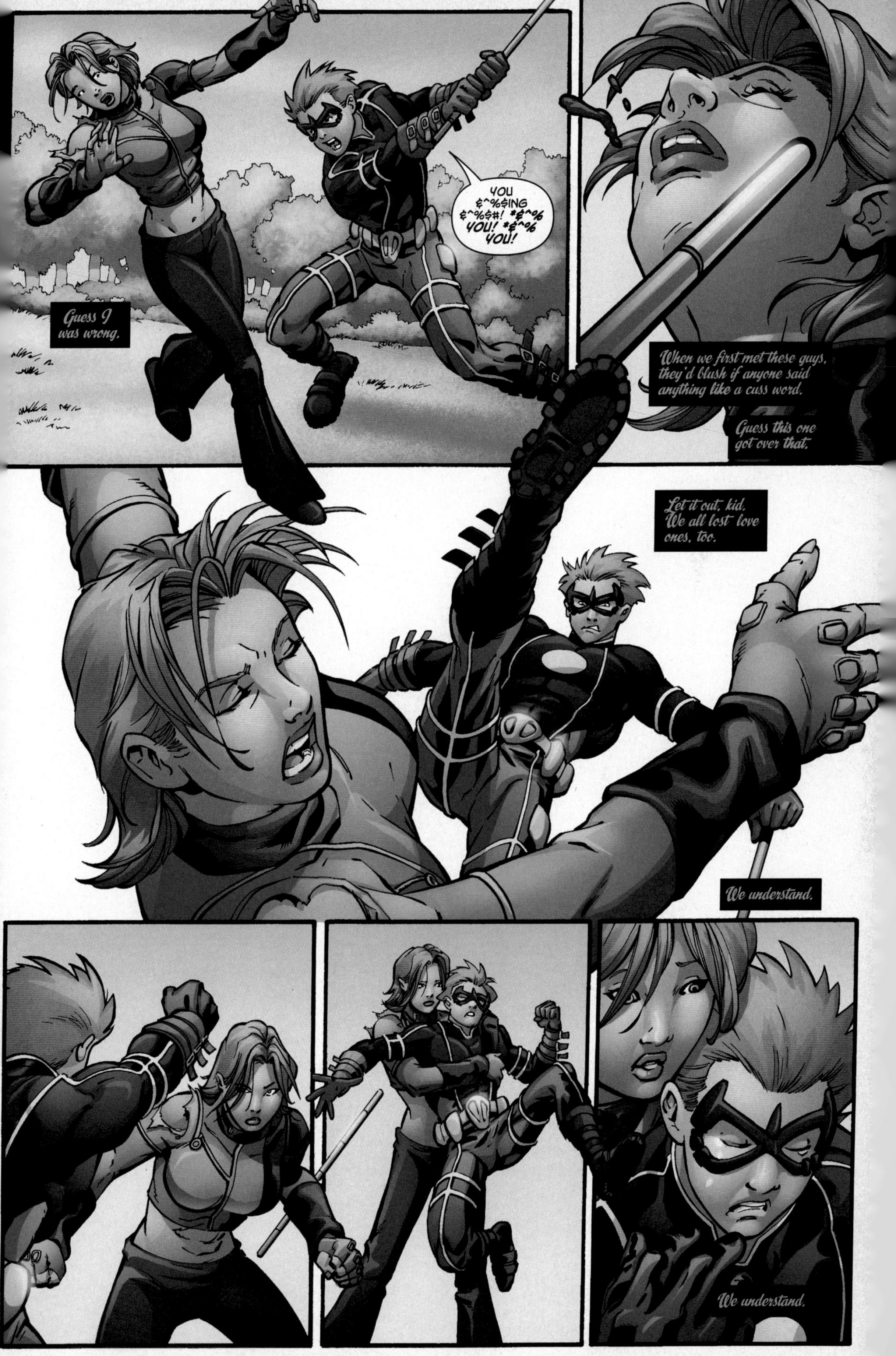

YOU &^%$ING &^%$#! *&^% YOU! *&^% YOU!
Guess I was wrong.
When we first met these guys, they'd blush if anyone said anything like a cuss word.
Guess this one got over that.
Let it out, kid. We all lost love ones, too.
We understand.
We understand.

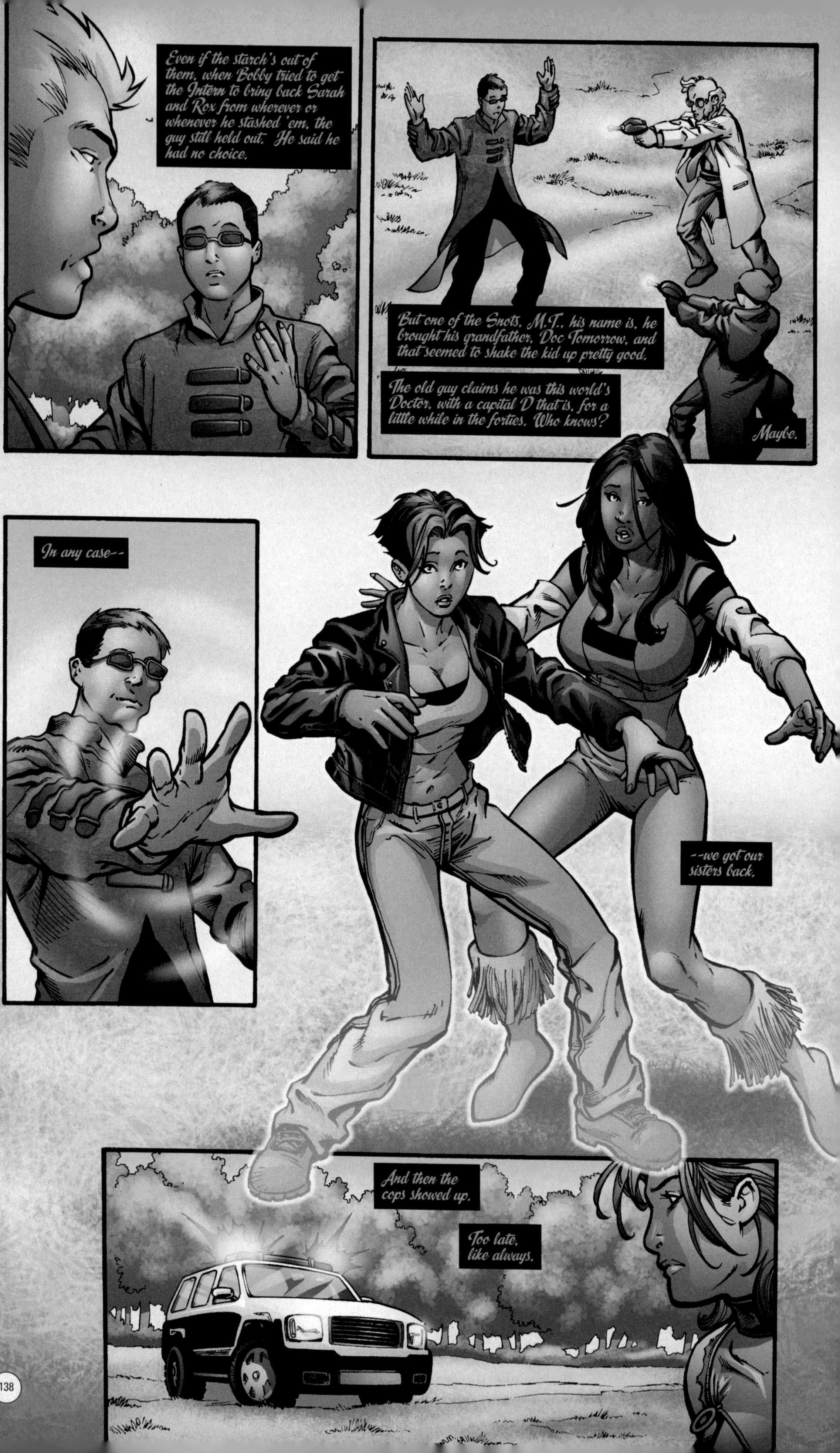
Even if the starch's out of them, when Bobby tried to get the Intern to bring back Sarah and Rox from wherever or whenever he stashed 'em, the guy still held out. He said he had no choice.
But one of the Snots, M.T., his name is, he brought his grandfather, Doc Tomorrow, and that seemed to shake the kid up pretty good.
The old guy claims he was this world's Doctor, with a capital D that is, for a little while in the forties. Who knows?
Maybe.
In any case--
--we got our sisters back.
And then the cops showed up.
Too late, like always.

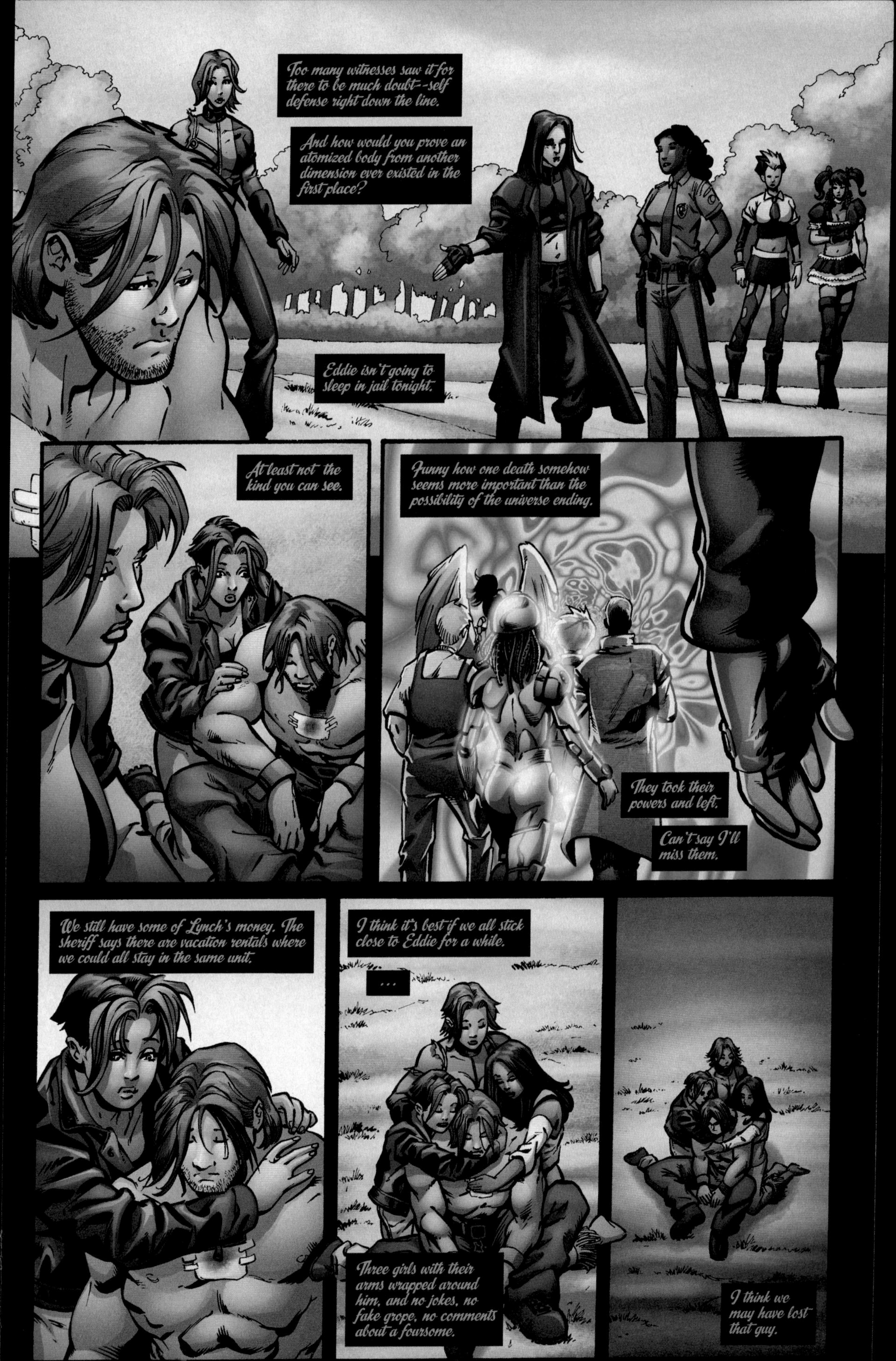
Too many witnesses saw it for there to be much doubt--self defense right down the line.
And how would you prove an atomized body from another dimension ever existed in the first place?
Eddie isn't going to sleep in jail tonight.
At least not the kind you can see.
Funny how one death somehow seems more important than the possibility of the universe ending.
They took their powers and left.
Can't say I'll miss them.
We still have some of Lynch's money. The sheriff says there are vacation rentals where we could all stay in the same unit.
I think it's best if we all stick close to Eddie for a while.
...
Three girls with their arms wrapped around him, and no jokes, no fake grope, no comments about a foursome.
I think we may have lost that guy.

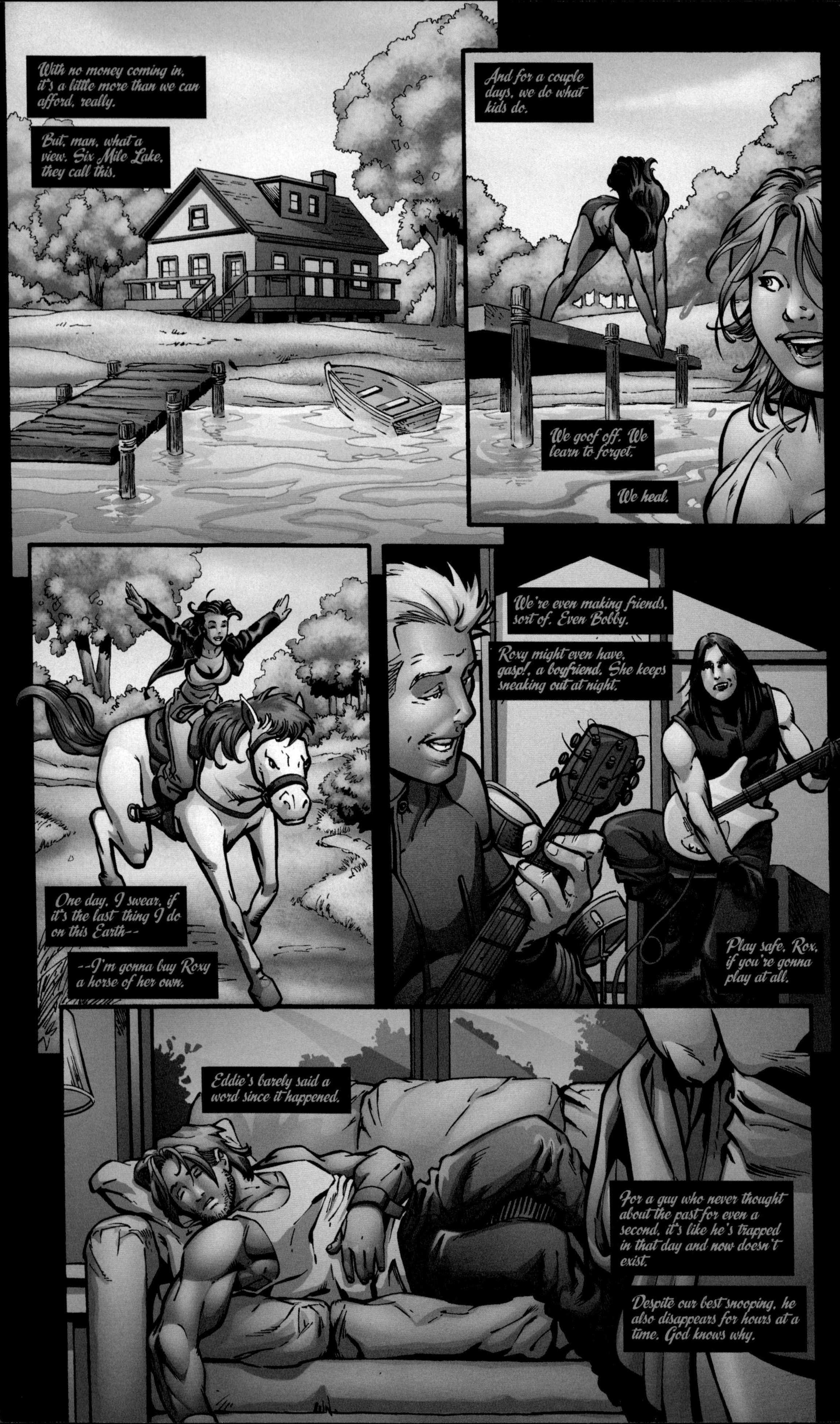
With no money coming in, it's a little more than we can afford, really.
But, man, what a view. Six Mile Lake, they call this.
And for a couple days, we do what kids do.
We goof off. We learn to forget.
We heal.
One day, I swear, if it's the last thing I do on this Earth--
--I'm gonna buy Roxy a horse of her own.
We're even making friends, sort of. Even Bobby.
Roxy might even have, gasp!, a boyfriend. She keeps sneaking out at night.
Play safe, Rox, if you're gonna play at all.
Eddie's barely said a word since it happened.
For a guy who never thought about the past for even a second, it's like he's trapped in that day and now doesn't exist.
Despite our best snooping, he also disappears for hours at a time. God knows why.

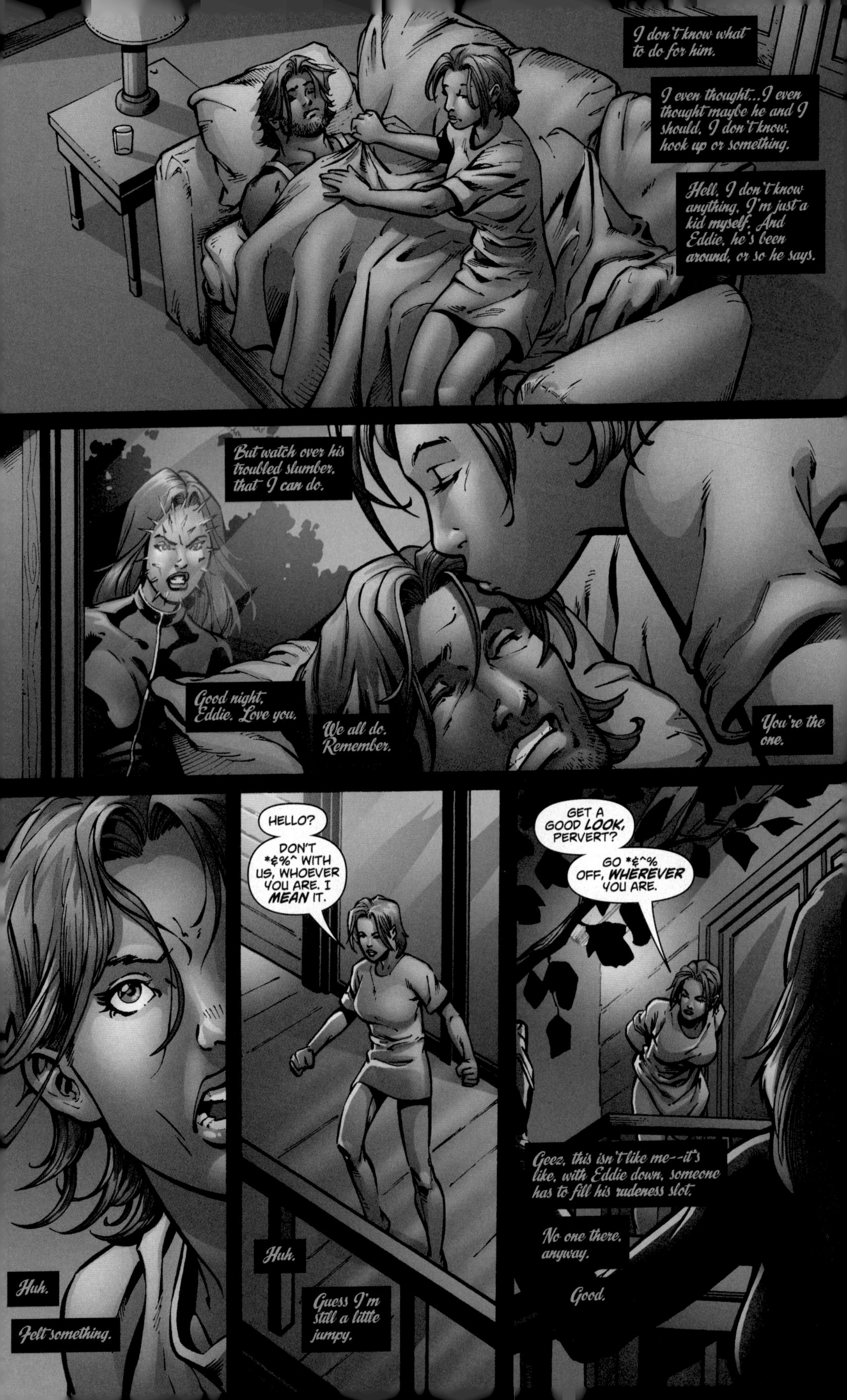
I don't know what to do for him.
I even thought...I even thought maybe he and I should, I don't know, hook up or something.
Hell, I don't know anything. I'm just a kid myself. And Eddie, he's been around, or so he says.
But watch over his troubled slumber, that I can do.
Good night, Eddie. Love you.
We all do. Remember.
You're the one.
Huh.
Felt something.
HELLO?
DON'T *&%^ WITH US, WHOEVER YOU ARE. I MEAN IT.
Huh.
Guess I'm still a little jumpy.
GET A GOOD LOOK, PERVERT?
GO *&^% OFF, WHEREVER YOU ARE.
Geez, this isn't like me--it's like, with Eddie down, someone has to fill his rudeness slot.
No one there, anyway.
Good.

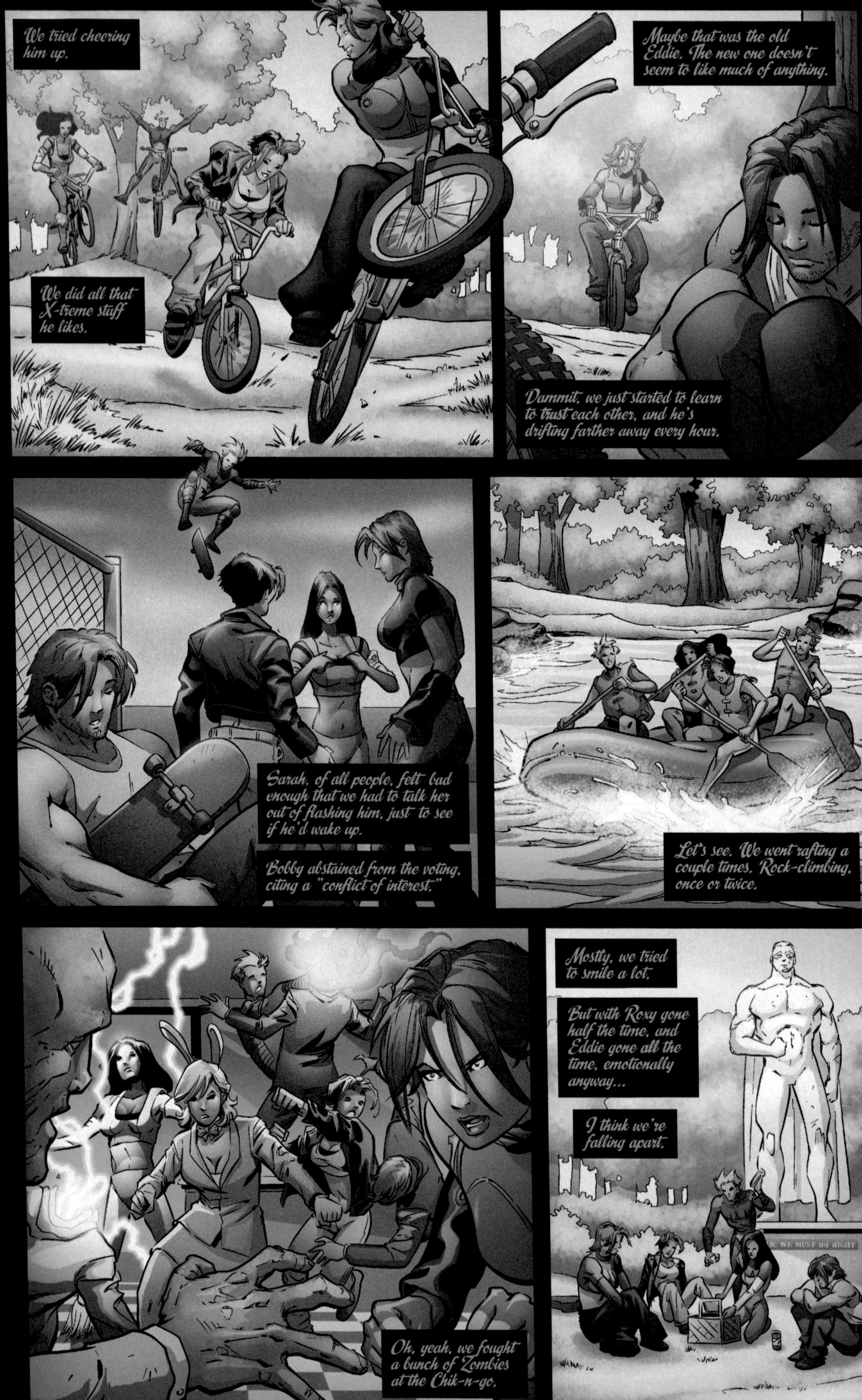
We tried cheering him up.
We did all that X-treme stuff he likes.
Maybe that was the old Eddie. The new one doesn't seem to like much of anything.
Dammit, we just started to learn to trust each other, and he's drifting farther away every hour.
Sarah, of all people, felt bad enough that we had to talk her out of flashing him, just to see if he'd wake up.
Bobby abstained from the voting, citing a "conflict of interest."
Let's see. We went rafting a couple times. Rock-climbing, once or twice.
Oh, yeah, we fought a bunch of Zombies at the Chik-n-go.
Mostly, we tried to smile a lot.
But with Roxy gone half the time, and Eddie gone all the time, emotionally anyway...
I think we're falling apart.

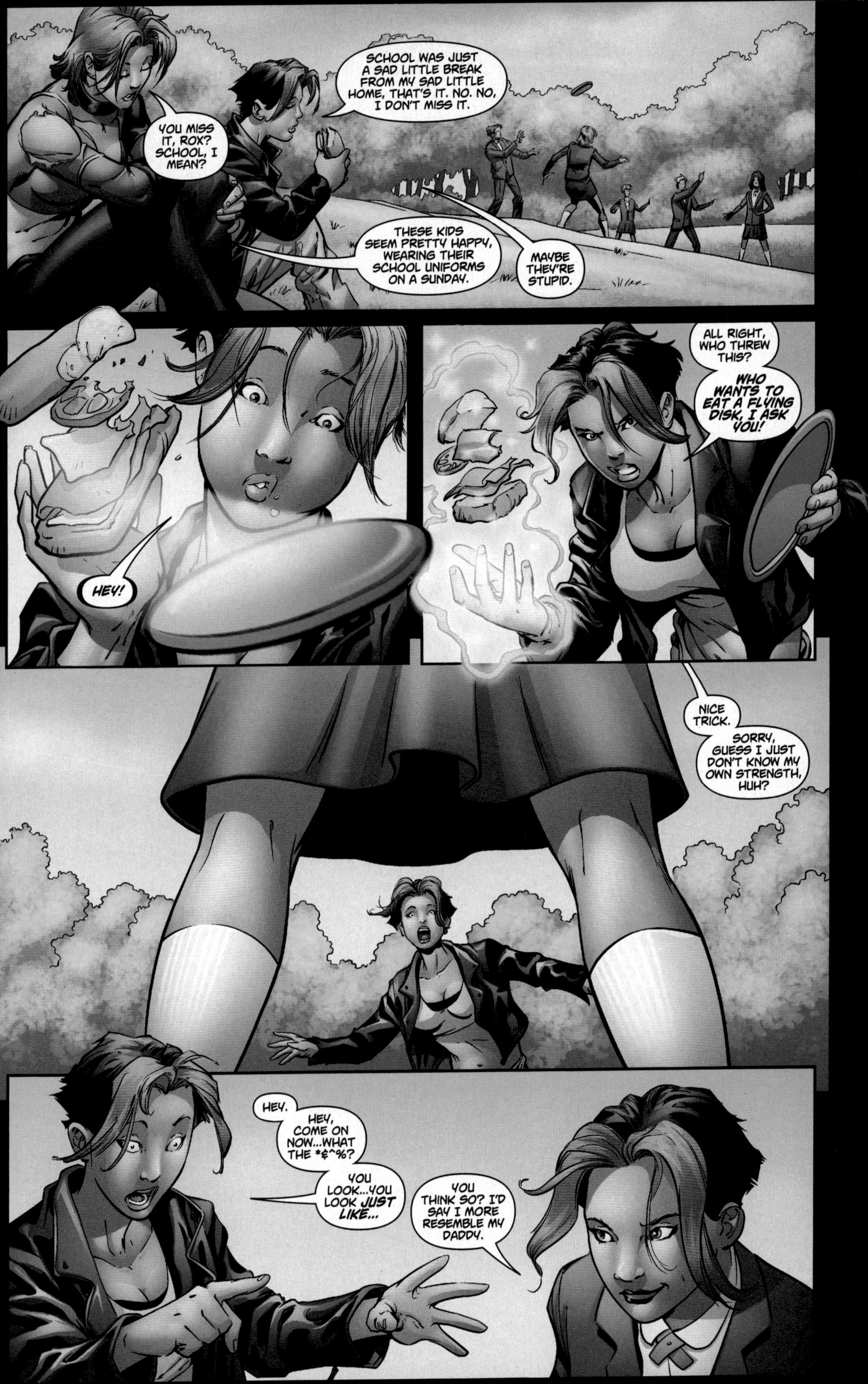

YOU MISS IT, ROX? SCHOOL, I MEAN?
SCHOOL WAS JUST A SAD LITTLE BREAK FROM MY SAD LITTLE HOME, THAT'S IT. NO. NO, I DON'T MISS IT.
THESE KIDS SEEM PRETTY HAPPY, WEARING THEIR SCHOOL UNIFORMS ON A SUNDAY.
MAYBE THEY'RE STUPID.
HEY!
ALL RIGHT, WHO THREW THIS?
WHO WANTS TO EAT A FLYING DISK, I ASK YOU!
NICE TRICK.
SORRY, GUESS I JUST DON'T KNOW MY OWN STRENGTH, HUH?
HEY.
HEY, COME ON NOW...WHAT THE *¢^%?
YOU LOOK...YOU LOOK JUST LIKE...
YOU THINK SO? I'D SAY I MORE RESEMBLE MY DADDY.

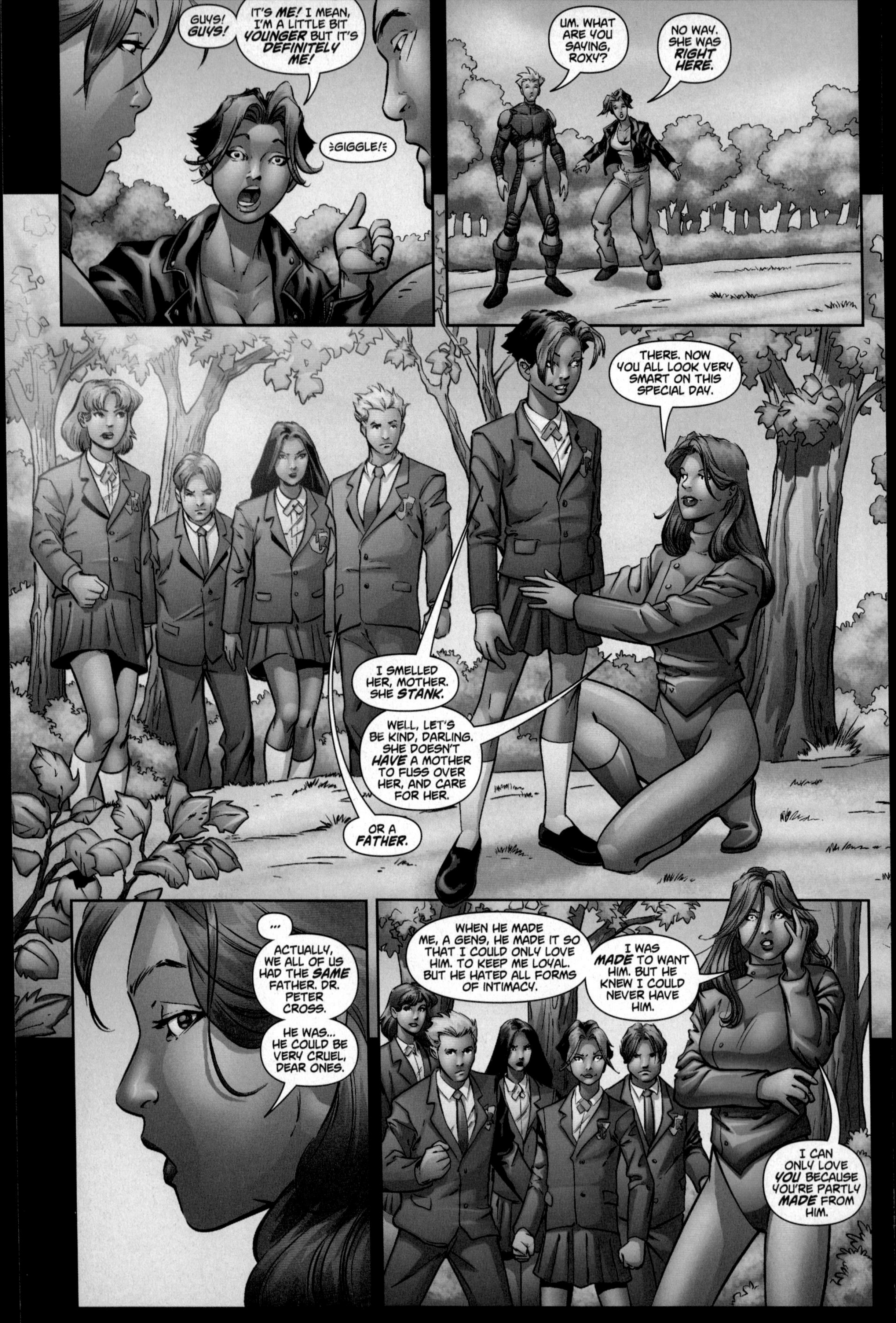
GUYS! GUYS!
IT'S ME! I MEAN, I'M A LITTLE BIT YOUNGER BUT IT'S DEFINITELY ME!
GIGGLE!
UM. WHAT ARE YOU SAYING, ROXY?
NO WAY. SHE WAS RIGHT HERE.
THERE. NOW YOU ALL LOOK VERY SMART ON THIS SPECIAL DAY.
I SMELLED HER, MOTHER. SHE STANK.
WELL, LET'S BE KIND, DARLING. SHE DOESN'T HAVE A MOTHER TO FUSS OVER HER, AND CARE FOR HER.
OR A FATHER.
...
ACTUALLY, WE ALL OF US HAD THE SAME FATHER. DR. PETER CROSS.
HE WAS... HE COULD BE VERY CRUEL, DEAR ONES.
WHEN HE MADE ME, A GENS, HE MADE IT SO THAT I COULD ONLY LOVE HIM. TO KEEP ME LOYAL. BUT HE HATED ALL FORMS OF INTIMACY.
I WAS MADE TO WANT HIM. BUT HE KNEW I COULD NEVER HAVE HIM.
I CAN ONLY LOVE YOU BECAUSE YOU'RE PARTLY MADE FROM HIM.

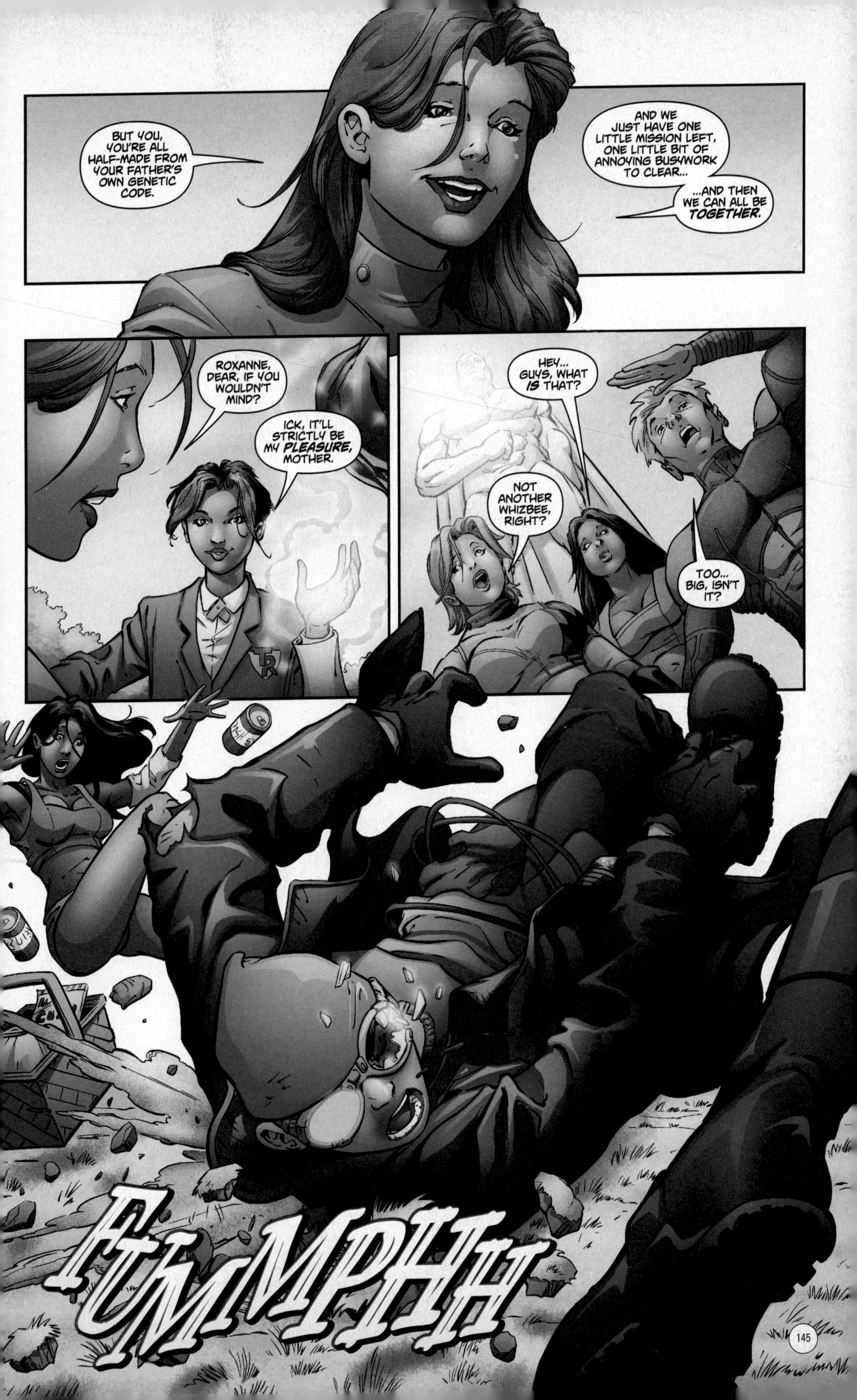
BUT YOU, YOU'RE ALL HALF-MADE FROM YOUR FATHER'S OWN GENETIC CODE.
AND WE JUST HAVE ONE LITTLE MISSION LEFT, ONE LITTLE BIT OF ANNOYING BUSYWORK TO CLEAR...
...AND THEN WE CAN ALL BE *TOGETHER.*
ROXANNE, DEAR, IF YOU WOULDN'T MIND?
ICK, IT'LL STRICTLY BE MY *PLEASURE,* MOTHER.
HEY... GUYS, WHAT *IS* THAT?
NOT ANOTHER WHIZBEE, RIGHT?
TOO... BIG, ISN'T IT?
FUMMPHH

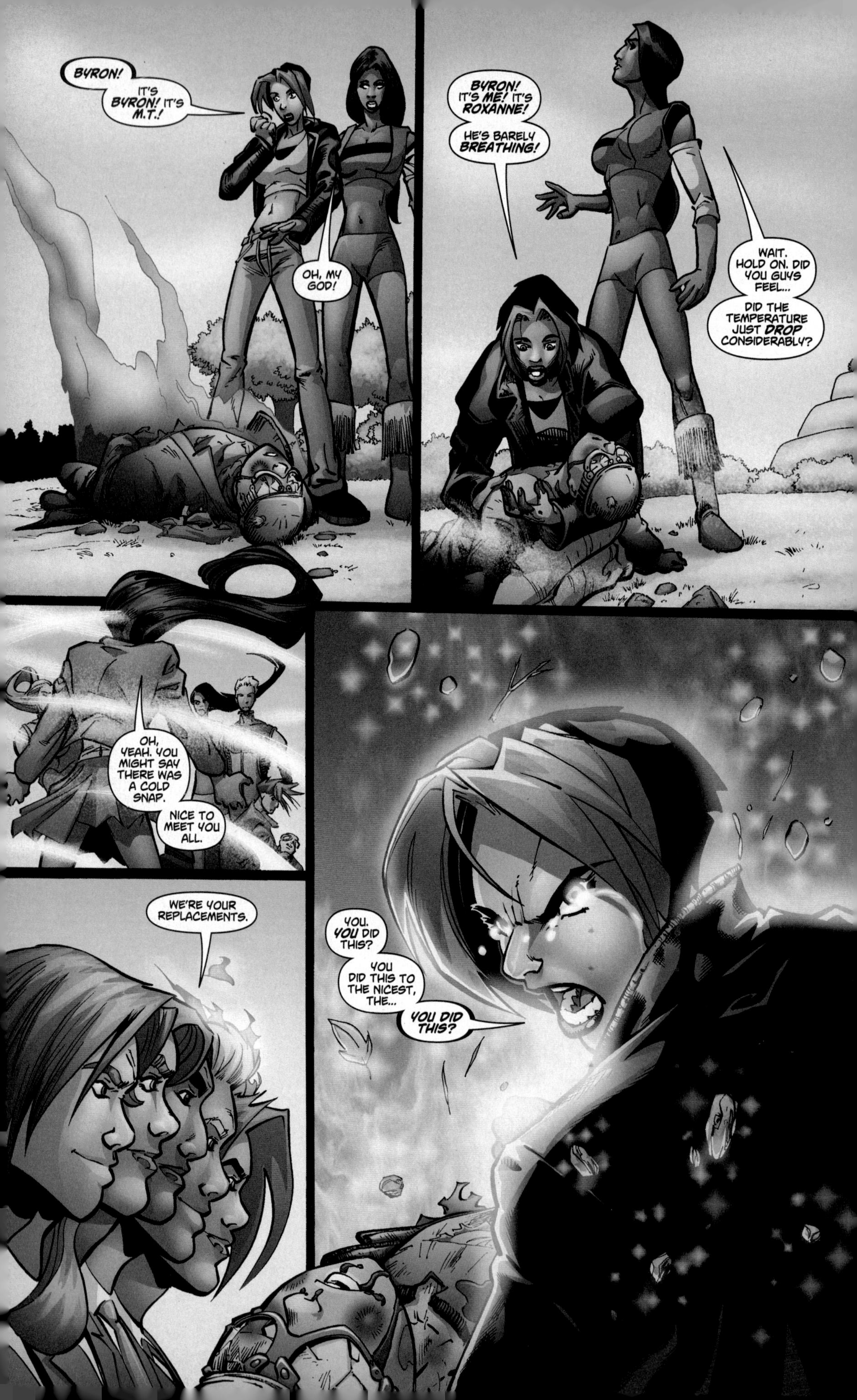

BYRON!
IT'S BYRON! IT'S M.T.!
OH, MY GOD!
BYRON! IT'S ME! IT'S ROXANNE!
HE'S BARELY BREATHING!
WAIT. HOLD ON. DID YOU GUYS FEEL...
DID THE TEMPERATURE JUST DROP CONSIDERABLY?
OH, YEAH. YOU MIGHT SAY THERE WAS A COLD SNAP.
NICE TO MEET YOU ALL.
WE'RE YOUR REPLACEMENTS.
YOU. YOU DID THIS?
YOU DID THIS TO THE NICEST, THE...
YOU DID THIS?

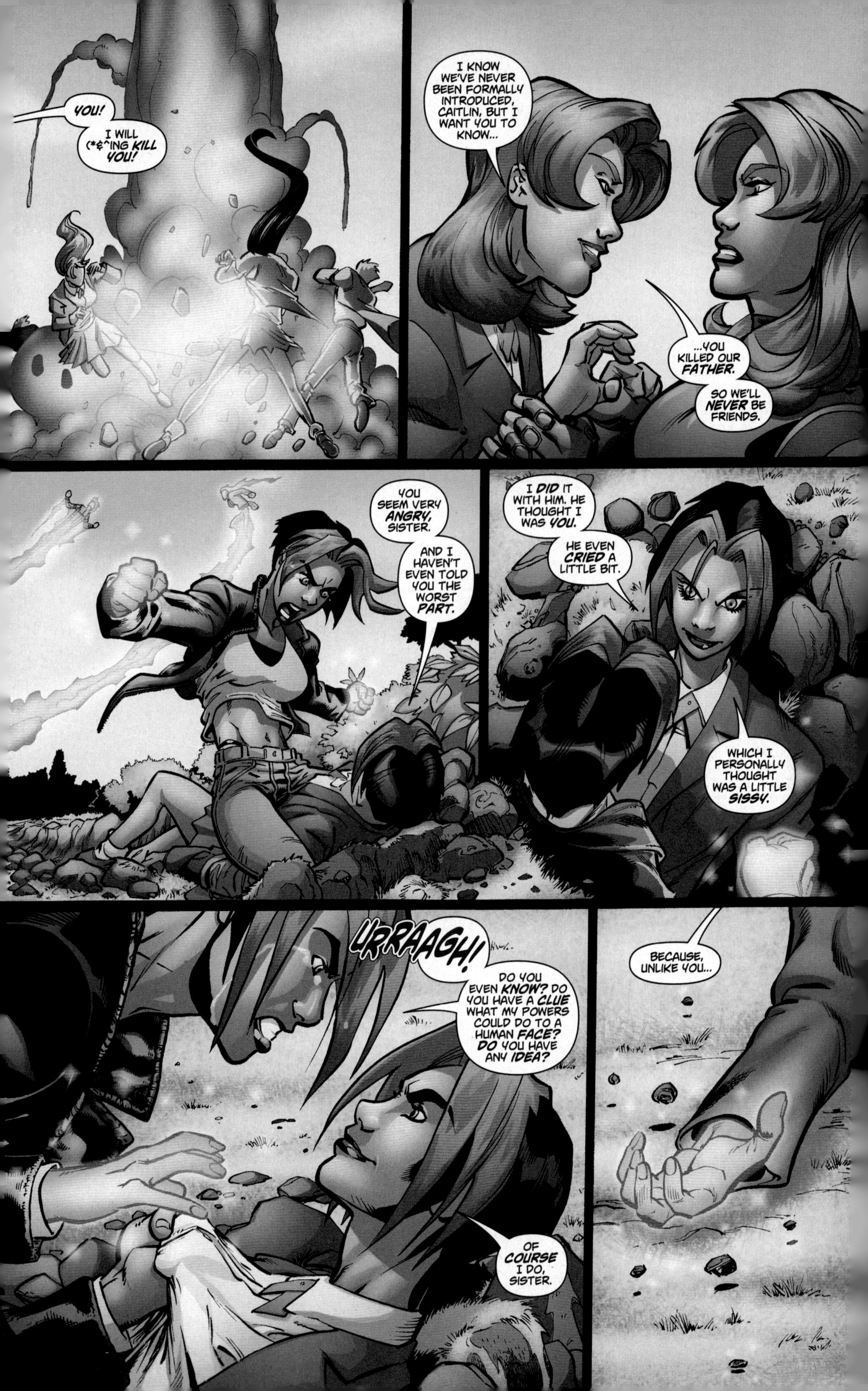
YOU!
I WILL (*&^ING KILL YOU!
I KNOW WE'VE NEVER BEEN FORMALLY INTRODUCED, CAITLIN, BUT I WANT YOU TO KNOW...
...YOU KILLED OUR FATHER.
SO WE'LL NEVER BE FRIENDS.
YOU SEEM VERY ANGRY, SISTER.
AND I HAVEN'T EVEN TOLD YOU THE WORST PART.
I DID IT WITH HIM. HE THOUGHT I WAS YOU.
HE EVEN CRIED A LITTLE BIT.
WHICH I PERSONALLY THOUGHT WAS A LITTLE SISSY.
URRAAGH!
DO YOU EVEN KNOW? DO YOU HAVE A CLUE WHAT MY POWERS COULD DO TO A HUMAN FACE? DO YOU HAVE ANY IDEA?
OF COURSE I DO, SISTER.
BECAUSE, UNLIKE YOU...

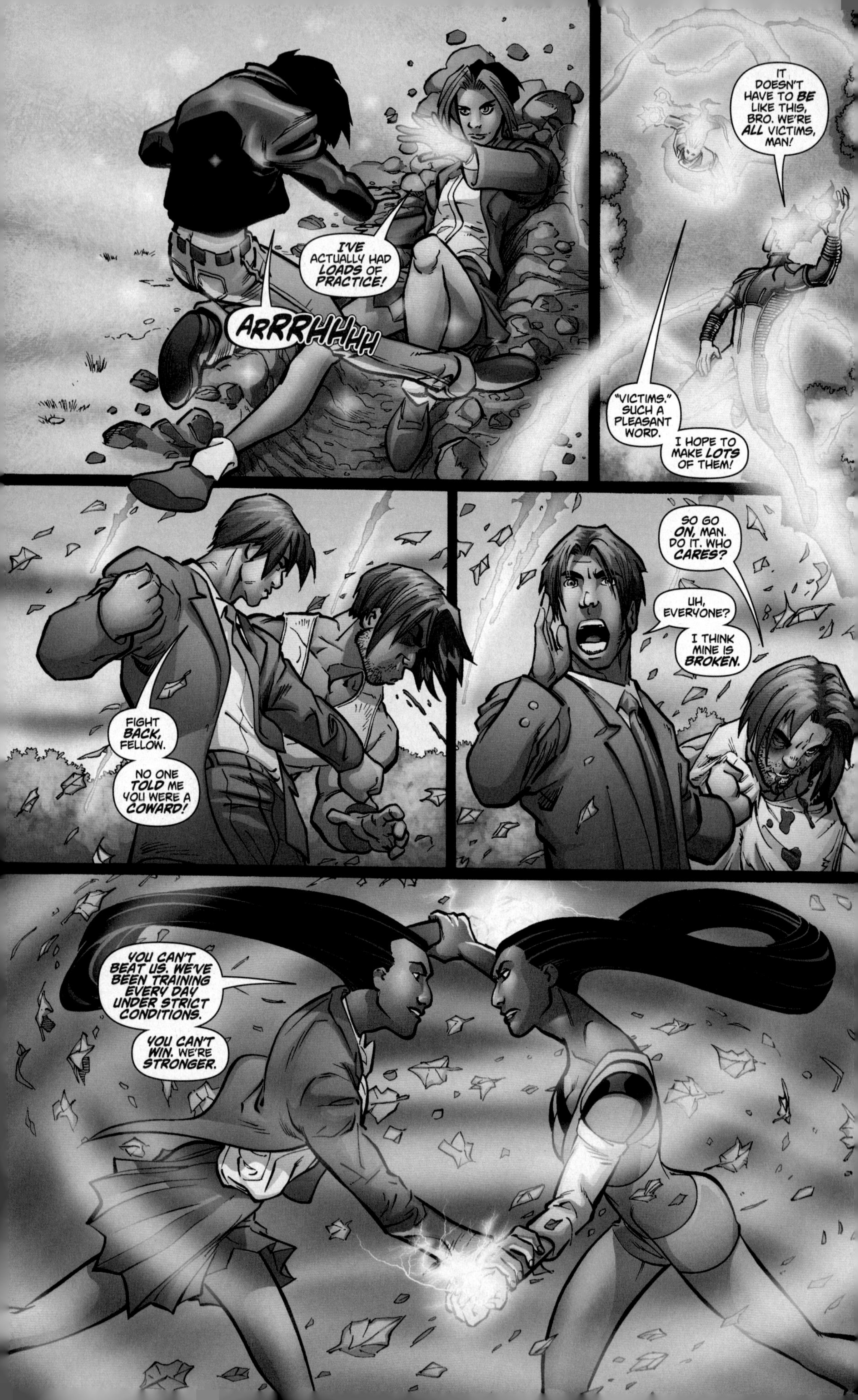
I'VE ACTUALLY HAD LOADS OF PRACTICE!
ARRRHHHH
IT DOESN'T HAVE TO BE LIKE THIS, BRO. WE'RE ALL VICTIMS, MAN!
"VICTIMS." SUCH A PLEASANT WORD.
I HOPE TO MAKE LOTS OF THEM!
FIGHT BACK, FELLOW.
NO ONE TOLD ME YOU WERE A COWARD!
SO GO ON, MAN. DO IT. WHO CARES?
UH, EVERYONE?
I THINK MINE IS BROKEN.
YOU CAN'T BEAT US. WE'VE BEEN TRAINING EVERY DAY UNDER STRICT CONDITIONS.
YOU CAN'T WIN. WE'RE STRONGER.

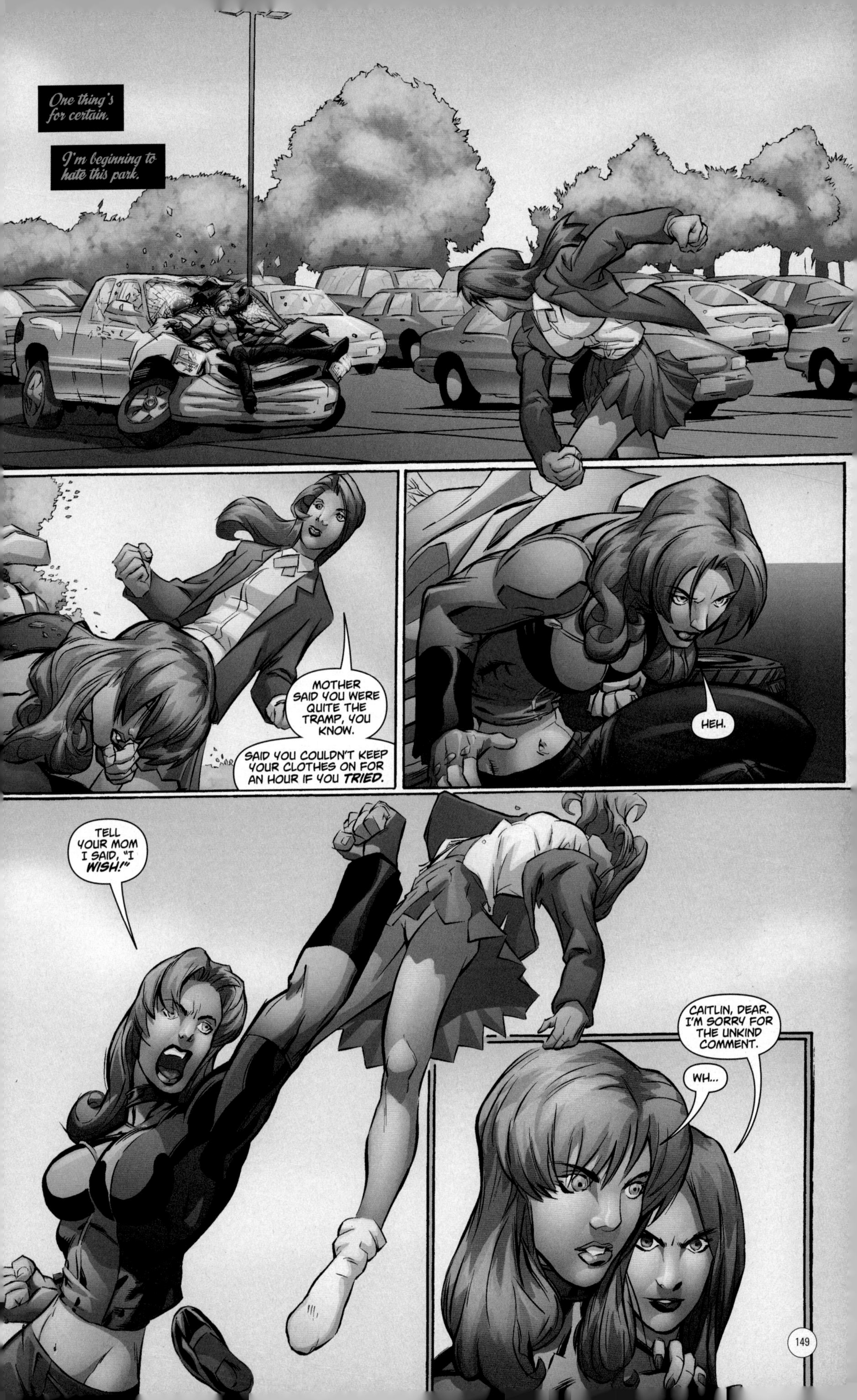

One thing's for certain.
I'm beginning to hate this park.
MOTHER SAID YOU WERE QUITE THE TRAMP, YOU KNOW.
SAID YOU COULDN'T KEEP YOUR CLOTHES ON FOR AN HOUR IF YOU TRIED.
HEH.
TELL YOUR MOM I SAID, "I WISH!"
CAITLIN, DEAR. I'M SORRY FOR THE UNKIND COMMENT.
WH...

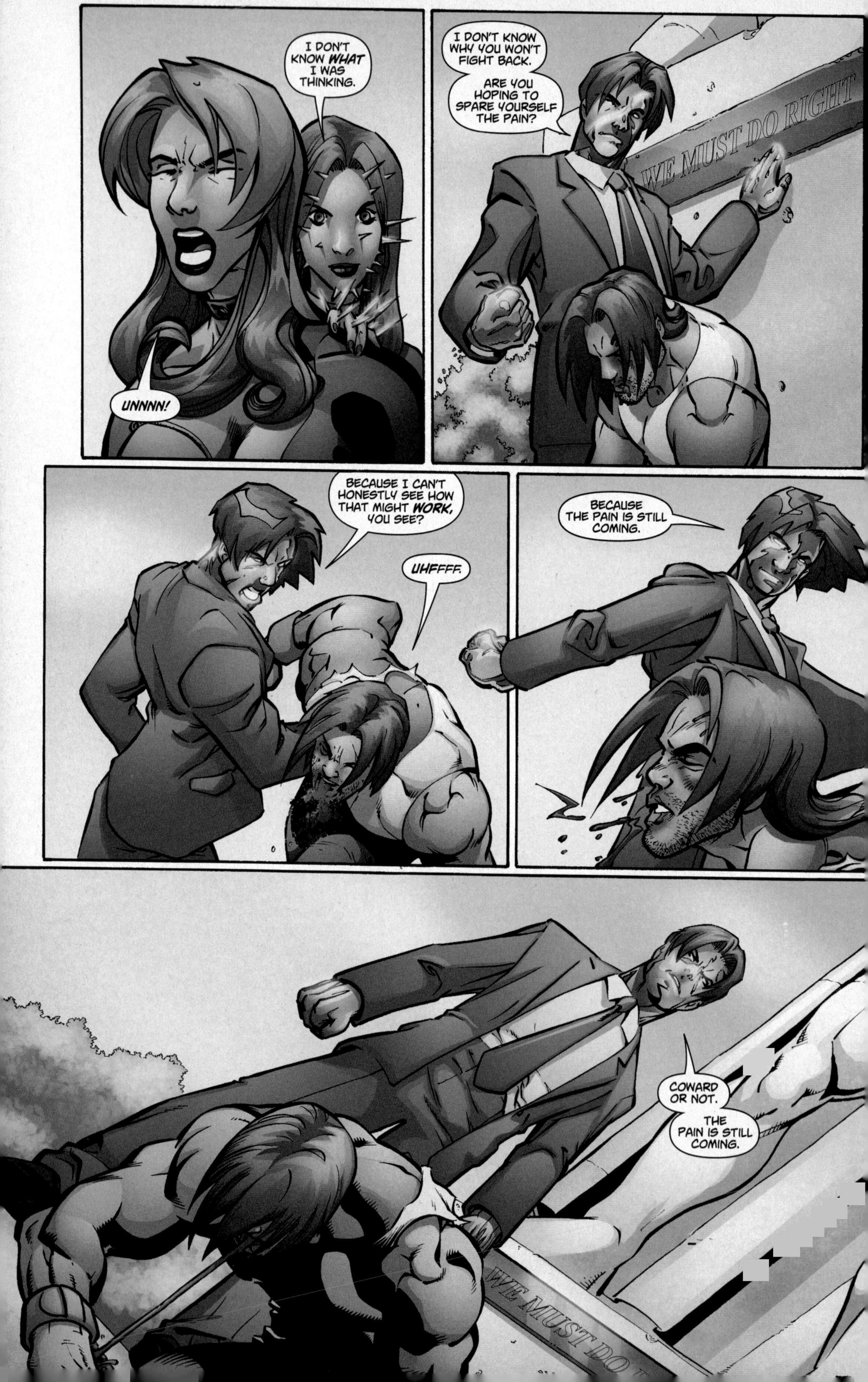
I DON'T KNOW WHAT I WAS THINKING.
UNNNN!
I DON'T KNOW WHY YOU WON'T FIGHT BACK.
ARE YOU HOPING TO SPARE YOURSELF THE PAIN?
WE MUST DO RIGHT
BECAUSE I CAN'T HONESTLY SEE HOW THAT MIGHT WORK, YOU SEE?
UHFFFF.
BECAUSE THE PAIN IS STILL COMING.
COWARD OR NOT.
THE PAIN IS STILL COMING.

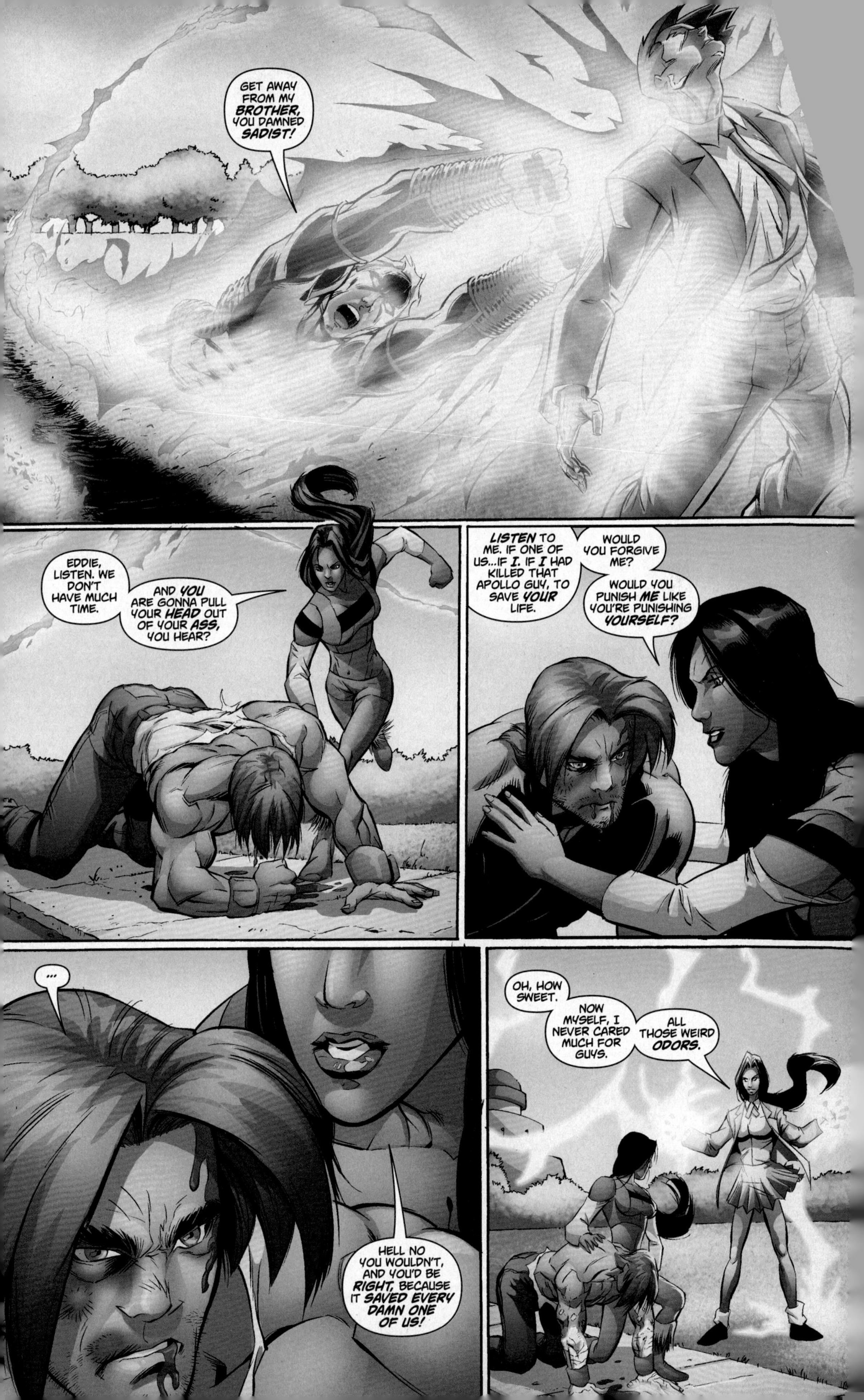
GET AWAY FROM MY BROTHER, YOU DAMNED SADIST!
EDDIE, LISTEN. WE DON'T HAVE MUCH TIME.
AND YOU ARE GONNA PULL YOUR HEAD OUT OF YOUR ASS, YOU HEAR?
LISTEN TO ME. IF ONE OF US...IF I. IF I HAD KILLED THAT APOLLO GUY, TO SAVE YOUR LIFE.
WOULD YOU FORGIVE ME?
WOULD YOU PUNISH ME LIKE YOU'RE PUNISHING YOURSELF?
...
HELL NO YOU WOULDN'T, AND YOU'D BE RIGHT, BECAUSE IT SAVED EVERY DAMN ONE OF US!
OH, HOW SWEET.
NOW MYSELF, I NEVER CARED MUCH FOR GUYS.
ALL THOSE WEIRD ODORS.

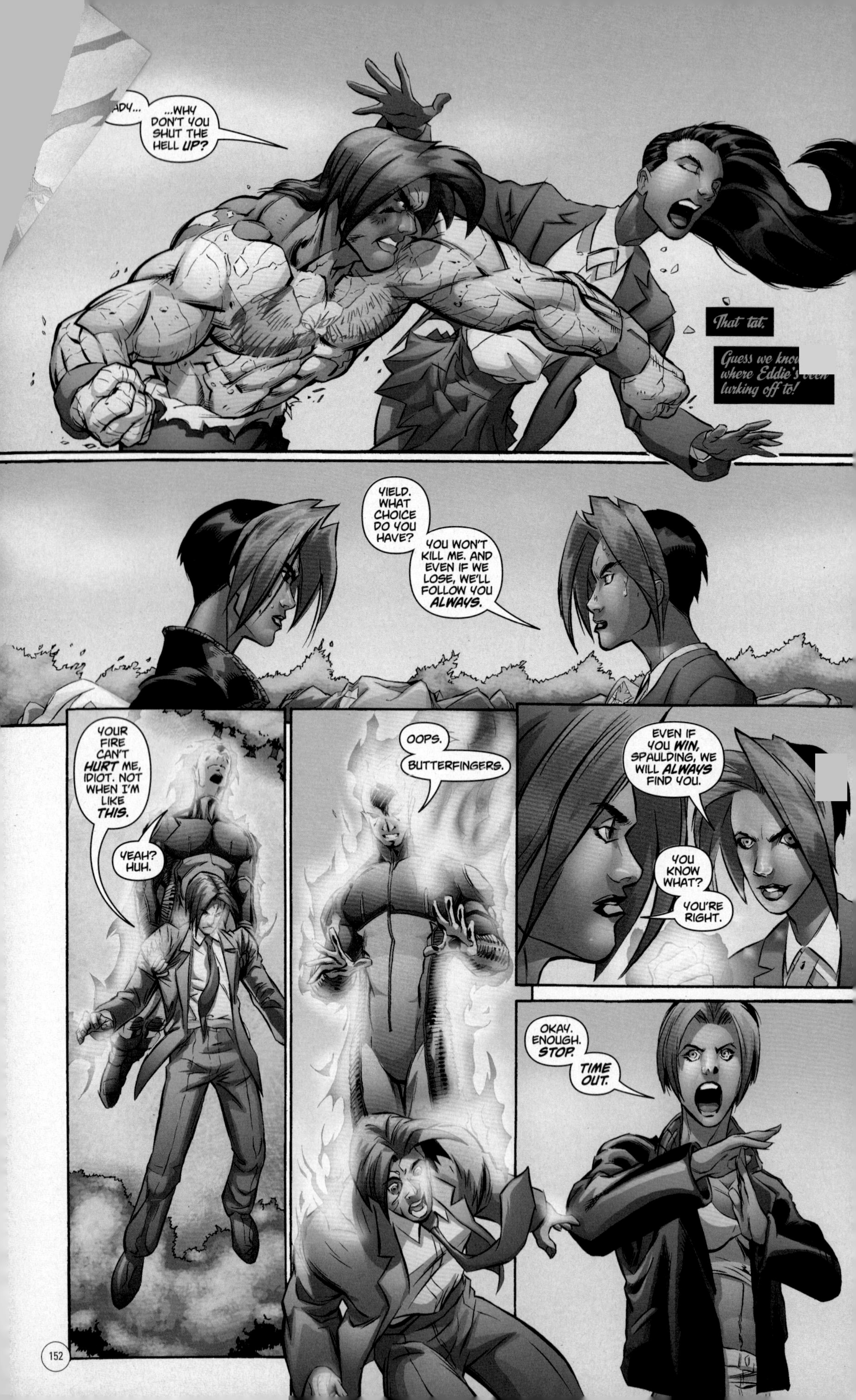
ADY...
...WHY DON'T YOU SHUT THE HELL UP?
That tat.
Guess we kno
where Eddie's
lurking off to!
YIELD. WHAT CHOICE DO YOU HAVE?
YOU WON'T KILL ME. AND EVEN IF WE LOSE, WE'LL FOLLOW YOU ALWAYS.
YOUR FIRE CAN'T HURT ME, IDIOT. NOT WHEN I'M LIKE THIS.
YEAH? HUH.
OOPS.
BUTTERFINGERS.
EVEN IF YOU WIN, SPAULDING, WE WILL ALWAYS FIND YOU.
YOU KNOW WHAT?
YOU'RE RIGHT.
OKAY. ENOUGH. STOP.
TIME OUT.

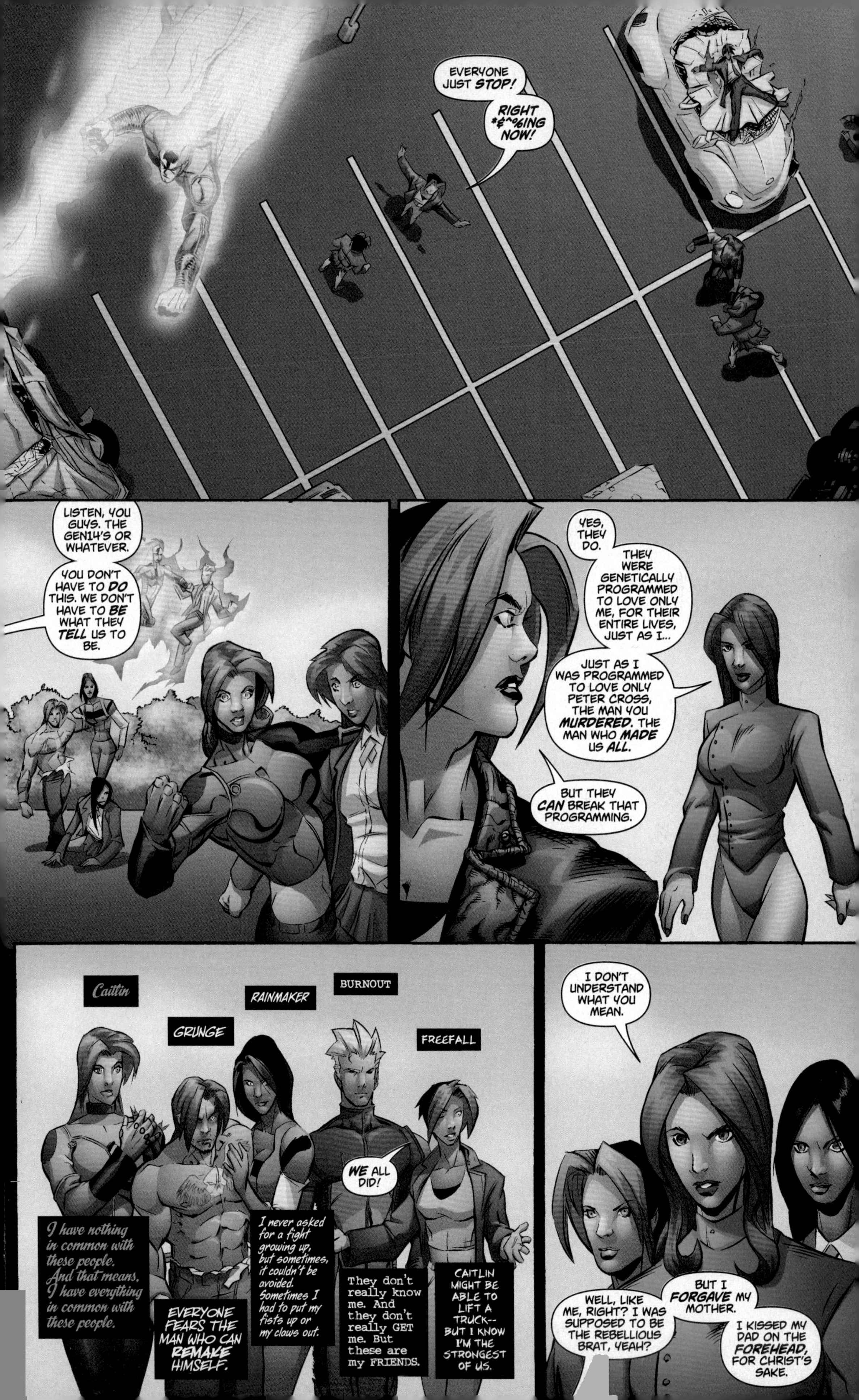
EVERYONE JUST STOP!
RIGHT *$^%ING NOW!
LISTEN, YOU GUYS. THE GEN14'S OR WHATEVER.
YOU DON'T HAVE TO DO THIS. WE DON'T HAVE TO BE WHAT THEY TELL US TO BE.
YES, THEY DO.
THEY WERE GENETICALLY PROGRAMMED TO LOVE ONLY ME, FOR THEIR ENTIRE LIVES, JUST AS I...
JUST AS I WAS PROGRAMMED TO LOVE ONLY PETER CROSS, THE MAN YOU MURDERED. THE MAN WHO MADE US ALL.
BUT THEY CAN BREAK THAT PROGRAMMING.
Caitlin
GRUNGE
RAINMAKER
BURNOUT
FREEFALL
I have nothing in common with these people. And that means, I have everything in common with these people.
EVERYONE FEARS THE MAN WHO CAN REMAKE HIMSELF.
I never asked for a fight growing up, but sometimes, it couldn't be avoided. Sometimes I had to put my fists up or my claws out.
WE ALL DID!
They don't really know me. And they don't really GET me. But these are my FRIENDS.
CAITLIN MIGHT BE ABLE TO LIFT A TRUCK-- BUT I KNOW I'M THE STRONGEST OF US.
I DON'T UNDERSTAND WHAT YOU MEAN.
WELL, LIKE ME, RIGHT? I WAS SUPPOSED TO BE THE REBELLIOUS BRAT, YEAH?
BUT I FORGAVE MY MOTHER.
I KISSED MY DAD ON THE FOREHEAD, FOR CHRIST'S SAKE.

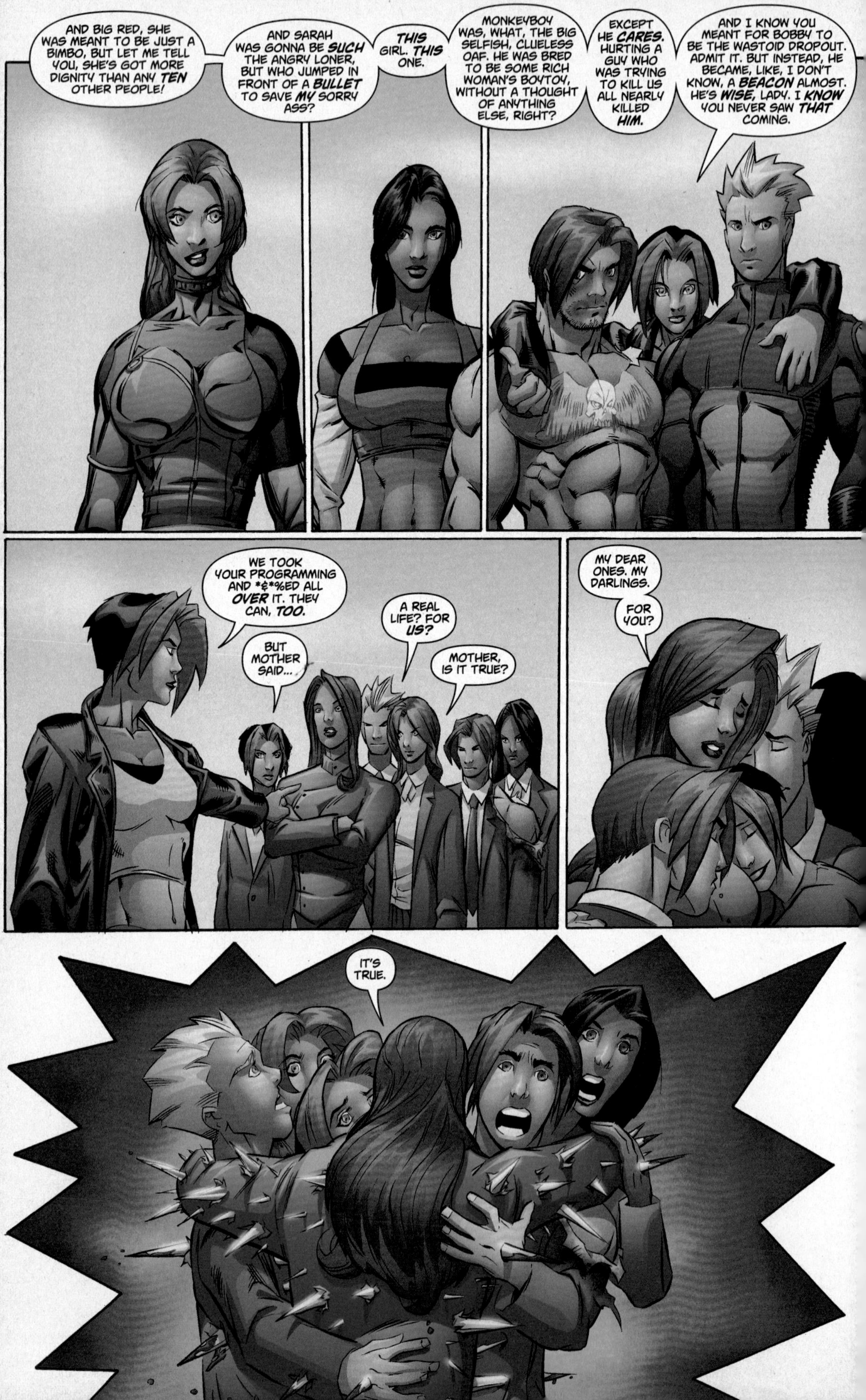

AND BIG RED, SHE WAS MEANT TO BE JUST A BIMBO, BUT LET ME TELL YOU, SHE'S GOT MORE DIGNITY THAN ANY TEN OTHER PEOPLE!
AND SARAH WAS GONNA BE SUCH THE ANGRY LONER, BUT WHO JUMPED IN FRONT OF A BULLET TO SAVE MY SORRY ASS?
THIS GIRL. THIS ONE.
MONKEYBOY WAS, WHAT, THE BIG SELFISH, CLUELESS OAF. HE WAS BRED TO BE SOME RICH WOMAN'S BOYTOY, WITHOUT A THOUGHT OF ANYTHING ELSE, RIGHT?
EXCEPT HE CARES. HURTING A GUY WHO WAS TRYING TO KILL US ALL NEARLY KILLED HIM.
AND I KNOW YOU MEANT FOR BOBBY TO BE THE WASTOID DROPOUT. ADMIT IT. BUT INSTEAD, HE BECAME, LIKE, I DON'T KNOW, A BEACON ALMOST. HE'S WISE, LADY. I KNOW YOU NEVER SAW THAT COMING.
WE TOOK YOUR PROGRAMMING AND *$*%ED ALL OVER IT. THEY CAN, TOO.
BUT MOTHER SAID...
A REAL LIFE? FOR US?
MOTHER, IS IT TRUE?
MY DEAR ONES. MY DARLINGS.
FOR YOU?
IT'S TRUE.

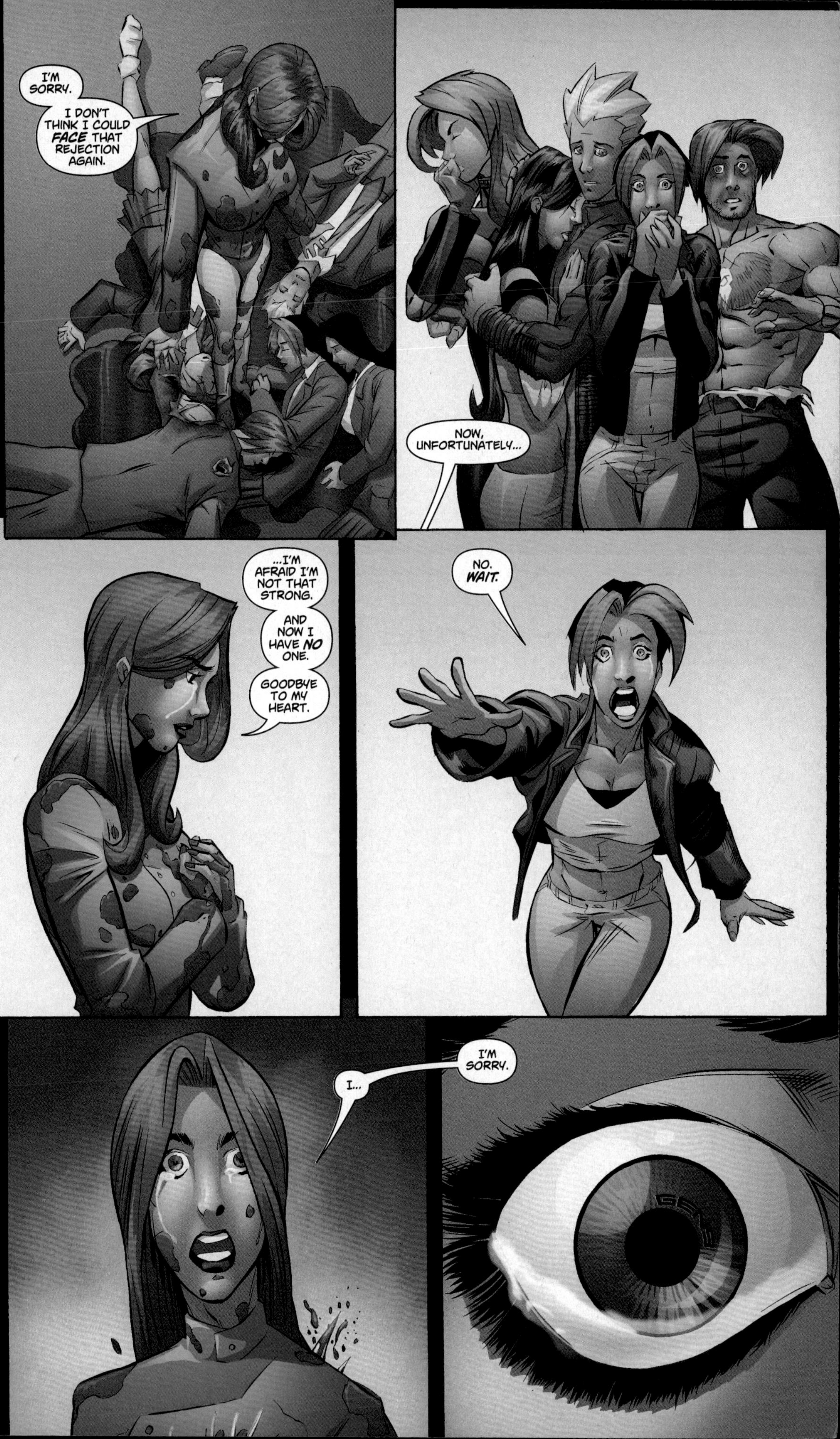
I'M SORRY.
I DON'T THINK I COULD FACE THAT REJECTION AGAIN.
NOW, UNFORTUNATELY...
...I'M AFRAID I'M NOT THAT STRONG.
AND NOW I HAVE NO ONE.
GOODBYE TO MY HEART.
NO. WAIT.
I...
I'M SORRY.

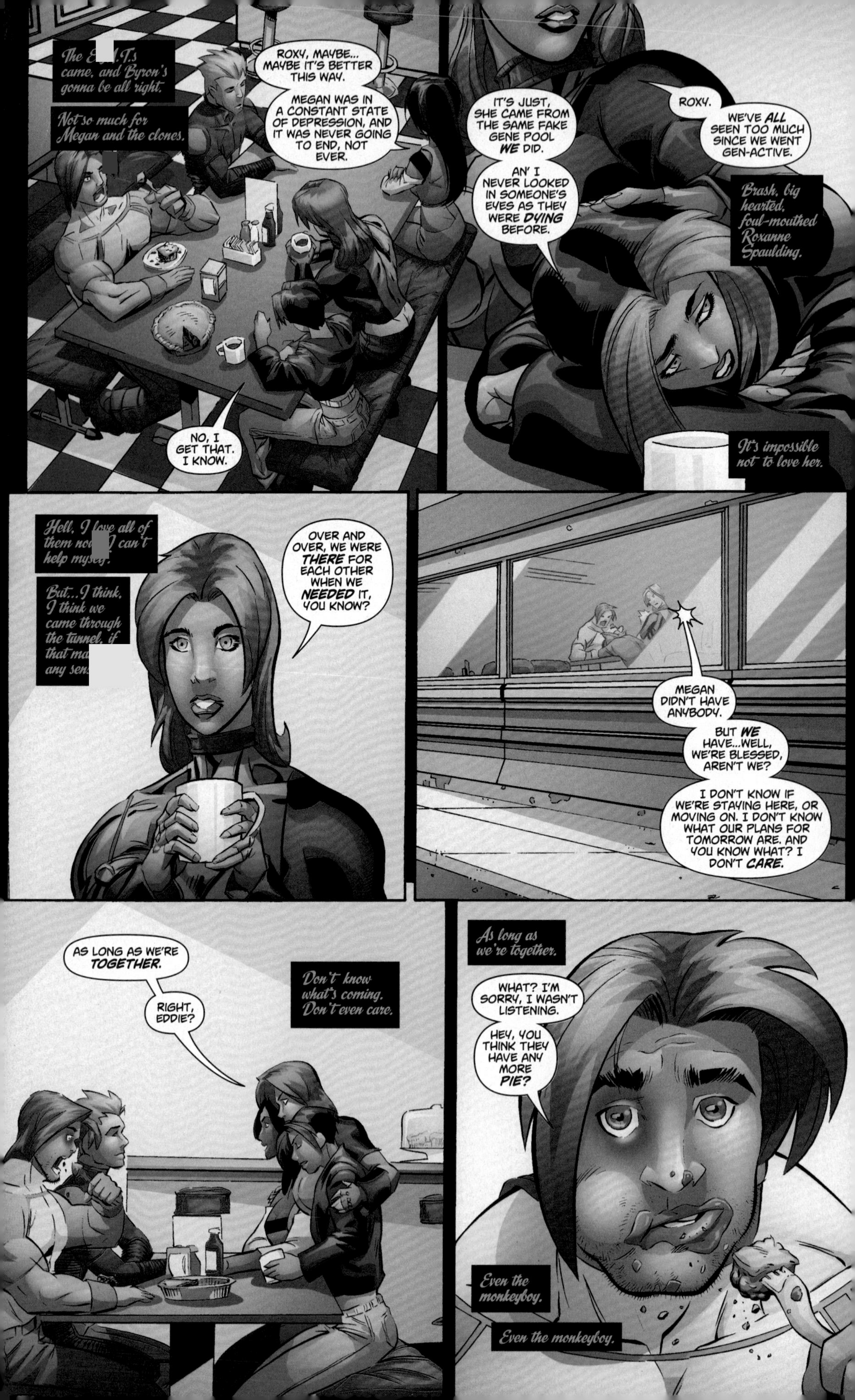

The E T.s came, and Byron's gonna be all right.
Not so much for Megan and the clones.
ROXY, MAYBE... MAYBE IT'S BETTER THIS WAY.
MEGAN WAS IN A CONSTANT STATE OF DEPRESSION, AND IT WAS NEVER GOING TO END, NOT EVER.
NO, I GET THAT. I KNOW.
IT'S JUST, SHE CAME FROM THE SAME FAKE GENE POOL WE DID.
AN' I NEVER LOOKED IN SOMEONE'S EYES AS THEY WERE DYING BEFORE.
ROXY.
WE'VE ALL SEEN TOO MUCH SINCE WE WENT GEN-ACTIVE.
Brash, big hearted, foul-mouthed Roxanne Spaulding.
It's impossible not to love her.
Hell, I l ve all of them no I can't help mys f.
But...I think, I think we came through the tunnel, if that ma any sen
OVER AND OVER, WE WERE THERE FOR EACH OTHER WHEN WE NEEDED IT, YOU KNOW?
MEGAN DIDN'T HAVE ANYBODY.
BUT WE HAVE...WELL, WE'RE BLESSED, AREN'T WE?
I DON'T KNOW IF WE'RE STAYING HERE, OR MOVING ON. I DON'T KNOW WHAT OUR PLANS FOR TOMORROW ARE. AND YOU KNOW WHAT? I DON'T CARE.
AS LONG AS WE'RE TOGETHER.
RIGHT, EDDIE?
Don't know what's coming. Don't even care.
As long as we're together.
WHAT? I'M SORRY, I WASN'T LISTENING.
HEY, YOU THINK THEY HAVE ANY MORE PIE?
Even the monkeyboy.
Even the monkeyboy.

COVER #8

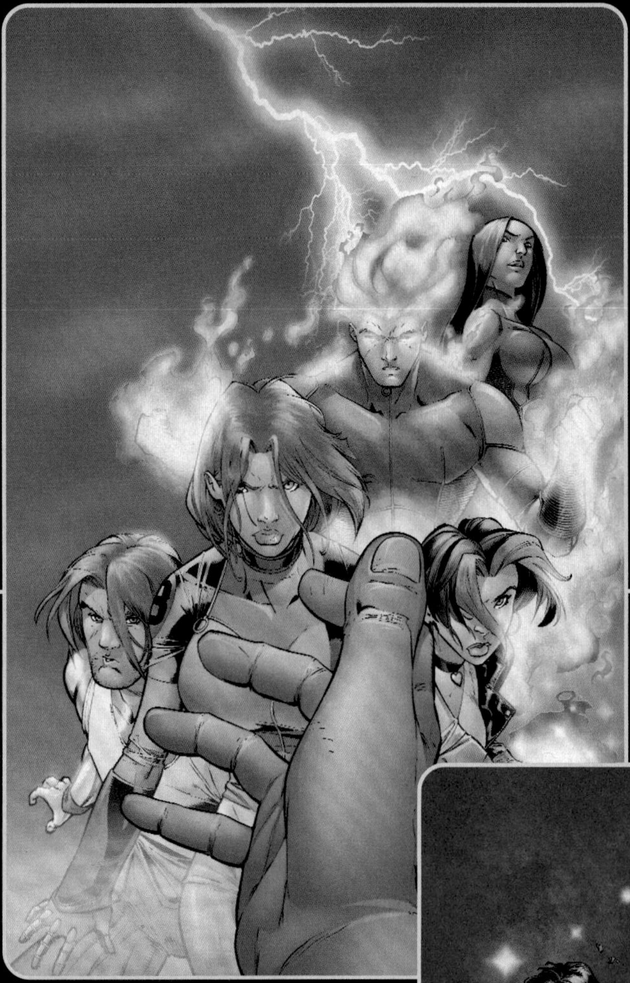

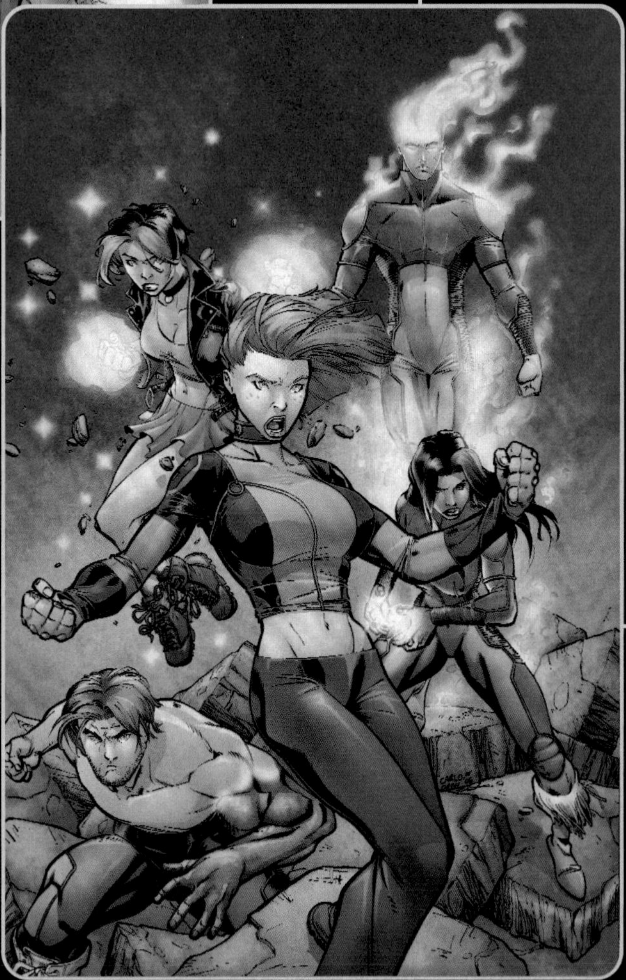

COVER #9

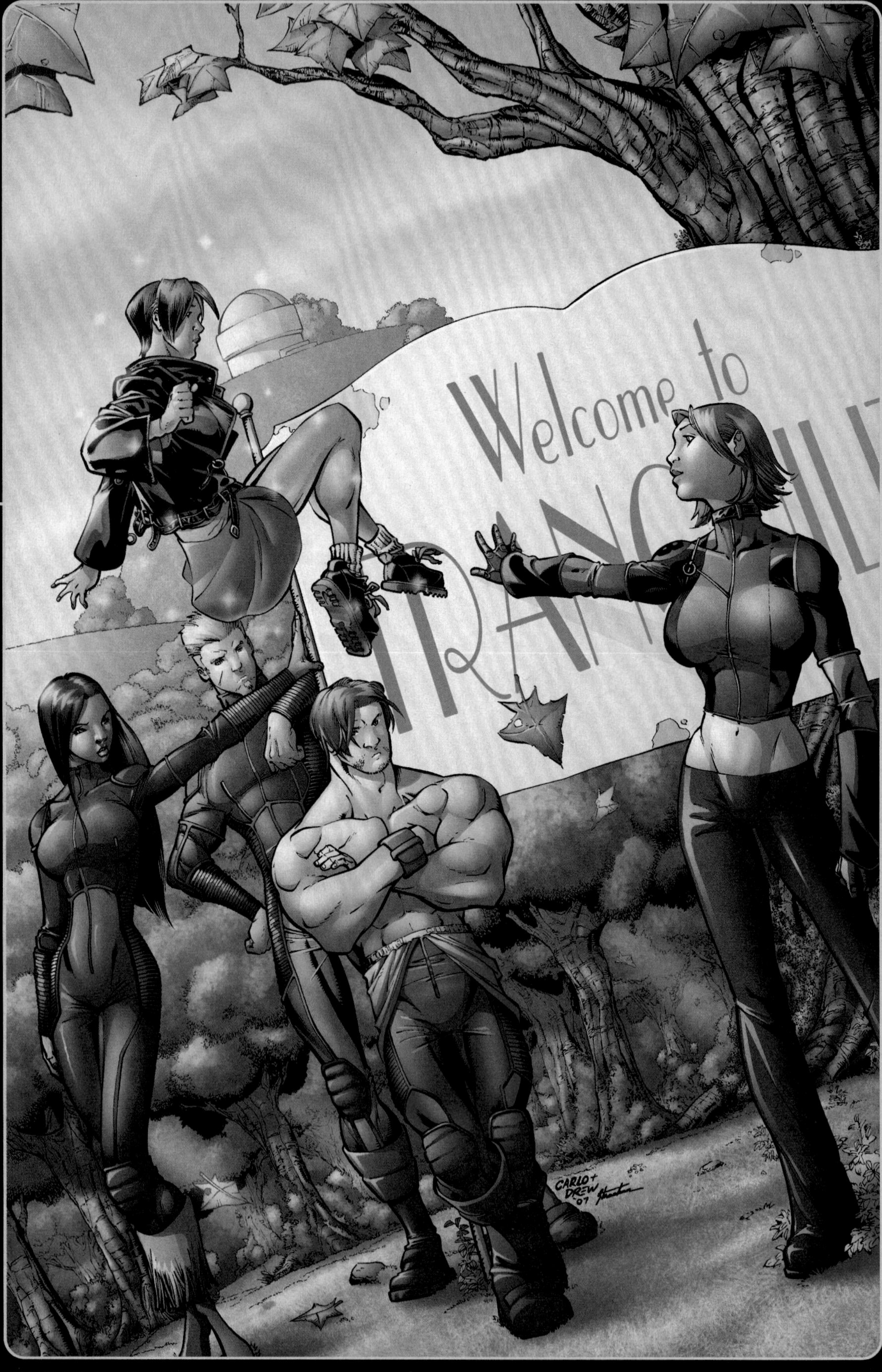
Welcome to
CARLO + DREW '07

COVER #10

COVER #11

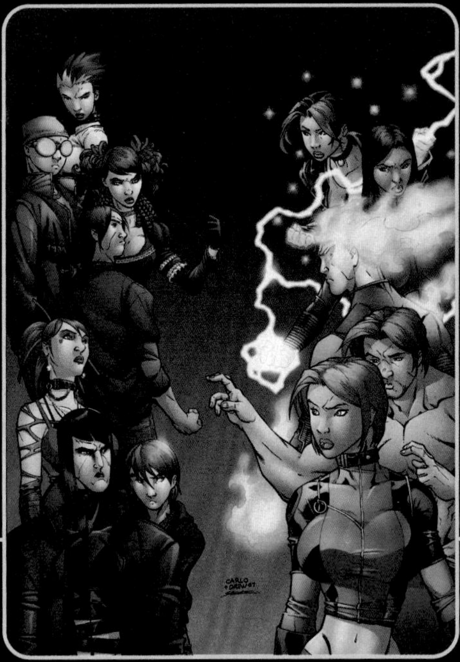

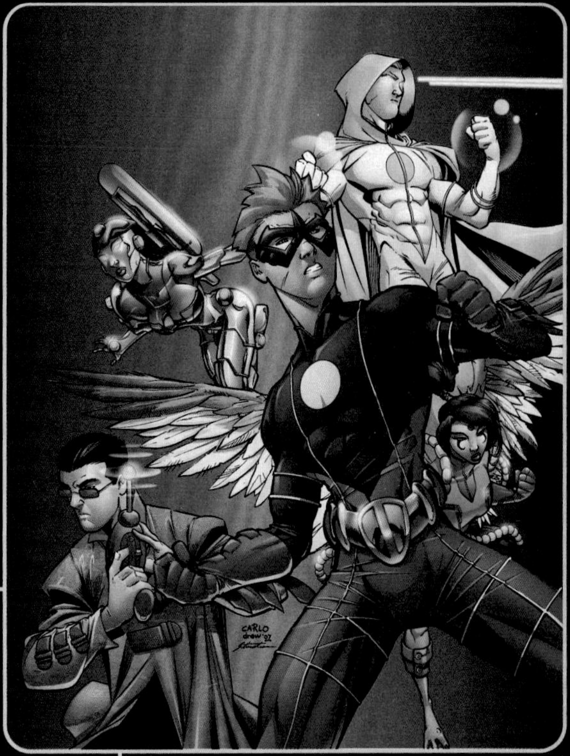

COVER #12

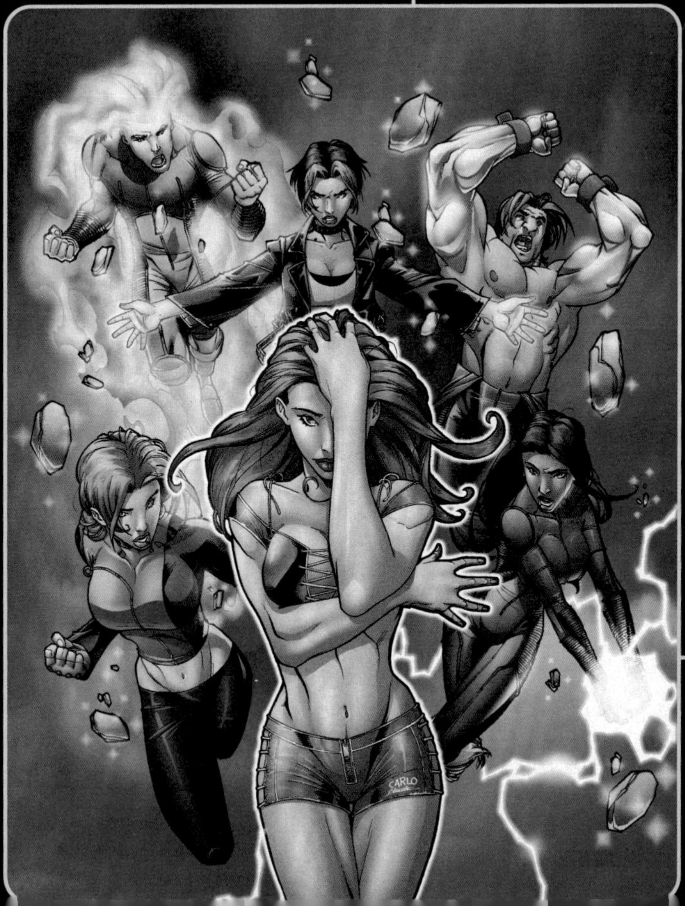

COVER #13

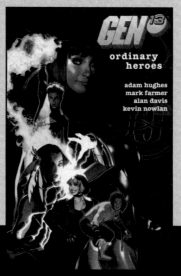